AHS
PLANTS
FOR EVERY
SEASON

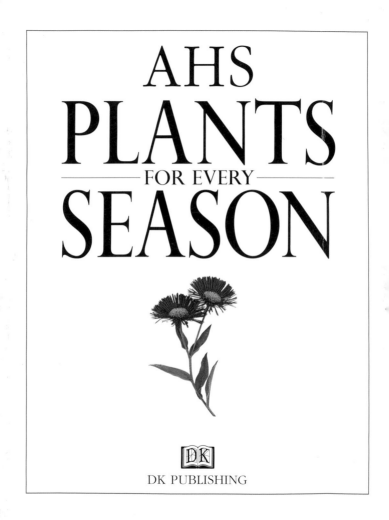

DK

DK PUBLISHING

LONDON, NEW YORK, MUNICH, MELBOURNE, and DELHI

WRITERS **Martin Page, Andrea Loom**
PROJECT EDITOR **Helen Fewster**
US PROJECT MANAGER **Jill Hamilton**
US EDITOR **Ray Rogers**
US Editorial Assistants **Katie Zien, Madeline Farbman**
ART EDITOR **Ann Thompson**
PROJECT ART EDITOR **Alison Lotinga**
MANAGING EDITOR **Anna Kruger**
MANAGING ART EDITOR **Lee Griffiths**
DTP DESIGN **Louise Waller**
US DTP DESIGN **Milos Orlovic**
PRODUCTION **Mandy Inness**

First American Edition, 2003

03 04 05 10 9 8 7 6 5 4 3 2

Published in the United States by
DK Publishing, Inc.
375 Hudson Street
New York, New York 10014

A catalog record for this book is available from the Library of Congress.
ISBN 0–7894–9437–X

Color reproduction by Colourscan.
Printed and bound in Italy by Graphicom.

see our complete catalog at
www.dk.com

CONTENTS

USING THE GUIDE

THE AIM OF THIS BOOK is to help you select plants for your garden that will provide color and interest throughout the year. There are seven chapters, based on the six seasons of the gardening year plus a final section suggesting plants that offer year-round interest. This "All Seasons" chapter will help you choose some plants that give shape and structure to the garden or that have evergreen foliage. They may be used to create a permanent framework, into which other flowering plants can be introduced.

It will come as no surprise to learn that the largest chapters relate to late spring and to early and late summer, but you may be interested to discover how many plants are of interest at other times of year. Use this book to plan ahead so your garden has autumn interest as well as color in winter and early spring.

In each chapter, the plants have been divided into color categories – white, pink, red, purple, blue, green, yellow, and orange – and then presented in alphabetical order. Some may flower over a long period or have several seasons of interest, but here they are placed in the season in which they make the

most significant impact. Thus a flowering cherry may have found its way into "Autumn" due to its attractive foliage, while firethorns may be grown for their early summer flowers as well as their bright clusters of winter berries.

SYMBOLS USED

SOIL MOISTURE PREFERENCES/TOLERANCES

◊ Well-drained soil

◖ Moist soil

● Wet soil

SUN/SHADE PREFERENCES/TOLERANCES

☼ Full sun

◐ Partial shade; either dappled shade or shade for part of the day

◑ Full shade

NB Where two symbols appear from the same category, the plant is suitable for a range of conditions.
f Fragrant flowers or aromatic leaves.

USDA HARDINESS ZONE RATINGS
A plant's generally accepted cold tolerance is given as a range (for example, Z5–8), based on the system developed by the US Department of Agriculture. See the front endpaper.

AHS HEAT ZONE RATINGS
A plant's generally accepted heat tolerance is given as a range (for example, H9–1), based on the AHS Heat Zone Map. See the back endpaper.

PLANNING YOUR GARDEN

IT IS A GOOD IDEA to plan before you plant by making a rough drawing of your existing garden and plotting in various permanent plants and features such as paths, a patio, or a shed. Computer programs are available to help you visualize how your garden will look, but a sheet of graph paper and a pencil can perform the same task at a much lower cost. Hard landscaping, for example paths and patios, should be installed before the garden is planted. It is also important to take into account your garden's use: do you need space for entertaining, or maybe areas for pets and children to play? Once your priorities are established, then turn to the plants.

SELECT IN ORDER

Start by choosing trees and shrubs. These provide the backbone of the garden. Boundary hedges or mixed shrub screens give shelter and privacy, and they buffer noise. Shrubs and trees need enough room to develop unhindered. They can grow to a considerable size, so it is usually better to plant one or two modest specimens and allow them to grow naturally rather than spoil their appearance by heavy pruning or, worse, needing to remove them after a few years.

Once these long-term plants are in place you can turn your attention to the small shrubs and herbaceous perennials. Often simplicity is the key to achieving a harmonious garden. Rather than using lots of different plants, it is better to plant groups of three or five of the same variety, which will merge together and create more impact. The final elements are the bulbs and annuals, all of which give instant color in their first year and are invaluable for filling gaps. Some annuals can be sown *in situ*, and bulbs can be naturalized under trees and in grass.

YEAR-ROUND INTEREST

There are no set times when the seasons begin and end. It depends on the climate where you live, your garden situation, and the weather. In mild years, flowers start to open between one and two weeks earlier than in others, and the entire garden can be brought to an abrupt halt by severe drought or an early frost.

To achieve year-round interest in the garden, start by choosing a few plants for winter, when the choice is most limited: perhaps a tree with

DUAL PURPOSE
*Bergenias make
an easy going
groundcover
in sun or light
shade. This one
has bright pink
spring flowers,
and the foliage
turns color
in winter.*

interesting bark or a cluster of
winter-flowering shrubs and some
early bulbs. Then select for early
spring and autumn; some plants will
double up with spring flowers and
bright autumn tints. Move on to
make your selection for late spring
before looking through the summer
sections. Consider planting a few
containers for each season; again,
there is a huge choice for summer,
but some plants, such as pansies
may go throughout the year.

COLOR

Many people enjoy lots of color,
but some of the most appealing
borders, containers, or garden areas
have a color theme. You might
choose shades of one color (but
this can be dull) or use a limited
palette. White and pastel colors are
cool and show up well at dusk –
good near a patio or path. Blues
and mauves are hazy and give a
sense of distance, whereas hot reds,
oranges, and yellows appear closer.

ASSESSING YOUR SITE

Planting a new garden can be an exciting prospect, but before you rush to the garden center it is wise to assess your site by testing the soil and identifying areas of sun and shade. If your site is bare, one way of finding out what grows well in your locality is to look at what succeeds in neighboring gardens, or ask at the garden center. Try to select plants that meet the conditions rather than fighting against nature;

this helps prevent expensive disappointments, and the plants will be healthier and need less attention.

If you have acquired a garden that is well established, try to stem your enthusiasm and observe it for

FOCAL POINTS
The variegated Yucca gloriosa *is a superb architectural plant and provides a strong focus in a border in well-drained, sunny gardens. It may also be grown in containers.*

a year. In doing so, you discover its hidden delights, such as bulbs, and see how plants perform through the seasons. Only then should you consider changes. If possible, keep established trees for the maturity they give, but smaller plants can be moved in spring or autumn.

TESTING THE SOIL

The soil is critical in determining which plants will grow well in your garden, so you need to establish its characteristics. Sandy soil drains quickly, is low in nutrients, and feels gritty if you rub it between your fingers. At the other extreme is clay soil, which is smooth and malleable when handled. It is nutrient-rich but sticky when wet, becomes rock hard when dry, and often has poor drainage. The ideal soil is moist and well-drained, retaining water but without becoming waterlogged. Much can be done to improve soil conditions. Sandy soils can be improved by adding plenty of well-rotted manure or compost on a regular basis. Clay soil may be lightened by deep digging and by adding coarse sand and organic matter, such as compost or leaf mold.

To test whether your soil has poor drainage, dig a hole about 3ft (1m) square and fill it with water.

If the water has not drained away within a few hours, the site is badly drained. You then have the option of growing moisture-loving plants and perhaps creating a bog garden, or installing subsurface drainage.

You should also test the pH of your soil to find out whether it is acidic or alkaline. Soil-testing kits are available from many garden centers, and this simple test can save you money in the long term, since some plants, such as rhodo-dendrons and many heathers, will thrive only on acidic or neutral soil.

EXPOSURE

The orientation of your house and garden is another important factor that determines which plants grow best. In a north-facing garden the area close to the house will always be in shadow, and it is likely to be relatively colder in winter. This limits the choice of plants to those that tolerate shade. South-facing gardens have much more light but can be hot in summer, so unless you plant shade trees, confine your choice to sun-lovers. East- and west-facing gardens offer their own particular mix of shade and sun. In windy situations (and often by the coast) it is advisable to plant a windbreak or erect a screen.

CARING FOR PLANTS

ALL PERENNIALS, especially trees and shrubs, need well-prepared sites. Dig the soil (but not when it is wet), attempt to remove all traces of perennial weeds, and incorporate plenty of well-rotted organic matter. Although most plants are sold in containers throughout the year, deciduous trees and shrubs, including roses, are best planted in the dormant seasons of late autumn and early spring, when the soil is neither frozen or sodden. Conifers and evergreens are best left until spring. Plant herbaceous perennials in autumn, while the soil is still warm, or (better for plants of borderline hardiness) in spring.

PLANTING

Water plants in containers an hour or two before transplanting them; after planting, water again. Then cover the root area, particularly around shrubs and trees, with a thick mulch of organic matter, such as bark chips, to conserve soil moisture and suppress weeds. Make sure they never lack for water in dry periods during the first year, or two or three years for shrubs and trees. Bulbs are normally planted in autumn, but some are planted in spring. They need a well-drained site and, as a rule of thumb, plant them at three times their depth (measured from the soil surface to the top of the bulb).

AFTERCARE

Remove winter debris in spring, clearing away the dead growth of perennials and ornamental grasses before new shoots begin to show. Weed and fork over the bare soil of beds and borders to aerate it, taking care not to damage emerging bulbs. Rake in balanced fertilizer and then, when the soil is moist and temperatures are rising, mulch with organic matter. Insert stakes and supports so they will be covered by the expanding foliage.

Once frosts are over, bedding and tender plants such as dahlias, gladiolus, begonias, and cannas can be put out, but be prepared to cover them in case temperatures fall to near freezing at night.

Deadheading is the main job for summer: it keeps plants neat and may stimulate the development of new buds and more flowers. Containers and hanging baskets will need daily watering and fertilizing every 10–14 days unless a slow-release fertilizer was mixed in at planting time. Water plants in borders, particularly those recently planted. Irrigate thoroughly to encourage deep roots; watering little and often results in surface roots and exposes plants to drought and damage.

In autumn the remains of annuals can be cleared away and perennials neatened for winter. Perennials with hollow stems, such as lupines, should be cut down to the ground, but others, including grasses and those not entirely hardy, are better left intact for protection. These and shrubs of marginal hardiness benefit from a protective mulch of straw or loose leaves; keep it in position throughout winter. Move tender plants under cover for winter and lift dahlias, begonias, cannas, and gladiolus to store in a cool, frost-free place over winter.

REPEAT PERFORMANCE
Large herbaceous borders are glorious during the summer. Deadhead plants regularly to extend the display.

EARLY SPRING

WINTER'S COLD GRIP seems to loosen as the bulbs begin to flower. Their growth initially can be quite slow, but the first warm day stirs them from their slumber. It is often very cold at night, and the earliest flowers of magnolias and camellias, for example, may be damaged in exposed areas. Keep newspaper and row cover on hand to protect smaller plants.

The flowers opening beneath deciduous trees and shrubs are a feature of early spring. Bulbs, hellebores, primroses, and starry blue hepaticas in mixed and woodland borders take advantage of the light before the leaves on overhanging branches unfurl. In more open sites and lawns, naturalized crocuses and daffodils make drifts of mauve, white, or sunny yellow. Allow the foliage of bulbs to die down naturally wherever they grow to make sure they flower well in future.

Magnolias are the monarchs of the spring garden, but not all are slow to flower or large: 'Star Wars' will bloom from a very young age, and the smaller *M. stellata* is ideal in an urban garden. Other trees and shrubs in blossom at this time are fragrant corylopsis and daphnes, early-flowering apricots and cherries (*Prunus*), and Japanese quince (*Chaenomeles*).

FOLIAGE FOUNDATIONS

Dramatic foliage is always an asset. The bright purple-red leaves of *Photinia × fraseri* 'Red Robin' stand out like beacons in spring sunshine; this plant makes an unusual hedge. Many pieris, such as 'Wakehurst', also boast brilliant red leaves, but they go through shades of pink and cream before maturing to mid- to dark green.

Hellebores have flowers in a wide range of subtle colors, but *Helleborus foetidus* and *H. × sternii* also make valuable foliage plants, adding height and structure to the garden at the start of the year.

ANEMONE BLANDA
'White Splendour'

Perennial

A spreading plant with knobby tubers and irregularly lobed leaves. The petals of the flowers are white, with a pink tint underneath. It enjoys a sunny site and well-drained soil and will quickly spread to form a large clump. Plant the tubers in autumn, at a depth of about 3in (8cm), and then leave undisturbed to naturalize.

◊ ☼ Z4–8 H9–3
‡ to 4in (10cm) ↔ to 6in (15cm)

ERICA ARBOREA
VAR. ALPINA

Evergreen shrub

This attractive tree heather bears masses of fragrant flowers from the end of winter to midspring. Perfect for adding height to a rock or heather garden, this variety prefers to be grown in full sun in well-drained, slightly acidic soil, but it will tolerate mildly alkaline conditions. The first year after planting, prune back by about two-thirds after flowering to form a bushy plant. After that, further pruning is not necessary.

◊ ☼ *f* Z9–10 H10–9
‡ to 6ft (2m) ↔ to 34in (85cm)

ERICA × DARLEYENSIS
'White Glow'

Evergreen shrub

The Darley Dale heath is compact and bushy with fine, lance-shaped leaves. Masses of white flowers with reddish brown tips appear in late winter and early spring. It benefits from a sunny position and well-drained, preferably acidic soil, although slightly alkaline soils are acceptable. Trim off the previous season's growth after it has flowered to keep the plant neat.

◊ ☀ Z5–7 H7–5
↕ to 10in (25cm) ↔ to 20in (50cm)

HELLEBORUS × HYBRIDUS

Perennial

These hybrid hellebores have leathery green leaves. The nodding flowers are white, pink, green, or purple and are often covered with small red spots. Vigorous, variable plants, they prefer heavy, moist, neutral or alkaline soil that is rich in organic matter. They will tolerate full sun but are best planted in the dappled shade of a woodland border or beneath the branches of deciduous trees or shrubs. Although they regularly self-seed, the best plants are purchased from specialist nurseries.

◊ ☀ ◑ Z6–9 H9–6
↕↔ to 18in (45cm)

HYACINTHUS ORIENTALIS *'White Pearl'*

Bulbous perennial

The large, pure white, rather waxy, bell-shaped flowers of this bulbous plant are intensely fragrant and emerge in early spring on stiff stems among bright green leaves. Plant the bulbs at a depth of 4in (10cm), about 3in (8cm) apart, in sun or partial shade in deep, well-drained fertile soil, and group them in clumps or use in bedding. Bulbs planted in pots of bulb fiber can be forced into flower early to create an indoor show for the winter months.

◊ ☼ ☀ *f* Z5–9 H9–1
‡ to 12in (30cm) ↔ to 3in (8cm)

LEUCOJUM VERNUM

Bulbous perennial

The spring snowflake is one of the earliest bulbs to bloom. Leafless stalks produce one or two green-tipped white flowers amid clumps of strap-shaped, glossy green leaves. For the greatest impact, plant groups of bulbs in moist soil, rich in organic matter, in the partial shade below deciduous trees or shrubs. Propagate by division in the spring, or sow seed in autumn.

◊ ☼ Z4–8 H8–1
‡ to 6in (15cm) ↔ to 4in (10cm)

LYSICHITON CAMTSCHATCENSIS

Perennial

The white skunk cabbage bears large white, hooded flowerheads in early spring. Large, dark green leaves follow shortly after, which eventually grow taller than the flowers. The thick roots require deep, permanently moist, fertile soil, so it is not ideal for growing in containers, but it can be used beside a pond as a marginal plant or planted in a bog garden. Allow space for clumps to develop and the leaves to expand.

◊ ◑ ☼ ◐ Z7–9 H9–7
‡ to 30in (75cm) ↔ to 24in (60cm)

MAGNOLIA STELLATA

Deciduous shrub

The star magnolia is a vigorous and free-flowering shrub or tree suitable for even the smallest of gardens. Left to its own devices it forms a broad-spreading shrub, covered in winter with fat, silky-haired flower buds. The star-shaped spring flowers open on bare branches and are composed of numerous narrow white petals. Plant this magnolia in a sheltered position in sun or light shade and moist, well-drained, fertile soil. It rarely requires pruning.

◊ ◑ ☼ ◐ Z5–9 H9–1
‡ to 10ft (3m) ↔ to 12ft (4m)

NARCISSUS
'Cheerfulness'

Bulbous perennial

An attractive, early-flowering daffodil with white outer petals that surround a cluster of smaller petals in the center. The long-lasting blooms have a strong fragrance and are good for cutting. For maximum visual impact, plant the bulbs in bold groups in late summer to early autumn in well-drained, fertile soil. The bulbs should be planted three times their depth below the soil surface.

◊ ☼ *f* Z3 –9 H9–1
‡ to 16in (40cm) ↔ to 6in (15cm)

NARCISSUS
'Merlin'

Bulbous perennial

The blooms of this dainty daffodil are good for cutting and have pure white, rounded petals and a flat, cup-shaped yellow trumpet with a reddish orange rim. It prefers a sunny site and well-drained soil. It flowers in the middle of spring. The bulbs should be planted as for 'Cheerfulness' (see above) in a herbaceous border, or it can be grown in grass and left to naturalize.

◊ ☼ Z3–9 H9–1
‡ to 18in (45cm) ↔ to 6in (15cm)

NARCISSUS
'Thalia'

Bulbous perennial

This vigorous daffodil will form large
clumps and is suitable for naturalizing
in the border or rock garden. Deep,
long-lasting, funnel-shaped flowers with
milky white petals, often with three or
more blooms per stem, are produced
in early to midspring. They also make
excellent cut flowers. Plant the bulbs as
for 'Cheerfulness' (see left) in a sunny
position and well-drained, fertile soil.

◊ ☼ Z3–9 H9–1
↕ to 14in (35cm) ↔ to 6in (15cm)

NARCISSUS TRIANDRUS

Bulbous perennial

Angel's tears is a dwarf narcissus that
bears nodding, pale cream flowers with
reflexed petals and rounded cups. The
leaves are green and strap-shaped. A
small-growing plant, it performs well
in containers and will naturalize, if the
conditions are right, in a sunny rock
garden or raised bed in well-drained
soil. There is also a white-flowered
variety, *albus*. Plant the bulbs as for
'Cheerfulness' (see above left).

◊ ☼ Z3–9 H9–1
↕ to 10in (25cm) ↔ to 3in (8cm)

ORNITHOGALUM OLIGOPHYLLUM

Bulbous perennial

In early spring, this slender plant produces up to five star-shaped white flowers with a yellowish green stripe down the outside of each petal. It also bears a pair of leaves that grow close to the ground. Plant the bulbs in groups in autumn in a sunny site and well-drained soil.

◊ ☼ Z7–10 H10–7
‡ to 3in (8cm) ↔ to 4in (10cm)

OSMANTHUS X BURKWOODII

Evergreen shrub

This slow-growing shrub has oval, dark green, slightly glossy, leathery leaves. In midspring it produces small clusters of fragrant white flowers which, on a still, sunny day, will fill the garden with a sweet scent. Plant this shrub in full sun or partial shade in fertile, well-drained soil. It can be used as a hedging plant that needs clipping only once a year, in summer.

◊ ☼ ☀ *f* Z7–9 H9–7
‡↔ to 10ft (3m)

PRUNUS SPINOSA

Deciduous tree

Blackthorn is nature's answer to the barbed-wire fence. A vigorous shrub or small tree, it bears star-shaped white flowers that open on bare branches in early and midspring. The branches are armed with sharp thorns, making a superb impenetrable hedge. It bears purple fruits (sloes) in autumn, which can be used to make a tasty liqueur. It grows happily in full sun on moist, well-drained soils and can be cut back hard in early spring. Hedges can be pruned at any time.

◊ ◊ ☼ Z5–9 H9–5
‡ to 15ft (5m) ↔ to 12ft (4m)

PULMONARIA
'Sissinghurst White'

Perennial

The leaves of this lungwort are elliptic and covered with small white spots. The flowers are pale pink when in bud and open in spring to form pure white, funnel-shaped blooms. It makes a good groundcover and is ideal for planting beneath deciduous trees in organic, moist but well drained soil. Cut back after it has flowered to encourage fresh foliage. To keep the plant vigorous, it is a good idea to divide and replant it every few years.

◊ ◊ ☼ ☀ Z6–8 H8–6
‡ to 12in (30cm) ↔ to 18in (45cm)

SANGUINARIA CANADENSIS *'Plena'*

Perennial

Bloodroot is aptly named, since its fleshy roots exude a red sap when cut. The white spring flowers, often tinted pink on the reverse, are succeeded by waxy, heart- or kidney-shaped, grayish green leaves that provide an excellent groundcover in damp, shaded sites. Divide large clumps after flowering.

◊ ☼ ☀ Z3–9 H9–1
‡ to 6in (15cm) ↔ to 12in (30cm)

TULIPA BIFLORA

Bulbous perennial

Well suited to a sunny site in a rock garden, the fragrant, star-shaped flowers of this dwarf tulip are creamy white or ivory with bright yellow centers. The blooms are produced from late winter and persist through early spring. Plant the bulbs in groups in late autumn in a light, fertile, well-drained soil, and leave undisturbed so clumps can develop. The bulbs like to be dry in the summer, so do not plant where neighbors may need watering.

◊ ☼ *f* Z4–7 H7–1
‡ to 4in (10cm) ↔ to 5in (13cm)

TULIPA
'Schoonoord'

Bulbous perennial

This is a relatively small tulip, ideal for
an urban garden where space is at a
premium. The wide-spreading, double,
pure white flowers open in the middle
of spring. The bulbs need a sunny site
and should be planted in late autumn
in a well-drained, fertile soil. *Tulipa*
'Peach Blossom', which grows to the
same height, has double, deep rose-
pink flowers and makes a comple-
mentary planting companion for
displays in pots and beddings.

◊ ☼ Z4–7 H7–1
‡ to 12in (30cm)

TULIPA TURKESTANICA
Bulbous perennial

A tulip with star-shaped white flowers
and a yellow (or occasionally orange)
center. The flowers have an unpleasant
aroma and are produced in early or
midspring. Choose a sunny site that is
dry in summer, such as a hot border or
by a sunny wall, and plant the bulbs in
autumn in groups in well-drained, light,
reasonably fertile soil.

◊ ☼ Z4–7 H8–1
‡ to 12in (30cm)

ANEMONE BLANDA
'Radar'

Perennial

The leaves of this spreading perennial
are deeply divided, and in early spring
it produces star-shaped, deep magenta
flowers with white centers. It grows
best on very well-drained sandy soil in
full sun. Plant the small, knobby tubers
in autumn in groups, then leave them
undisturbed to naturalize.

○ ☼ Z4–8 H9–3
↕ to 4in (10cm) ↔ to 6in (15cm)

BELLIS PERENNIS
'Pomponette'

Perennial

A selected form of the English daisy,
this perennial is frequently grown as a
biennial for spring bedding. The double
pink, white, or red flowers have quill-
like petals and measure up to 1½in
(4cm) across. Grow in a sunny position
in a well drained, fertile soil for spring
bedding, as edging, or in pots or
windowboxes. Deadhead regularly to
extend the flowering period.

○ ☼ ☀ Z4–8 H8–1
↕↔ to 8in (20cm)

BERGENIA
'Sunningdale'

Evergreen perennial

An early flowering plant, the deep pink
blooms are borne on stiff red stems.
The rounded, leathery leaves become
bronze-colored in the autumn. It should
be grown in full sun or partial shade,
and it is suitable for planting beneath
shrubs and deciduous trees. Propagate
it by division in spring after the flowers
have finished, and remove tattered
leaves at this time, too.

◊ ◊ ☼ ☼ Z3–8 H8–1
‡ to 18in (45cm) ↔ to 24in (60cm)

CAMELLIA × WILLIAMSII
'Donation'

Evergreen shrub

This camellia is valued for its deep
pink, double flowers that appear in
late winter and persist through spring.
A vigorous, free-flowering shrub, it also
boasts glossy, dark green foliage.
Plant it in partial shade, away from the
early morning sun, in moist but well-
drained, neutral or acidic soil mixed
with plenty of organic matter, or grow
it in containers of acidic soil mix.
For perfect blooms, grow in an
unheated greenhouse or conservatory.

◊ ◊ ☼ Z7–8 H8–7
‡ to 15ft (5m) ↔ to 8ft (2.5m)

CHAENOMELES SPECIOSA
'Moerloosei'

Deciduous shrub

This flowering quince can be used as
a free-standing shrub or trained on
a wall. It produces a tangle of spiny
stems covered with glossy, dark green
leaves and clusters of saucer-shaped
white and pink flowers. The blooms are
followed in autumn by edible, greenish
yellow fruits that can be made into
jelly. Cut back after flowering if grown
against a wall.

◊ ☼ ☀ Z5–8 H8–4
‡ to 8ft (2.5m) ↔ to 15ft (5m)

CHIONODOXA
'Pink Giant'

Bulbous perennial

This medium-sized bulbous perennial
produces soft pink, star-shaped flowers
with white centers. It is ideal for a rock
garden or for planting beneath shrubs,
where the bulbs can be left to naturalize.
It prefers a sunny site and well-drained
soil. Plant bulbs in autumn in groups,
and propagate by dividing established
clumps or by seed.

◊ ☼ Z3–9 H9–1
‡ to 10in (25cm) ↔ to 2in (5cm)

CLEMATIS ARMANDII
'Apple Blossom'

Climber

The glossy, dark, evergreen leaves of this vigorous climber are accompanied in spring by large clusters of pink-tinged, scented white flowers with deeper pink undersides that pale to pinkish white. It often benefits from a sunny position against a south- or west-facing wall in a well-drained soil. Purchase plants from a reputable source; inferior seedlings are sometimes offered. It can be pruned back after flowering, but not into old, dark wood.

◊ ☼ *f* Z7–9 H9–7
‡ to 15ft (5m)

DAPHNE CNEORUM
'Eximia'

Evergreen shrub

A prostrate shrub with small, oval, dark green leaves. The rose-pink flowers are highly fragrant and borne in clusters at the end of the branches. To grow well it needs a rich soil, which should be mixed with well-rotted compost or leaf mold when planting. All parts of the plant are harmful if ingested, and the sap can irritate the skin on contact.

◊ ☼ *f* Z5–7 H7–5
‡ to 4in (10cm) ↔ to 20in (50cm)

ERICA × DARLEYENSIS
'Kramer's Rote'

Evergreen shrub

Bronze-tinted green foliage and bright magenta spring flowers are features of this bushy heather. It should be grown in moist but well-drained, organic or peaty soil. It prefers acidic conditions but tolerates slightly alkaline soil, and it is a useful groundcover plant. Trim off the previous season's growth after flowering to keep the plant neat. 'Archie Graham' is similar heather with mauve-pink flowers.

◊ ◊ ☼ Z7–8 H8–7
↕ to 12in (30cm) ↔ to 24in (60cm)

HYACINTHUS ORIENTALIS
'Queen of the Pinks'

Bulbous perennial

This is one of the best pink hyacinths, with bright green leaves and highly fragrant flowers borne on robust stems in spring. Plant the bulbs in autumn in fertile, well-drained soil at a depth of 4in (10cm) and about 3in (8cm) apart. They can be grown in informal clumps, used in bedding, or grown in pots. Fertilize after flowering to help the bulbs build up their strength.

◊ ☼ ☀ f Z5–9 H9–1
↕ to 12in (30cm) ↔ to 3in (8cm)

MAGNOLIA × LOEBNERI
'Leonard Messel'

Deciduous shrub

A substantial shrub or small tree with large, rounded leaves. It bears fragrant flowers that boast a dozen lilac-pink, strap-shaped petals, the color of which is most intense during warm springs. It grows happily on most soils and tolerates alkaline soil. Plant where it has adequate space to spread, since magnolias resent disturbance. It rarely needs pruning.

○ ◐ ☼ ◑ *f* Z5–9 H9–5
‡ to 25ft (8m) ↔ to 20ft (6m)

MAGNOLIA
'Star Wars'

Deciduous tree

This recently introduced magnolia bears massive, deep pink blooms at a very early age. It was named after the shape of the flowers, which can measure up to 12in (30cm) across, with petals pointing in many different directions. 'Star Wars' grows in most soils; in time, this vigorous plant may grow to form a medium-sized, pyramid-shaped tree. Plant where it has plenty of space to develop unhindered.

○ ◐ ☼ ◑ Z5–9 H9–5
‡ to 30ft (10m) ↔ to 25ft (8m)

NARCISSUS *'Passionale'*

Bulbous perennial

This vigorous daffodil has milky white petals and a large pink cup. It makes a superb spring cut flower. Plant the bulbs in well-drained, fertile soil at three times their depth in late summer or early autumn. They will perform well in a sunny situation and can be used in a border planting or formal bedding. Deadhead the plants after flowering, and divide large clumps after 3–5 years.

○ ☼ Z3–9 H9–1
↕ to 16in (40cm) ↔ to 6in (15cm)

PAEONIA CAMBESSEDESII

Perennial

The Majorcan peony is one of the first peonies to bloom. It has grayish green leaves with deep red undersides and wavy margins, while the flowers have five pale magenta-pink petals and deeper pink veins. Plant it in full sun in a well-drained soil. It needs protection from late frosts, and it is often best grown in the shelter of a south-facing wall with extra winter protection.

○ ☼ Z7–8 H8–7
↕↔ to 22in (55cm)

PRUNUS
'Accolade'

Deciduous tree

A beautiful flowering cherry, 'Accolade' has midgreen leaves that turn orange-red in autumn before they fall. Its wide-spreading branches produce clusters of three semidouble, pale pink flowers that emerge from deep pink buds. It needs a sunny situation and should be planted in deep, well-drained, fertile soil. This tree rarely requires pruning.

◊ ☼ Z6–8 H8–6
‡↔ to 25ft (8m)

PRUNUS MUME
'Beni-chidori'

Deciduous tree

Japanese apricots are spreading trees suitable for small gardens. The almond-scented, double, deep pink flowers of 'Beni-chidori' appear in late winter or early spring and become paler as they age. The tree may also later produce small orange fruit, which look a little like apricots but are very bitter. Plant it in a sunny, sheltered position, where frost is unlikely to damage the blooms, in deep, well-drained, fertile soil. Little pruning is required.

◊ ☼ *f* Z6–8 H8–6
‡↔ to 28ft (9m)

PRUNUS
'Okame'

Deciduous tree

The toothed, oval, dark green leaves of this flowering cherry turn brilliant shades of orange and red in autumn. The cup-shaped, single, deep pink flowers provide a longer display than most cherries. It is best planted in a sunny position in a deep, moist, well-drained, fertile soil, and it will only occasionally need to be pruned.

◊ ◐ ☼ Z5–8 H8–5
‡ to 30ft (10m) ↔ to 25ft (8m)

PRUNUS × YEDOENSIS

Deciduous tree

The beautiful Yoshino cherry grows to form a medium-sized, round-headed tree with gently arching branches. It bears clusters of five or six single, pale pink flowers that gradually fade to white in the sun. It should be planted in deep, fertile, well-drained soil. Little pruning is required.

◊ ☼ Z6–8 H8–6
‡ to 50ft (15m) ↔ to 30ft (10m)

TULIPA
'Pink Beauty'

Bulbous perennial

Tulips are an invaluable addition to the spring border and are used to create a spectrum of color relatively early in the year. There is plenty of choice, with different varieties bursting into flower throughout spring and early summer, providing a range of sizes, colors, and flower shapes. The deep pink petals (with a brushstroke of white) and cup-shaped flowers of 'Pink Beauty' appear early. It makes a particularly eye-catching bedding plant.

◊ ☼ Z4–7 H7–1
‡ to 24in (60cm) ↔ to 5in (13cm)

VIOLA X WITTROCKIANA
Ultima Series

Perennial

Pansies have been widely hybridized to produce a range of long-flowering plants. The Ultima Series starts to flower in winter and continues through spring. They are available in a range of bright colors including pink, and they make a superb choice for brightening up the garden. Use them as bedding and in pots and windowboxes in a sunny site in fertile, well-drained soil.

◊ ☼ Z4–8 H8–1
‡ to 9in (23cm) ↔ to 12in (30cm)

CAMELLIA JAPONICA
'Coquettii'

Evergreen shrub

In early to midspring the arching stems of this slow-growing shrub are covered with deep red, semidouble or double flowers. It makes an elegant addition to a border and will complement plantings in a woodland garden, but it can also be grown as a specimen in containers. Choose a partially shaded site, out of the early morning sun, in moist but well-drained, organic, acidic soil. Use an acidic soil mix in containers.

◊ ◊ ☼ Z7–8 H8–7

↕ to 28ft (9m) ↔ to 25ft (8m)

CHAENOMELES × SUPERBA
'Crimson and Gold'

Deciduous shrub

The deep crimson flowers with golden yellow anthers are produced by this Japanese quince from spring to early summer; they are often followed in autumn by yellow-green fruit. Its wide-spreading habit makes it a useful shrubby groundcover, planting against walls or in a border, or grown as an informal, low, flowering hedge. Quinces trained against walls or used as hedges should be cut back after flowering.

◊ ☼ Z5–8 H9–4

↕ to 3ft (1m) ↔ to 6ft (2m)

CORYDALIS SOLIDA
'George Baker'

Perennial

This attractive tuberous perennial has deeply dissected, grayish green leaves. In spring it produces bright red (with a hint of orange) tubular flowers. Plant it in a rock or gravel garden in full sun or partial shade and well-drained, fertile soil. Divide in autumn if clumps become too large.

◊ ☼ ☼ Z5–7 H7–5
↕ to 10in (25cm) ↔ to 8in (20cm)

ERYSIMUM
'Blood Red'

Perennial

Although perennial, wallflowers are often grown as biennial bedding plants, planted in combination with tall-stemmed tulips. Left alone, they will live for several years but can become woody and leggy with age. This variety has vivid, deep red flowers in spring and is ideal for growing against a dry wall or to brighten up the front of a sunny border or raised bed. Plant it in autumn in very well-drained, neutral to alkaline soil.

◊ ☼ Z5–8 H8–5
↕↔ to 12in (30cm)

PAEONIA TENUIFOLIA

Perennial

Fernleaf peonies are among the earliest species to flower, producing beautiful deep red, single flowers in spring amid dark green, ferny leaves. There are also other forms with double white, red, and pink flowers. Plant it in a sunny site in well-drained, sandy soil. This delicate-looking plant may be grown in rock or gravel gardens or a herbaceous border.

◊ ☀ Z5–8 H8–5
↕↔ to 28in (70cm)

PHOTINIA × FRASERI
'Red Robin'

Evergreen shrub

The glossy young leaves of this shrub are bright purplish red, turning dark bronze-green as the season progresses. From midspring it produces clusters of small white flowers. It prefers fertile, well-drained soil; the foliage is easily damaged by cold winds, so plant it in a sunny, sheltered position. It can be used as a hedging plant or free-standing shrub. Trim hedges two to three times a year to keep up the show of bright young foliage.

◊ ◊ ☀ ◐ Z8–9 H9–8
↕↔ to 15ft (5m)

PIERIS FORMOSA
'Wakehurst'

Evergreen shrub

The brilliant red young foliage of this beautiful shrub gradually turns various shades of pink and creamy white and then finally goes dark green. Small, urn-shaped white flowers hang in pendent clusters. 'Wakehurst' does best in semi-shade and needs protection from cold winds and late frosts. Plant it in moist, slightly acidic, organic soil in a shrub or woodland border. Prune lightly after it has flowered to maintain its shape.

○ ◑ ☼ ☼ Z7–9 H9–7
↕ to 15ft (5m) ↔ to 12ft (4m)

PRIMULA JAPONICA

Perennial

The Japanese primrose is a robust perennial with a rosette of spoon-shaped, pale green leaves. In spring it produces a thick stem with up to six tiers of many white, pink, red, or purplish red flowers. It needs organic, damp to wet soil and is ideal for a bog or waterside garden and moist woodland.

◑ ● ☼ ☼ Z3–8 H8–1
↕ ↔ to 18in (45cm)

PRIMULA
'Crescendo Bright Red'

Evergreen perennial

Polyanthus primroses are often planted
in autumn for a spring bedding display.
They produce rosettes of evergreen
leaves and often start flowering at the
end of winter. The Crescendo Series is
available in a range of bright colors
including vivid red. They prefer a sunny
position but will tolerate some shade,
and they should be planted in
reasonably fertile, moist but well-
drained soil.

◊ ◊ ☼ ☼ Z4–8 H8–1
‡ to 6in (15cm) ↔ to 12in (30cm)

PULMONARIA RUBRA
'Redstart'

Perennial

This attractive herbaceous perennial has
bright green, hairy leaves and funnel-
shaped, coral-red flowers. It begins to
flower early in the year, with blooms
often appearing in late winter and
continuing into spring. It forms a loose
clump and makes an excellent groundcover for damp, shady positions. Plants
are vigorous and should be divided
after two or three years. Cut back after
flowering to encourage a flush of bright
new foliage.

◊ ☼ ☼ Z5–8 H8–4
‡ to 16in (40cm) ↔ to 36in (90cm)

TULIPA
'Red Riding Hood'

Bulbous perennial

The bright red flowers of this striking
tulip have black marks at the base of
the petals, and its lance-shaped leaves
are strongly marked with purple stripes.
Plant bulbs in late autumn in a sunny
situation in well-drained, fertile soil in a
border or rock garden, where they can
be left for years. Alternatively, plant
them in containers, moving the bulbs
out into the garden after flowering. For
a bold bedding display, plant with a
deep yellow tulip, such as 'Yokahama'.

◊ ☼ Z4–7 H7–1
‡ to 8in (20cm) ↔ to 6in (15cm)

TULIPA
'Apeldoorn'

Bulbous perennial

Darwin tulips, such as 'Apeldoorn', are
easy to grow, and their rounded flowers
look equally at home in spring bedding
displays as they do when used as cut
flowers. 'Apeldoorn' has scarlet-red
flowers with black centers surrounded
by yellow. Plant bulbs in late autumn in
a sunny site in well-drained, fertile soil.
It looks superb when partnered with a
yellow tulip, such as 'Daydream'.

◊ ☼ Z4–7 H7–1
‡ to 24in (60cm) ↔ to 5in (13cm)

CROCUS
TOMMASINIANUS

Cormous perennial

This crocus gives the impression of being rather delicate, but its slender appearance is deceptive. It produces purple, violet, or lilac flowers from late winter to early spring, and it grows easily from seed. Plant the corms in autumn in a sunny site with well-drained soil, in groups to create drifts of color at the front of a border, or naturalize in short grass.

◊ ☼ Z3–8 H8–1
‡ to 4in (10cm) ↔ to 1in (2.5cm)

HARDENBERGIA
COMPTONIANA

Climber

Clusters of small mauve or purplish blue flowers appear on this vigorous climber with woody stems from early spring. It prefers a sunny position in moist, well-drained, neutral or acidic soil. Where not hardy, it will need to be kept in a greenhouse or conservatory over winter. In mild areas it can be used to complement exisiting plantings by growing it through larger shrubs and up small trees, or train it on a wall.

◊ ◊ ☼ Z13–15 H12–9
‡ to 8ft (2.5m)

HELLEBORUS ORIENTALIS
Early Purple Group

Perennial

Often sold under its former name of
H. atrorubens, this variable hellebore
flowers very early in the year. It has
deep purple, saucer-shaped, pendent
flowers that emerge from late winter
to early spring. The deciduous, palm-
shaped leaves are midgreen, flushed
with purple. It thrives on rich, moist,
well-drained soil, and its preference for
partial shade makes it a good choice for
a shrub border or a woodland garden.

◊ ◊ ☀ ☀ Z9–9 H9–1
‡ to 12in (30cm) ↔ to 18in (45cm)

PRIMULA AURICULA
'Adrian'

Evergreen perennial

A rosette-forming perennial, this alpine
auricula primrose has fleshy, pale green
leaves. In spring it bears beautiful
flowers with purple-blue petals, slightly
paler at the edges, and a white eye.
Alpine auriculas are extremely tough
plants, but they do best in a sunny or
partially shaded site in moist, well-
drained soil. Grow them in a rock or
gravel garden, raised beds, or in pots of
gritty, soil-based potting mix.

◊ ◊ ☀ ☀ Z3–8 H8–1
‡↔ to 4in (10cm)

RHODODENDRON DAURICUM

Evergreen shrub

The leaves of this semi-evergreen shrub are green with a dark brown underside. It starts flowering in late winter, when the funnel-shaped, bright pinkish purple blooms bring a dramatic burst of color to perhaps an otherwise gloomy garden. Plant it in a sunny site in well-drained, organic, acidic soil, and mulch it annually with leaf mold or bark chips. This sturdy rhododendron is suitable for exposed sites and may be used to create an informal screen.

△ ◑ ☼ ☀ Z4–8 H8–1
↕↔ to 5ft (1.5m)

RHODODENDRON 'Praecox'

Evergreen shrub

This is among the first rhododendrons to bloom, flowering from late winter and continuing into early spring. It is normally evergreen, but it will shed some of its leaves during winter. The pinkish purple flowers appear in clusters of two or three. The flowers may be damaged by late frost. It makes a spectacular flowering hedge but is equally at home in the border. Plant in full sun or partial shade in moist, well-drained, acidic soil.

△ ◑ ☼ ☀ Z6–8 H8–6
↕↔ to 4½ft (1.3m)

TULIPA HUMILIS
Violacea Group

Bulbous perennial

This tulip has large, purple, star-shaped flowers with a bright yellow blotch at the base of the petals, and narrow, grayish green leaves. Plant bulbs in late autumn in a sunny position in light, well-drained soil. It is ideal for the rock garden or to make a colorful display in raised beds. Leave undisturbed so clumps can build up; they like to be dry during summer.

◊ ☼ Z9–7 H7–1
‡↔ to 10in (25cm) ↔ to 5in (13cm)

VIOLA ODORATA

Perennial

Sweet violets may be small, but their very aromatic blue-purple or white flowers will perfume the garden in late winter and early spring. They self-seed and will quickly become established, particularly when allowed to naturalize in a woodland setting or among deciduous shrubs. Plant in a sunny position or in dappled shade in well-drained, organic soil. They can also be divided and replanted in spring.

◊ ☼ ☼ *f* Z7–9 H9–7
‡ to 8in (20cm) ↔ to 12in (30cm)

ANEMONE BLANDA
'Atrocaerulea'

Perennial

The deep-blue, daisylike flowers of this
anemone are striking when naturalized
in grass or beneath the bare branches
of deciduous trees. It has a low, clump-
forming habit that also makes it a
suitable plant for the front of a border.
Plant the knobby tubers in autumn
in full sun or partial shade and organic,
well-drained soil.

◊ ☼ ☀ Z4–8 H9–3
↕ to 4in (10cm) ↔ to 6in (15cm)

ANEMONE NEMOROSA
'Robinsoniana'

Perennial

This wood anemone bears numerous
pale lavender-blue flowers with a light
gray reverse to the petals. The midgreen leaves die back after flowering.
It is a low, creeping plant, useful for
underplanting or naturalizing. A native
of European woods, it does best in a
woodland situation, but it will grow in
most positions, given dappled or partial
shade and a moist but well-drained,
organic soil.

◊ ◗ ☀ Z4–8 H8–1
↕ to 6in (15cm) ↔ to 12in (30cm)

AUBRIETA
'Cobalt Violet'

Perennial

A mat-forming perennial with masses
of small, hairy leaves. In spring it
produces profuse quantities of small
violet-blue flowers. It is ideal for trailing
over the edge of a raised bed or stone
wall or for growing in a rock garden.
Plant it in fertile, well-drained, neutral
or alkaline soil, and cut it back after
flowering to keep it neat.

◊ ☼ Z5–7 H7–5
‡ to 4in (10cm) ↔ to 8in (20cm)

BRUNNERA MACROPHYLLA

Perennial

This spreading perennial has coarse,
long-stalked, heart-shaped leaves and
bright blue flowers in spring. It will
eventually form a large clump and is
good as a groundcover in semi-shaded
situations. It needs moist, well-drained,
organic soil. 'Hadspen Cream' has
partially variegated leaves with creamy
white margins that will brighten a dull
corner. Propagate it by seed in autumn
or division in spring.

◊ ◑ ☼ Z3–7 H7–1
‡ to 18in (45cm) ↔ to 24in (60cm)

CHIONODOXA LUCILIAE

Bulbous perennial

In spring, glory-of-the-snow bears up
to three violet-blue, star-shaped flowers,
each with a small white eye. It comes
from the stony slopes of Turkey and is
at home in a rock garden, raised bed,
or naturalized under deciduous trees or
at the front of a border. Plant the bulbs
in autumn in a sunny site in well-drained
soil. Established clumps benefit from a
mulch of leaf mold or well-rotted
compost in autumn.

○ ☼ Z3–9 H9–1
‡ to 6in (15cm) ↔ to 1¼in (3cm)

CLEMATIS ALPINA
'Frances Rivis'

Climber

A deciduous, early flowering climber
with midblue, bell-shaped flowers in
spring to early summer and feathery
seedheads in autumn. It tolerates fairly
exposed situations. Prune it back after
flowering. Provide support in the form
of wires or a trellis attached to a wall or
fence, or train it over an arch or tripod.
Grow it in well-drained, fertile,
preferably alkaline soil, with the roots
in shade and its head in the sun.

○ ☼ ☀ Z7–9 H9–7
‡ to 10ft (3m) ↔ to 5ft (1.5m)

HEPATICA NOBILIS
VAR. JAPONICA

Perennial

This is a slow-growing perennial that
retains it leathery leaves during most
winters. The star-shaped flowers, with
blue-purple, pink, or white petals that
open in spring, sit above three small,
dark green leaves. It requires partial
shade and moist, organic soil and is
well suited to a woodland setting or
a shady border.

◊ ☼ Z5–8 H8–4
↕ to 3in (8cm) ↔ to 5in (12cm)

HYACINTHUS ORIENTALIS
'Blue Jacket'

Bulbous perennial

This is one of the best blue flowered
hyacinths, with wonderfully fragrant,
navy blue blooms. The petals have a
waxy texture and purple veins. Plant it
in autumn in deep, well-drained, fertile
soil in sun or partial shade. Hyacinths
are perfect for creating colorful spring
bedding displays and are also useful
container or windowbox plants. Grow
them either outside or forced in pots
for indoor display.

◊ ☼ ☼ ƒ Z5–9 H9–1
↕ to 12in (30cm) ↔ to 3in (8cm)

IRIS HISTRIOIDES
'Major'

Bulbous perennial

The vivid blue flowers of this vigorous dwarf iris open in early spring. Its lower petals are marked with a bright yellow ridge, which is surrounded by dark blue lines, and the squarish leaves are very short at the beginning of the year but extend to 12in (30cm) after flowering. Plant it in a sunny location in well-drained, fertile soil. Dwarf irises are an excellent choice for a rock garden, raised beds, or containers.

◊ ☼ Z5–8 H8–5
↕ to 6in (15cm) ↔ to 3in (7cm)

IRIS
'Joyce'

Bulbous perennial

A superb plant for a rock garden, this is a reticulata iris that flowers very early in the spring. It bears sky blue flowers with a bold yellow flare down the center of the petals. Plant bulbs in autumn in a sunny situation and well-drained, neutral or alkaline soil. 'Joyce' will also grow happily in containers or troughs of gritty, soil-based potting mix. Keep the bulbs on the dry side during summer, or you can lift them and replant in autumn.

◊ ☼ Z5–8 H8–5
↕ to 5in (12cm) ↔ to 3in (7cm)

IRIS
'Katharine Hodgkin'

Bulbous perennial

This vigorous dwarf iris flowers from late winter. Its upper petals are covered with fine, deep blue veins, while the broad lower petals have a yellow center and are heavily marked with blue lines and speckles. Plant the bulbs in autumn on a sunny bank or in other well-drained situation, making sure the bulbs are kept on the dry side during summer. It does best in neutral or slightly alkaline soil.

◊ ☼ Z5–8 H8–5
‡ to 5in (12cm) ↔ to 3in (7cm)

IRIS
'Cantab'

Bulbous perennial

Another reticulata iris (see 'Joyce'), this one has pale blue flowers with slightly darker lower petals marked by a deep yellow crest. The blooms start to appear in late winter. These iris are vigorous, but the bulbs often divide after they have flowered and then take a couple of years to grow large enough to bloom again. Plant the bulbs in autumn in a sunny situation and fertile, well-drained soil, such as in a rock garden or trough filled with gritty soil-based potting mix.

◊ ☼ Z5–8 H8–5
‡ to 5in (12cm) ↔ to 3in (7cm)

MUSCARI ARMENIACUM

Bulbous perennial

The grape hyacinth is one of the most widely grown spring-flowering bulbs, used to create spectacular bedding displays and in the border. Each stem carries a dense spike of small, deep blue flowers above narrow, bright green leaves. In the right conditions, it spreads quickly and may occasionally be invasive. The bulbs can become overcrowded and will benefit from division in summer every few years. Plant bulbs in autumn in full sun and fertile, moist but well-drained soil.

◊ ◑ ☼ Z4–8 H8–1
‡ to 8in (20cm) ↔ to 4in (10cm)

OMPHALODES CAPPADOCICA

Evergreen perennial

The forget-me-not-like flowers of this evergreen are azure blue with white eyes and are borne on slender stems from early spring. It has creeping roots and forms clumps of heart-shaped, slightly hairy leaves, which make an ideal groundcover for shady places. Grow it in full or partial shade and slightly moist, well-drained, organic, fertile soil.

◊ ◑ ☼ ☀ Z6–8 H8–6
‡ to 10in (25cm) ↔ to 16in (40cm)

PULMONARIA
'Lewis Palmer'

Perennial

This deciduous groundcover plant has
slightly hairy, lance-shaped leaves with
greenish white spots and small funnel-
shaped flowers that are pink when they
open in spring and then turn a vibrant
blue. Lungwort should be grown in
organic, moist soil in partial or full
shade. It attracts bees and makes an
excellent choice for a wildlife garden,
or use it to enhance a shady woodland
or shrub border. Cut it back after it has
flowered to refresh the foliage.

◊ ☼ ☀ Z5–8 H8–5
‡ to 14in (35cm) ↔ to 18in (45cm)

PUSCHKINIA SCILLOIDES

Bulbous perennial

The pale blue, bell-like flowers of this
bulbous perennial are set off by a fine
blue line down the center of each petal.
Its compact spikes make an attractive
addition to a rock garden or shrub
border. Plant it in a sunny or partially
shaded site in well-drained, fertile soil.

◊ ☼ ☀ Z3–9 H9–1
‡ to 6in (15cm) ↔ to 2in (5cm)

RHODODENDRON
Blue Tit Group

Evergreen shrub

This remarkably compact rhododendron bears abundant small, funnel-shaped, grayish blue flowers. Its leaves are initially yellow-green but darken to midgreen as the plant matures. Like many dwarf rhododendrons, 'Blue Tit' will bloom happily in a container or in a rock or gravel garden, given full sun and moist, well-drained, acidic soil or acidic soil mix.

◊ ◊ ☼ ☀ Z5–8 H8–5
‡↔ to 3ft (1m)

SCILLA BIFOLIA

Bulbous perennial

This is a distinctive flowering bulb that looks wonderful naturalized in grass or under deciduous shrubs and trees. It has narrow, strap-shaped, bright green leaves and star-shaped flowers borne on one side of the stem. This species has blue or violet-blue flowers, but there are also varieties with white ('Alba') and pink ('Rosea') blooms. Plant it in fertile, organic, well-drained soil in full sun or partial shade.

◊ ☼ Z3–8 H8–1
‡↔ to 6in (15cm)

SCILLA MISCHTSCHENKOANA

Bulbous perennial

The pale blue, bell-shaped flowers of
this bulbous perennial have a dark blue
stripe down the center of each petal.
They are carried above broad, strap-
shaped, arching leaves on rather short
stems, which grow longer as the
flowers open in early spring. Naturalize
it in grass or plant in a rock or gravel
garden or raised bed in a sunny
position with well-drained soil.
Plant bulbs in autumn.

◊ ☼ Z6–9 H9–6
‡ to 6in (15cm) ↔ to 2in (5cm)

SCILLA SIBERICA
'Spring Beauty'

Bulbous perennial

This bulbous perennial has small spikes
of bell-shaped, violet-tinted, deep blue
flowers borne on one side of the stem.
Ideal for a rock garden or a mixed
herbaceous border beneath deciduous
shrubs or trees, it prefers sandy, well-
drained, fertile soil in slight shade or
full sun. Divide large clumps after
flowering during summer. Plant bulbs
in autumn.

◊ ☼ ☀ Z5–8 H8–5
‡ to 8in (20cm) ↔ to 2in (5cm)

EUPHORBIA CHARACIAS SUBSP. WULFENII

Evergreen shrub

A large rounded bush with grayish green leaves. The huge, globe-shaped heads filled with small yellow-green flowers appear from early spring. It is ideal for the back of a border, gravel garden, or gaps in paving, but it needs a sunny site and well-drained soil. Buy young plants from a reliable source to avoid inferior, less brightly colored seedlings. Cut out the old flowerheads in autumn, and wear gloves: the sap may cause an allergic skin reaction.

◊ ☼ Z7–10 H12–7
↕↔ to 4ft (1.2m)

EUPHORBIA MYRSINITES

Evergreen perennial

This is a sprawling, evergreen perennial suitable for planting in a rock or gravel garden, gaps in paving, or at the edge of a raised bed or on a stone wall. The fleshy, blue-green leaves are arranged in a spiral around the stems. In spring, the stems are topped with clusters of yellowish green flowers that turn a grayish pink as they fade. Plant it full sun in well-drained soil. It may self-seed if not deadheaded (removal of the dead flowers) after flowering.

◊ ☼ Z5–8 H8–5
↕ to 4in (10cm) ↔ to 12in (30cm)

HELLEBORUS ARGUTIFOLIUS

Evergreen perennial

The Corsican hellebore bears bright green, slightly nodding, cup-shaped flowers from late winter to early spring. Its evergreen leaves are divided into three toothed, grayish green leaflets. One of the largest hellebores, it grows best on moist, well-drained, alkaline or neutral soil in full sun or partial shade. Choose it for a mixed border or allow to naturalize in a woodland setting, since it self-seeds freely.

◊ ☼ ☀ Z6–9 H9–6
‡ to 4ft (1.2m) ↔ to 36in (90cm)

HELLEBORUS FOETIDUS

Evergreen perennial

The stinking hellebore is a vigorous, clump-forming perennial with dark evergreen, deeply divided, somewhat leathery leaves; it is named for the unpleasant smell that emanates from them when they are crushed. The bell-shaped, slightly fragrant green flowers are produced in clusters on tall, erect stems from late winter to early spring. Equally at home in full sun or partial shade, it can be planted in a variety of situations in the garden and is happy on moist, alkaline soils.

◊ ☼ ☀ ƒ Z6–9 H9–6
‡ to 32in (80cm) ↔ to 18in (45cm)

ADONIS VERNALIS

Perennial

This clump-forming perennial originates from Europe, where it is often found in rocky, exposed sites. In spring it produces golden yellow flowers above deeply dissected, bright green leaves. Grow it in a raised bed or rock or gravel garden in full sun and well-drained, preferably alkaline soil.

◊ ☼ Z4–7 H7–1
‡↔ to 12in (30cm)

ANEMONE × LIPSIENSIS

Perennial

The pale sulfur yellow flowers of this carpet-forming wood anemone appear in spring. Its dark green leaves are deeply toothed and lie close to the soil surface. Best grown in partially shaded situations beneath deciduous trees or shrubs, this natural hybrid prefers a organic, well-drained soil and will tolerate alkaline conditions.

◊ ◗ ☼ Z5–8 H8–5
‡ to 6in (15cm) ↔ to 18in (45cm)

ANEMONE RANUNCULOIDES

Perennial

This spreading perennial received its species name because of its similarity to buttercups (*Ranunculus*). It has deeply divided midgreen leaves and bright yellow flowers with five or six petals. It enjoys a site in partial shade and is ideal for a mixed border or naturalizing in a woodland or wild garden. Plant it in moist but well-drained, organic soil.

◌ ◗ ☀ Z4–8 H8–1
‡ to 4in (10cm) ↔ to 18in (45cm)

CALTHA PALUSTRIS

Perennial

The kingcup, or marsh marigold, is a vigorous, clump-forming perennial with serrated, glossy green leaves. It is one of the earliest aquatic plants to come into bloom and has large, bright golden yellow flowers. Thriving in full sun in wet soil, it makes an excellent choice for a bog garden, but it may also be grown in a permanently moist border or shallow water at the edge of a pond, contained in a perforated basket. 'Flore Pleno' is slightly less vigorous and has double yellow flowers.

◗ ◗ ☀ Z3–7 H7–1
‡ to 16in (40cm) ↔ to 18in (45cm)

CORYLOPSIS PAUCIFLORA

Deciduous shrub

This bushy, deciduous plant produces small, very fragrant, pale yellow, bell-shaped flowers in spring. The young leaves appear after the flowers; they are dark pink when they open but turn green as they age. Although other corylopsis species tolerate alkaline conditions, *C. pauciflora* requires acidic soil. Given plenty of room, it will grow into a pleasing, spreading shape and enhance a woodland garden or a shrub border in dappled shade. The flowers can be damaged by late frosts.

◊ ◊ ☼ *f* Z6–9 H9–6
‡ to 5ft (1.5m) ↔ to 8ft (2.5m)

CORYLUS AVELLANA 'Aurea'

Deciduous shrub

In late winter and early spring, this decorative hazel bears dangling yellow catkins. It forms a broad, spreading shrub or small tree with bright yellow-green, sharply toothed leaves, and in late summer the rounded hazelnuts are favored by squirrels. A relatively small variety, it is suitable for a shrub border and contrasts well with the purple-leaved hazel, *C. avellana* 'Purpurea'.

◊ ☼ ☼ Z3–9 H9–1
‡↔ to 15ft (5m)

CROCUS CHRYSANTHUS
'E.A. Bowles'

Cormous perennial

This dainty crocus has deep lemon yellow, goblet-shaped flowers with purple feathering on the outer petals. The leaves are dark green with a white stripe. Plant the corms in groups in autumn in well-drained soil at the front of a sunny border for an early splash of spring color, or grow in raised beds and containers.

◊ ☼ Z3–8 H8–1
‡ to 3in (7cm) ↔ to 2in (5cm)

CROCUS CHRYSANTHUS
'Cream Beauty'

Cormous perennial

This compact crocus has golden-throated, rich cream-colored flowers that darken at the base to a greenish gold. Plant the bulbs as for 'E.A Bowles' (above) in a sunny position in well-drained, gritty soil. It is suitable for a rock garden and may also be naturalized in grass.

◊ ☼ Z3–8 H8–1
‡ to 3in (7cm) ↔ to 2in (5cm)

ERANTHIS HYEMALIS

Perennial

The winter aconite begins flowering
in late winter and continues into early
spring. Its bright yellow blooms perch
on a ruff of deeply divided, leaflike
bracts. Ideal for naturalizing in grass
and woodland borders, it will create
a colorful carpet beneath deciduous
trees and shrubs. Plant the tubers in
autumn in fertile, moist, well-drained
soil that does not dry out in summer.
Large clumps can be divided after they
have flowered.

◊ ◐ ☼ Z4–9 H9–1
↕ to 3in (8cm) ↔ to 2in (5cm)

ERYSIMUM
'Moonlight'

Evergreen perennial

A mat-forming perennial wallflower
with evergreen, grayish green, lance-
shaped leaves, throughout spring and
early summer it produces clusters of
slightly fragrant, pale sulfur yellow
flowers. It is rather short-lived, but it
makes an excellent subject for a dry
wall, gravel or raised bed, or rock
garden. Plant it in full sun in
poor, gritty, very well-drained soil.

◊ ☼ ☼ ƒZ5–8 H7–1
↕ to 12in (30cm) ↔ to 18in (45cm)

ERYTHRONIUM
'Pagoda'

Bulbous perennial

This dog's-tooth violet bears drooping
clusters of up to five sulfur yellow
flowers in spring. A vigorous plant with
mottled, glossy green leaves, it is
suitable for planting beneath shrubs or
in the dappled shade of a woodland
garden in moist, organic, well-drained
soil. Plant the bulbs in autumn. Large
clumps can be divided after the leaves
have died; replant immediately to
prevent the bulbs from drying out.

◊ ◊ ☼ Z4–9 H9–8
‡ to 14in (35cm) ↔ to 8in (20cm)

FORSYTHIA × INTERMEDIA
'Lynwood'

Deciduous shrub

Forsythias are free flowering, medium-
sized shrubs, the upright branches of
which are covered with large, bright
yellow flowers before the leaves
unfurl. Plant them in a row to create a
spectacular hedge, or grow one as a
freestanding shrub in a border. Cut
hedges and prune back the shoots of
shrubs after flowering to promote new
growth and flowers the following year.
Choose a site in full sun or light shade
in fertile, well-drained soil.

◊ ☼ Z6–9 H9–6
‡ ↔ to 10ft (3m)

HYACINTHUS ORIENTALIS
'City of Haarlem'

Bulbous perennial

With spikes of primrose yellow, waxy, bell-shaped flowers, this is one of only a few yellow hyacinths. Its intense scent makes it an appealing houseplant when forced into bloom in the winter months. Outdoors, it looks wonderful in spring bedding displays, where it needs full sun and free-draining soil. Forced bulbs grown for indoor display should be fertilized regularly after flowering and then planted outside. The flower spikes will be smaller in subsequent years.

◊ ☼ *f* Z5–9 H9–1

‡ to 12in (30cm) ↔ to 3in (8cm)

IRIS DANFORDIAE

Bulbous perennial

This is an extremely attractive dwarf iris with bright yellow spring flowers. It is best considered as a disposable plant, because although it flowers well in the first season, the bulbs then split into tiny bulblets that rarely bloom again. Ideal for containers, troughs, or raised beds, the bulbs should be planted in late summer or early autumn in a sunny position and well-drained soil.

◊ ☼ Z5–8 H8–5

‡ to 4in (10cm) ↔ to 2in (5cm)

IRIS WINOGRADOWII

Bulbous perennial

The pale yellow flowers of this dwarf iris emerge in early spring. Its leaves are very short at flowering time, but they lengthen afterward. Suitable for a rock or gravel garden or a raised bed; grow it in full sun in well-drained but moisture-retentive soil. Do not allow the bulbs to dry out during summer.

◊ ◑ ☼ Z5–8 H8–5
‡ to 4in (10cm) ↔ to 3in (7cm)

MAHONIA AQUIFOLIUM
'Apollo'

Evergreen shrub

This suckering shrub has large, red-stalked leaves divided into spiny leaflets. Leaves take on coppery tones in autumn. Its bright yellow flowers are carried in compact clusters, which are succeeded by bluish black berries. The Oregon grape will thrive in the dry soil beneath trees; grown in sun or shade, it provides a superb groundcover that should be cut almost to the ground after flowering every other year.

◊ ◑ ☼ ☀ Z6–9 H9–3
‡ to 24in (60cm) ↔ to 4ft (1.2m)

NARCISSUS
'Ambergate'

Bulbous perennial

This striking daffodil bears flowers with a large, deep orange cup surrounded by warm yellow petals in midspring. The flowers can measure as much as 4in (10cm) across, making it a dramatic choice for cut flowers. It may also be planted in groups in a mixed border or naturalized in grass. Plant bulbs in late summer to three times their depth in a sunny site in well-drained, reasonably fertile soil.

◊ ☼ Z3–9 H9–1
↕ to 16in (40cm) ↔ to 6in (15cm)

NARCISSUS BULBOCODIUM

Bulbous perennial

The diminutive hoop-petticoat daffodil produces dark green, almost cylindrical leaves and funnel-shaped yellow flowers. Tiny, pointed petals appear halfway down the flower funnel, so that it looks like a lady wearing a long yellow ball gown. It grows best in a sunny position and can be planted among fine-leaved grasses or in a raised bed. The variety *conspicuus* bears deep golden yellow flowers. Plant bulbs as for 'Ambergate' (see above).

◊ ☼ Z3–9 H9–1
↕ to 6in (15cm) ↔ to 2in (5cm)

NARCISSUS CYCLAMINEUS

Bulbous perennial

This early-flowering daffodil produces
deep yellow, vase-shaped flowers with
strongly swept-back petals, and bright
green leaves. Grow in a sunny position,
in well-drained neutral to acidic soil.
It makes an excellent choice for
containers, a woodland border, or
for naturalizing in grass. Plant bulbs
as for 'Ambergate' (see left).

◊ ☼ Z3–9 H9–1
↕ to 8in (20cm) ↔ to 3in (8cm)

NARCISSUS
'February Gold'

Bulbous perennial

A widely grown daffodil, 'February
Gold' is extremely vigorous and
produces nodding, large, golden yellow
flowers with slightly swept-back petals.
The flowers are set off by midgreen,
strap-shaped leaves. It is suitable for
planting in borders or for naturalizing
in grass. Plant bulbs as for 'Ambergate'
(see above left).

◊ ☼ Z3–9 H9–1
↕ to 12in (30cm) ↔ to 3in (8cm)

PRIMULA PALINURI

Evergreen perennial

This is an attractive, rosette-forming primrose with rather fleshy, spoon-shaped leaves. In early spring it bears often large, cowslip-like clusters of slightly fragrant yellow flowers. Grow it in a sunny site in reasonably fertile, moist, well-drained, preferably alkaline soil, and mulch with grit. It suffers in cold, wet winters, so it is best to grow it in pots of gritty soil-based potting mix with protection from excessive moisture.

○ ◑ ☼ ƒ Z5–8 H8–5
↕↔ to 12in (30cm)

PRIMULA VULGARIS

Evergreen perennial

This primrose is often regarded as a harbinger of spring. Each stem of this rosette-forming perennial carries up to 25 single, pale yellow flowers with an orange spot at the base of each petal. It prefers a position in partial shade and moist, well-drained, organic soil. An excellent plant for growing in containers, it will also be happy in woodland and shrub borders and rock gardens. Propagate it from seed or divide during early spring or autumn.

○ ◑ ☼ Z4–8 H8–1
↕ to 8in (20cm) ↔ to 14in (35cm)

RANUNCULUS FICARIA
'Brazen Hussy'

Perennial

This celandine boasts glossy, bronze-colored, heart-shaped leaves that lie close to the ground, and bright yellow flowers that emerge in spring. Given wet soil in winter it can be invasive, but it is easy to remove unwanted portions, and it dies back completely during the summer. It will thrive in partial shade and moist soil in a shrub border or in a woodland setting. The variety *aurantiacus* bears single orange flowers.

◑ ☼ Z4–8 H8–1
‡ to 2in (5cm) ↔ to 8in (20cm)

RHODODENDRON LUTESCENS

Evergreen shrub

An attractive medium-to-large evergreen shrub with bronzy-green leaves, its clusters of primrose yellow flowers start to open in late winter and continue into early spring. Ideal for brightening up a shady woodland situation, it should be protected from strong winds and planted in moist, well-drained, organic, acidic soil. Mulch it annually with leaf mold or bark chips.

○ ◑ ☼ ☼ Z7–9 H9–7
‡ ↔ to 15ft (5m)

SALIX CAPREA
'Kilmarnock'

Deciduous tree

Salix caprea is usually a tall, vigorous tree, but the Kilmarnock willow rarely exceeds a height of 6ft (2m), making it ideal for planting in small gardens or large containers. It has a weeping habit and bears numerous, rounded yellow catkins in late winter and early spring. Plant it in deep, moist, well-drained soil in a sunny site. The branches can become congested; in late winter prune out surplus ones and remove shoots that appear on the trunk.

◊ ◖ ☼ Z6–8 H8–6
‡↔ to 6ft (2m)

TULIPA KAUFMANNIANA

Bulbous perennial

The flowers of the waterlily tulip have narrow, pointed, yellow or cream petals that are tinted orange or pink on the outside. Its tall stems bear up to five blooms carried above lance-shaped, grayish green leaves. A long-lived bulb, it is best grown in a rock garden. Plant the bulbs in late autumn in full sun in fertile, well-drained soil at a depth of 4in (10cm).

◊ ☼ Z4–7 H8–1
‡ to 10in (25cm) ↔ to 6in (15cm)

TULIPA URUMIENSIS
Bulbous perennial

The cheerful, star-shaped, golden yellow flowers of this low-growing tulip appear in early spring above a rosette of waxy green leaves; much of its stem remains below ground. Its petals are flushed with green and red on the outside. Grow it in a raised bed or rock garden, where clumps can develop undisturbed and the soil is well-drained and fairly dry in summer. Plant the bulbs in late autumn at a depth of about 4in (10cm).

◊ ☀ Z4–7 H8–1
‡ to 6in (15cm) ↔ to 5in (13cm)

VALERIANA PHU
'Aurea'
Perennial

The main feature of valerian is its bright butter yellow foliage that appears in early spring. The leaves turn lime green after a few weeks and then mature to midgreen. After these exciting foliage effects, its small white summer flowers are rather unimpressive. It provides the perfect foil for blue spring flowers in the herbaceous border. Plant it in full sun in any reasonably fertile, well-drained soil, and divide it in autumn.

◊ ☀ Z5–9 H9–5
‡↔ to 15in (38cm)

LATE SPRING

As TEMPERATURES RISE and light levels increase, the garden seems to burst into life. Flower buds open, and spring-flowering shrubs with bright new foliage add color and scent to borders and beds. As the bulbs continue their seasonal show, leaves of perennials pushing through the soil hint at the drama to come.

However, new growth can be damaged by late frosts, so keep covers handy to protect young plants, and do not be tempted to put out tender bedding or summer displays in containers too early. Slugs and snails are lurking in the damp conditions, and the succulent shoots of many perennials are vulnerable to their feeding. Entice birds, toads, and frogs to help control the pests by providing a pond; with candelabra primroses and other moisture-loving plants in bloom, there is plenty for the gardener to enjoy, too.

Ornamental cherries (*Prunus*) and crabapples (*Malus*) do double duty in your garden: many will reward you with autumn interest. The massive blooms of tree peonies make a big impact, but the rhododendrons, with hundreds to choose from and flowers in almost every shade, provide the most excitement. If you lack the acidic conditions they enjoy, try early-flowering clematis and fragrant lilacs (*Syringa*).

ALPINES AND BULBS

The rock garden is at its best as the season begins, studded with jewel-like flowers of arabis, gold dust (*Aurinia*), spring gentians, and small species tulips. Tulips also dominate late-spring bulb displays, with larger-flowered varieties creating bold swaths of color in beds, borders, and containers. Clumps of quamash (*Camassia*) and tall, stately crown imperials (*Fritillaria imperialis*) make imposing centerpieces in the border, while the delicate snake's head fritillary (*Fritillaria meleagris*) is superb naturalized in grass.

ARABIS ALPINA *SUBSP.* CAUCASICA *'Variegata'*

Evergreen perennial

This mat-forming plant has rosettes of grayish green, spoon-shaped leaves. The fragrant white flowers are produced in loose clusters over a long period from late spring to early autumn. It is very sturdy and will flower well when grown in poor, well-drained soil in full sun, making it ideal for a rock or scree garden. 'Variegata' has the added bonus of green leaves with pale yellow margins.

◊ ☼ *f* Z4–8 H8–1
↕↔ to 6in (15cm)

CAMASSIA LEICHTLINII

Bulbous perennial

The white form of quamash flowers from late spring to early summer. The tall flowering stems make a striking addition to the herbaceous border. The bulbs should be planted at a depth of 4in (10cm) in autumn. Plant quamash in groups in deep, moist but well-drained soil in a sunny or slightly shaded position. Where marginally hardy, place a thick, loose mulch over the area where the bulbs have been planted.

◊ ◊ ☼ ☀ Z4–10 H12–1
↕ to 4.5ft (1.3m) ↔ to 12in (30cm)

CASSIOPE
'Edinburgh'

Evergreen shrub

This compact plant has small, slightly
hairy, dark green leaves and nodding,
bell-shaped white flowers with swept-
back tips, similar to those of lily-of-the-
valley. It is closely related to heathers
and needs a moist, fertile, acidic soil
in a sunny or partially shaded spot.
Cassiopes are fairly demanding plants,
but 'Edinburgh' is the least fussy.

◊ ☼ ☀ Z2–6 H6–1
‡ ↔ to 8in (20cm)

CHOISYA TERNATA

Evergreen shrub

The Mexican orange blossom is a fast-
growing shrub with glossy, dark green
foliage. The leaves are aromatic when
crushed. It produces a profusion of
fragrant, star-shaped white flowers –
a light pruning after these have faded
can often stimulate a second flush of
blooms in autumn. Grow in fertile,
well-drained soil in full sun. 'Sundance'
has bright yellow-green leaves.

◊ ☼ *f* Z8–10 H10–8
‡ ↔ to 8ft (2.5m)

CONVALLARIA MAJALIS

Perennial

Lily-of-the-valley is a delightful spring-flowering plant with arching stems of sweetly scented, bell-shaped white flowers that appear between the dark green leaves. It makes an ideal ground-cover plant for shady, damp situations and spreads very quickly by means of creeping roots. 'Albostriata' has gold-striped leaves, and 'Fortin's Giant' is slightly taller, growing to a height of 12in (30cm).

◊ ☼ ☀ *f* Z2–7 H7–1
‡ to 9in (23cm) ↔ to 12in (30cm)

CORNUS FLORIDA
'White Cloud'

Deciduous tree

The flowering dogwood forms an attractive, spreading tree that looks as if it is adorned with large white flowers in late spring. In fact, these "flowers" consist of four creamy white, petal-like bracts surrounding a cluster of tiny green flowers. An additional feature of this beautiful plant are the slightly twisted green leaves that turn bright orange and red iin autumn.

◊ ☼ Z5–8 H8–5
‡ to 20ft (6m) ↔ to 25ft (8m)

DAVIDIA INVOLUCRATA

Deciduous tree

In full bloom, the branches of the dove tree or ghost tree are hung with what look like hundreds of crisp white linen squares. These are, in fact, showy bracts that surround the tiny flowerheads. It needs shelter from strong winds and will grow in most situations, but it prefers moist but well-drained, fertile soil and a sunny position. When mature it can be quite large, making it less suitable for small gardens.

◊ ◊ ☼ Z6–8 H8–6
↕ to 50ft (15m) ↔ to 30ft (10m)

ERYTHRONIUM OREGONUM

Bulbous perennial

This dog's-tooth violet forms a clump of dark green leaves with paler mottling. In spring, it produces stems bearing two or three pendent flowers with creamy white reflexed petals and yellow anthers. Suitable for a woodland garden or beneath deciduous shrubs in fertile, moist but well-drained soil. Divide clumps in summer after the flowers have faded.

◊ ◊ ☼ Z3–9 H9–1
↕ to 14in (35cm) ↔ to 5in (12cm)

HALESIA MONTICOLA

Deciduous tree

The fast-growing snowdrop tree forms an attractive cone shape. Often before the leaves emerge, bell-shaped white blooms appear in clusters along the branches. These are followed in summer by winged green fruit measuring up to 2in (5cm) long. In autumn the leaves may take on a strong yellow color before falling. Plant in moist but well-drained, neutral or slightly acidic soil in a sunny (or partially shaded), sheltered position.

◊ ◊ ☼ ☀ Z6–9 H9–6
‡ to 40ft (12m) ↔ to 25ft (8m)

IRIS CONFUSA

Perennial

This is one of the crested irises. The leaves, which are green and sword-shaped, are held in fans on bamboo-like stems. In late spring and early summer it bears abundant, small, flattened white flowers measuring about 2in (5cm) across. *Iris confusa* should be grown in a sunny or slightly shaded position, with some shelter where marginally hardy. Soil should be moist and fertile. Mulch after flowering every year.

◊ ☼ ☀ Z8–10 H12–8
‡ to 3ft (1m) ↔ to indefinite

MAGNOLIA STELLATA *'Waterlily'*

Deciduous tree

The star magnolia is a fairly compact tree that is suitable for smaller gardens: just make sure it has sufficient space to spread its branches. 'Waterlily' bears an abundance of pure white, slightly fragrant flowers These are made up of numerous straplike petals. Give this magnolia a sunny or partially shaded spot and moist, well-drained soil.

○ ◐ ☼ ☽ *f* Z5–9 H9–5
↕ to 10ft (3m) ↔ to 12ft (4m)

MAGNOLIA WILSONII

Deciduous tree

This elegant magnolia forms a large shrub or small tree. In late spring and early summer it produces fragrant white flowers with a ring of crimson stamens in the center. It benefits from a sheltered spot in full sun or light shade and a moist, well-drained soil. As with all magnolias, give it plenty of space to develop unhindered.

○ ◐ ☼ ☽ *f* Z7–9 H9–7
↕ ↔ to 20ft (6m)

MALUS TORINGO
SUBSP. SARGENTII

Deciduous tree

This crabapple produces a profusion of white flowers in spring, giving rise in the autumn to bright red fruit. It has dark green, three-lobed leaves. Give it a spot in full sun or light shade and, although tolerant of a wide range of soil types, it prefers moderately fertile, moist, well-drained soil.

◊ ◖ ☼ ☀ Z5–9 H9–5
‡ to 12ft (4m) ↔ to 15ft (5m)

NARCISSUS POETICUS
VAR. RECURVUS

Bulbous perennial

The old pheasant's eye narcissus obtained its common name from the short, red-rimmed yellow cup in the center of the flower. This particular variety has fragrant, long-lasting flowers with swept-back, pure white petals and greenish yellow throats. It flowers slightly later in spring than many other daffodils and can be grown in borders, large containers, or naturalized in grass. Plant it in well-drained soil in full sun or dappled shade.

◊ ☼ ☀ *f* Z3–9 H9–1
‡ to 14in (35cm) ↔ to 4in (10cm)

OSMANTHUS DELAVAYI

Evergreen shrub

A large, rounded evergreen, this plant
has arching stems from which hang
clusters of tubular flowers in mid- to
late spring. The highly fragrant white
blooms are set off by dark green,
glossy, toothed foliage. Later in the
year, small blue-black berries appear.
Grow this bush in well-drained soil in
full sun or partial shade, and protect it
from drying winds. Prune it after the
flowers have faded.

◊ ☼ ☀ *f* Z7–9 H9–7
‡ to 20ft (6m) ↔ to 12ft (4m)

PAEONIA SUFFRUTICOSA
'Godaishu'

Deciduous shrub

This decorative white tree peony is well
worth searching for. It has dark green,
slightly waxy leaves and large semidouble flowers with pure white soft
petals that surround yellow stamens.
For the best results, plant it in well-
drained soil in full sun or partial shade.

◊ ☼ ☀ Z5–8 H8–5
‡ ↔ to 6ft (2m)

POLYGONATUM × HYBRIDUM

Perennial

Solomon's seal is an elegant plant with small, tubular white flowers that hang gracefully from arching green stems. It adds a touch of class to late-spring herbaceous borders and woodland gardens and needs a cool, shaded position and fertile, well-drained soil. 'Striatum' has variegated leaves. Divide clumps in early spring or autumn.

◊ ☀ Z6–9 H9–6
↕ to 4ft (1.2m) ↔ to 3ft (1m)

PRIMULA DENTICULATA
VAR. ALBA

Perennial

Drumstick primroses have neat, globe-shaped flowerheads composed of many small blooms. This variety has white flowers, each with a bright yellow eye, although drumstick primroses also come in shades of pale lilac, pink, and deep purple. All thrive in moist, well-drained, neutral to slightly acidic soil and fare best if the soil dries out a little in summer. They are ideal for use in a herbaceous border or among shrubs, and they are easy to raise from seed.

◊ ◖ ☀ ☀ Z2–8 H8–1
↕↔ to 18in (45cm)

PRUNUS LUSITANICA
SUBSP. AZORICA

Evergreen tree

This vigorous Portugal laurel forms an
evergreen shrub or small tree with
large, glossy leaves. It produces free-
flowering spikes of small, scented white
blooms in late spring and early summer.
In autumn it bears red cherrylike fruits
that turn black when ripe. This plant
grows well even on shallow alkaline
soil and will flourish when planted in a
sheltered position in full sun. It makes
a good specimen plant, but it is often
trimmed as a hedge.

◊ ◊ ☼ Z7–9 H9–7
‡ ↔ to 70ft (20m)

PRUNUS PADUS
'Watereri'

Deciduous tree

The bird cherry has a decorative habit,
with spreading branches that carry
pendent stems of cup-shaped, almond-
scented white flowers in late spring.
These are then followed by small black
fruits that are loved by birds. This
vigorous tree should be grown in full
sun or light shade in a well-drained,
moist soil. The bird cherry makes an
excellent specimen for the middle of a
lawn or in a mixed border.

◊ ◊ ☼ ☀ *f* Z4–8 H8–1
‡ to 50ft (15m) ↔ to 30ft (10m)

PYRUS SALICIFOLIA
'Pendula'

Deciduous tree

An ornamental pear, 'Pendula' has
attractive weeping branches covered
with oval silvery leaves. These are
accompanied in mid- to late spring by
clusters of creamy white flowers. Small,
inedible green fruit may also appear in
late summer. It needs full sun and well-
drained soil and makes a decorative
specimen for a lawn or a mixed border.

◊ ☼ Z5–9 H9–5
‡ to 25ft (8m) ↔ to 20ft (6m)

RHODODENDRON
'Fragrantissimum'

Evergreen shrub

This rhododendron has highly fragrant,
funnel-shaped white flowers that
contrast beautifully with the slightly
hairy, evergreen foliage. Grow it in sun
or partial shade in a well-drained, acidic
to neutral soil or in a pot filled with
acidic potting mix. Mulch generously
with bark or leaf mold.

◊ ◊ ☼ ☀ ƒ Z9–10 H10–9
‡ ↔ to 6ft (2m)

RHODODENDRON 'Loderi King George'

Evergreen shrub

One of the best white rhododendrons, this slow-growing plant can grow to 12ft (4m) in height. The pale pink flower buds open in late spring to form large clusters of fragrant white flowers with green markings. It is best planted in a woodland garden and, like most rhododendrons, needs a moist, well-drained, acidic soil. Mulch it every year with bark or leaf mold, especially when young.

◊ ◐ ☼ ☼ *f* Z7–9 H9–7
‡ ↔ to 12ft (4m)

SAXIFRAGA 'Southside Seedling'

Perennial

This saxifrage bears densely packed rosettes of pale green, spoon-shaped leaves. It flowers freely, producing branched stems of red-centered white blooms. The leaf rosettes die after flowering. 'Southside Seedling' requires a very well-drained, slightly alkaline soil, preferably with coarse sand or grit added to it, and it prefers a sunny position.

◊ ☼ Z4–6 H6–1
‡ to 12in (30cm) ↔ to 8in (20cm)

SMILACINA RACEMOSA

Perennial

The false Solomon's seal is a slow-spreading plant that bears tall stems topped with conical clusters of small, slightly scented white flowers. The large leaves are also attractive. To grow well, false Solomon's seal requires a shady site, perhaps in a woodland garden setting or a moist shady border. It will do best in a moist, slightly acidic soil. Divide large clumps in spring.

◐ ☼ ☼ *f* Z4–9 H9–1
‡ to 36in (90cm) ↔ to 24in (60cm)

SPIRAEA
'Arguta'

Deciduous shrub

Known as bridal wreath because of its arching stems that are covered in late spring with small white flowers that create a light, delicate effect. The blooms are borne among lance-shaped, bright green leaves. Bridal wreath is perfect for a low hedge or in a mixed shrub border and needs a moist, well-drained soil in full sun. The flowers are produced on the previous year's wood, and the stems should be pruned back in early summer after flowering.

◊ ◊ ☼ Z5–8 H8–5
‡ to 6ft (2m) ↔ to 5ft (1.5m)

SYRINGA VULGARIS
'Madame Lemoine'

Deciduous shrub

Lilacs are large shrubs with branched, upright stems covered with dark green, heart-shaped leaves. 'Madame Lemoine' has large, cone-shaped clusters of pure white, highly scented flowers, which are produced in abundance during spring. Tolerant of pollution and most soils, except very acidic soil, it is ideal for growing in an urban garden. If lilacs become leggy, cut them back hard to 3ft (1m) above the ground after they have flowered.

○ ◑ ◐ ☼ *f* Z4–8 H8–1
‡ ↔ to 22ft (7m)

TRILLIUM GRANDIFLORUM
Perennial

The great white trillium produces large flowers with three distinctive, clear white petals (that turn pale pink as they age) and bright yellow stamens. The blooms contrast beautifully with the deep green leaves that eventually form a large clump. Trilliums need moist, well-drained soil and a slightly shaded position. They do best in a deciduous woodland, but they can also be used in a rock garden.

○ ◑ ☼ Z5–8 H8–4
‡ to 16in (40cm) ↔ to 12in (30cm)

TROLLIUS × CULTORUM
'Alabaster'

Perennial

Most globeflowers have bright yellow
or orange flowers, but those of
'Alabaster' are much paler. It has bowl-
shaped, deep cream-colored flowers
held on slim, upright stems. It will grow
happily in wet soil (as long as it dries
out slightly in summer) and is suitable
for waterside plantings or bog gardens.
Large clumps can be divided immediately after flowering.

◐ ◖ ☼ ☀ Z5–8 H8–4
‡ to 24in (60cm) ↔ to 16in (40cm)

TULIPA
'White Triumphator'

Bulbous perennial

This elegant, pure white lily-flowered
tulip is stunning planted *en masse* in
a mixed herbaceous border or in
bedding. Alternatively, you could
plant a few in a large containers for a
sophisticated patio display. The bulbs
should be planted in late autumn in full
sun and fertile, well-drained soil.
In bedding displays it is often easier
to lift bulbs and discard them after
flowering rather than letting the foliage
die naturally.

◌ ☼ Z4–7 H7–1
‡ to 28in (70cm)

VIBURNUM PLICATUM
'Mariesii'

Deciduous shrub

The broad-spreading branches of this viburnum are held in several layers, one above the other. It bears clusters of small, fertile flowers surrounded by sterile, showier flowers with large white petals. The flowers are followed by small red fruits that turn black in summer. Plant it in a shrub border or woodland garden in full sun or partial shade and moist, well-drained soil.

○ ◐ ☼ ◑ Z4–8 H8-1
‡ to 10ft (3m) ↔ to 12ft (4m)

WISTERIA SINENSIS
'Alba'

Climber

The Chinese wisteria – one of the most beautiful of the spring-flowering climbers – can be grown against a wall, on a large, sturdy trellis or pergola, or through a tree. Twisted stems produce large leaves with up to 13 leaflets, and the white, scented, pealike blooms are borne on long, pendent flower stems. Plant it in a fertile, well-drained, moist soil in sun or partial shade, and prune back new shoots in summer after it has flowered to restrict their growth.

○ ◐ ☼ ◑ Z5–8 H8–4
‡ to 28ft (9m)

AESCULUS × NEGLECTA
'Erythroblastos'

Deciduous tree

The emerging spring foliage of the aptly named sunrise horse chestnut is bright pink, later turning pale green. Just after the leaves unfurl, 'Erythroblastos' produces cones of pink or peach flowers. This slow-growing tree also puts on an impressive autumn display of bright yellow and orange leaves. Grow it in deep, moist, well-drained soil in full sun or partial shade.

◊ ◑ ☼ ◑ Z5–8 H8–5
‡ to 30ft (10m) ↔ to 25ft (8m)

ANAGALLIS TENELLA
'Studland'

Perennial

This bog pimpernel forms a low mat of bright green leaves covered with small, lightly scented, deep pink flowers. It requires a moist, free-draining soil to survive and will die if it is allowed to dry out in summer. Suitable for a rock garden where the soil is moist, this dainty plant can also be used as a groundcover. A short-lived plant, it can be propagated by taking cuttings in late summer.

◊ ☼ *f* Z5–7 H7–5
‡ to ½in (1cm) ↔ to 6in (15cm)

AQUILEGIA VULGARIS
'Nora Barlow'

Perennial

This unusual columbine has double
pink and white flowers with pale green-
tipped petals that are slightly swept
back when the flower is fully open. It
needs a well-drained, moist soil in full
sun and makes a stunning addition to
a spring herbaceous border. Plant it in
bold groups of at least 3-5 plants for
the best effect.

◊ ◑ ☼ Z3–8 H8–1
‡ to 30in (75cm) ↔ to 20in (50cm)

ARMERIA MARITIMA
'Vindictive'

Evergreen perennial

Thrift is a seaside plant that will grow
happily in a rock garden. It forms a
rounded cushion of deep green, grasslike leaves and bears large numbers of
bright pink flowers in spring. Its deep
taproot allows it to survive the driest of
summers, and care should be taken
when weeding to avoid damage to this
root, which may kill the plant. Thrift is
suitable for either coastal or inland
gardens as long as it is given
a sunny site and well-drained soil.

◊ ☼ Z3–9 H9–1
‡ to 4in (10cm) ↔ to 6in (15cm)

CERCIS SILIQUASTRUM

Deciduous tree

The Judas tree opens its flowers before the heart-shaped leaves emerge. The pealike blooms are magenta in bud, turning pink as they open, and are followed by purple seedpods during summer. The leaves turn yellow in autumn. The Judas tree comes from the Mediterranean and flowers best after a long, hot summer. Give it a sheltered site, since late frosts may damage the young leaves and flower buds. Plant it in moist, free-draining soil in sun or partial shade.

◊ ◊ ☼ Z6–9 H9–6
‡↔ to 30ft (10m)

CLEMATIS MACROPETALA *'Markham's Pink'*

Climber

Deep pink, semidouble flowers adorn this beautiful plant in late spring and early summer. Not as vigorous as many early-flowering clematis, it is ideal for a small urban garden. It blooms on the previous year's wood; if necessary, it should be pruned after flowering to remove any dead wood and to keep it within bounds. This clematis is very sturdy and will tolerate an exposed site in sun or partial shade. It prefers well-drained soil.

◊ ☼ ☼ Z6–9 H9–6
‡ to 10ft (3m)

CLEMATIS MONTANA
'Elizabeth'

Climber

Like all *Clematis montana*, this vigorous plant is perfect for growing up a large, sturdy trellis, a good-sized mature tree, or up wires attached to a house, fence, or wall. Just as the lobed leaves unfurl, it produces masses of fragrant pink blooms along its climbing stems. It needs a sheltered situation in full sun and well drained soil. It may need pruning after it has flowered to keep it under control.

○ ☼ ◑ *f* Z6–9 H9–6
‡ to 22ft (7m)

CLEMATIS MONTANA
VAR. RUBENS

Climber

This vigorous plant will soon cover an ugly wall or scramble up a large tree. It produces a huge number of single, pale pink flowers with creamy yellow anthers. Grow it in free-draining soil in a sunny or partially shaded site, and prune it after flowering to keep it in check.

○ ☼ ◑ Z6–9 H9–6
‡ to 30ft (10m)

DARMERA PELTATA

Perennial

The umbrella plant is a waterside plant that flowers before the large umbrella-shaped leaves emerge. Clusters of tiny, pale pink blooms, held on thick stems, are produced in mid- to late spring. Grow it in permanently wet soil, such as beside a pond or in a bog garden, in a sunny or partially shaded position. It can eventually cover a large area.

◊ ▲ ☼ ◐ Z5–9 H9–4
↕ to 6ft (2m) ↔ to 3ft (1m)

DICENTRA SPECTABILIS

Perennial

This elegant plant has many common names, including bleeding heart, lady's locket, and lady-in-the-bath. The leaves are pale green and deeply lobed, and delicate pink and white heart-shaped flowers hang from long, arching stems. For the best results, plant it in a partially shaded position in moist, well-drained, fertile soil. Where summers are hot and dry it will go dormant – all of the top-growth will die back to the ground – in summer.

◌ ◊ ◐ Z3–9 H9–1
↕ to 4ft (1.2m) ↔ to 18in (45cm)

EPIMEDIUM × RUBRUM

Perennial

This carpet-forming plant has attractive, heart-shaped leaves tinted reddish brown in spring as they unfurl, which then color yellow in autumn. It bears small crimson-pink, star-shaped flowers with long yellow spurs. Epimediums need a partially shaded position and moist but well-drained fertile soil. Propagate clumps by division in early spring or autumn.

○ ◐ ☼ Z9–8 H8–1
↕↔ to 12in (30cm)

ERICA AUSTRALIS

Evergreen shrub

The Spanish heath produces small, bell-shaped, purple-pink flowers from mid-spring to the beginning of summer and has dark green, needlelike foliage. Where marginally hardy, plant it in a sheltered position. Young plants benefit from some winter protection until they are established. Although tolerant of alkaline conditions, it prefers slightly moist, acidic or neutral soil in full sun.

◐ ☼ Z9–10 H10–9
↕ to 6ft (2m) ↔ to 3ft (1m)

ERYTHRONIUM DENS-CANIS

Bulbous perennial

The dog's-tooth violet has distinctive purple, pink, or white pendent flowers with reflexed petals. The decorative, oval-shaped green leaves have pinkish brown mottling on the upper surface. Dog's-tooth violets can be planted in woodland or grass and grow best in well-drained, fertile soil in partial shade. To propagate, lift and divide the clumps of bulbs after flowering, then replant them immediately in fertile soil.

◊ ☀ Z3–9 H9–1
‡ to 6in (15cm) ↔ to 4in (10cm)

GERANIUM CINEREUM
'Ballerina'

Perennial

This semi-evergreen, mound-forming hardy geranium, or cranesbill, has deeply divided, gray-green leaves. One of the first cranesbills to bloom, it bears many cup-shaped, pinkish purple flowers with distinctive purple veins and dark eyes. It makes a good rock- or gravel-garden plant, and it flowers over a long period. Plant it in full sun in well-drained soil, and divide plants in the spring.

◊ ☀ Z5-9 H9–5
‡ to 4in (10cm) ↔ to 12in (30cm)

KOLKWITZIA AMABILIS
'Pink Cloud'

Deciduous shrub

One of the prettiest of the spring-flowering shrubs, *Kolkwitzia* deserves its common name, beauty bush. It has arching branches clothed with tapering, dark green leaves and clusters of bell-shaped deep pink flowers with yellow-tinted throats. Plant it in a sunny site in fertile, well-drained soil. The newly emerging leaves may be damaged by late frosts, so it is best to choose a sheltered site in exposed sites.

○ ☼ Z5-9 H9–5
‡ to 10ft (3m) ↔ to 12ft (4m)

LAMIUM ORVALA

Perennial

This pretty variety of deadnettle forms clumps of triangular, midgreen leaves. The hooded flowers are bronzy pink and borne in tiers around the stem. It needs shade and a moist, well-drained soil to do well, and it is never invasive, unlike other deadnettles. There is also an attractive white-flowered form called 'Album'.

○ ◑ ☼ Z4–8 H8–1
‡ to 24in (60cm) ↔ to 12in (30cm)

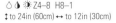

LEWISIA COTYLEDON

Evergreen perennial

Lewisias are rosette-forming alpines
from the mountains of North America.
The funnel-shaped flowers of this
species are produced in vivid pink,
white, red, apricot, or yellow and are
borne from late spring to early summer.
Unlike many lewisias, which are often
best grown under cover, *L. cotyledon*
can be planted outside in crevices in a
drystone wall, or in a rock garden.
Plant it in full sun and a very well-
drained, fertile soil.

◊ ☼ Z6–8 H8–6
‡ to 12in (30cm) ↔ to 6in (15cm)

MAGNOLIA X SOULANGEANA

Deciduous tree

This is probably the most widely grown
of all magnolias. Fast growing, it will
quickly form a small tree with wide-
spreading branches. The goblet-shaped
flowers are pink to pinkish purple, but
there are also forms with white and
reddish purple blooms. The flowers
appear before the leaves. Select a
planting position in full sun or partial
shade, where the tree has plenty of
space to develop its spreading shape.
It also needs a moist, well-drained soil.

◊ ◑ ☼ ☼ Z5–9 H9–5
‡↔ to 20ft (6m)

MALUS FLORIBUNDA

Deciduous tree

The Japanese crabapple grows to form a large shrub or small, spreading tree with graceful, pendent branches. The flower buds are red, opening in mid- to late spring to a very pale pink, with small fruits ripening yellow in autumn. It is not fussy about the soil conditions, as long as the site is not waterlogged. Grow this crabapple in sun or partial shade, and use it as a specimen tree in a lawn or in a mixed border.

◊ ☼ ☀ Z4–8 H8–1
↕ ↔ to 30ft (10m)

OXALIS ADENOPHYLLA

Perennial

This mat-forming tuberous perennial has grayish green leaves divided into heart-shaped leaflets, and purplish pink flowers with conspicuous purple veins. Plant the tubers in a rock or gravel garden or in troughs, in well-drained, gritty soil in full sun. It is easily propagated by division in autumn or early spring.

◊ ☼ Z6–8 H8–6
↕ to 2in (5cm) ↔ to 4in (10cm)

PAULOWNIA TOMENTOSA

Deciduous tree

The Empress tree has extremely large, rounded leaves. In mid- to late spring, the lilac, foxglovelike, scented flowers appear. The flower buds may be damaged by unusually cold winters. It can be treated as a foliage plant by cutting it down to ground level in late winter, which stimulates growth of even larger leaves . If this is done annually, apply a balanced fertilizer, and mulch after pruning. Plant it in well-drained soil in a sunny, sheltered site.

◊ ☼ *f* Z5–8 H8–5
‡ to 40ft (12m) ↔ to 30ft (10m)

PHLOX SUBULATA
'Marjorie'

Perennial

A pretty cushion-forming plant with narrow green leaves, the rose-pink flowers of this creeping phlox have five notched petals and a dark eye. It is ideal for a spring display in a rock or gravel garden or raised bed, and it will perform well when planted in well-drained, fertile soil in a sunny position.

◊ ☼ Z3–8 H8–1
‡ to 4in (10cm) ↔ to 8in (20cm)

PRIMULA ROSEA

Perennial

This primrose forms a rosette of
toothed, bronze-green leaves and
produces clusters of beautiful, clear
pink flowers. It needs moist, neutral to
acidic, fertile soil and will do well in a
bog garden or the damp soil beside a
pond. It can be grown in full sun, as
long as the soil is permanently moist.

● ◊ ☼ ☀ Z3–8 H8–1
↕↔ to 8in (20cm)

PRIMULA SIEBOLDII

Perennial

This primrose has long been cultivated
in Japan, and there are many different
forms from which to choose. The wild
plant has pinkish purple flowers with
white eyes, but there are also cultivars
with pink or white flowers, and some
have attractively fringed petals.
The blooms are held above a rosette
of bright green leaves. Plant it in a
moist, fertile soil, preferably in partial
shade, or in full sun if the soil remains
moist all summer.

◊ ☼ ☀ Z3–8 H8–1
↕ to 12in (30cm) ↔ to 18in (45cm)

PRUNUS
'Kanzan'

Deciduous tree

This pretty flowering cherry has upright branches when young, but they spread more widely as the tree matures, so this habit must be considered before planting. Double, deep pink flowers are produced just before the reddish brown leaves appear in mid- to late spring. Grow it in moist, fertile, well-drained soil in full sun.

○ ◐ ☼ Z6–8 H8–6
‡↔ to 30ft (10m)

PRUNUS
'Kiku-shidare-zakura'

Deciduous tree

Often sold as 'Cheal's Weeping', the graceful, weeping branches of this flowering cherry are covered in spring with clusters of double, bright pink flowers. It is quite tolerant of pollution and can make an attractive feature when planted as a street tree.

○ ◐ ☼ Z6–8 H8–6
‡↔ to 12ft (3m)

RHODODENDRON
'Pink Pearl'

Evergreen shrub

This is a very popular rhododendron, grown for its large clusters of pale pink flowers. While the plant is generally very vigorous, the branches are rather weak and have a tendency to droop. Plant it among other shrubs or in a woodland garden. It should be grown in a sunny or partially shaded position in deep, moist, well-drained, acidic soil. Mulch annually with bark chips or leaf mold.

○ ◊ ☼ ◑ Z7–9 H9–7
↕ ↔ to 12ft (4m)

RHODODENDRON
YAKUSHIMANUM

Evergreen shrub

A compact, sturdy rhododendron, this variety forms a domed bush of dark green, glossy leaves. It is covered with funnel-shaped, rose-pink flowers that fade to pale pink and then to white. Plant it in full sun or partial shade in moist, well-drained, fertile, acidic soil, and mulch annually with bark chips or leaf mold. This shrub is suitable for containers filled with an acidic soil mix.

○ ◊ ☼ ◑ Z5–9 H9–5
↕ ↔ to 6ft (2m)

SYMPHYTUM × UPLANDICUM *'Variegatum'*

Perennial

Russian comfrey is a vigorous, clump-forming perennial ideal as a ground-cover in wild gardens. 'Variegatum' has rather coarse, hairy green leaves with a broad cream margin. The small, tubular pink flowers are borne on tall stems and eventually turn blue. 'Variegatum' is far less vigorous than the normal green form. Both will flourish in moist soil in sun or partial shade. Divide in early spring.

◊ ☼ ☀ Z3–9 H9–1
‡ to 3ft (1m) ↔ to 2ft (60cm)

SYRINGA MEYERI *'Palibin'*

Deciduous shrub

This slow-growing lilac is the perfect choice for a small garden, where the much more common *Syringa vulgaris* may grow too large. It forms a compact bush that is covered from late spring to early summer with clusters of very fragrant, pale lavender-pink flowers. Plant it in full sun in well-drained soil, or in a large container of soil-based potting mix.

◊ ☼ ƒZ4–7 H7–1
‡↔ to 5ft (1.5m)

TULIPA
'Don Quichotte'
Bulbous perennial

This bright cherry pink tulip makes a
dramatic statement when planted in
large groups and used as a bedding
plant. Its vivid color combines well with
cream or white tulips, such as 'White
Triumphator' (see page 86), or forget-
me-nots. Plant the bulbs in late autumn
in well-drained soil in full sun.

◊ ☼ Z4–7 H7–1
‡ to 16in (40cm)

TULIPA
'Groenland'
Bulbous perennial

The viridiflora tulips are named for
the bright green stripe in the middle
of the outer petals. 'Groenland' has soft
pink petals marked with a triangular
green brush stroke. It can be used in
groups in a herbaceous border, or as a
bedding plant. Like all tulips, the bulbs
need to be planted in late autumn in a
sunny position in well-drained soil.

◊ ☼ Z4–7 H7–1
‡ to 18in (45cm)

ACER PALMATUM
'Corallinum'

Deciduous tree

This compact form of *Acer palmatum* grows slowly to form a bushy shrub or small tree. It is particularly dramatic in spring, when the bright red young shoots appear together with vivid shrimp pink leaves, which gradually turn pale green. In autumn the leaves turn orange, red, and yellow. It is best planted in sun or partial shade in moist, well-drained, acidic soil.

◊ ◖ ☼ Z5-8 H8–2
↕ to 4ft (1.2m) ↔ to 3ft (1m)

ANEMONE X FULGENS

Perennial

This striking tuberous plant bears vivid balck-centered scarlet flowers that resemble poppies. The flowers are held on thick stems above deeply lobed leaves. For the best effect, plant it in groups in sandy, very well-drained soil and a sunny position, since it can be damaged while dormant in summer by persistently wet soil conditions.

◊ ☼ Z8–10 H10–8
↕ to 12in (30cm) ↔ to 4in (10cm)

CAMELLIA JAPONICA
'Rubescens Major'

Evergreen shrub

This very old form of the Japanese
camellia produces double crimson-red
flowers with darker veins. It forms a
compact bush with glossy, rounded,
dark green leaves. There are several
other good camellias with red flowers,
such as the semidouble 'Paul's Apollo'
and 'R. L. Wheeler'. Plant 'Rubescens
Major' in a slightly shaded site,
preferably away from early morning
sun, in deep, moist, well-drained,
acidic soil.

◊ ◐ ☼ Z7–8 H8–7
‡↔ to 30ft (10m)

CRATAEGUS LAEVIGATA
'Paul's Scarlet'

Deciduous tree

Similar in shape to the English haw-
thorn, this small tree is covered with
double, deep pink flowers. These are
sometimes followed in late summer by
small red fruits. The leaves are shiny
and deeply lobed. It will grow well in
most soils (as long as they are not
waterlogged) in a sunny or lightly
shaded location. Mature trees are
particularly attractive.

◊ ◐ ☼ ☀ Z5–8 H8–5
‡↔ to 25ft (8m)

DICENTRA
'Bacchanal'

Perennial

Bleeding hearts are perennials with
finely divided leaves. 'Bacchanal' bears
its dangling, deep crimson-red flowers
on arching stems. Plant it in fertile soil
in partial shade underneath shrubs or in
a mixed border. Try to combine it with
plants that will hide its foliage as it dies
back in summer.

◊ ◊ ☼ Z3–9 H9–1
↕ to 14in (35cm) ↔ to 18in (45cm)

GEUM RIVALE

Perennial

Water avens grows naturally beside
rivers and streams, making it ideal for
bog gardens and pondsides. This
species produces clumps of hairy,
dark green divided leaves and single,
nodding, bell-shaped flowers on
arching stems. Plant it in damp soil
in full sun, and divide clumps
in autumn.

◊ ◊ ☼ Z3–8 H8–1
↕↔ to 24in (60cm)

LEPTOSPERMUM SCOPARIUM
'Red Damask'

Evergreen shrub

The New Zealand tea tree has arching branches covered with aromatic, lance-shaped leaves. From late spring to early summer it produces masses of beautiful double, saucer-shaped red flowers. It benefits from the protection of a south- or west-facing wall where marginally hardy. Where not hardy, grow it in a container of soil-based potting mix and move it under cover for the winter. This shrub also needs a free-draining soil.

◊ ☼ ◑ *f* Z9–10 H10–9
‡ ↔ to 10ft (3m)

PAEONIA
'Buckeye Belle'

Perennial

'Buckeye Belle' is a peony with semi-double, deep red flowers. It is a vigorous plant and will eventually form a large clump. Peonies need to be grown in well-drained, fertile soil, but they require relatively little aftercare. They are generally pest free but may be attacked by peony blight, a fungal disease. *Paeonia* 'Belle Center' is very similar to 'Buckeye Belle' but flowers two weeks later.

◊ ◊ ☼ ◑ Z3–8 H8–1
‡ ↔ to 34in (85cm)

PRIMULA JAPONICA
'Miller's Crimson'

Perennial

Candelabra primroses are ideal for a bog garden or planting by a pond. They are grown for their colorful flowers that are arranged in tiers up the stem. 'Miller's Crimson' bears striking crimson-red flowers, and there are other selections in other shades of red, plus white. It prefers a shaded spot in moist soil and looks best when planted in groups. Divide candelabra primroses in early spring.

◐ ◑ ● ☀ Z3–8 H8–1
↕ ↔ to 18in (45cm)

RHODODENDRON
'Elizabeth'

Evergreen shrub

'Elizabeth' is a dwarf rhododendron, making it an excellent choice for small gardens. In late spring it bears trumpet-shaped, bright red flowers that measure up to 3in (7.5cm) across. These large blooms are borne in clusters of five or six and create an eye-catching display. Grow this shrub in sun or partial shade in moist, well-drained, acidic soil, and mulch annually with leaf mold or bark chips.

◐ ◑ ☀ ☀ Z7–9 H9–7
↕ ↔ to 5ft (1.5m)

RHODODENDRON
'Hotspur'

Deciduous shrub

Deciduous azaleas are unsurpassed for vivid spring color, and 'Hotspur' is no exception, with its clusters of flame red flowers. The brightly colored autumn foliage adds to this plant's decorative qualities. Plant it in full sun or partial shade in moist, fertile, acidic soil, and mulch annually with leaf mold or bark chips. 'Silver Slipper' is a similar azalea with white flowers.

◐ ☼ ☀ Z6–9 H9–6
↕↔ to 6ft (2m)

RHODOHYPOXIS
'Douglas'

Perennial

This is a clump-forming plant with narrow, lance-shaped, grayish green leaves. In late spring and early summer it produces masses of deep red flowers on short stems. It should be grown in a sunny situation in slightly fertile, well-drained soil. It is suitable for a rock or gravel garden or a screebed, where its roots will be protected from excessive moisture in winter.

◊ ☼ Z9–10 H10–9
↕↔ to 4in (10cm)

RIBES SANGUINEUM *'Pulborough Scarlet'*

Deciduous shrub

Flowering currants create a dazzling display when their stems are clothed in masses of small flowers arranged in clusters. This variety has an upright habit, dark green, aromatic leaves, and dark red, pendent flowers with white centers. It is suitable for an informal hedge and needs only a light trim after flowering. Flowering currants will grow almost anywhere but prefer a sunny site and moderately fertile soil.

○ ◐ ☼ ☀ Z6–8 H8–6
↕ to 6ft (2m) ↔ to 8ft (2.5m)

SCHISANDRA RUBRIFLORA

Climber

This climber has red shoots and lance-shaped or oval, dark green leaves. It produces striking, deep red flowers measuring up to 1in (2.5cm) across, followed on female plants by fleshy red fruits. It grows well in moist, well-drained soil in sun or partial shade.

○ ◐ ☀ Z7–9 H9–7
↕ to 20ft (6m)

TRILLIUM SESSILE

Perennial

Wake robin is a clump-forming plant with three large, irregularly marked leaves. The flowers consist of three upright, narrow, maroon petals surrounded by three smaller, spreading sepals. It will do well when grown in dappled shade or woodland in moist, fertile, well-drained soil. It benefits from an annual mulch of leaf mold or well-rotted compost. Divide it after the leaves have died.

Z4–8 H8–1
↕ to 15in (38cm) ↔ to 18in (45cm)

TULIPA SPRENGERI

Bulbous perennial

Many species tulips are (undeservedly) not widely grown, but their simplicity and elegance are hard to beat. This species is one of the latest to flower in spring and has single, bright red flowers with sharply pointed petals. It self seeds and will naturalize if planted in deciduous woodland, preferring a sunny or lightly shaded site and well-drained, acidic soil.

Z4–7 H7–1
↕ to 20in (50cm)

ALLIUM HOLLANDICUM
'Purple Sensation'

Bulbous perennial

This is a superb ornamental flowering
onion with long, strap-shaped, grayish
green leaves. In late spring and early
summer it produces large flowerheads
that are good for cutting, consisting of
50 or more tiny, star-shaped, deep
violet florets. The decorative seedheads
last well into late summer, although any
self-sown plants that result may be
inferior to the original. Plant the bulbs
in autumn in a sunny position in fertile,
well-drained soil.

◊ ☼ Z4–9 H9–1
‡ to 30in (75cm) ↔ to 8in (20cm)

ALLIUM UNIFOLIUM

Bulbous perennial

This is a decorative ornamental onion
from Oregon. Each small bulb produces
a single grayish green leaf that dies
before bright pinkish purple, six-petaled
flowers appear. Plant the bulbs in
autumn in a sheltered, sunny position
in well-drained, fertile soil. It does well
in a rock or gravel garden and should
be grown in bold groups for best effect.

◊ ☼ Z4–9 H9–1
‡ to 12in (30cm) ↔ to 4in (10cm)

FRITILLARIA MELEAGRIS

Bulbous perennial

The snake's head fritillary produces pendent, bell-shaped purple or white flowers with a distinctive checkerboard pattern on the petals. It grows well when naturalized in grass and will often self-seed. Take care when mowing, since the young seedlings look very much like grass. It should be planted in a moist, well-drained, ideally slightly alkaline soil. If the bulbs become congested, mark the position so they can be lifted in the autumn and replanted elsewhere.

◊ ◑ ☼ ☀ Z3–8 H8–1
‡ to 12in (30cm) ↔ to 3in (8cm)

FRITILLARIA GRAECA

Bulbous perennial

This unusual fritillary is a native of Southern Greece. It has a delicate habit, bearing slim flower stems from which hang pendent, brownish purple, bell-shaped flowers with a bold green stripe down the center of the petals. It needs to be planted in a sunny site and in soil with very good drainage. It will add interest to a rock garden or raised bed Plant the bulbs in groups in autumn.

◊ ☼ Z6–9 H9–6
‡ to 8in (20cm) ↔ to 2in (5cm)

IPHEION UNIFLORUM

Bulbous perennial

In mid- to late spring, this vigorous, clump-forming plant produces violet, blue, or white star-shaped flowers. The narrow leaves smell of onions when bruised. Plant bulbs in autumn in a fertile, moist, well-drained soil in a sunny, sheltered situation, where they will naturalize. Where marginally hardy, provide a loose, light winter mulch.

◊ ◊ ☼ Z6–9 H9–6
↕ to 8in (20cm) ↔ to 1in (2cm)

LUNARIA ANNUA

Biennial

Honesty (or money plant) is a fast-growing biennial that will often flower in its first year. It has tall stems and toothed, heart-shaped, dark green leaves. Small flowers with four petals come in shades of purple or white (sometimes both on the same flower). It often self-seeds and will thrive in a woodland garden, preferring a site in partial shade or sun and moist, well-drained soil. Honesty is frequently grown for its round, silvery seedpods for use in dried flower arrangements.

◊ ◊ ☼ ☀ Z5–9 H9–5
↕ to 30in (75cm) ↔ to 12in (30cm)

PHLOX DOUGLASII
'Crackerjack'

Perennial

A reliable plant, this dwarf phlox forms
a mound of narrow, dark green leaves
covered with small, bright purplish
magenta flowers. Grow this variety in
full sun in well-drained, fertile soil. It is
ideally suited to a rock garden, the
cracks of a drystone wall, or between
the slabs of a stone path.

○ ☼ Z5–7 H7–5
↕ to 3in (8cm) ↔ to 8in (20cm)

PRIMULA PULVERULENTA

Perennial

This species is one of the most striking
of the candelabra primroses. It bears
tiers of deep reddish purple flowers
with a bright red or purple eye. The
plants form rosettes of toothed, midgreen leaves, and their stems are
covered with a grayish green, downy
material called "farina." Plant it in
partial shade in fertile, moist soil. It will
tolerate full sun, provided the soil
remains moist throughout summer.
Candelabra primroses look best when
they are planted in a group near water.

◐ ☼ ☀ Z4–8 H8–1
↕ to 3ft (1m) ↔ to 24in (60cm)

PULSATILLA VULGARIS

Perennial

This is an extremely beautiful clump-forming pasqueflower with attractive divided, feathery foliage. The pendent, bell-shaped flowers have bright purple petals and golden yellow stamens. Ideal for a rock garden, it needs gritty, very well-drained soil and a sunny position, growing best in alkaline soil. Pasqueflowers do not like to have their roots disturbed and are best left undisturbed after planting. Propagate by seed.

◊ ☼ Z5–7 H7–5
↕ ↔ to 8in (20cm)

RHODODENDRON *'Hatsugiri'*

Evergreen shrub

This small, compact evergreen azalea produces a profusion of bright reddish purple flowers borne in clusters of three blooms. It is suitable for a container on a patio, or the front of a border, and it will tolerate full sun, unlike many of its relatives. Plant it in a free-draining, organic, acidic soil or soil mix. In the open garden, mulch it generously with leaf mold or bark chips.

◊ ☼ ☀ Z6–9 H9–6
↕ ↔ to 24in (60cm)

TULIPA
'Blue Parrot'

Bulbous perennial

This robust tulip is not truly blue but more violet. It has single flowers with slightly twisted petals. Use it in borders and as a cut flower. *Tulipa* 'Greuze' also has violet-purple flowers, but they are more uniform in shape. The bulbs of both should be planted in late autumn in free-draining soil in full sun.

◊ ☀ Z4–7 H7–1
‡ to 24in (60cm)

TULIPA
'Queen of Night'

Bulbous perennial

'Queen of Night' is an elegant hybrid tulip with large, dark maroon-purple flowers. The single cup-shaped blooms are borne on elegant, long green stems above lance-shaped, grayish green leaves. It looks particularly effective when planted with an ivory-colored variety, such as 'Maureen'. Plant bulbs of this reliably perennial tulip in late autumn in a sunny position and free-draining soil.

◊ ☀ Z4–7 H7–1
‡ to 24in (60cm)

Anemone Coronaria
'Lord Lieutenant'

Perennial

This striking plant originates from the Mediterranean region. The cultivar 'Lord Lieutenant' bears superb, velvety, semi-double, deep blue flowers with black eyes, which open in mid- to late spring and are good for cutting. The divided foliage adds to this plant's charms. Plant the small tubers in autumn, preferably in light, sandy soil in full sun.

◊ ☼ Z8–10 H10–8
‡ to 18in (45cm) ↔ to 6in (15cm)

Aquilegia Alpina

Perennial

The alpine columbine has an upright habit and is suitable for planting in a herbaceous border, rock garden, or raised bed. It produces long stems that bear slightly nodding, deep blue flowers. The stems rise up above finely divided, bluish green, ferny foliage. Grow it in a sunny or partially shaded position in fertile, moist, well-drained, gritty soil.

◊ ◊ ☼ ☀ Z4–7 H7–1
‡ to 18in (45cm) ↔ to 12in (30cm)

CEANOTHUS ARBOREUS
'Trewithen Blue'

Evergreen shrub

There are very few blue-flowered large
shrubs or small trees that will grow well
in a temperate climate. The California
lilacs are among the best of these and
are suitable for a wide range of soils,
including alkaline. 'Trewithen Blue' is
one of the most vigorous and soon
forms a small tree. It produces large
heads of midblue flowers from late
spring to early summer. Where
marginally hardy, it is best to grow
it against a warm wall.

○ ◐ ☼ ☼ Z9–10 H10–9
‡ to 20ft (6m) ↔ to 25ft (8m)

CORYDALIS FLEXUOSA

Perennial

This plant has waxy, light green, ferny
leaves and produces clusters of long,
tubular, bright blue flowers. The
growing position should be marked to
avoid damaging the delicate rootstock
during cultivation or weeding. It needs
partial shade and should be grown in
fertile, moist, well-drained soil.

○ ◐ ☼ Z6–8 H8–6
‡ to 12in (30cm) ↔ to 8in (20cm)

GENTIANA ACAULIS

Evergreen perennial

The trumpet gentian is a beautiful rock plant that bears vivid, trumpet-shaped, deep blue flowers with green-spotted throats. The blooms appear above rosettes of evergreen, glossy leaves that form a slightly raised mound. 'Coelestina' has Cambridge blue blooms. The trumpet gentian needs to be planted in moist, very well-drained, acidic soil in a partly shaded situation.

○ ◐ ☀ Z5–8 H8–5
↕ to 3in (8cm) ↔ to 12in (30cm)

HYACINTHOIDES NON-SCRIPTA

Bulbous perennial

In late spring, few sights compare with the beauty of a deciduous woodland carpeted with the fragrant flowers of English bluebells. Replicate these shady conditions, and bluebells will self seed and spread throughout the garden. For the best results, plant the bulbs in autumn in moist, acidic, fertile soil, although they will tolerate slightly alkaline conditions. Cultivars with white and mauve flowers are also available.

◐ ☀ ☀ *f*Z4–9 H9–1
↕ to 16in (40cm) ↔ to 3in (8cm)

MUSCARI LATIFOLIUM
Bulbous perennial

This is an unusual grape hyacinth with a spike of tiny, bicolored, urn-shaped flowers. The lower flowers are purplish black, while the upper, smaller, infertile flowers are pale blue. The lance-shaped leaves are broader than those of most other muscaris. Plant the small bulbs in a sunny, sheltered site in a well-drained soil, and use at the front of a border or in a rock garden. Established clumps can be divided, or sow seed in summer.

◊ ☼ Z4-8 H8–1
‡ to 8in (20cm) ↔ to 2in (5cm)

ROSMARINUS OFFICINALIS *'Sissinghurst Blue'*
Evergreen shrub

Widely grown as a culinary herb and for its aromatic foliage, rosemary makes a decorative shrub that can be grown as a low hedge. 'Sissinghurst Blue' is a dwarf variety that bears small, pale blue flowers in late spring. It favors a sunny, sheltered location and well-drained soil. Rosemary will respond well to pruning, and straggly old plants can be cut back hard in the spring. Propagate by semi-ripe cuttings in summer.

◊ ☼ ƒ Z8–10 H10–8
‡ ↔ to 20in (50cm)

SYRINGA VULGARIS
'Katherine Havemeyer'

Deciduous shrub

A double-flowered form of the common lilac that produces clusters of pink buds that develop into lavender-blue, sweetly scented flowers. It grows quickly to form a spreading shrub or small tree, performing well when planted in a moist, well-drained fertile soil in full sun or partial shade. Young plants do not need pruning, but rejuvenate old lilac bushes by cutting them back hard after they have flowered. Lilacs are also tolerant of pollution.

◊ ◊ ☼ ◑ ƒ Z4–8 H8–1
↕ ↔ to 22ft (7m)

TECOPHILAEA
CYANOCROCUS

Cormous perennial

This low-growing plant has slightly erect, lance-shaped leaves, and in spring produces one or two brilliant gentian blue flowers with white throats. Grow it in a sunny site in very well-drained, sandy soil in a rock garden or raised bed. It is better grown in a cold frame where marginally hardy.

◊ ☼ Z7–9 H9–7
↕ to 4in (10cm) ↔ to 3in (8cm)

VERONICA PEDUNCULARIS

Perennial

Masses of small, saucer-shaped, deep
blue flowers open over a long period
from spring to early summer on this
mat-forming, low-growing veronica.
The glossy, purple-tinted green leaves
are also an attractive feature. Grow it in
a well-drained soil in a sunny location,
such as a rock garden or raised bed.
Stocks can be increased by dividing it
in the autumn.

◊ ☼ Z6–8 H8–6
‡ to 4in (10cm) ↔ to 24in (60cm)

WISTERIA SINENSIS

Climber

Chinese wisteria is a stunning climber
suitable for growing against a wall, up
a large tree, or over a pergola. The
brilliant lilac-blue, fragrant, pealike
flowers are produced in long, pendent
clusters during the late spring and early
summer. It is a vigorous plant, but it
can be restricted by careful pruning in
summer after flowering, as well as in
winter. Plant it in full sun or partial
shade in fertile, moist, well-drained soil.

◊ ◑ ☼ ◑ ƒ Z5–8 H8–4
‡ to 100ft (30m)

ARUM CRETICUM

Perennial

This spring-flowering arum is a native
of Crete. It has a large yellow or white
bract, or spathe, from which protrudes
a deep yellow spike composed of a
mass of tiny, slightly fragrant flowers.
The large, arrow-shaped, glossy leaves
contrast well with the spring blooms.
Plant tubers in full sun in well-drained,
fertile soil. Large clumps can be divided,
or raise plants from seed sown
in early autumn.

◊ ☼ *f* Z8–10 H10–8
↕ to 20in (50cm) ↔ to 12in (30cm)

AURINIA SAXATILIS

Evergreen perennial

Gold dust, formerly known as *Alyssum
saxatile*, is an evergreen with grayish
green leaves. In spring it produces
masses of small, bright yellow flowers.
Other gold dusts include 'Citrina', which
bears bright lemon yellow flowers, and
'Compacta', a small variety with golden
yellow blooms. It needs a sunny, well-
drained situation and can be grown on
a wall, spilling over the front of a raised
bed, or in a rock garden.

◊ ☼ Z4–8 H8–1
↕ to 9in (23cm) ↔ to 12in (30cm)

BERBERIS × STENOPHYLLA

Evergreen shrub

This vigorous, spiny plant forms an
elegant, spreading bush with arching
branches covered with clusters of deep
yellow flowers. The blooms are
followed in summer by waxy black
fruit. Plant it in full sun in a well-
drained, fertile soil. It is most useful
when grown as a dense, intruder-proof
hedge, which should be trimmed after
flowering has finished.

◊ ☼ Z6–9 H9–6
‡ to 10ft (3m) ↔ to 15ft (5m)

BERBERIS THUNBERGII
'Aurea'

Deciduous shrub

A beautiful barberry with bright golden-
yellow leaves, this is much shorter than
other varieties and is suitable for small
gardens. In late spring it bears clusters
of pink-tinged, pale yellow flowers,
which are followed in autumn by bright
red berries. While it needs good light,
bright sun can scorch the yellow leaves,
but in dense shade the foliage will turn
green. It grows happily in most soils.

◊ ◑ ☼ ☼ Z5–8 H8–3
‡ to 5ft (1.5m) ↔ to 6ft (2m)

COLCHICUM LUTEUM

Cormous perennial

Colchicums are best known for their bright pink flowers produced in the autumn, but this species is different: it has golden yellow, goblet-shaped flowers . It needs very good drainage and should be planted in gritty, fertile soil in full sun. It can be quite difficult to grow outdoors, because the corms need to be kept completely dry when they are dormant. In wet climates, grow it in pots in a cold frame, and take it outside in the spring.

◊ ☼ Z4–9 H9–1

‡ to 4in (10cm) ↔ to 3in (8cm)

CYTISUS × PRAECOX *'Allgold'*

Evergreen shrub

This small, free-flowering broom bears a profusion of dark yellow blooms from mid- to late spring. Ideal for growing in a sunny mixed border, it needs a deep, slightly fertile, well-drained soil. After flowering, it can be trimmed back to keep it in shape, although pruning is not essential. 'Warminster' has a similar habit to 'Allgold', but it produces creamy yellow flowers.

◊ ☼ Z6–9 H9–6

‡ to 4ft (1.2m) ↔ to 5ft (1.5m)

DIONYSIA TAPETODES

Evergreen perennial

This alpine plant forms a tight cushion of small, grayish green leaves, and in late spring and early summer bright yellow, upward facing flowers appear above the foliage. It needs dry, very well-drained soil and full sun to succeed. In its natural environment, it grows in the crevices of rocks. It is best grown in pots of alpine soil mix under cover to protect it from a damp environment and winter moisture.

◊ ☼ Z5–7 H7–5
↕ to 2in (5cm) ↔ to 8in (20cm)

DORONICUM × EXCELSUM
'Harpur Crewe'

Perennial

Bright, golden yellow, daisylike flowers adorn this leopard's bane in late spring. The blooms are held on tall, erect stems above decorative, heart-shaped, basal leaves. Plant it in a moist, fertile soil in partial shade, and grow it in groups to enliven an early herbaceous border or woodland garden with dazzling color. Leopard's bane can be propagated by division in autumn.

◊ ☼ Z4–8 H8–1
↕↔ to 24in (60cm)

ENKIANTHUS CAMPANULATUS

Deciduous shrub

A member of the heather family, this shrub can grow to form a small tree. The stems are covered with dense clusters of pendent, pale creamy yellow, bell-shaped flowers with pink tips and pink veins. The toothed foliage turns wonderful shades of red, yellow, and orange in autumn. It will grow well in sun or partial shade in a fertile, acidic, moist but well-drained soil.

○ ◐ ☼ ☼ Z5–8 H8-4
↕ ↔ to 15ft (5m)

EPIMEDIUM PINNATUM *SUBSP.* COLCHICUM

Evergreen perennial

An attractive clump-former, this plant produces rounded leaves divided into five leaflets. The golden yellow, single flowers are relatively large for an epimedium, measuring up to ¾in (18mm) across. It prefers a semi-shaded situation and heavy, moisture-retentive, fertile soil. Although slower to spread than the species, it still makes an excellent groundcover. The appearance of the plant will be improved if the old foliage is cut back in late winter.

◐ ☼ Z5–9 H9–5
↕ ↔ to 12in (30cm)

ERIGERON AUREUS
'Canary Bird'

Perennial

A slow-growing fleabane, this form has
rounded, grayish green leaves, and in
late spring and early summer it bears
daisylike, canary yellow flowers. Grow
it in a sunny site where there is some
protection from the full strength of the
summer sun, and plant it in moist, well-
drained soil that does not dry out.
When plants begin to lose their vigor,
divide them in spring.

◊ ◔ ☼ Z5-8 H8–5

‡ to 4in (10cm) ↔ to 6in (15cm)

EUPHORBIA POLYCHROMA

Perennial

This plant is guaranteed to brighten up
a dull spring morning. The stems are
clothed in bright green leaves, which
form a rounded clump, and from late
spring and well into summer it bears
acid yellow flowers surrounded by a
collar of striking, greenish yellow
bracts. A tolerant plant, it will grow on
most well-drained soils and can be used
at the front of a border or in a
woodland garden. Care should be taken
when pruning the stems, because the
latex they exude can irritate the skin.

◊ ☼ ☀ Z4–9 H9–1

‡ ↔ to 20in (50cm)

FREMONTODENDRON
'California Glory'

Evergreen shrub

Large, golden yellow flowers bloom from late spring to midautumn, set off by dark green, five-lobed foliage, making this plant a valuable addition to any garden. It grows happily on alkaline, free-draining soil and can be pruned lightly in early spring. This shrub often does best when trained against a sheltered, south-facing wall. Contact with the foliage may cause an allergic reaction.

◊ ☼ Z8–10 H10–8
‡ to 20ft (6m) ↔ to 12ft (4m)

FRITILLARIA IMPERIALIS
'Maxima Lutea'

Bulbous perennial

The value of crown imperials in the spring garden is beyond question. The tall stems carry a tuft of shiny green, leafy bracts at the top, beneath which hang a number of bright yellow, bell-shaped flowers. The bulbs should be planted in late summer in full sun and a deep, well-drained soil where they will not be disturbed. 'Rubra' is more robust, with orange-red flowers and purple-tinged stems.

◊ ☼ Z5–9 H9–5
‡ to 5ft (1.5m) ↔ to 12in (30cm)

GENISTA HISPANICA

Deciduous shrub

A mound-forming shrub, Spanish gorse produces a profusion of small, pealike, golden yellow flowers on prickly green stems in late spring and early summer. Plant it in a well-drained soil and sunny position, such as the front of a raised bed. Where marginally hardy, plant it in a sheltered position by a warm wall to lessen its chances of being severely damaged in winter.

◊ ☼ Z7–9 H9–7
‡ to 30in (75cm) ↔ to 5ft (1.5m)

IRIS
'Golden Harvest'

Bulbous perennial

This iris produces pure golden yellow flowers that are good for cutting from the middle of spring to early summer. It requires a very well-drained, neutral or slightly alkaline soil and a sunny site, since they may not survive wet conditions while they are dormant. Large clumps should be divided as soon as possible after flowering.

◊ ☼ Z3–9 H9–1
‡ to 32in (80cm) ↔ to 6in (15cm)

KERRIA JAPONICA
'Golden Guinea'

Deciduous shrub

Kerria is an easy-to-grow and vigorous shrub with graceful, arching green stems. One of the most popular forms is 'Pleniflora', which has double, deep yellow flowers. 'Golden Guinea' is less vigorous, with single yellow blooms. It grows best in free-draining soil and full sun but can tolerate light shade. Kerria spreads by suckers, which can be dug up in autumn to propagate it. Cut back the stems after flowering to keep it within bounds.

◊ ☼ ❄ Z4–9 H9–1
‡ to 6ft (2m) ↔ to 8ft (2.5m)

LABURNUM ANAGYROIDES

Deciduous tree

The laburnum is valued for its long, pendent clusters of pealike, bright yellow flowers. Laburnums will grow in almost any soil as long as it is not waterlogged, but they need full sun to flourish. They are easily propagated from seed sown in autumn – but remember that laburnum seeds are very poisonous. *L.* x *watereri* 'Vossii' has larger blooms held in longer clusters.

◊ ◖ ☼ Z6–8 H8–6
‡↔ to 25ft (8m)

MECONOPSIS CAMBRICA

Perennial

The Welsh poppy has single lemon
yellow or orange flowers that bloom
from late spring to autumn. The flowers
are borne on long stems above fern-
like, grayish green foliage. 'Flore Pleno'
has double yellow flowers and comes
true from seed. Welsh poppies are
happiest in partial shade and moist,
acidic soil, although they will tolerate
alkaline conditions. They have a
tendency to self-seed and will spread
quickly unless the seedheads are cut
off before they ripen.

◊ ☼ Z6–8 H8–6
‡ to 18in (45cm) ↔ to 12in (30cm)

NARCISSUS JONQUILLA

Bulbous perennial

Wild jonquils are valued for their sweet
fragrance and small yellow blooms that
appear in spring. Each stem produces
five or six bright yellow flowers above
linear, almost cylindrical leaves. These
bulbs look lovely naturalized in grass or
beneath deciduous trees and also make
wonderful container plants for a patio,
where their fragrance can be enjoyed at
close range. Plant the bulbs in free-
draining soil in sun for best results.

◊ ☼ Z3–9 H9–1
‡ to 12in (30cm) ↔ to 3in (8cm)

PAEONIA DELAVAYI
VAR. LUDLOWII

Deciduous shrub

When given the correct conditions, the Tibetan tree peony will eventually form a broad, spreading bush. It bears bright yellow flowers and has decorative, lobed, deeply cut foliage borne on graceful, arching stems. Grow this tree peony in a full sun or light shade on moist, well-drained soil. Cut out one or two of the older stems in late winter to rejuvenate established plants. It is easily propagated from seed.

○ ◑ ☼ ☀ Z5–8 H8–1
‡ to 6ft (2m) ↔ to 9ft (3m)

PAEONIA
MLOKOSEWITSCHII

Perennial

There are few more desirable peonies than "Molly-the-Witch," with its large, primrose yellow flowers and glaucous green, divided foliage. The stems are tinted pink or red. Slow-growing at first, it can eventually form a wide-spreading clump. It grows happily in full sun or dappled shade, although a well-drained soil is essential. Propagate it from seed. Although peonies tend to resent being disturbed, large clumps can be divided in autumn.

○ ☼ ☀ Z5–8 H8–5
‡↔ to 30in (75cm)

PRIMULA PROLIFERA

Evergreen perennial

This candelabra primrose forms rosettes of pale green, evergreen leaves with serrated edges, above which fragrant, golden yellow flowers appear. Like all candelabra primroses, it requires deep, fertile, neutral or slightly acidic soil that does not dry out in summer. It looks particularly striking when planted in a large group near water. Divide congested clumps in the early spring or grow plants from seed.

◐ ☼ ƒ Z4–8 H8–1
‡↔ to 24in (60cm)

PRIMULA VERIS

Evergreen perennial

The cowslip, a long-beloved spring flower, produces clusters of pale yellow, fragrant blooms. The erect flower stems are surrounded by a rosette of evergreen, deeply veined leaves. Cowslips should be planted in a partly shaded site in well-drained, moist soil. They can be grown in full sun as long as the soil remains permanently moist. Grow it from seed in spring, or divide large clumps in autumn or early spring.

◌ ◐ ☼ ☼ ƒ Z3–8 H8–1
‡↔ to 10in (25cm)

RHODODENDRON LUTEUM

Deciduous shrub

This widely grown deciduous azalea
bears large numbers of strongly
fragrant, funnel-shaped, bright yellow
flowers. The lance-shaped leaves turn
shades of purple, red, and orange in
autumn. This azalea prefers full sun
but will tolerate a little shade. Plant it
with the root ball just above the surface
in moist, well-drained, acidic soil,
and mulch it annually with leaf mold
or bark chips.

◊ ◊ ☼ ☼ *f* Z7–9 H9–7
‡↔ to 12ft (4m)

RHODODENDRON MACABEANUM

Evergreen tree

Many people consider this to be the
finest of all the yellow rhododendrons.
In mid- to late spring it produces large
clusters of deep yellow flowers with
purple spots on the inside. It eventually
grows into a substantial tree, making it
suitable only for large gardens, where it
is best planted in dappled shade
beneath deciduous trees. It enjoys
moist, well-drained, acidic soil. Mulch
annually with leaf mold or bark chips.

◊ ◊ ☼ Z6–9 H9–6
‡ to 45ft (13.5m) ↔ to 45ft (13.5m)

RIBES ODORATUM

Deciduous shrub

The clove currant is an upright shrub
with attractive three-lobed, bright green
leaves. From mid- to late spring, clusters
of small, fragrant, tubular, golden yellow
flowers with bright red anthers appear,
followed in summer by black berries. In
autumn its foliage turns various shades
of red and purple. Plant it in full sun
or light shade in well-drained soil. It is
easy to propagate by taking hardwood
cuttings during winter.

○ ☼ ☀ *f* Z5–8 H8–5
↕ ↔ to 6ft (2m)

SAXIFRAGA × ELIZABETHAE

Perennial

A free-flowering, cushion-forming plant,
this saxifrage is covered in bright
yellow flowers borne on very short
stems, which rarely exceed 1in (2.5cm)
in height. Plant it in a semi-shaded
situation in well-drained soil. It makes
a superb rock garden plant, thriving in
the gaps between the stones.

○ ☀ Z7–8 H8–7
↕ to 1in (2.5cm) ↔ to 6in (15cm)

TRILLIUM LUTEUM

Perennial

This clump-forming plant has silver-green mottled leaves with pointed tips. Its fragrant yellow flowers are composed of three narrow green sepals and three upright, pale yellow petals. It is a good choice for a woodland garden and should be grown in a shaded position in moist, well-drained, acidic soil. In autumn, mulch it with well-rotted leaf mold.

○ ◐ ☼ ☀ *f* Z5–8 H8–5
‡ to 16in (40cm) ↔ to 12in (30cm)

TROLLIUS EUROPAEUS

Perennial

The European globeflower is a reliable plant for moist soils. Resembling a large buttercup, the spherical, lemon yellow flowers appear in late spring and early summer. It also has attractive, glossy, divided foliage. This globeflower can be planted in full sun or partial shade and is suitable for bog gardens, since it does particularly well in fertile soil that never dries out. 'Canary Bird' is one of the best cultivars. European globe-flowers can be grown from seed or divided in autumn.

◐ ☼ ☀ Z5–8 H8–5
‡ to 24in (60cm) ↔ to 18in (45cm)

TULIPA
'Golden Apeldoorn'

Bulbous perennial

This widely grown single-flowered tulip
has bright golden yellow flowers, with
the inner petals marked with a large
black patch that disguises the black
stamens. Plant it in well-drained, fertile
soil in a sunny position. Most tulips
look best when grown with a
contrasting color; this yellow variety
would look good with the cherry red
'Apeldoorn' or scarlet 'Oxford' in a
bedding design.

◊ ☼ Z4–7 H7–1
‡ to 24in (60cm)

TULIPA
'West Point'

Bulbous perennial

This is a striking lily-flowered tulip, the
golden yellow flowers of which have
pointed petals that curve dramatically
outward at the tips. It should be
planted in a sunny situation in well-
drained, fertile soil, and it looks
stunning when combined with a
bright red tulip, such as the lily-
flowered 'Mariette'.

◊ ☼ Z4–7 H7–1
‡ to 20in (50cm)

Uvularia grandiflora

Perennial

An unusual, spreading plant, the large merrybells has erect stems that droop at the tip and carry narrow, bell-shaped yellow flowers. It should be planted in deep, moist, well-drained soil. Merrybells will perform well when grown in a shady border or in the dappled shade of a woodland garden.

◊ ◊ ☼ Z3–7 H7–1
‡ to 24in (60cm) ↔ to 12in (30cm)

Vestia foetida

Evergreen shrub

With glossy, dark green, elliptic leaves and bright tubular flowers, *Vestia* is a valuable asset to the late spring garden. Where marginally hardy, this shrub should be planted against a sunny west- or south-facing wall in a well-drained soil. Where not hardy, grow it in a large container and bring it under cover during winter.

◊ ☼ Z8–10 H10–8
‡ to 6ft (2m) ↔ to 5ft (1.5m)

VIOLA BIFLORA

Perennial

A dwarf violet with attractive kidney- or heart-shaped leaves, this plant spreads slowly by creeping roots. In spring and early summer it produces solitary or paired small, deep lemon yellow flowers, the lower petals of which have purple-brown streaks that radiate out from the center. It performs well when planted in well-drained, moist soil in a partially shade situation and is suitable for a woodland garden.

◊ ◊ ☼ Z4–8 H8–1
‡ to 3in (8cm) ↔ to 8in (20cm)

VIOLA
'Jackanapes'

Evergreen perennial

This violet has toothed, bright green leaves and spreading stems that bear bicolored flowers in late spring and throughout the summer. The small blooms are deep maroon-purple at the top and bright yellow at the base, with purple streaks radiating from the center. 'Jackanapes' should be grown in moist, well-drained soil in full sun or partial shade. It is short-lived and needs to be propagated regularly by taking stem-tip cuttings in late summer.

◊ ◊ ☼ Z4–8 H8–1
‡ to 5in (12cm) ↔ to 12in (30cm)

BERBERIS LINEARIFOLIA
'Orange King'

Evergreen shrub

This attractive barberry has glossy, dark green leaves and strong, upright, spiny stems. The cup-shaped, bright orange flowers borne in small clusters are followed in late summer by waxy black fruit. It will grow well in full sun and deep, moist, well-drained soil. To propagate it, take softwood cuttings in late summer.

◊ ◗ ☀ Z6–9 H9–6
↕↔ to 8ft (2.5m)

PRIMULA × BULLEESIANA

Evergreen perennial

This beautiful candelabra primrose is a hybrid between *P. bulleyana* and *P. beesiana*. Plants may have orange, yellow, pink, red, or purple flowers borne in tiers around thick stems. Plant it in a slightly shaded situation in moist, neutral or slightly acidic soil. The plant overwinters as a rosette of midgreen leaves and can be divided, or grown from seed, in spring.

◗ ☀ Z5–8 H8–5
↕↔ to 24in (60cm)

PRIMULA BULLEYANA

Perennial

Clusters of crimson flowers that quickly change to bright orange are borne on this striking candelabra primrose. The toothed, rounded, lance-shaped, mid-green leaves form a tight rosette at the base of the plant. It is good for waterside plantings and bog gardens: it enjoys partial shade and deep, moist, fertile, neutral or slightly acidic soil that does not dry out in summer. It can be propagated by division in spring.

◊ ☼ Z6–9 H9–6
↕ ↔ to 24in (60cm)

RHODODENDRON
'*Frome*'

Deciduous shrub

A medium-sized deciduous azalea, this form has orange-yellow, frilly, funnel-shaped flowers with red marks on their throats. It forms a large, dome-shaped bush and is suitable for the middle or back of a mixed border or beneath deciduous trees. It needs a moist, well-drained, fertile, acidic soil in partial shade. Mulch it annually with leaf mold or bark chips.

◊ ◊ ☼ Z5–8 H8–5
↕ ↔ to 5ft (1.5m)

EARLY SUMMER

Not a day goes by without more flowers opening somewhere in the garden. Hanging baskets and containers brimming with geraniums, verbenas, and other tender plants can be put out, now that all danger of frost has passed. The herbaceous border reaches a peak of perfection: peonies and delphiniums surround their supports, holding their flowers up against the weather for pure enjoyment, while bearded irises, daylilies, starry alliums, and hardy geraniums bloom in profusion and dazzling shades.

In the light shade of trees, making cool leafy groundcover, grow hostas, heucheras, and bugle (*Ajuga*). Feathery clumps of goatsbeard (*Aruncus*) and monkshood (*Aconitum*) will thrive in moist conditions, but, for permanently wet soil and pond margins, the beauty of the Japanese iris is without peer.

Mediterranean shrubs such as genistas, thymes, and phlomis revel in the hot, dry conditions.

More dramatic bursts of color are provided by sun-loving annuals, especially those sown in autumn, such as eschscholzia and cosmos. Snapdragons and salvias can be used for bedding or to fill gaps, perhaps replacing Oriental poppies after their flowers have gone. All will flower into autumn if they are deadheaded: this is the key to extending the display of many annuals and, or course, roses.

SUMMER ROMANCE

Most evocative of summer are the roses, gracing many garden situations with fragrance and color throughout the season. Modern shrub roses are easier-going than hybrid teas, often having the characteristics of old roses but flowering longer. Groundcover roses are healthy and very versatile; many will trail over sunny banks or walls but are also at home in a large pot or hanging basket, and some can even make a spectacular thorny hedge.

ACANTHUS SPINOSUS

Perennial

The distinctive, tubular, purple-hooded white flowers of bear's breeches are held on tall spikes. Its deeply divided leaves are a glossy dark green. Grow it in fertile, well-drained soil, close to a warm wall or in a herbaceous border in full sun. In partial shade it will produce lusher foliage. Divide clumps in spring or autumn. When given plenty of space, this clump-forming perennial makes a striking architectural plant. The flowers dry well when left on the plant or cut.

◊ ☼ ☀ Z5–9 H9–5
↕ to 4ft (1.2m) ↔ to 24in (60cm)

ACHILLEA PTARMICA
'The Pearl'

Perennial

Sneezewort is a slender perennial with narrow, serrated, dark green leaves. From early to late summer, 'The Pearl' bears abundant small, pompon-shaped flowers with tiny white petals. It is happiest when planted in a sunny position in well-drained fertile soil. Propagate it by division in autumn. The flowerheads dry well.

◊ ☼ Z3–8 H8–1
↕↔ to 30in (75cm)

ACTINIDIA KOLOMIKTA

Climber

This deciduous, woody-stemmed climber, with its green, white, and pink variegated leaves, is ideal for clothing a pergola or a wall. Fragrant white flowers are borne in clusters in early summer and are sometimes followed by yellow-green fruits. Plant in fertile, well-drained soil, and provide shelter from strong winds. It will grow in partial shade, but full sun will give the best leaf color. Propagate by semi-ripe cuttings in late summer. Prune lightly in early spring to keep it within bounds.

◊ ☼ ◑ ƒ Z5–8 H8–5
‡ to 12ft (4m)

ARUNCUS DIOICUS

Perennial

Goatsbeard forms large clumps of fern-like, midgreen foliage. From early to midsummer tiny, star-shaped white flowers appear on fluffy plumes up to 20in (50cm) long. An easy-going plant, it is tolerant of sun or shade and moist or dry, reasonably fertile soil. It does well in a sunny border, moist ground by water, or a woodland border. Divide plants in early spring or autumn.

◊ ◊ ☼ ◑ Z3–7 H7–1
‡ to 6ft (2m) ↔ to 4ft (1.2m)

CARDIOCRINUM GIGANTEUM

Bulbous perennial

The giant lily is an impressive plant, with up to 20 fragrant, trumpet-shaped blooms on top of a tall, sturdy stem that does not require staking. It forms a rosette of dark green, glossy leaves at the base. For the best results, give it a shady, sheltered position in moist, organic soil. Although the lily dies after flowering, the bulb forms plenty of small bulblets that can be dug up and replanted immediately. They will be ready to flower in three to five years. Protect new growth over winter with a loose, dry mulch.

💧 ☀ *f* Z7–9 H9–7
↕ to 12ft (4m) ↔ to 18in (45cm)

CISTUS LADANIFER

Evergreen shrub

This is a substantial, though often short-lived, upright shrub. The branches are covered with aromatic leaves, and from early summer it bears large quantities of white, saucer-shaped flowers with yellow centers. Each papery petal carries a crimson spot at its base. A native of the Mediterranean, this shrub thrives in full sun and well-drained soil and grows happily in a gravel garden or a site close to a sunny wall, especially in coastal gardens. Established plants will not tolerate being moved.

💧 ☼ *f* Z8–10 H10–8
↕ to 6ft (2m) ↔ to 5ft (1.5m)

CLEMATIS FLORIDA
VAR. SIEBOLDIANA

Climber

This clematis is widely grown for its
striking flowers made up of creamy
white petals and rich purple stamens.
Cold weather may damage early top
growth, so plant it in a sheltered spot
in organic, well-drained soil or in a
container of soil-based potting mix.
In early spring, prune stems back to a
strong pair of buds, approximately 8in
(20cm) above the ground. Train it along
supporting wires, up a trellis, or over a
tripod or similar frame.

○ ☼ ☀ Z6–9 H9–6
↕ to 8ft (2.5m)

CLEMATIS
'Silver Moon'

Climber

Large, silvery white flowers with a hint
of mauve make this among the most
attractive of the early summer-flowering
clematis. Rarely growing taller than 6ft
(2m), it is ideal for a small garden. It
needs a sheltered spot in sun or partial
shade, with its roots in shade, and well-
drained, organic, fertile soil. Provide it
with a support or allow it to scramble
through shrubs. In early spring, remove
dead stems and prune back the other
shoots to a couple of strong buds.

○ ☼ ☀ Z4–9 H9–1
↕ to 6ft (2m)

CORNUS CANADENSIS

Subshrub

Spreading by means of underground stems, the creeping dogwood will provide a low-growing carpet of lush greenery beneath shrubs or trees. The bright green, oval leaves, which grow in opposite pairs, are a perfect foil for the creamy white, petal-like bracts that surround the tiny green-red flowers. It does best on moist but well-drained, slightly acidic soil in partial shade. Divide established plants in early spring or autumn.

◊ ☼ Z2–7 H7–1
‡ to 6in (15cm) ↔ to 12in (30cm)

CORNUS
'Norman Hadden'

Deciduous tree

'Norman Hadden' bears masses of large, creamy white, petal-like bracts in early summer that, after a few weeks, turn a deep shade of pink. The blooms are followed in autumn by strawberry-like fruits. Yet another of its attractions is that, with age, its bark will start to peel, creating a handsome effect. For best results, plant in a sunny or partially shaded position, protected from strong winds, in well-drained, neutral to acidic, fertile soil.

◊ ☼ ☼ Z5–8 H8–5
‡↔ to 25ft (8m)

CRAMBE CORDIFOLIA

Perennial

This extremely vigorous perennial has large, dark green, crinkled leaves. In wonderful contrast, small, highly fragrant, star-shaped flowers are borne in a white froth on stiffly branching, slender stems. To accommodate its sprawling habit, provide it with plenty of space. Although it will tolerate poor soil, it prefers a sunny position in well-drained, fertile soil. Plant it in a gravel garden or herbaceous border.

◊ ☼ ☀ *f* Z6–9 H9–6
‡ to 8ft (2.5m) ↔ to 5ft (1.5m)

DELPHINIUM
'Butterball'

Perennial

In summer, this vigorous perennial bears tall spikes of semidouble white flowers with deep yellow eyes. For the greatest impact, plant in groups in well-drained, fertile soil in full sun. The stems will need supporting with stakes from a young age to prevent them from snapping in strong winds. If you fertilize the plants in spring and remove the faded flowerheads, you may well be rewarded with a second, smaller burst of flowers.

◊ ☼ Z3–7 H7–1
‡ to 5ft (1.5m) ↔ to 36in (90cm)

DEUTZIA GRACILIS

Deciduous shrub

An upright, spreading shrub, slender
deutzia bears clusters of fragrant, pure
white flowers. Plant it in a sunny site in
fertile, well-drained soil. Prune back the
old shoots after flowering has finished.
Take softwood cuttings in summer and
hardwood cuttings in late autumn.

◊ ☼ ƒ Z5–8 H8–5
↕↔ to 3ft (1m)

DIANTHUS
'Haytor White'

Perennial

This white modern pink is widely
grown for cutting and will fill a room
with its delicious clove scent. The
double flowers have deeply serrated
petals. Pinks do best in a sunny position
at the front of a border or by stones and
should be planted in reasonably fertile,
well-drained soil. In spring, pinch out
the growing tips to promote bushy
growth. Deadheading will help prolong
its bloom season. Take cuttings from
nonflowering stems in early spring.

◊ ☼ Z7–10 H10–7
↕ to 18in (45cm) ↔ to 16in (40cm)

DIGITALIS PURPUREA
F. ALBIFLORA

Biennial

This foxglove will grow easily in most gardens, provided you give it moist but well-drained soil and a little shade. In the first year it produces a large rosette of oval-shaped, deep green leaves, followed next year by a tall spire of pure white flowers. Sow seed in spring, and plant out the young seedlings in autumn. Foxgloves look best when planted in groups in front of a dark background (such as shrubs) or in a dappled woodland.

◊ ◐ ☼ Z4–8 H8–1
↕ to 6ft (2m) ↔ to 24in (60cm)

DRYAS OCTOPETALA

Evergreen shrub

The dainty flowers of the mountain avens belie its tough nature – this plant can cope with the harsh conditions on top of windswept, stony slopes and cliffs. What it lacks in height it more than makes up for in spread; its glossy, dark green leaves will quickly fill crevices between rocks, plug gaps in drystone walls, or form large mats in a gravel garden. Grow it in well-drained, gritty soil in sun or partial shade.

◊ ☼ ☼ Z3–6 H6–1
↕ to 4in (10cm) ↔ to 3ft (1m)

ERICA VAGANS
'Lyonesse'

Evergreen shrub

The Cornish heath forms a nicely rounded, spreading bush suitable as a groundcover, with bright green, needle-like leaves. The long spikes of small white flowers, which appear in summer and continue into early autumn, are a favorite of hoverflies and butterflies. Plant it in full sun in moist, well-drained, organic, acidic soil, although it tolerates slightly alkaline soils. After flowering, cut off the dead flowers to keep the plant more compact and neat.

◊ ◊ ☼ Z7–9 H9–7
‡ to 10in (25cm) ↔ to 20in (50cm)

GALEGA OFFICINALIS
'Alba'

Perennial

An ideal plant for the back of a sunny border, this goat's rue bears small, pea-like white flowers. For the best results, plant it in sun or partial shade in moist, well-drained soil. If the soil is rich the stems will be floppy and the plant will need supporting, either with stakes inserted in late spring or by allowing it to grow through open, sturdy shrubs. Propagate by dividing established plants between late autumn and spring.

◊ ◊ ☼ ☀ Z5–10 H10–5
‡ to 5ft (1.5m) ↔ to 36in (90cm)

GILLENIA TRIFOLIATA

Perennial

This is an upright, herbaceous perennial
with red-tinted, branched stems and
small, single white to pinkish white
flowers that are good for cutting.
Plant it in a well-drained, fertile soil.
Native to North American woodlands,
it needs the light or dappled shade
of a woodland garden or shady border
beneath deciduous trees. The tall, wiry
stems will need supporting early in the
year if the site is exposed. Divide large
clumps in spring or autumn.

◊ ◑ ☼ Z5–9 H9–5
↕ to 3ft (1m) ↔ to 24in (60cm)

GLADIOLUS CALLIANTHUS

Cormous perennial

This gladiolus may be sold under its
former name of *Acidanthera*. The
fragrant white flowers, borne on tall,
arching stems, have deep red or purple
throats and are good for cutting. Plant
the corms in a sunny border in well-
drained, fertile soil. They will rot
quickly in wet conditions, and it is
advisable to mix coarse sand with
heavier soil when planting. Where not
hardy, dig up the corms in early
autumn, dry them, then store in a frost-
free place until replanting in spring.

◊ ☼ *f* Z8–10 H12–1
↕ to 3ft (1m) ↔ to 2in (5cm)

x HALIMIOCISTUS SAHUCII

Evergreen shrub

A spreading shrub with narrow, dark green, downy leaves, this hybrid bears a profusion of saucer-shaped white flowers from early summer to autumn. It makes a welcome addition to a gravel or rock garden or a raised bed, where it will enjoy basking in the full heat of the sun. It does well in poor soils, and very well-drained conditions are a must. If in doubt, improve drainage by adding coarse sand to the soil.

◊ ☼ Z7–9 H9–7

‡ to 18in (45cm) ↔ to 36in (90cm)

HEBE
'Pewter Dome'

Evergreen shrub

A rounded, spreading shrub, this hebe bears grayish green leaves and spikes of small white flowers for several weeks from early summer. Grow in reasonably fertile, well-drained soil in sun or partial shade. Provide some shade from strong sun, which can burn the leaves. It is suitable for a rock garden or a mixed border and is good for seaside gardens. It can be used as a low hedge, clipped lightly after flowering.

◊ ☼ ☀ Z9–11 H12–9

‡ to 16in (40cm) ↔ to 24in (60cm)

HELIANTHEMUM
'Wisley White'

Evergreen shrub

Rock roses are attractive dwarf shrubs that bear an abundance of small, saucer-shaped flowers all summer. The papery flowers of 'Wisley White' are pure white with yellow stamens, offset by grayish green leaves. Rock roses thrive in well-drained soil on sun-baked banks, in paving cracks, and in gravel gardens. Trim after flowering to keep the shape of the bush neat. Propagate by semi-ripe cuttings in early summer.

◊ ☼ Z6–8 H8–6
‡ to 8in (20cm) ↔ to 12in (30cm)

HEMEROCALLIS
'Joan Senior'

Perennial

'Joan Senior', with its near white flowers tinged green at the throat, is something quite different from the more familiar yellow or orange daylily. Although each bloom lasts only a day, flowers continue to be produced from early to midsummer. It does best in fertile, moist but well-drained soil in a sunny situation. When the plants become congested, divide the clumps in late summer or early spring.

◊ ◊ ☼ Z3–10 H10–1
‡ to 24in (60cm) ↔ to 30in (75cm)

HESPERIS MATRONALIS *VAR.* ALBIFLORA

Perennial

The tall flower spikes of sweet rocket are a favorite with butterflies. Make the most of the heavenly scent – which, incidentally, grows stronger after dusk – by planting it alongside a path or patio. It is short-lived and best grown as a biennial. Plants are easy to raise from seed sown *in situ* outdoors. Grow in full sun or light shade in fertile, moist, well-drained soil. It is also tolerant of poor soil.

◊ ◊ ☼ *f* Z4–9 H9–1
‡ to 30in (75cm) ↔ to 24in (60cm)

IBERIS AMARA

Annual

In summer, this fast-growing annual produces masses of white to purplish white, scented flowers borne in dense, flattish clusters. Enjoying a sunny site and well-drained soil, it is perfect for edging a path or planting in a gravel garden or raised bed. Sow seed *in situ* in spring or autumn.

◊ ☼ *f* Z0 H9–1
‡ to 12in (30cm) ↔ to 6in (15cm)

IRIS
'Bold Print'

Perennial

Bearded iris come in a huge range of
colors and color combinations. 'Bold
Print' has striking white flowers that are
edged and lightly veined with deep
purple. Grow it in full sun in a well-
drained, neutral to slightly acidic soil.
Divide congested clumps in late
summer. When planting, make sure that
the tops of the rhizomes are exposed
to the sun.

◊ ☼ Z3–9　H9–1
‡ to 22in (55cm) ↔ indefinite

JASMINUM OFFICINALE
'Argenteovariegatum'

Climber

This jasmine is semi-evergreen, with
cream-edged green leaves. The highly
fragrant, pure white flowers appear in
clusters from early summer to early
autumn. Grow it in full sun or partial
shade in fertile, well-drained soil. Once
flowering is over, thin old or congested
stems. During summer, take semi-ripe
cuttings. Where marginally hardy, plant
it in a sheltered position or by a warm
wall. It can also be grown in containers
of soil-based potting mix.

◊ ☼ ◑ *f* Z9–10　H10–9
‡ to 40ft (12m)

LAMIUM MACULATUM
'White Nancy'

Perennial

Ideal as a groundcover in shady areas and beneath trees and shrubs, this attractive deadnettle may retain its green-edged silver leaves throughout winter. In early summer it produces dainty spikes of hooded white flowers. Plant it in moist but well-drained soil in full or partial shade. Divide large clumps in autumn or early spring.

◊ ◊ ☀ ☀ Z4–8 H8–1
‡ to 6in (15cm) ↔ to 3ft (1m)

LAVATERA × CLEMENTII
'Barnsley'

Perennial

This tree mallow is a vigorous, free-flowering, semi-evergreen shrub with lobed green leaves. From early summer until the first frosts, 'Barnsley' steadily produces clusters of funnel-shaped white flowers with distinctive red eyes. Choose a spot for it in full sun in well-drained, ideally light, fertile soil. Provide shelter from strong winds, since the branches are brittle. Propagate by softwood cuttings in summer. It is suitable for gardens in coastal areas.

◊ ☀ Z6–8 H8–6
‡↔ to 6ft (2m)

LEUCANTHEMUM × SUPERBUM
'Wirral Supreme'

Perennial

A stalwart of the herbaceous border, this vigorous plant produces masses of double, daisylike flowers on stiff, erect stems held above dark green, lance-shaped leaves. The blooms make good cut flowers. In exposed sites, the tall stems may need support. Happiest in fairly fertile, well-drained but moist soil in full sun or partial shade, it will eventually spread to form a large clump. Divide every few years in early spring or late summer.

◊ ◊ ☼ ☀ Z5–8 H8–4
‡ to 36in (90cm) ↔ to 30in (75cm)

LEUCOJUM AESTIVUM
'Gravetye Giant'

Bulbous perennial

If left undisturbed in a lightly shaded spot in damp, fertile soil, the summer snowflake will quickly spread to form a large clump of glossy, dark green leaves. From spring to early summer, 'Gravetye Giant' produces up to eight slightly pendent white flowers tipped with green; they have a faint chocolate scent. Plant the bulbs in autumn, preferably in a waterside setting.

◊ ☀ *f* Z4–9 H9–1
‡ to 36in (90cm) ↔ to 3in (8cm)

LILIUM
'Mont Blanc'

Bulbous perennial

From early to midsummer, this sturdy Asiatic lily produces bunches of ivory-white flowers with brown-spotted throats. Its compact stems make it ideal for growing in containers or in a raised bed. Plant bulbs in full sun in fertile, well-drained soil from late autumn to early spring. The flowers are good for cutting, but care must be taken because the pollen stains clothing and damages polished surfaces.

◊ ☼ Z3–8 H8–1
‡ to 28in (70cm)

MATTHIOLA
'Hansens Park'

Perennial

Their sweet fragrance makes stocks a popular bedding plant and cut flower. Most have narrow, grayish green leaves and erect stems. Sow seed in spring in pots of soil-based potting mix. Over-winter young plants in a cold frame before planting out the following spring in moist but well-drained, slightly fertile soil. *M. fructiculosa* 'Alba', also in white, is a compact form that is ideal for containers.

◊ ◊ ☼ *f* Z6–10 H10–6
‡ to 18in (45cm) ↔ to 12in (30cm)

PAEONIA LACTIFLORA
'Baroness Schröder'

Perennial

This superb Chinese peony produces a
bold clump of dark green leaves and
very large, almost globe-shaped flowers.
The petals are blushed pink when they
first open but turn snow white as they
mature. Plant in fertile, moist but well-
drained soil in full sun or partial shade.
The blooms are heavy, so provide support
for them before they open. The fragrant
flowers are excellent for cutting.

◊ ◖ ☼ ☼ ƒ Z4–8 H8–1
↕↔ to 36in (90cm)

PASSIFLORA CAERULEA
'Constance Elliot'

Climber

This passionflower bears pure white,
lightly scented flowers followed by
orange-yellow fruit. It is a fast-growing
climber, especially when grown in the
protection of a warm wall. Where
marginally hardy, mulch the root area;
come spring, new shoots should grow
again. Plant it in fertile, moist but well-
drained soil in full sun or light shade.

◊ ◖ ☼ ☼ Z6–9 H9–6
↕ to 30ft (10m) or more

PHILADELPHUS
'Belle Etoile'

Deciduous shrub

This mockorange is a superb, freely flowering shrub with sprays of large, fragrant white flowers. When weighted down with bloom the branches arch over, giving the shrub a graceful, spreading outline. Plant it in full sun or partial shade in reasonably fertile, well-drained soil. Each year after it has finished flowering, prune some of the older branches down to the ground to encourage new shoots.

◊ ☼ ☀ *f* Z5–8 H8–5
‡ to 4ft (1.2m) ↔ to 8ft (2.5m)

PYRACANTHA
'Watereri'

Evergreen shrub

This upright shrub combines glossy, dark green leaves with an abundance of small white flowers. These are followed in autumn and winter by shiny red berries. A good choice for a boundary hedge, its sharp spines will deter intruders; or train it against a wall. Plant it in a sheltered position in well-drained, fertile soil in full sun or shade. Shorten nonblooming sideshoots to two or three leaves after flowering, and trim hedges in spring and summer.

◊ ☼ ☀ ☀ Z7–9 H9–7
‡↔ to 8ft (2.5m)

RHEUM
'Ace of Hearts'

Perennial

A close relative of edible rhubarb, this
imposing plant has large, heart-shaped,
dark green leaves with red undersides.
In summer it produces tall, branching
stems laden with masses of tiny, star-
shaped white flowers. A lover of deep,
fertile, moist soil, it does well in the
dappled shade of a woodland garden or
the sunny banks of a stream or pond.
Divide large clumps if necessary in
spring, and mulch annually with well-
rotted compost.

◊ ☼ ☀ Z5–9 H9–5
‡ to 4ft (1.2m) ↔ to 36in (90cm)

RODGERSIA AESCULIFOLIA

Perennial

This sizeable, clump-forming plant has
creeping roots and large, dark, bronzy
green leaves that are similar in shape
to a horsechestnut leaf. In summer it
produces tall plumes of fragrant white
or pinkish white flowers. Plant in moist,
fertile soil in full sun. A perfect pond-
side plant, it will also grow well in a
bog garden. If given partial shade it will
tolerate slightly drier soil. Propagate by
dividing established plants in autumn.

◊ ☼ ☀ *f* Z5–8 H8–5
‡ to 6ft (2m) ↔ to 3ft (1m)

ROMNEYA COULTERI

Deciduous shrub

The California tree poppy is a vigorous shrub with large, poppylike, fragrant flowers and gray-green leaves. It can be difficult to establish, but in the right conditions it will spread extensively. Plant it in a sunny site in deep, well-drained soil, and provide protection during cold winters – where marginally hardy, grow plants in the shelter of a sunny wall or fence; it will die down each year but should reshoot in spring. Mature plants resent disturbance and are best left to grow unhindered.

◊ ☼ *f* Z7–8 H8–7

↕ to 8ft (2.5m) ↔ indefinite

ROSA
'Blanc Double de Coubert'

Deciduous shrub

This shrub rose flowers from early summer to early autumn, producing semidouble, fragrant white blooms. Occasionally it will go on to develop bright red hips in autumn. Suitable for a mixed border, it can also be used as a hedge. It tolerates a wide range of conditions but prefers full sun and an open site on fairly fertile, moist but well-drained soil. In early spring, cut out a few of the oldest stems, and lightly trim back flowering shoots.

◊ ◑ ☼ *f* Z3–9 H9–1

↕ to 5ft (1.5m) ↔ to 4ft (1.2m)

ROSA
'Madame Hardy'

Deciduous shrub

Ideal for a mixed border, this extremely attractive shrub rose has vibrant green, leathery foliage and forms a rounded mound. It flowers only once, producing rosette-shaped blooms that have a green button eye and carry a spicy fragrance. A sunny site and fairly fertile, moist but well-drained soil are ideal, although it will tolerate a wide range of growing conditions. Prune it in early spring, removing only the old stems or lightly trimming it into shape.

◊ ◖ ☼ *f* Z4–9 H9–1
‡ to 5ft (1.5m) ↔ to 4ft (1.2m)

SISYRINCHIUM STRIATUM
'Aunt May'

Evergreen perennial

A very striking clump-forming plant whose sword-shaped, variegated leaves are boldly striped with creamy yellow. The cream flowers, lined on the reverse with purple, are borne on stiff, upright spikes. Choose a spot in full sun in poor to moderately fertile, well-drained soil. Protect it from excessive moisture in winter.

◊ ☼ Z7–8 H8–7
‡ to 20in (50cm) ↔ to 10in (25cm)

TANACETUM PARTHENIUM *'Aureum'*

Perennial

In summer and again in autumn, golden feverfew produces clusters of daisylike white flowers with dark yellow centers, borne on upright stems above aromatic, golden yellow leaves. Grow in a sunny border, herb garden, or gravel garden in well-drained soil. Deadhead regularly to prevent it from self-seeding freely around the garden.

◊ ☼ Z4–9 H9–1
‡↔ to 18in (45cm)

VERATRUM ALBUM

Perennial

A statuesque plant with large, pleated green leaves and tall spikes of small, star-shaped white flowers lightly tinged with green. Tolerant of shade and happy in organic, moist but well-drained soil, it is ideal for a woodland garden or shady border. Provided the soil never dries out, it will also cope with full sun. Protect it from cold, drying winds, and divide congested clumps in autumn or early spring. All parts of this plant are toxic.

◊ ◑ ☼ ◐ Z5–9 H9–5
‡ to 6ft (2m) ↔ to 24in (60cm)

ZANTEDESCHIA AETHIOPICA 'Crowborough'

Bulbous perennial

This calla lily has shapely flowers held on stiff stems above luxuriant, dark green leaves. 'Crowborough' can be planted in shallow water at the edge of a pond, or try it in a border in deep, moist, fertile soil in sun or dappled shade. In the latter situation, protect the root area over winter with a thick layer of mulch. When grown in a container, move under cover when frost threatens.

◊ ♦ ☼ ☀ Z8–10 H10–8
‡ to 36in (90cm) ↔ to 24in (60cm)

ZENOBIA PULVERULENTA

Deciduous shrub

From early to midsummer, this attractive shrub produces anise-scented, bell-shaped white flowers that are similar to those of lily-of-the-valley. Its leaves are glossy green above and waxy beneath. Given a sheltered spot, it may retain some leaves in winter. It prefers an organic, acidic, moist soil, preferably in partial shade. It will grow in a sunny situation, provided the soil never dries out.

◊ ☼ ☀ ƒZ5–8 H8–5
‡ to 6ft (2m) ↔ to 5ft (1.5m)

ALLIUM CERNUUM

Bulbous perennial

The nodding onion is a graceful plant with erect, strappy, pungently scented leaves. Stiff stems, arching at the top, produce loose clusters of 25–40 deep pink, bell-shaped flowers. A good plant for a gravel garden or the front of a border, it prefers fertile, well-drained soil in full sun. Plant the bulbs in groups in autumn in groups at a depth of 2–4in (5–10cm).

◊ ☼ Z4–10 H10–4
‡ to 24in (60cm) ↔ to 2in (5cm)

ALLIUM SCHOENOPRASUM

Bulbous perennial

Chives are widely grown as a kitchen herb, but the plant is pretty enough to use in a herbaceous border or edge a bed. In summer, small, dark pink or occasionally lavender-white flowers appear on the top of narrow stems among the grayish green leaves. Cut back after flowering to encourage fresh leaves to sprout. Chives prefer full sun and well-drained soil. Large clumps may be divided in spring.

◊ ☼ Z3–9 H9–1
‡ to 24in (60cm) ↔ to 2in (5cm)

ARGYRANTHEMUM
'Vancouver'

Perennial

With its fernlike foliage and unusual rose-pink blooms, 'Vancouver' is a particularly striking marguerite daisy. It has a long flowering period from early summer until early autumn, making it excellent for borders, bedding, and container displays. Pinching out the growing tips will help maintain a neat, bushy habit. Where marginally hardy, plant it in a sheltered spot in well-drained soil and full sun. If potted up, it is easily moved under cover for winter.

◊ ☼ Z10–11 H10–1
‡ to 36in (90cm) ↔ to 32in (80cm)

ASTILBE
'Straussenfeder'

Perennial

Sprays of coral-pink flowers and dark green leaves – bronze-tinted when young – of this astilbe will provide an attractive groundcover for a permanently moist border, by water, or in a bog garden. Astilbes prefer moist, fertile soil in full sun. Plant in groups for maximum impact. A fast grower, clumps will need dividing every few years in early spring to maintain vigor. The faded flower-heads remain attractive through autumn.

◊ ● ☼ ☼ Z4–9 H8–2
‡ to 36in (90cm) ↔ to 24in (60cm)

ASTILBE *'Venus'*

Perennial

The limited spread of this astilbe makes it ideal for a small garden. Tall sprays of bright pink flowers are borne above vibrant green foliage. It grows best in moist, fertile soil in full sun and is excellent for a bog garden or moist soil beside a pond. In drier soils, grow in partial shade. Divide clumps every few years in early spring to keep plants strong and to encourage more flowers. The bleached flowerheads dry well and continue to look attractive on the plants through autumn.

◑ ◐ ☼ ☀ Z4–9 H9–1
↕ to 3ft (1m) ↔ to 18in (45cm)

ASTRANTIA MAJOR

Perennial

Hattie's pincushion is a clump-forming plant with toothed, midgreen leaves. The tiny flowers are pink or green and surrounded by a pinkish white, papery collar. Astrantias prefer moist, fertile soil in full sun or light shade. They are good for a slightly shaded herbaceous border, a woodland garden, or moist ground beside a pond or stream. Dead-head to prevent self-seeding. Large clumps may be divided in spring.

◑ ☼ ☀ Z4–7 H7–1
↕ to 24in (60cm) ↔ to 18in (45cm)

CAMPANULA LACTIFLORA

Perennial

This upright bellflower has thin, mid-green leaves. In summer, tall stems carry clusters of large, pale pink, white, or blue bell-shaped flowers. In exposed sites they may need supporting with stakes. Choose a spot in full sun or partial shade in fertile, moist but well-drained soil. Divide in spring or autumn to keep the plant healthy and vigorous.

◊ ◑ ☼ ☀ Z5–7 H7–5
↕ to 5ft (1.5m) ↔ to 24in (60cm)

CAMPANULA PUNCTATA

Perennial

This low-growing bellflower thrives in moist but well-drained, fertile, fairly light soil, particularly if it gets plenty of sun. In early summer, dusky to shell pink flowers hang from erect stems. Their inner surfaces are freckled red and covered in a fuzz of soft hairs. The dark green, semi-evergreen leaves are heart-shaped at the base. Cut back after flowering to encourage a second flush of blooms and to prevent self-seeding, .

◊ ◑ ☼ ☀ Z4–8 H8–1
↕ to 12in (30cm) ↔ to 16in (40cm)

CENTAUREA HYPOLEUCA *'John Coutts'*

Perennial

This upright plant has grayish green, wavy-edged leaves. The long-lasting, fragrant flowers are borne singly on long stems throughout early summer. The outer florets are star-shaped, with bright pink thistlelike centres. Plant in a border or rock garden in full sun and well-drained soil. Divide big clumps in spring or autumn.

◊ ☼ *f* Z4–8 H8–1
‡↔ to 24in (60cm)

CENTRANTHUS RUBER

Perennial

Red valerian will grow in some of the most exposed places: on cliffs, walls, and at the edge of roads. It is also grown successfully as a border perennial, where it is valued for its long flowering season. It has fleshy, bright green leaves and, throughout summer, branching stems covered with small, star-shaped pink, red, or white flowers. Plant in poor, well-drained soil in full sun, and deadhead regularly. Suitable for coastal gardens.

◊ ☼ Z5–8 H8–5
‡↔ to 3ft (1m)

CISTUS × ARGENTEUS
'Peggy Sammons'

Evergreen shrub

Each bloom on a rock rose lasts for
only one day, but they are produced
constantly from early to late summer.
'Peggy Sammons' has large, purplish
pink flowers and grayish green leaves.
It thrives on well-drained soil, including
poor, in full sun. Grow in containers,
around paved areas, on sunny banks,
or in a border. Rock roses do well in
coastal gardens.

◊ ☼ Z8–10 H10–8
↕↔ to 3ft (1m)

CLEMATIS
'Comtesse de Bouchaud'

Climber

A vigorous, deciduous clematis with pale
green leaves. Many pinkish mauve
flowers are produced, with dark lines
radiating out from their yellow centers.
Grow in well-drained fertile soil in sun
or partial shade, with the roots in
shade. Cut back in early spring to a pair
of strong buds 8in (20cm) above soil
level to promote heavy flowering.
Clematis are often grown through roses
and other shrubs or trees and used to
clothe trellises, walls, and arches.

◊ ☼ ◗ Z6–9 H9–6
↕ to 10ft (3m)

CLEMATIS
'Nelly Moser'

Climber

In early summer this deciduous clematis
bears large, pinkish purple flowers with a
reddish stripe down the center of each
petal. The foliage is a pretty, pale green.
It is best grown in well-drained fertile
soil in a slightly shaded position, since
the blooms fade in strong sun. Grow it
through a tree or shrub or over a trellis
or an arch. To encourage lots of flowers,
remove any dead stems in early spring
and prune the remaining shoots back to
a pair of strong buds.

◊ ☀ Z4–9 H9–1
‡ to 10ft (3m)

CORDYLINE AUSTRALIS
'Torbay Red'

Evergreen tree

The exotic-looking cabbage palm has
an erect stem topped by a crown of
strap-shaped, pink- and red-striped
leaves. Where marginally hardy, plant it
in a position sheltered from strong
winds and wrap the crown in burlap
and mulch the soil generously before
winter. It also makes a good container
plant that can be brought into a frost-
free greenhouse or conservatory during
the winter months.

◊ ☀ ☀ Z10–11 H12–1
‡ to 10ft (3m) ↔ to 3ft (1m)

CORNUS KOUSA 'Satomi'

Deciduous tree

This dramatic dogwood has many attractions, including decorative bark, deep purplish red leaves in autumn, and a handsome outline. Perhaps most striking, though, is its display of masses of dark pink bracts against the dark green foliage. The bracts surround a cluster of tiny flowers. Plant in a sunny or partially shaded site in neutral or acidic, well drained, organic soil.

◊ ☼ ☀ Z5–8 H8–5
‡ to 22ft (7m) ↔ to 15ft (5m)

COSMOS BIPINNATUS *Sensation Series*

Annual

This elegant annual is perfect for an annual or mixed border, where it is valued for its feathery, midgreen leaves and large, showy blooms. The long-stemmed, daisylike flowers come in white and a range of pinks and are good for cutting. Prolong flowering by deadheading regularly. It prefers a sunny position in moist but well-drained soil. For early flowering, sow seed in autumn or early spring.

◊ ◊ ☼ Z0 H12–1
‡ to 36in (90cm) ↔ to 18in (45cm)

DEUTZIA × ELEGANTISSIMA *'Rosealind'*

Deciduous shrub

Thousands of star-shaped, pale pink flowers adorn this shrub. Deutzias are stunning when grown in the border or as a specimen plant; choose a position in full sun and fertile, well-drained soil. Maintain this shrub's neat shape by pruning out old flowered shoots after the blooms have faded.

◊ ☼ Z6–8 H8–6
‡ to 4ft (1.2m) ↔ to 5ft (1.5m)

DIANTHUS ALPINUS *'Joan's Blood'*

Perennial

Alpine pinks are compact, tuft-forming evergreens with narrow, shiny, dark green leaves. In summer, 'Joan's Blood' is almost completely covered by large, deep pink flowers with toothed petals. This decorative plant is ideal for planting at the front of borders, in raised beds and rock gardens, and between paving slabs. Choose a sunny spot in organic, well-drained soil.

◊ ☼ Z3–8 H8–1
‡ to 3in (8cm) ↔ to 4in (10cm)

DIANTHUS
'Houndspool Ruby'

Perennial

This bold pink has double, rose-pink
flowers with a splash of red at the
center of their delicately fringed petals.
Modern pinks bloom throughout
summer, are good in a border, and are
excellent for cutting. They form dense
mounds of narrow, gray-green, evergreen leaves. Choose a position in full
sun with well-drained soil.

◊ ☼ Z4–10 H10–4
↕ to 18in (45cm) ↔ to 16in (40cm)

DIANTHUS
'Doris'

Perennial

With its pale pink, wavy-edged petals
and raspberry-colored center, this is one
of the prettiest pinks. Often two or
three flushes of clove-scented blooms
will be borne from early summer to
autumn above a mound of gray-green
leaves. The flowers are decorative in
a border and very long lasting when
cut. Pinks thrive in well-drained soil
and full sun.

◊ ☼ *f* Z5–10 H10–5
↕ to 18in (45cm) ↔ to 16in (40cm)

DICTAMNUS ALBUS
VAR. PURPUREUS

Perennial

The gas plant produces aromatic oils that can ignite on a hot, very still summer evening. Long spikes of large pink flowers with dark purple veins are produced. The foliage is lemon-scented, but take care, since contact with its leaves may irritate the skin. Plant in well-drained soil in sun or partial shade and avoid transplanting, because it resents disturbance.

◊ ☼ ☀ *f* Z3–8 H8–1
‡ to 36in (90cm) ↔ to 24in (60cm)

DIERAMA PULCHERRIMUM

Bulbous perennial

Angel's fishing rod is so named because the bright pink, bell-shaped flowers hang from graceful, arching stems in summer. The narrow leaves are grayish green and grasslike. It is especially pretty grown beside a pond, where the water will reflect its slender form, or in a border. Choose a sunny situation in reliably moist but well-drained soil, planting the bulbs 2–3in (5–7cm) deep in spring.

◊ ◑ ☼ Z8–10 H10–8
‡ to 5ft (1.5m) ↔ to 24in (60cm)

DIGITALIS × MERTONENSIS

Perennial

This foxglove has large, strawberry-colored, funnel-shaped flowers borne on sturdy spikes. It forms clumps of handsome, glossy green leaves. Foxgloves prefer moist, well-drained soil in partial shade but will tolerate a wide range of conditions. They are equally happy in a border or naturalized beneath deciduous trees. Allow plants to self-seed, or sow seed in late spring.

◊ ◐ ☼ ☼ Z3- 8 H8–1
↕ to 36in (90cm) ↔ to 12in (30cm)

EREMURUS ROBUSTUS

Perennial

From a clump of strappy, bluish green leaves, this impressive plant produces a tower of pale pink flowers on top of a tall, leafless stem. Foxtail lilies are effective when several are grouped together in a border. Grow in a sunny position in sandy, very well-drained soil, since the roots will die if they get too wet in winter. The flower spikes may need support, especially in exposed areas. If frost threatens in late winter and spring, mulch with straw or row cover to protect emerging shoots.

◊ ☼ Z5–8 H8–5
↕ to 10ft (3m) ↔ to 4ft (1.2m)

ESCALLONIA
'Apple Blossom'

Evergreen shrub

A bushy shrub with rounded, glossy green leaves, this escallonia bears small, clear pink flowers with white centers in early summer. Grow it in a border, against a wall, or as a hedge or windbreak. It will also thrive in coastal areas. To help retain a neat shape, trim lightly in mid- to late spring.

○ ☼ Z8–9 H9–8
↕↔ to 8ft (2.5m)

FRAGARIA
Pink Panda

Perennial

This vigorous groundcover plant is related to the strawberry but rarely fruits. Deep pink flowers are produced for a long period during summer. The leaves are bright green, deeply veined, and almost evergreen. It does well in full sun or partial shade and prefers moist but well-drained, fertile soil. Ideal for the front of a herbaceous border. If it threatens to spread out of bounds, control it by removing unwanted runners (the horizontal stems).

○ ◖ ☼ ☀ Z5–9 H9–5
↕ to 6in (15cm) ↔ indefinite

GERANIUM ENDRESSII

Perennial

A clump-forming hardy geranium, or cranesbill, with trumpet-shaped, pale pink flowers with notched petals. The evergreen leaves are hairy and wrinkly. Cranesbills tolerate a wide range of soil types and growing conditions, coping well in full sun or partial shade – a rock garden, the front of a mixed border, or a wild garden are ideal. Cut back after flowering to encourage fresh growth and more flowers. *G. endressii* combines well with a blue-flowering geranium such as *G. ibericum.*

◊ ◑ ☼ ☀ Z4–8 H9–1
‡ to 18in (45cm) ↔ to 24in (60cm)

GERANIUM × RIVERSLEAIANUM *'Russell Prichard'*

Perennial

This hardy geranium has trailing, creeping stems, making it a good groundcover plant. In summer it has deeply divided, slightly hairy, grayish green leaves and deep magenta flowers. It prefers to be planted in full sun in well-drained, slightly fertile soil, but it will tolerate a wide range of conditions. Cut back after flowering to encourage fresh growth and more flowers.

◊ ☼ Z6–8 H8–6
‡ to 12in (30cm) ↔ to 3ft (1m)

GLADIOLUS
'Rose Supreme'

Cormous perennial

Tall spikes can hold as many as 24
flowers above a fan of sword-shaped
leaves. Each rose-pink bloom has a
cream throat and dark pink edges. Plant
it in full sun in fertile, well-drained soil,
and support it with a stake. Gladioli are
superb for adding height to a border
and make excellent cut flowers. Lift
corms in autumn, store dry over winter,
and replant in spring in soil enriched
with organic matter.

◊ ☼ Z8–10 H12–1
‡ to 5½ft (1.7m) ↔ to 10in (25cm)

HELIANTHEMUM
'Rhodanthe Carneum'

Evergreen shrub

A wide-spreading rock rose with silver-
gray leaves. In summer it produces
numerous flat, pale pink flowers
marked with yellow in the center. Grow
it at the front of a border, in a raised
bed, alongside paving, or in a rock or
gravel garden. Choose a position in
fertile, well-drained soil and full sun.
Prune after flowering to prevent it from
becoming leggy or sprawly.

◊ ☼ Z6–8 H8–6
‡ to 12in (30cm) ↔ to 18in (45cm)

HEMEROCALLIS
'Joylene Nichole'

Perennial

The daylily is so called because its flowers open for just one day. 'Joylene Nichole' is unusual in that it unfurls its flowers late in the afternoon, and they stay open throughout the night. It has large, pink flowers with a yellowish green throat and lined with deep pink veins. The flowers are borne above a large clump of almost evergreen, bluish green leaves. Plant in moist but well-drained soil in a sunny border.

○ ◑ ☼ Z3–10 H12–1
‡ to 20in (50cm) ↔ to 3ft (1m)

IMPATIENS WALLERIANA
'Tempo Lavender'

Perennial

With its vivid, lavender-pink, long-lasting flowers and light green leaves, 'Tempo Lavender' is a particularly pretty summer bedding plant. Available in a wide range of colors, impatiens are tender perennials that are usually grown as annuals. For the best flowers, choose a spot in partial shade in moist but well-drained soil. They also make excellent container plants.

○ ◑ ☼ Z9–15 H12–1
‡↔ to 10in (25cm)

INCARVILLEA DELAVAYI

Perennial

Here is an exotic-looking plant with large flowers held on strong stems above a rosette of lush, midgreen leaves. The flowerhead consists of up to 10 trumpet-shaped, rose-pink or purple blooms. Grow it in fertile, moist, well-drained soil in a bright, sunny position, preferably one that avoids direct midday sun. A good choice for a gravel garden or mixed or herbaceous border.

◊ ◊ ☼ Z6–8 H8–6
‡ to 24in (60cm) ↔ to 12in (30cm)

IRIS
'Carnaby'

Perennial

Bearded irises are grown mostly for their flamboyant flowers that come in a huge range of colors. This variety has large flowers with peach-pink upper petals and pink-purple lower petals that are furred with an orange "beard." Divide congested clumps of iris after flowering, replanting only plump sections of rhizome in a sunny spot in well-drained fertile soil and making sure their tops are exposed to the sun.

◊ ☼ Z3–9 H9–1
‡ to 3ft (1m) ↔ indefinite

KALMIA LATIFOLIA

Evergreen shrub

Mountain laurel is an excellent choice
for slightly acidic soil, where your
reward will be large heads of pink or
white flowers. It forms a nicely rounded
bush with oval, dark green leaves.
Kalmias prefer organic, moist but well-
drained, acidic soil in partial shade,
although they will tolerate full sun
where the ground remains moist in
summer. Mulch annually with leaf mold
or bark chips.

◊ ◊ ☼ ☀ Z5–9 H9–5
↟↔ to 10ft (3m)

LATHYRUS GRANDIFLORUS

Climber

The everlasting pea is a herbaceous
perennial that will climb through
shrubs, over banks, or along a trellis
using clinging tendrils. In the summer
it produces small clusters of red or
purple-pink flowers and pairs of oval
leaves. It is best grown in a sunny
position in well-drained, fertile soil.
This pea spreads underground; if
unwanted shoots emerge, remove them
at ground level.

◊ ☼ Z6–9 H9–6
↕ to 5ft (1.5m)

LAVATERA × CLEMENTII *'Bredon Springs'*

Deciduous shrub

Mallows are short-lived plants grown for their profuse flowers borne throughout the summer months. 'Bredon Springs' is almost evergreen, with gray-green leaves and deep, dusky pink blooms. Position it in full sun in fertile, well-drained soil, sheltered or staked against the wind. When the flowers have finished, prune back hard to a strong bud close to the base of the plant. Suitable for coastal gardens.

◊ ☼ Z10–11 H12–9
‡↔ to 6ft (2m)

LAVATERA MARITIMA

Shrub

This shrubby perennial has rounded, grayish green leaves with shallow lobes. In summer it bears solitary, saucer-shaped pink flowers with deep magenta veins radiating out from the center. It prefers a spot in full sun in fertile, well-drained soil, sheltered or staked against the wind. To encourage healthy growth the following year, after flowering cut back to a strong bud close to the base. Mallows tend to be short lived but are good for seaside gardens.

◊ ☼ Z6–8 H8–6
‡ to 5ft (1.5m) ↔ to 3ft (1m)

MATTHIOLA INCANA
Cinderella Series

Perennial

Stocks are extremely fragrant flowers that, although botanically perennial, are usually grown as a biennial or annual. The Cinderella Series has double white, deep pink, purple, or lavender flowers produced from early summer. Plant in a sunny position in fertile, well-drained, neutral or slightly alkaline soil. Stocks are excellent as annual bedding and as cut flowers.

◊ ☼ *f* Z7–8   H8–1
‡↔ to 10in (25cm)

MORINA LONGIFOLIA
Perennial

A spiny-toothed, evergreen perennial with dark green, aromatic leaves that overwinter as a thistlelike rosette. In early summer it produces a spike of small, dangling, tubular flowers – these open white, turn pink after they have been fertilized, then eventually change to red before falling. Plant in a sunny position in poor, very well-drained soil to guard against rot in winter.

◊ ☼ *f* Z6–9   H9–6
‡ to 36in (90cm) ↔ to 12in (30cm)

NECTAROSCORDUM SICULUM *SUBSP.* BULGARICUM

Bulbous perennial

An elegant perennial with pendulous, pink-flushed, bell-shaped flowers that are borne on tall stems. These emerge from a clump of garlic-smelling, linear leaves. It can be grown in full sun or partial shade and prefers a slightly fertile, well-drained soil. This bulb is ideal for a wild garden, where it may freely self-seed. To control its spread in a herbaceous border, simply deadhead it diligently.

◊ ☼ ☀ Z6–10 H10–6
↕ to 4ft (1.2m) ↔ to 18in (45cm)

NEILLIA THIBETICA

Deciduous shrub

This shrub grows well in a border or beneath deciduous trees, spreading by suckers to form a dense thicket. The arching branches have glossy green leaves and long clusters of bright pink, bell-shaped flowers. Grow in full sun or partial shade in fertile, well-drained soil. To encourage strong new growth the following year, prune after flowering by cutting branches back to a strong pair of buds and removing a quarter of the stems down to the base.

◊ ☼ Z6–9 H9–6
↕↔ to 6ft (2m)

ONOPORDUM ACANTHIUM

Biennial

The Scotch thistle is an architectural
plant that is good for a large border or
a wild or gravel garden. In its first year,
an impressive rosette of spiny, grayish
green leaves is formed. During the
second year, a strong, prickly stem
covered with white hairs is produced.
The stem is crowned with thistlelike
flowerheads composed of many small,
deep pink or occasionally white
flowers. Grow in full sun in fertile,
well-drained, neutral or alkaline soil.
It will readily self-seed.

◊ ☼ Z6–9 H9–6
‡ to 6ft (1.8m) ↔ to 3ft (1m)

OSTEOSPERMUM JUCUNDUM

Perennial

Free-flowering and extremely decorative,
this is a superb perennial for any border.
It has pretty mauvish pink or magenta
daisylike blooms that are produced
throughout summer above a clump
of grayish green leaves. Grow in well-
drained, fertile soil in full sun. Regular
deadheading will help extend the
flowering period.

◊ ☼ Z9–10 H10–1
‡ to 20in (50cm) ↔ to 3ft (1m)

PAEONIA LACTIFLORA
'Monsieur Jules Elie'

Perennial

This herbaceous peony forms bold clumps of glossy, dark green leaves and deep pink, double flowers that are good for cutting. Grow in a border in sun or partial shade in deep, fertile, well-drained soil. For the best blooms, mulch generously with organic matter in autumn. The blooms, which reach over 8in (20cm) across, may need some support – encircling stakes are ideal. Clumps are best left undisturbed.

○ ◑ ☼ ◐ Z4–8 H8–1
↕↔ to 3ft (1m)

PAPAVER ORIENTALE
'Cedric Morris'

Perennial

The Oriental poppy is a vigorous plant that will provide a spectacular splash of color in any border. It forms a large clump of lobed, gray-haired leaves and tall stems that bear very large, soft pink flowers with a black mark at the base of each petal. After the decorative seed pods appear, the plant dies down – make sure it is masked by other plants during this unattractive phase. Plant in full sun in fertile, well-drained soil; divide in late summer.

○ ☼ Z4–9 H9–1
↕↔ to 36in (90cm)

PAPAVER SOMNIFERUM
'Paeony Flowered'

Annual

Although grown mainly for its beautiful flowers, the opium poppy also has handsome blue-green leaves and decorative seedpods. In summer, the 'Peony Flowered' type bears huge, rounded, frilly blooms in shades of pink or purple. Sow *in situ* in spring in a sunny situation in very well-drained soil in an annual border or in gaps in a herbaceous or mixed border.

◊ ☼ Z0 H9–1
↕ to 4ft (1.2m) ↔ to 12in (30cm)

PERSICARIA BISTORTA
'Superba'

Perennial

Bistort is a vigorous plant that is often used in a border or wild garden or as a groundcover. Numerous flower spikes are held well above clumps of broad, midgreen leaves. They are made up of many tiny, densely packed, soft pink flowers. Although it will tolerate dry soil, it prefers moist ground in full sun or partial shade. Divide large clumps in spring or autumn.

◊ ◊ ☼ ☼ Z4–8 H8–1
↕↔ to 36in (90cm)

PETUNIA
Surfinia Pink Vein

Annual

The Surfinia Series is well known for their large flowers and vigorous growth. Their trailing habit makes them ideal for containers and hanging baskets. They can also be used as bedding, but the flowers may be damaged by heavy rain. In a border, provide a sunny position and well-drained soil. Deadhead regularly and fertilize container-grown plants with a tomato fertilizer every 10–14 days to prolong flowering.

◊ ☼ Z0 H12–1
‡ to 16in (40cm) ↔ to 36in (90cm)

PRIMULA VIALII

Perennial

Grow this unusual-looking primrose beside a pond or in any moist site in sun or, preferably, partial shade. In summer, from a rosette of hairy leaves, it produces a thick stem topped with a tight spike of small pink flowers that emerge from crimson buds. *P. vialii* is happiest in organic, neutral or acidic soil. Although perennial, it can be rather short-lived: sow in spring to renew your stock, or allow to self-seed.

◊ ☼ ☀ Z5–8 H8–5
‡ to 24in (60cm) ↔ to 12in (30cm)

ROSA
'Blessings'

Deciduous shrub

If deadheaded regularly, this hybrid
tea rose will produce many urn-shaped
pink, scented blooms up through
autumn. Prune the main stems to 10in
(25cm) above ground in early spring,
then apply a balanced fertilizer and
mulch generously with well-rotted
manure to encourage the production of
lots of flowers. Roses should be planted
in a sunny situation in fertile, organic,
well-drained soil, preferably slightly
acidic or neutral.

◊ ◊ ☼ *f* Z5–9 H9–5
‡ to 3ft (1m) ↔ to 24in (60cm)

ROSA
'Frühlingsmorgen'

Deciduous shrub

A healthy, upright shrub rose with
dark, grayish green leaves. The single,
light pink, hay-scented flowers are
produced in early summer. It can be
grown up a pillar, in mixed borders, or
as hedging and will even tolerate light
shade. It needs less rich conditions than
hybrid teas and other bush roses. To
maintain a neat shape, lightly trim the
bush after flowering.

◊ ◊ ☼ *f* Z4–9 H9–1
‡ to 6ft (2m) ↔ to 5ft (1.5m)

ROSA
Gertrude Jekyll

Deciduous shrub

Named after the famous Edwardian
garden designer, this is a slender, large-
flowered shrub rose. It is grown for its
deep pink flowers, which are extremely
fragrant and start to appear in early
summer. With regular deadheading,
flowering may continue into early
autumn. This disease-resistant rose needs
rich growing conditions, so mulch
deeply in early spring with well-rotted
manure after lightly pruning it to shape
– although this is not essential.

◊ ◐ ☼ *f* Z5–9　H9–5
‡ to 5ft (1.5m) ↔ to 3ft (1m)

ROSA
'Madame Knorr'

Deciduous shrub

An old variety of Portland rose with
large, lilac-pink, very fragrant flowers
throughout the summer months. It is an
easy-going rose with midgreen foliage
and thorny stems. It does well on most
well-drained soils and even in poor
conditions. When used as hedging, trim
it back in late winter or early spring.

◊ ◐ ☼ *f* Z5–9　H9–5
‡ to 4ft (1.2m) ↔ to 3ft (1m)

ROSA
Surrey

Deciduous shrub

Groundcover roses are chosen for their
low, spreading habit and abundant,
healthy foliage. They can be used in
many situations: in a border, trailing
down a bank or over a wall, and in a
container or large hanging basket. Surrey
is disease resistant, grows quickly, and
is very free flowering, with double,
soft pink blooms. Grow in moist but
well-drained, fertile soil in full sun. Trim
in late winter or early spring to keep it
within bounds.

◊ ◊ ☼ Z5–9 H9–5
↕ to 32in (80cm) ↔ to 4ft (1.2m)

SALVIA VIRIDIS
'Claryssa Pink'

Annual

Clary sage is an aromatic plant with
upright, branching stems. Seed is
available in single shades or in
mixtures. The bracts of 'Claryssa Pink'
are a particularly bright, rose-pink hue.
Sow seeds *in situ* in midspring in well-
drained soil. It can be used as a long-
lasting cut or dried flower.

◊ ◊ ☼ ☼ Z0 H9–1
↕ to 16in (40cm) ↔ to 9in (23cm)

SANGUISORBA OBTUSA

Perennial

Burnet is a clump-forming plant with bold, grayish green leaves and thin, wiry stems tipped with spikes of tiny pink flowers resembling bottlebrushes. Grow them in a border or next to a pond in moist but well-drained soil in full sun or partial shade. Both the flowers and leaves are good for cutting.

◊ ◐ ☼ ☀ Z4–8 H8–1
‡ to 4ft (1.2m) ↔ to 24in (60cm)

SAPONARIA OFFICINALIS
'Rosea Plena'

Perennial

Before commercial detergents became available, soapwort was used as a soap substitute for washing delicate fabrics. Today it is still often used in natural shampoos. A robust plant with rough, rounded leaves, this form has double pink flowers. It can spread rapidly and may need to be kept in check in a border to prevent it from overwhelming other plants. It is best in well-drained neutral to alkaline soils in a sunny or very lightly shaded position.

◊ ☼ Z3–9 H9–1
‡ to 24in (60cm) ↔ to 20in (50cm)

SIDALCEA
'Elsie Heugh'

Perennial

This false mallow forms clumps of rounded, basal leaves and upright stems that bear purple-pink, fringed flowers with the texture of satin. They are excellent for cutting. Grow in a sunny border in well-drained, neutral to slightly acidic, fertile soil.

◊ ◑ ☼ ☀ Z6–8 H8–6
‡ to 36in (90cm) ↔ to 18in (45cm)

TAMARIX RAMOSSISSIMA
'Pink Cascade'

Deciduous shrub

This tamarisk is an attractive small tree with graceful, arching branches and feathery foliage covered with tiny pink flowers. It makes a superb windbreak or hedge in coastal areas; in inland areas it may need a more sheltered position. To prevent plants from becoming straggly, cut back in early spring. It grows best in sandy, well-drained soil in full sun.

◊ ☼ Z3–8 H8–1
‡ to 12ft (4m) ↔ to 11ft (3.5m)

TANACETUM COCCINEUM
'Eileen May Robinson'

Perennial

This painted daisy is a bushy plant with silver-haired, balsam-scented leaves that can be used as a cut flower and to make potpourri. It produces an abundance of soft pink flowers. Cut back after flowers fade to encourage a second flush. It will tolerate any light, well-drained soil in full sun.

○ ☼ Z5–9 H9–5
‡ to 30in (75cm) ↔ to 18in (45cm)

THYMUS SERPYLLUM
'Annie Hall'

Evergreen shrub

This thyme forms a mat of creeping branches covered with numerous tiny, pale pink flowers. Its small, dark green leaves are highly aromatic when crushed, making it ideal for planting in paving crevices, where its pungent oils are released when it is lightly stepped on. Alternatively, plant it in an herb or rock garden or in containers, choosing a sunny position and very well-drained soil of average fertility.

○ ☼ *f* Z4–9 H9–1
‡ to 10in (25cm) ↔ to 18in (45cm)

VERBASCUM
'Helen Johnson'

Perennial

This mullein produces tall spikes of pinkish brown, saucer-shaped flowers in early to midsummer. They emerge from an evergreen rosette of downy, grayish green leaves. Plant in a border or gravel garden in a sunny position with well-drained soil. 'Helen Johnson' can be short-lived, so propagate new plants by division in autumn.

◊ ☼ Z6–9 H9–5
‡ to 36in (90cm) ↔ to 12in (30cm)

VERBENA
'Sissinghurst'

Perennial

This sprawling verbena is ideal for containers and especially hanging baskets. It has dark green leaves and, from summer and into autumn, large, round clusters of bright, magenta-pink flowers. Often grown as an annual, it can be potted up and taken into a greenhouse over winter. It is easily raised from semi-ripe cuttings of non-flowering shoots taken in late summer.

◊ ◑ ☼ Z7–11 H12–1
‡ to 8in (20cm) ↔ to 3ft (1m)

ADONIS ANNUA

Annual

Pheasant's eye is a striking plant with finely divided leaves and bright scarlet, cup-shaped flowers with a black spot in the center. It makes a superb addition to an annual border or hot-hued herbaceous border, where it will fill the gaps left by early spring bulbs. It likes a sunny situation in well-drained, preferably alkaline soil. Sow seed *in situ* in autumn or spring.

◊ ☼ Z0 H12–1
‡ to 18in (45cm) ↔ to 12in (30cm)

ASTILBE × ARENDSII *'Fanal'*

Perennial

This dramatic herbaceous plant bears plumes of tiny red flowers. Its divided, toothed, deep green foliage contrasts well with the blooms and is a feature in its own right. Astilbes flourish in organic, fertile soil in a permanently moist border, at the edge of a woodland garden, in a bog garden, or by water. They prefer a position in partial shade, although they will grow in full sun as long as the soil never dries out.

◊ ♦ ☼ ☀ Z4–9 H9–1
‡ to 24in (60cm) ↔ to 18in (45cm)

ASTRANTIA
'Hadspen Blood'

Perennial

This plant forms a clump of deeply lobed green leaves and bears sprays of tiny dark red flowers, surrounded by petal-like bracts, from early to midsummer. Plant astrantias beside a stream, in a damp border, or in a deciduous woodland garden in moist, fertile soil in full sun or partial shade. Large clumps can be divided in spring.

◑ ☼ ◐ Z4–7 H7–1
‡ to 36in (90cm) ↔ to 18in (45cm)

CIRSIUM RIVULARE
'Atropurpureum'

Perennial

The thistlelike flowers and informal habit of this plant make it ideal for growing in a wild garden, a damp meadow, or in association with ornamental grasses. It forms clumps of narrow, lance-shaped leaves covered beneath with soft hairs, and tall stems of reddish purple blooms. It needs to be planted in a sunny situation in moist, well-drained soil. Divide it in autumn or early spring.

○ ◐ ☼ Z4–8 H8–1
‡ to 4ft (1.2m) ↔ to 24in (60cm)

DIANTHUS BARBATUS
'Dunnet's Dark Crimson'

Biennial

Sweet Williams are valued for their
early summer flowers and wonderful
fragrance, and 'Dunnet's Dark Crimson'
is a particularly decorative variety. Its
dark, bronzy green leaves contrast well
with the dense clusters of deep red
flowers. Sweet Williams will grow well
in a sunny herbaceous border in fertile,
well-drained, neutral to alkaline soil.
Good for cutting.

◊ ☼ Z3–9 H9–1
‡ to 24in (60cm) ↔ to 12in (30cm)

DIANTHUS
Telstar Series
'Telstar Crimson'

Biennial

This bushy, compact plant bears small,
deep red flowers in clusters on short
stems above dark green leaves. It is
much smaller than the more vigorous
Sweet William, and when planted in
groups makes a good bedding plant.
It is also useful for the front of a
herbaceous border. Sow *in situ* in
autumn in full sun and well-drained,
fertile soil.

◊ ☼ Z4–10 H10–1
‡ to 10in (25cm) ↔ to 9in (23cm)

ECCREMOCARPUS SCABER

Climber

The Chilean glory flower is a vigorous
evergreen with tubular, bright orange-
red flowers that appear early in summer
and continue to autumn. A short-lived
tender perennial, it is often grown as an
annual where not hardy. Use it to
clothe a trellis or pergola, or train it on
wires up a house wall. Plant it in full
sun in well-drained, fertile soil.

◊ ☼ Z10–11 H12–7
‡ to 12ft (4m)

GAILLARDIA
'Dazzler'

Perennial

As the name suggests, the flowers of
this plant will certainly catch the eye in
a bed or border. Their petals are deep
orange-red tipped with yellow, while
the centers resemble a maroon
pincushion. The blooms appear in early
summer and continue until frost. Grow
'Dazzler' in a sunny position in fertile,
well-drained soil, and remove the dead
flowers to prolong blooming. Excellent
for cutting.

◊ ☼ Z3–8 H8–1
‡ to 34in (85cm) ↔ to 18in (45cm)

HELIANTHEMUM
'Fire Dragon'

Evergreen shrub

This rock rose flowers for many months
from early summer and quickly spreads
to form a dense mound of linear, gray-
green leaves that set off the bright
orange-red, cup-shaped blooms. It will
inject color into a sunny bank, a rock
or gravel garden, or a raised bed. It will
flourish in full sun and a well-drained,
alkaline soil, and it should be trimmed
after flowering to maintain its shape.

◊ ☼ Z6–8 H8–6
↕↔ to 12in (30cm)

HEMEROCALLIS
'Stafford'

Perennial

A beautiful daylily, 'Stafford' produces
deep red flowers with golden yellow
centers, borne above a clump of straplike, midgreen leaves. It flowers from
early to midsummer and will help fire
up a gravel garden or the front of a
border. Alternatively, it can be grown in
a large container if well watered in the
summer. Plant it in full sun or partial
shade in moist, well-drained soil.

◊ ◊ ☼ Z3–10 H10–1
↕ to 28in (70cm) ↔ to 3ft (1m)

LEPTOSPERMUM SCOPARIUM 'Kiwi'

Evergreen shrub

This New Zealand tea tree has aromatic, lance-shaped, purple-tinged leaves and produces masses of dark, crimson-red flowers from late spring to early summer. Where not hardy, it can be overwintered in a container in a cool greenhouse. Otherwise, grow it outside in well-drained soil, ideally near a sheltered patio or terrace where the flowers can be fully appreciated. Suitable for coastal gardens.

◊ ☼ *f* Z9–10 H10–9
↔ to 10ft (3m)

LILIUM CHALCEDONICUM

Bulbous perennial

The scarlet turkscap lily is a tall plant with deep green leaves arranged in a spiral up the stem. It flowers from early to midsummer and has bright scarlet petals, which are strongly swept back, while the long stamens with bright red anthers drop down from the center of the flower. This unusual lily makes a valuable addition to a sunny or partially shaded herbaceous border and will grow in almost any well-drained soil.

◊ ☼ Z7–9 H9–7
↕ to 5ft (1.5m)

LONICERA SEMPERVIRENS
Climber

The beautiful trumpet honeysuckle is semi-evergreen in mild winters, and from summer to autumn it produces clusters of tubular, orange-red flowers with a yellow throat. The oval, paired leaves help highlight their intense color. In autumn, the plant is covered with bright red berries, giving it a long season of interest. Use it to cover a wall or to brighten up a drab spot in the garden. Plant it in full sun or partial shade in fertile, well-drained soil.

◊ ☼ ☀ Z4–9 H9–1
↕ to 12ft (4m)

LUPINUS
'Inverewe Red'
Perennial

Bold spikes of deep red flowers appear on this lupine above clumps of palmate leaves. Plant in groups in a herbaceous border or as a superb addition to a cottage-style garden. Encourage a second flush of flowers by deadheading. Lupines need a site in full sun or partial shade and should be planted in well-drained, fertile soil. They usually benefit from staking, and the succulent new growth is favored by slugs and snails.

◊ ☼ ☀ Z5–8 H8–5
↕ to 4ft (1.2m) ↔ to 18in (45cm)

MECONOPSIS NAPAULENSIS

Perennial

The satin poppy is a very large plant that can take several years to grow to flowering size. When mature, it will produce clusters of large red, purple, or pink bowl-shaped flowers from early to midsummer, after which the plant will die. It is good in a woodland garden or the back or a wild area. Plant it in semi-shade in neutral or acidic, moist soil. Sow fresh seed annually in autumn or spring to provide a continual supply of mature plants that will be ready to bloom in summer.

◊ ◊ ☼ Z8–9 H9–8
‡ to 8ft (2.5m) ↔ to 36in (90cm)

MONARDA
'Cambridge Scarlet'

Perennial

Bee balm, or bergamot,, is a clump-forming herb with aromatic, toothed leaves. 'Cambridge Scarlet' has vivid red, hooded, spidery-looking flowers and, like all bee balms, is attractive to bees. Perfect for a sunny border or prairie garden, it spreads quickly in a moist but well-drained soil that does not dry out in summer or become waterlogged in winter. It can be divided in spring.

◊ ◊ ☼ *f* Z4–9 H9–1
‡ to 3ft (1m) ↔ to 18in (45cm)

PAEONIA DELAVAYI

Deciduous shrub

The flowers of this tree peony have dark red petals and yellow stamens. The handsome, deeply dissected, blue-green foliage provides color and structure long after the flowers have faded. It is perfect for the back of a herbaceous or mixed border and prefers a sunny or partially shaded situation in moist, well-drained soil. Best left alone, apart from occasionally cutting out one or two of the oldest stems in autumn or early spring.

◊ ◊ ☼ ☀ Z5–8 H8–1
‡↔ to 6ft (2m)

PAPAVER COMMUTATUM 'Ladybird'

Annual

This distinctive annual poppy bears numerous glossy, brilliant red flowers. Grow it in groups in a gravel garden or a border with a fiery color theme, in full sun and well-drained soil. It does not need staking. It will self-seed naturally, or seed can be gathered and sown in spring where it is to flower. Alternatively, remove the unripe green seedpods to prevent seed set and to prolong the flowering season.

◊ ☼ Z0 H9–1
‡ to 18in (45cm) ↔ to 6in (15cm)

PAPAVER ORIENTALE
Goliath Group
'Beauty of Livermere'

Perennial

Large scarlet blooms with black centers are borne on the long, sturdy stems of this poppy from early to midsummer. Its vibrant colors contrast well a sunny border, where it can help disguise the dying foliage of spring bulbs. It in turn dies back early after flowering and should be grown close to late-flowering perennials that will fill the gap later in the year. Plant it in well-drained soil.

◊ ☼ Z4–9 H9–1
‡ to 4ft (1.2m) ↔ to 36in (90cm)

PELARGONIUM
'Caligula'

Perennial

This small-growing zonal geranium bears dark green leaves and double, bright scarlet flowers that are produced from early summer up to the first frosts, provided they are deadheaded regularly. Its compact size and long flowering season combine to make it an excellent plant for containers, although it can also be used as bedding when planted in full sun in free-draining soil. It is tender and must be kept in a frost-free place in winter.

◊ ☼ Z8–15 H12–1
‡ to 5in (12cm) ↔ to 4in (10cm)

PERSICARIA AMPLEXICAULIS *'Firetail'*

Perennial

This Himalayan bistort is a vigorous, clump-forming plant with decorative, large, dark green, lance-shaped leaves. From the beginning of summer to autumn 'Firetail' produces tall spikes of small, bright red flowers. It likes moist soil conditions and offers a long season of interest in a damp border or an area partially shaded by deciduous trees. Its foliage also makes a good groundcover.

◐ ☼ ☀ Z5–8 H8–5
↕↔ to 4ft (1.2m)

POTENTILLA *'Gibson's Scarlet'*

Perennial

A profusion of single, bright scarlet flowers appear on this cinquefoil from early to late summer. The blooms are produced on long stems above clumps of soft green, palmate foliage. It is an excellent plant for the front of a sunny border, or use it in a raised bed or gravel garden. It needs a sunny position in poor or moderately fertile, well-drained soil.

◐ ☼ Z5–8 H8–5
↕ to 18in (45cm) ↔ to 24in (60cm)

POTENTILLA
'Red Ace'

Evergreen shrub

This shrubby cinquefoil bears orange-red, saucer-shaped, single flowers that contrast well with the small, divided leaves. It blooms from late spring to midautumn and makes a wonderful low informal hedge or gravel-garden plant. Grow it in a sunny position (with some afternoon shade to help retain the red flower color) in well-drained, poor to moderately fertile soil, and trim after flowering, removing weak shoots and cutting dead wood back to the base.

◊ ☼ Z3–7 H7–1
‡ to 3ft (1m) ↔ to 5ft (1.5m)

RHEUM PALMATUM
'Atrosanguineum'

Perennial

Chinese rhubarb is a large, spreading plant with huge, deeply cut, rough-textured green leaves that are crimson-purple when young. The spectacular foliage is accompanied by tall stems of feathery, pinkish red flowers that provide a focal point in a damp border or beneath deep-rooted deciduous trees. This plant is happy in full sun or partial shade in moist soil. Mulch plants annually in spring with well-rotted compost.

◑ ☼ ◐ Z5–9 H9–5
‡ to 8ft (2.5m) ↔ to 6ft (2m)

ROSA GALLICA
VAR. OFFICINALIS

Deciduous shrub

The crimson damask rose produces
lightly scented, pink-red flowers from
early summer. These are followed in
autumn by orange-red hips. Plant this
compact rose with other old-fashioned
roses or in a shrub or mixed border,
perhaps with hardy geraniums.
Alternatively, use it as a low hedge
that can be cut back lightly after bloom.
Plant it in full sun in fertile, moist, well-
drained soil.

◊ ◊ ☼ *f* Z3–9 H9–1
‡ to 32in (80cm) ↔ to 3ft (1m)

ROSA
L.D. Braithwaite

Deciduous shrub

This superb modern shrub rose is
covered from early summer to autumn
with crimson flowers. The blooms are
slightly scented when they first open
but develop a stronger fragrance as
they age. This rose has a compact habit
and is ideally suited to small gardens,
where it can be planted as a specimen
or in a border. It will do best when
grown in full sun in fertile, moist, well-
drained soil. Lightly trim to shape in
late winter or early spring.

◊ ◊ ☼ *f* Z5–9 H9–5
‡ to 36in (90cm) ↔ to 4ft (1.2m)

ROSA
'Roseraie de l'Haÿ'
Deciduous shrub

A rugosa shrub rose with heavily
scented, purple-red flowers from early
summer to autumn. The blooms are
complemented by the light green,
healthy foliage. It makes a prickly-
stemmed hedge ideal for a house
boundary, or it can be used as a
specimen plant or grown in a mixed
border. It prefers full sun and a deep,
fertile, moist but well-drained soil.
Trim hedges to shape in early spring;
otherwise, little pruning is required.

◊ ◊ ☼ ƒ Z4–9 H9–1
‡ to 7ft (2.2m) ↔ to 6ft (2m)

ROSA
Royal William
Deciduous shrub

This hybrid tea rose is very free
flowering and produces fragrant,
double, velvety, deep crimson blooms
from early summer to autumn. The
flowers contrast well with the dark
green leaves. Grow several of these
compact, upright bush roses together in
a bed. As a standard it makes a central
focal point for a bed. Plant it in full sun
in a deep, fertile, well-drained soil.
Prune and mulch as for 'Blessings' (see
p.195).

◊ ◊ ☼ ƒ Z5–9 H9–5
‡ to 3ft (1m) ↔ to 30in (75cm)

SALVIA FULGENS

Perennial

This tender plant produces tall, dark red stems that bear scarlet flowers from early to midsummer. It will add color and height to a bedding design or container planting. It can be over-wintered in a frost-free greenhouse, or alternatively grow it as an annual; gather the seed in autumn and sow it under cover the following spring to flower the same year. It prefers full sun and a moist, reasonably fertile, well-drained soil or soil-based potting mix.

◊ ☼ ☀ Z9–10 H10–1

↕ to 3ft (1m) ↔ to 36in (90cm)

SEMPERVIVUM TECTORUM

Perennial

Often overlooked as a garden plant, the common hen and chickens forms rosettes of pointed, bristle-tipped, blue-green leaves, which often turn a rich purple-red in summer. The star-shaped, red-pink flowers appear in early summer, after which the leafy rosettes die but are replaced by new growth. Plant hen and chickens in a sunny situation in a rock garden or a trough, or on a dry stone wall. Good drainage is also essential, and they should be grown in gritty, well-drained soil.

◊ ☼ Z4–8 H8–1

↕ to 6in (15cm) ↔ to 20in (50cm)

TROPAEOLUM SPECIOSUM

Climber

The flame nasturtium has beautiful rounded leaves that resemble flower petals. Throughout the summer and into autumn it bears long-spurred vermilion flowers that are followed by round blue fruit. It looks best grown on a trellis or through an evergreen shrub, which has the benefit of possibly providing some winter protection. Otherwise use a thick, loose winter mulch. Plant it in moist but well-drained, fertile, neutral to acidic soil in full sun or dappled shade.

◊ ◊ ☼ ☼ Z8–10 H10–8
‡ to 10in (3m)

VERATRUM NIGRUM

Perennial

This large herbaceous plant has highly decorative, pleated, bright green leaves. In the summer it produces branched stems covered with small, star-shaped, red-purple flowers. It forms a statuesque plant for a wild garden or woodland setting, and it will grow well when planted in partial shade and a moist but well-drained, fertile soil. Divide congested clumps in spring. All parts of this plant are toxic.

◊ ◊ ☼ ☼ Z6–9 H9–6
‡ to 4ft (1.2m) ↔ to 24in (60cm)

ALLIUM
'Globemaster'

Bulbous perennial

The large flowerheads of this ornamental onion are made up of numerous small, intense purple flowers grouped together in a huge globe that can reach 8in (20cm) across. The gray basal leaves are slightly hairy and arch over at the tips. For maximum impact, plant the bulbs in autumn, in groups of at least five, in well-drained, fertile soil. Although good for cutting fresh, the globes look most dramatic when left to dry on the plant.

◊ ☼ Z6–10 H10–6
‡ to 32in (80cm) ↔ to 8in (20cm)

ALLIUM CRISTOPHII

Bulbous perennial

The clusters of pinkish purple flowers on this ornamental onion look like a firework. When the sun catches them, they take on a metallic sheen. The flowers top a 24in (60cm) stalk that emerges from dark green, strap-shaped leaves. This allium looks best when planted in a group of at least ten bulbs – that may sound extravagant, but the effect is well worth it. Plant the bulbs in autumn in full sun and fertile, well-drained soil. Allow the flowerheads to dry on the plant before cutting.

◊ ☼ Z5–8 H8–5
‡ to 24in (60cm) ↔ to 7in (19cm)

ALLIUM CYATHOPHORUM VAR. FARRERI

Bulbous perennial

Another beautiful ornamental onion, daintier in form than the flamboyant 'Globemaster' and *A. cristophii*. Up to 30 small, bell-shaped violet flowers dangle from the top of a 12in (30cm) stem. The slightest breeze will set them swaying and nodding. In keeping, the midgreen, grasslike leaves are delicate, too. To enjoy its subtle charms, plant small groups of bulbs in autumn at the front of a border in fertile, well-drained soil in full sun.

◊ ☼ Z4–9 H9–1
↕ to 12in (30cm) ↔ to 2in (5cm)

ANGELICA GIGAS

Perennial

The double pleasures of purple flowers and burgundy flower stems make this short-lived perennial well worth growing in a large border. Closely related to culinary angelica, be sure to give its lush, midgreen leaves plenty of room to spread. It is ideally suitable for an informal woodland garden and, as a lover of moist but well-drained, fertile soil, it is at home around the margins of a large pond. It will tolerate sun and partial shade. Grow from seed, because mature plants resent being disturbed.

◊ ☼ ☼ Z4–9 H9–1
↕ to 6ft (2m) ↔ to 4ft (1.2m)

BUDDLEJA ALTERNIFOLIA

Deciduous shrub

Clusters of sweetly scented, pale lilac flowers wreathe the arching branches of this shrub in early summer. So many are produced that they nearly hide the silvery green, lance-shaped leaves. It flowers on the previous year's wood and should be pruned back to strong buds after flowering. Cut out around a quarter of the old branches each year to stimulate new growth. It can be also be trained as a standard tree, as shown here. Grow in fertile, well-drained, preferably alkaline soil in full sun.

◊ ☼ *f* Z6–9 H9–4
↕↔ to 12ft (4m)

BUDDLEJA DAVIDII
'Black Knight'

Deciduous shrub

The butterfly bush is well named for its ability to attract butterflies like a magnet. This vigorous shrub has long, arching branches and lance-shaped, midgreen leaves. From early summer to autumn it produces large conical spikes of tiny, deep purplish blue, fragrant flowers. In early spring, prune it back hard to a low framework of branches to improve flowering later in the year. Grow it in a sunny position in moist but well-drained, fertile soil.

◊ ☼ *f* Z6–9 H10–4
↕ to 10ft (3m) ↔ to 15ft (5m)

CAMPANULA LATILOBA
'Hidcote Amethyst'

Perennial

The pale mauve of this rosette-forming bellflower is a good mixer in the busy color palette of the herbaceous border. Tall flower stems carry the large, bell-shaped flowers well above the broad, lance-shaped leaves. Plant in any fertile, neutral to alkaline soil that is also moist but well drained. Light shade is preferable, although a spot in full sun is fine (but the flower color may fade). Divide large clumps in autumn.

○ ◐ ☼ ☀ Z5–7 H7–5
‡ to 36in (90cm) ↔ to 18in (45cm)

CLEMATIS
'The President'

Climber

This free-flowering clematis deserves a prominent spot on a pergola or decorative trellis, where it can show off its amazing silver-backed, deep purple-blue blooms. These can measure up to 6in (15cm) across. It should be planted in fertile, well-drained soil in full sun or partial shade. Clematis grow best when their roots are in the shade. Remove any dead shoots in early spring, and prune the others back to a strong pair of buds.

○ ☼ ☀ Z6–9 H9–6
‡ to 10ft (3m)

CONVOLVULUS SABATIUS

Perennial

From summer to autumn, this trailing plant bears an endless supply of lavender-blue, funnel-shaped flowers on a cushion of bright green leaves. It thrives in the sharply drained conditions of a rock garden or sunny bank. Plant it in full sun in poor to moderately fertile, very well-drained soil. Where not hardy, enjoy it in a container and move it into a cool greenhouse for the winter.

◊ ☼ Z8–9 H9–8
‡ to 6in (15cm) ↔ to 20in (50cm)

CYNARA CARDUNCULUS

Evergreen perennial

Closely related to the globe artichoke, the cardoon is a fast-growing, large, architectural plant with grayish green, deeply divided, arching, evergreen leaves. The thistlelike purple flowers are borne on tall, robust stems from summer until autumn. If space allows, for real impact plant it in groups of 3 in a sheltered, sunny spot by a wall or fence in fertile, well-drained soil. A useful plant, it is attractive to bees, the flowers dry well, and, when blanched, the leaf stalks and midribs are edible.

◊ ☼ Z7–9 H9–7
‡ to 5ft (1.5m) ↔ to 4ft (1.2m)

DELPHINIUM
'Bruce'

Perennial

A mixed summer border would be incomplete without delphiniums. 'Bruce' produces deep violet-purple flowers on tall spires in early summer. An autumn flowering can often be encouraged if the faded flowering stems are cut back. Easily damaged by winds and rain, the plants should be supported when young with a strong stake and the stems tied in as they grow. Plant in a well-drained, fertile soil in full sun. Protect emerging foliage from slugs and snails.

◊ ☼ Z3–7 H7–1
↕ to 7ft (2.2m) ↔ to 36in (90cm)

DIPSACUS FULLONUM

Biennial

In its first season, the teasel produces a rosette of spiny, toothed leaves. The following year, it sends up tall stems topped with thistlelike globes composed of tiny, pinkish purple blooms. These make wonderful dried flowers. The stems carry pairs of glossy green leaves that form natural cups; rainwater collects in them, attracting small birds to drink. The teasel is also a favorite food plant of the goldfinch. Sow seed in a wild garden in sun or partial shade in moderately fertile soil, including clay.

◊ ◊ ☼ ☀ Z5–8 H8–5
↕ to 6ft (2m) ↔ to 32in (80cm)

ERIGERON
'Dunkelste Aller'

Perennial

Daisylike flowers always look so cheerful, and the blooms of fleabane are no exception. This one has a sunny yellow center fringed with violet petals. A clump-forming plant with lance-shaped, grayish green leaves, it does well in a mixed herbaceous border or rock garden. It also thrives in a coastal garden but will need staking on exposed sites. As a cut flower, it has great lasting qualities. Plant in fertile soil that does not dry out in summer.

◊ ☼ Z5–7 H7–5
‡ to 24in (60cm) ↔ to 18in (45cm)

ERODIUM MANESCAUI

Perennial

The delicate magenta-purple, saucer-shaped blooms of this clump-forming plant are very similar to those of hardy geraniums. Throughout summer, they are borne on long stalks in profuse clusters of up to 20. The top two petals of each flower are darkly freckled. The leaves are attractive, too, being deeply divided, lance-shaped, and slightly hairy. Plant it in gritty, very well-drained soil in full sun. A rock garden would suit it well, or plant it at the front of the herbaceous border. It self-seeds freely.

◊ ☼ Z6–8 H8–6
‡ to 18in (45cm) ↔ to 8in (20cm)

ERYSIMUM
'Bowles' Mauve'

Evergreen perennial

A long-flowering wallflower, 'Bowles
Mauve' produces tall spikes of mauve
blooms throughout much of the year; early
summer is when they are most profuse.
The flowers are set off by narrow, gray-
green leaves. Plant it in well-drained,
poor to moderately fertile, preferably
alkaline soil in full sun. Trim after
flowering, and take cuttings to make
more plants: it tends to be short lived.

◊ ☼ Z5–8 H8–5
↕ to 30in (75cm) ↔ to 24in (60cm)

GERANIUM PSILOSTEMON

Perennial

One of the largest hardy geraniums,
this fast-growing plant has deep
magenta-purple flowers with an almost
black eye. The toothed, midgreen
leaves are infused with crimson in
spring and autumn. A useful ground-
covering plant to fill in around shrubs
in a border, it grows well in most well-
drained soils in sun or partial shade.
Cut it back after flowering to encourage
new growth. In the right conditions it
will self seed freely; alternatively, divide
large clumps in spring.

◊ ☼ ◐ Z5–8 H8–5
↕ to 4ft (1.2m) ↔ to 24in (60cm)

GERANIUM SYLVATICUM
'Mayflower'

Perennial

With its white-centered, rich violet-blue, upward-facing flowers, 'Mayflower' is one of the most attractive geraniums available. Its deeply lobed, midgreen leaves form a shapely mound. It is a good naturalizer in open ground or under trees and shrubs. Plant it in moist but well-drained soil; although it tolerates shade, it would prefer full sun. Cut back after flowering to encourage new growth.

◊ ◊ ☼ ☼ Z4–8 H8–1
‡ to 30in (75cm) ↔ to 24in (60cm)

GLADIOLUS COMMUNIS
SUBSP. BYZANTINUS

Cormous perennial

The tall flower spikes of this gladiolus carry up to 20 magenta flowers that add zest to an early summer border, and they are good for cutting. The rich green, strappy leaves reach 28in (70cm) long. Unless you want huge swaths of these plants, take care if disturbing the soil around them, since small corms will break off and spread. Plant in full sun in fertile, well-drained soil. Where marginally hardy, cover the soil with a deep but loose winter mulch.

◊ ☼ Z8–11 H12–1
‡ to 3ft (1m) ↔ to 3in (8cm)

HELIOTROPIUM ARBORESCENS *'Marine'*

Evergreen shrub

Heliotrope is a tender, short-lived shrub usually grown as an annual. With its clusters of fragrant, violet-blue flowers, it looks good in pots and windowboxes or as front-of-the-border edging. Plant it in full sun in moist but well-drained, fertile soil. Take softwood cuttings in summer, and overwinter them in a cool greenhouse. You can also grow heliotropes as conservatory plants. Use a soil-based potting mix, and provide shading from strong summer sun.

○ ◑ ☼ *f* Z13–15 H12–1
‡↔ to 18in (45cm)

HEUCHERA MICRANTHA *'Palace Purple'*

Evergreen perennial

Heucheras are evergreen, or nearly evergreen, clump-forming plants grown primarily for their attractive foliage. 'Palace Purple' has glossy, deeply lobed, purplish red leaves and airy spikes of tiny, greenish cream flowers. It makes a sumptuous groundcover plant in a herbaceous or shrub border. Plant in full sun or partial shade in moist but well-drained, neutral to slightly acidic, fertile soil.

○ ◑ ☼ ☀ Z4–8 H8–1
‡↔ to 24in (60cm)

IRIS ENSATA
'Hue and Cry'

Perennial

Japanese irises are beautiful marginal-aquatic plants. 'Hue and Cry' has flat flowers with six large, white-veined lower petals, each with a central yellow "signal." Short periods of flooding are tolerated, but, rather than total immersion, this plant prefers permanently moist or wet, acidic soil and is eminently suitable for a bog garden.

◐ ◕ ☼ ☀ Z3–9 H9–1
‡ to 36in (90cm)

IRIS VERSICOLOR

Perennial

The richly colored petals of the blue flag iris have beautiful markings, with heavy purple veining and a large white signal at their base. Together with the vibrant green, sword-shaped leaves, this is an attractive plant for a bog garden, the shallow margins of a natural pond, or a moisture-retentive border. Plant the rhizomes in permanently moist or wet soil, but not underwater.

◐ ◕ ☼ ☀ Z3–9 H9–1
‡ to 32in (80cm)

IRIS × ROBUSTA
'Gerald Darby'
Perennial

Another stunning water iris, 'Gerald
Darby' has narrow, sword-shaped
leaves that are covered at the base with
purple spots. Its dark violet stems
produce four bluish purple flowers,
each marked with a patch of yellow.
Plant it in a moist border or at the edge
of a pond. Given the right conditions,
this vigorous clump-former can reach
the spectacular height of 6ft (1.8m);
however, it usually measures just under
half that.

◊ ◖ ☼ ☼ Z3–9 H9–1
‡ to 30in (75cm)

LATHYRUS PUBESCENS
Climber

This is an attractive perennial sweet pea
with pairs of lance-shaped, dark green
leaves and hairy stems. It is a strong-
growing plant that produces long-
stalked clusters of deep lilac-blue
flowers. Using its tendrils for support,
it will happily clamber up a trellis or
through shrubs or will sprawl over a
bank. Plant it in a sunny site in well-
drained, fertile soil. Where marginally
hardy, provide a deep mulch for winter.

◊ ☼ ☼ Z9–10 H10–9
‡ to 10ft (3m)

POLEMONIUM
'Lambrook Mauve'

Perennial

Jacob's ladder is a free-flowering plant that produces clusters of lilac-blue flowers on upright, branched stems. A neat, mound-forming perennial, it is ideally suited to the front of a mixed or herbaceous border. It also makes a lovely feature plant in formal planting or among low-growing grasses. Give it a spot in full sun or partial shade in a moist but well-drained, fertile soil. Deadhead regularly, and divide large clumps during the spring.

○ ◐ ☼ ☀ Z4–8 H8–1
‡↔ to 18in (45cm)

ROSA
Blue Moon

Deciduous shrub

The blooms of this large-flowered rose, in a delicate shade of lilac-mauve, are held on upright, thorny stems, which also bear dark green foliage. Its fragrant flowers are semidouble and good for cutting; to produce the best color, grow in full sun. Plant roses in fertile, well-drained soil, and apply a rose fertilizer regularly in the growing season. Prune the main stems to 8in (20cm) above the ground in late winter or early spring to ensure lots of flowers.

○ ◐ ☼ *f* Z5–9 H9–1
‡ to 3ft (1m) ↔ to 28in (70cm)

ROSCOEA HUMEANA

Perennial

This unusual tuberous plant has orchid-like flowers with a prominent, hooded upper petal. The lush, deep green, rounded leaves set the blooms off perfectly. A sheltered woodland garden would be the ideal home for this plant, since it grows best in damp shade in a cool climate. Where marginally hardy, cover the root area with a deep mulch, such as leaf mold.

◑ ☀ Z7–9 H9–7
‡ to 10in (25cm) ↔ to 6in (15cm)

STACHYS MACRANTHA
'Superba'

Perennial

Erect spikes of pink-purple, hooded flowers are held above rosettes of wrinkled, dark green, heart-shaped leaves An easy-going plant for the front of a herbaceous border, it flowers over a long period from early summer until early autumn. Plant it in well-drained, fertile soil. It is best in full sun but will tolerate some shade.

◔ ☀ ☀ Z5–7 H7–5
‡ to 24in (60cm) ↔ to 12in (30cm)

ACONITUM × CAMMARUM *'Bicolor'*

Perennial

This tall, elegant plant forms clumps of deeply lobed, midgreen leaves and spikes of bicolored blue and white, hooded flowers. It is a woodland plant and so thrives in a similar garden situation beneath deciduous trees or in a partially shaded border. However, it will tolerate a sunny site as long as the soil is reasonably moist and fertile. All parts of this plant are highly toxic.

◊ ☼ ☀ Z3–7 H7–1
‡ to 4ft (1.2m) ↔ to 12in (30cm)

ADENOPHORA BULLEYANA

Perennial

Reminiscent of a bellflower, this pretty herbaceous plant bears tall spikes of pendent, funnel-shaped, pale blue flowers. For the greatest impact, plant it in large groups in a herbaceous border or summer flower garden. It will do well when grown in moist but well-drained soil in full sun or partial shade. It resents being moved once planted, so position it carefully.

◊ ◊ ☼ ☀ Z4–8 H8–1
‡ to 4ft (1.2m) ↔ to 12in (30cm)

AGERATUM HOUSTONIANUM
'Adriatic'

Annual

The floss flower forms a mound of
downy, oval green leaves, above which
frothy-looking heads of tiny midblue
flowers are borne in summer and up
to the first frosts. It is widely grown as
a bedding plant and complements low-
growing annuals with bright yellow
flowers, such as marigolds. It is also
suitable for containers and hanging
baskets. Plant it in full sun in a moist,
well-drained soil. In containers, keep
it well watered when in flower.

◊ ◊ ☼ Z0 H12–1
‡ to 8in (20cm) ↔ to 12in (30cm)

AGERATUM HOUSTONIANUM
'Bavaria'

Annual

This decorative bedding or container
plant grows quickly in the spring. In
summer and up to the first frosts, it
produces branched clusters of pale blue
flowers with white centers. It can be
used to edge a border or path or grown
in containers, including hanging
baskets, within a pastel color scheme.
Grow as for 'Adriatic' (see above).

◊ ◊ ☼ Z0 H12–1
‡ to 10in (25cm) ↔ to 12in (30cm)

AJUGA REPTANS
'Variegata'

Evergreen perennial

Bugle is a useful, easy-going ground-cover plant that forms a carpet of evergreen leaves borne on spreading stems. 'Variegata' has gray-green leaves with a cream edge and cream markings. From late spring to early summer, bugle produces upright stems of small, dark blue tubular flowers. Plant it in any moist soil in partial shade. It will also tolerate full sun if the soil does not dry out during summer.

◐ ☼ ☼ Z3–9 H8–2
↕ to 6in (15cm) ↔ to 36in (90cm)

ALLIUM CAERULEUM

Bulbous perennial

A beautiful onion, this variety produces spherical heads of tiny bright blue, star-shaped flowers in early summer. The blooms are produced after the narrow leaves have died down on triangular, stiff green stems. Plant groups of bulbs in the autumn in a herbaceous border, gravel garden, or a large container in full sun and well-drained, fertile soil.

◊ ☼ Z4–10 H12–1
↕ to 24in (60cm) ↔ to 6in (15cm)

ANCHUSA AZUREA
'Loddon Royalist'

Perennial

This beautiful, early summer-flowering
plant forms a clump of lance-shaped
leaves and robust, branched stems of
deep blue flowers. The blooms are
attractive to bees, making it a good
candidate for a wild garden or a
herbaceous border. Plant it in groups
in full sun and moist, well-drained soil.
Young plants should be cut back after
flowering to promote the growth of
basal leaves. Deadhead mature plants
to encourage a second flush of flowers.

◊ ◊ ☼ Z3–8 H8–1
‡ to 36in (90cm) ↔ to 24in (60cm)

ANCHUSA AZUREA
'Blue Angel'

Perennial

A compact, bushy plant, 'Blue Angel'
produces a mass of pale blue flowers
that resemble those of forget-me-nots.
The leaves are rough-textured and
covered with bristles. It is a short-lived
perennial that can be grown as an
annual and can be used at the front
of a border, in a raised bed or rock
garden, or as a container plant. Plant
it in full sun and moist, well-drained,
fertile soil.

◊ ◊ ☼ Z3–8 H8–1
‡ to 8in (20cm) ↔ to 6in (15cm)

BAPTISIA AUSTRALIS

Perennial

False indigo is a spreading plant with midgreen leaves divided into three egg-shaped leaflets. It produces tall spikes of dark blue, pealike flowers that are often marked with white or cream. The flowers are followed in autumn by large seedpods suitable for drying. Plant it in an open, sunny site in deep, very free-draining, neutral to acidic soil. It is suitable for a herbaceous border, but once planted it is best left undisturbed. Stake tall plants unless the planting site is sheltered.

◊ ☼ Z3–9 H9–2

‡ to 5ft (1.5m) ↔ to 24in (60cm)

CAMPANULA BARBATA

Perennial

The bearded bellflower is so named because of the unusual hairs that edge the pendent, lavender-blue flowers. A short-lived perennial, it forms rosettes of hairy, lance-shaped, midgreen leaves beneath the erect flower stems. It is a suitable plant for a rock or gravel garden and should be planted in full sun or partial shade in moist but well-drained soil.

◊ ◊ ☼ ☼ Z5–8 H8–5

‡ to 8in (20cm) ↔ to 5in (12cm)

CAMPANULA PERSICIFOLIA
'Telham Beauty'

Perennial

One of the most vigorous bellflowers, this form bears rosettes of evergreen, lance-shaped, bright green leaves. Pale blue, bell-shaped flowers appear for many weeks on tall stems. Flowering can be prolonged by regular dead-heading. It is best planted in groups in a herbaceous or mixed border, or in a woodland or wildflower garden. Grow it in full sun or partial shade in fertile, well-drained, neutral or slightly alkaline soil.

◊ ☼ ☀ Z3–8 H8–1
‡ to 3ft (1m) ↔ to 12in (30cm)

CEANOTHUS
'Cynthia Postan'

Evergreen shrub

This California lilac forms a rounded bush with toothed, glossy, evergreen leaves. It is very free flowering and from late spring to early summer bears clusters of deep blue flowers. Plant it in a sheltered, sunny position in fertile, well-drained soil. Grow it in a mixed shrub border, as a specimen plant, or train it against a wall.

◊ ☼ Z9–10 H10–9
‡↔ to 8ft (2.5m)

CEANOTHUS × DELILEANUS
'Gloire de Versailles'

Deciduous shrub

Hardier than many other California
lilacs, 'Gloire de Versailles' has oval,
dark green leaves and clusters of tiny,
deep sky blue flowers held in open
spikes at the end of the stems. It
flowers in early summer and again in
the autumn. A good shrub for a mixed
border or a Mediterranean-style garden,
it prefers a position in full sun and a
well-drained soil. Overgrown specimens
can be cut back hard in spring.

◊ ☼ Z7–10 H10–8
‡↔ to 5ft (1.5m)

CENTAUREA CYANUS

Annual

Once a common weed of European
grain fields, the cornflower is now more
often found in borders, meadows, or
wild gardens. It has lance-shaped
leaves, and for several weeks in
summer it produces dark blue flowers
with violet-blue centers. Grow it in a
meadow or wild garden, combined with
Shirley poppies (*Papaver rhoeas*) and
corn cockles (*Agrostemma githago*). It is
also an excellent cut flower. Sow the
seed *in situ* in autumn or spring in full
sun and a well-drained soil.

◊ ☼ Z0 H12–1
‡ to 32in (80cm) ↔ to 6in (15cm)

CICHORIUM INTYBUS

Perennial

Chicory forms a clump of lance-shaped, toothed leaves and is sometimes grown as a salad vegetable. However, when left to flower, it is a decorative plant with branched stems of daisylike blue (rarely pink or white) flowers with toothed petals. Plant it in groups in a flower garden or mixed border in full sun and a well-drained, fertile soil.

◊ ☼ Z4–8 H8–1
↕ to 4ft (1.2m) ↔ to 24in (60cm)

CONSOLIDA AJACIS

Annual

The annual delphiniums, otherwise known as larkspurs, are fast-growing herbaceous plants with deeply divided, feathery leaves. They look similar to perennial delphiniums but tend to have shorter flowering stems. They produce spikes of violet-blue, pink, or white flowers with long spurs and are good for cutting. Ideal for filling gaps left by spring bulbs in a border, they grow best in full sun in light, well-drained soil. Sow the seed *in situ* from late winter through late spring or autumn.

◊ ☼ Z6–9 H9–1
↕ to 4ft (1.2m) ↔ to 12in (30cm)

DELPHINIUM
'Blue Nile'

Perennial

This beautiful delphinium has deeply divided green foliage and produces tall, elegant spikes of midblue flowers with white eyes. The flowerheads should be removed when they fade to allow the sideshoots to flower. Stake it firmly in spring when the foliage emerges, and tie in the flower stems as they grow. Plant it in groups at the back of a border in full sun, out of strong winds and in fertile, organic, well-drained soil.

◊ ☼ Z3–7 H7–1
‡ to 5ft (1.5m)

DELPHINIUM GRANDIFLORUM
'Blue Butterfly'

Perennial

A short-lived plant, this delphinium is often grown as an annual. It has deeply divided leaves and bears spikes of bright blue flowers. Grow it as bedding or at the front of a herbaceous border. It also makes a good cut flower. Plant this delphinium in well-drained, fertile soil in full sun. It is less demanding than the large-flowered varieties, such as 'Blue Nile'.

◊ ☼ Z3–7 H7–1
‡↔ to 12in (30cm)

ECHINOPS RITRO
'Veitch's Blue'

Perennial

Grown partly for its architectural, spiny, grayish green leaves, this vigorous plant also produces spherical, dark blue flowerheads on woolly gray stems. The lollipop-shaped flowerheads contrast well with flat-headed blooms, such as those of achillea, in a gravel garden or a herbaceous border. The flowers can be used fresh or dried in flower arrangements. Plant it singly or in groups of three or five in poor, well-drained soil in full sun.

○ ☼ ☀ Z3–9   H9–1
‡ to 36in (90cm) ↔ to 18in (45cm)

ECHIUM VULGARE
'Blue Bedder'

Biennial

The dwarf form of viper's bugloss has an upright habit and produces bristly, lance-shaped, dark-green leaves. It bears an abundance of blue flowers, which turn pink as they age. Plant it in a wildflower garden or use it as bedding. Viper's bugloss likes a sunny situation and reasonably fertile, well-drained soil.

◊ ☼ Z3–8   H8–1
‡ to 16in (40cm) ↔ to 12in (30cm)

ERYNGIUM GIGANTEUM

Biennial

Commonly known as 'Miss Wilmott's Ghost', this biennial or short-lived perennial forms a rosette of bluish green, spiny leaves. The tiny silver-blue flowers are borne in conelike clusters and are surrounded by a collar of large silver bracts. It works well in a hot gravel or Mediterranean-style garden, or grow it in a herbaceous border. Its skeletal form can be left to decorate the winter landscape. Plant it in full sun in well-drained soil, where it will self-seed freely.

◊ ☼ Z5–8 H8–5
‡ to 4ft (1.2m) ↔ to 12in (30cm)

ERYNGIUM × OLIVERIANUM

Perennial

This striking sea holly forms a clump of heart-shaped, midgreen, spiny leaves with distinctive silver veining. In summer and early autumn, branched stems produce lavender-blue, thistlelike flowers surrounded by spiny, linear, leaflike bracts. The whole plant is suffused with a steel blue coloration. Plant it in a sunny position in well-drained soil, and use it in a herbaceous border or gravel garden. The flower stems make excellent cut flowers, too, or they can be left to stand over winter.

◊ ☼ Z5–8 H8–5
‡ to 36in (90cm) ↔ to 18in (45cm)

GERANIUM
'Johnson's Blue'

Perennial

This is one of the most widely grown geraniums, favored for its deeply lobed, midgreen leaves and long flowering season. It bears deep lavender-blue, saucer-shaped flowers with pink centers. Plant it at the front of a herbaceous border, or use it as underplanting in a rose bed. It will grow in most soils but does best in well-drained, fertile soil in a sunny or partially shaded situation. Divide large clumps in autumn.

◊ ◊ ☼ ☀ Z4–8 H8–1
↕ to 18in (45cm) ↔ to 30in (75cm)

GERANIUM PRATENSE
'Mrs. Kendall Clark'

Perennial

The meadow cranesbill is a clump-forming plant with deeply lobed, midgreen leaves. The single flowers appear from early to midsummer and are blue-gray flushed with pale pink or sometimes violet-blue with delicate white veining. The meadow cranesbill is a beautiful plant for the front of a border, or use it as a groundcover. It grows well in most soils but prefers a well-drained, fertile soil in full sun or partial shade.

◊ ◊ ☼ ☀ Z4–8 H8–1
↕ to 36in (90cm) ↔ to 24in (60cm)

GERANIUM WALLICHIANUM
'Buxton's Variety'

Perennial

This hardy geranium, or cranesbill, forms a wide-spreading but compact clump of decorative, deeply divided, marbled leaves. It produces single, sky blue flowers with white centers, marked with prominent blue veins. Its carpeting foliage makes a good groundcover, and it does well in a sunny site at the front of a border or rock garden. For the best results, plant it in a well-drained, fertile soil.

◊ ☼ Z4–8 H8–1
‡ to 12in (30cm) ↔ to 4ft (1.2m)

HEMEROCALLIS
'Prairie Blue Eyes'

Perennial

A great many daylilies have yellow or orange blooms, but this one has deep lavender-blue flowers produced from early to midsummer. Semi-evergreen, it forms a clump of narrow, midgreen leaves that add structure and form to a sheltered border throughout the year. It can also be used in a large container or in gravel beds and prefers a sunny site and fertile, moist, well-drained soil.

◊ ◊ ☼ Z4–11, H12–1
‡ to 28in (70cm) ↔ to 30in (75cm)

HOSTA
'Halcyon'

Perennial

The thick, heart-shaped, blue-green leaves of this hosta may be slightly less susceptible to slug damage than some other varieties. In summer it bears spikes of grayish lavender, funnel-shaped flowers. The foliage color may fade in bright sun, so it is advisable to plant it in partial shade beneath shrubs or trees in moist, well-drained soil. In spring, mulch hostas with organic matter, such as composted bark, to conserve moisture in summer.

◊ ◊ ☼ Z3–8 H8–1
‡ to 16in (40cm) ↔ to 28in (70cm)

HYSSOPUS OFFICINALIS

Deciduous shrub

Hyssop is a pretty garden plant that can also be used for medicinal and culinary purposes. It has small, aromatic leaves, and the flowers vary in color from blue to violet, pink, and white. It blooms from early or midsummer to early autumn and will add color and form to an herb bed or the front of a border. It can also be grown in a large container or a gravel garden. Plant it in a sunny situation in well-drained soil.

◊ ☼ ƒ Z6–9 H9–6
‡ to 2ft (60cm) ↔ to 3ft (1m)

IRIS ENSATA
'Flying Tiger'

Perennial

Japanese irises are beautiful plants with striking, large, flat blooms. The flowers of 'Flying Tiger' measure up to 12in (30cm) across and have rounded petals marked with bold violet-blue veins and a splash of yellow radiating from the center. Although it is an aquatic plant, it will grow in a bog garden or moist border as long as the roots do not completely dry out in the summer. When grown in a border, it prefers a rich, moist, acidic soil.

◊ ♦ ☼ ☀ Z3–9 H9–1
‡ to 36in (90cm) ↔ indefinite

IRIS
'Jane Phillips'

Perennial

An elegant tall bearded iris, this variety has bluish green, sword-shaped leaves and midblue, fragrant flowers. To ensure a good show of flowers year after year, plant it in front of a sunny wall or in a hot border, where it can thrive in the summer sun. It grows well in neutral or slightly acidic, fertile, well-drained soil. Divide large clumps after flowering, then replant plump sections so that the top of the rhizomes are exposed to sun.

◊ ☼ *f* Z3–9 H9–1
‡ to 36in (90cm) ↔ to 24in (60cm)

IRIS LAEVIGATA

Perennial

The deep purple-blue flowers of this beardless water iris make a superb addition to a sunny or partially shaded bog garden or the margins of a pond in acidic soil. The blooms are set off by broad, midgreen, straplike leaves. This is a vigorous iris, and large clumps can be divided in the spring. 'Variegata' is an attractive cultivar with white- and green-striped leaves.

◊ ♦ ☼ ☼ Z4–9 H9–1
↕ to 32in (80cm) ↔ indefinite

IRIS PALLIDA
'Variegata'

Perennial

The dramatic, variegated, sword-shaped leaves of this iris provide structure, color, and form in a sunny herbaceous border from spring to autumn. The beautiful bearded, midblue flowers are a bonus and magnify this plant's charms. For the best results, plant it in groups in well-drained, neutral or slightly acidic soil.

◊ ☼ Z5–9 H9–4
↕ to 4ft (1.2m) ↔ indefinite

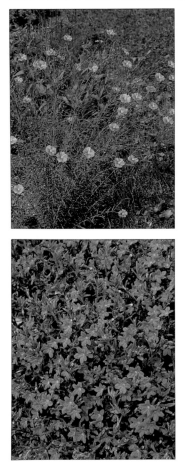

LINUM PERENNE

Perennial

The perennial flax is a clump-forming plant with narrow, bluish green, lance-shaped leaves and slender flower stems. Although each pale blue flower lasts for just one day and fades before evening, the blooms are produced in succession from early to midsummer. Grow it in groups in full sun and a well-drained, fertile soil, and use it in a flower garden or herbaceous border. It can be raised from seed sown in pots in a cold frame in autumn or early spring.

◊ ☼ Z5–8 H8–5
‡ to 12in (30cm) ↔ to 6in (15cm)

LITHODORA DIFFUSA
'Heavenly Blue'

Evergreen shrub

This prostrate plant produces trailing branches covered with small, elliptic, deep green leaves. In the summer it bears large numbers of rich azure blue flowers. It can be planted in a raised bed or a rock or gravel garden, and to grow well it needs an acidic, fertile soil and a sunny situation.

◊ ☼ Z6–8 H8–6
‡ to 6in (15cm) ↔ to 24in (60cm)

LOBELIA ERINUS
'Sapphire'

Annual

This dainty perennial plant is usually
treated as an annual and raised from
seed each year. It is grown for its
trailing stems of small, midgreen leaves
and abundant bright blue flowers with
striking white eyes. It flowers from
summer to midautumn and is an
excellent plant for containers, hanging
baskets, and borders. It should be
planted in full sun or partial shade in
moist, well-drained soil. When grown in
containers, fertilize every other week

◊ ◑ ☼ ◔ Z0 H7–1
↕ to 8in (20cm) ↔ to 6in (15cm)

LUPINUS ALBIFRONS

Evergreen shrub

A decorative tree lupine, this variety has
a rounded habit and attractive foliage
covered with silvery hairs. Throughout
summer it produces spikes of pealike
blue or reddish purple flowers. To
survive most winters it needs to be
planted in a sunny position in very
well-drained soil, such as by a wall or
in a sheltered raised bed or gravel
garden. Mulch generously with gravel.

◊ ☼ Z9–10 H10–9
↕↔ to 30in (75cm)

NEMOPHILA MENZIESII

Annual

Throughout summer, the aptly named baby blue-eyes produces bright blue, saucer-shaped flowers with darker veins and paler centers among downy, gray-green, divided foliage. It is suitable for the front of the herbaceous border or in hanging baskets and containers. Baby blue-eyes should be planted in fertile, moist, well-drained soil in full sun or partial shade. It will self-seed when planted in a border.

◊ ◖ ☼ ☼ Z0 H6–1
‡ to 8in (20cm) ↔ to 12in (30cm)

NIGELLA DAMASCENA
'Miss Jekyll'

Annual

A widely grown, self-seeding annual, love-in-a-mist has highly decorative, finely divided green leaves. 'Miss Jekyll' bears sky blue flowers surrounded by a "ruff" of threadlike leaves and is followed by attractive seedheads. In spring or autumn, sow the seed *in situ* in bold groups at the front of a mixed border, or grow with other annuals in a wildflower meadow. It needs to be grown in full sun and well-drained soil.

◊ ☼ Z0 H12–1
‡ to 18in (45cm) ↔ to 8in (20cm)

PASSIFLORA CAERULEA

Climber

The blue passionflower has woody stems and dark green, divided foliage. The exotic-looking flowers have white petals, which are sometimes tinged with pink, and a ring of purple-blue banded strands that radiate out from the center. In summer the blooms may be followed by round yellow fruit. Plant it in a sunny, sheltered site in moist, well-drained soil. The top-growth may be killed back over winter, but young shoots should appear from the base if the root area is mulched over winter.

◊ ◊ ☼ Z6–9 H9–6
‡ to 30ft (10m) or more

POLEMONIUM CAERULEUM

Perennial

Jacob's ladder has decorative, divided foliage and in early summer bears erect stems of clear blue, bell-shaped flowers. It is very adaptable and can be grown in an informal planting among low-growing grasses, or at the front of a herbaceous border, where it can help disguise the dying foliage of early spring bulbs. Plant it in full sun or partial shade in fertile, moist, well-drained soil. Deadhead regularly, and divide large clumps in spring.

◊ ◊ ☼ ◑ Z4–8 H8–1
↔ to 18in (45cm)

SALVIA PATENS
'Cambridge Blue'

Perennial

From summer to autumn this form of sage produces delicate, pale blue flowers. Beneath the flower stems it forms a clump of oval, midgreen leaves. Plant it in a sunny, sheltered border or by a wall, in well-drained soil. This salvia is better treated as an annual in cold areas. Sow seed under glass in spring, or overwinter mature plants in a frost-free greenhouse.

◊ ☼ Z3–9 H9–1
‡ to 24in (60cm) ↔ to 18in (45cm)

SCABIOSA CAUCASICA
'Clive Greaves'

Perennial

A beautiful scabiosa, 'Clive Greaves' has gray-green basal leaves and violet-blue flowers with cream-colored centers that attract bees and butterflies. It is perfect for a wildflower garden or a herbaceous border and needs a sunny position and well-drained, reasonably fertile, neutral to alkaline soil to thrive. Young plants flower most freely, so divide and replant them every spring to ensure a good display each summer. Deadhead the plants regularly, too.

◊ ☼ Z4–9 H9–1
‡↔ to 24in (60cm)

SISYRINCHIUM ANGUSTIFOLIUM

Perennial

Blue-eyed grass is a semi-evergreen plant that forms tussocks of grasslike leaves. The purplish blue flowers with bright yellow eyes are produced in succession throughout summer. It should be planted in full sun in well-drained soil, and it will provide a long season of interest in a rock or gravel garden or a raised bed.

◊ ☼ Z5–8 H8–5
↕ to 12in (30cm) ↔ to 6in (15cm)

VERONICA AUSTRIACA *'Crater Lake Blue'*

Perennial

This striking mat-forming perennial has hairy, grayish green leaves and spikes of vivid, deep blue, saucer-shaped flowers produced for many weeks in summer. Ideal for a herbaceous or mixed border or a rock garden, it will perform well when planted in full sun or partial shade in a well-drained, even poor soil.

◊ ☼ ☼ Z6–8 H8–6
↕↔ to 24in (60cm)

CAREX PENDULA

Perennial

The weeping sedge forms substantial clumps of relatively wide, straplike, midgreen leaves that are blue-green underneath. Arching, triangular stems bear pendent, catkinlike flower spikes that look attractive when hanging over water at the edge of a pond or in a damp border or woodland setting. Grow this sedge in permanently moist or wet soil in partial shade or sun. It can self-seed profusely.

◑ ▲ ◐ ☼ ☀ Z5–9 H9–5
↕ to 4½ft (1.4m) ↔ to 5ft (1.5m)

EUPHORBIA CHARACIAS

Evergreen shrub

This impressive spurge creates structure and form throughout the year, with its ascending stems clothed with grayish-green, narrow leaves. In spring and early summer it produces dome-shaped clusters of small green flowers with maroon eyes. A very variable plant, it is best to grow a named variety, and for best results plant it in a sunny position in a well-drained soil. Remove the old stems after they have flowered.

◐ ☼ Z7–10 H10–7
↕ to 4ft (1.2m) ↔ to 4ft (1.2m)

HOSTA
'Frances Williams'

Perennial

A widely grown hosta, this variety is
favored for its large, thick, blue-green,
heart-shaped leaves with yellow-green
margins. It has very pale lavender-gray
flowers borne in clusters on tall stems.
It is best to grow it in moist soil in a
partially shaded situation, because the
leaves have a tendency to scorch in
bright sun. Plant it to provide interest
beneath deciduous trees or in
a mixed or herbaceous border. Take
measures to prevent slug damage.

◊ ☼ Z3–8 H8–1
↕ to 24in (60cm) ↔ to 3ft (1m)

HOSTA PLANTAGINEA
VAR. JAPONICA

Perennial

The large, oval, light green leaves of
this hosta have a glossy texture and
distinctive raised veins. It grows well
in sun or partial shade in moist but
well-drained soil, and it can be used in
a herbaceous or mixed border or in the
light shade underneath deciduous trees.
The majority of hostas are grown for
their foliage, but this also has attractive,
trumpet-shaped, fragrant white flowers
borne on long stems in mid- to late
summer. Slugs may cause leaf damage.

◊ ◊ ☼ ◑ *f*Z3–8 H8–1
↕ to 24in (60cm) ↔ to 3ft (1m)

HOSTA SIEBOLDIANA
VAR. ELEGANS

Perennial

Few plants can compete with hostas for foliage effects, and this variety is particularly spectacular with large, blue-gray, crinkled leaves and deeply incised veins. Spikes of pale lilac, funnel-shaped flowers appear in late summer but can only just be seen above the leaves. Plant this hosta in partial shade in moist, fertile, well-drained soil, and propagate by dividing clumps in the spring. Like all hostas, it is prone to slug damage.

◊ ◗ ☼ ◑ Z3–8 H8–1
↕ to 3ft (1m) ↔ to 4ft (1.2m)

HOSTA UNDULATA
VAR. ALBOMARGINATA

Perennial

The clumps of relatively small, bright green leaves of this hosta are enlivened with creamy white margins that define their elliptic shape. Lavender, funnel-shaped flowers are borne on long stems from early to midsummer. This hosta will lighten up a partially shaded site in a herbaceous or mixed border, or use it in deciduous woodland. It prefers a moist, well-drained soil. Grow it in soil-based mix in a pot to reduce the chance of slug damage.

◊ ☼ ◑ Z3–8 H8–1
↕ to 22in (55cm) ↔ to 24in (60cm)

LIRIODENDRON TULIPIFERA

Deciduous tree

The tulip tree has a conical shape and bears unusual lobed, square leaves that appear as though they have been lopped off at the tips. The tulip-shaped flowers, produced only on mature trees, are yellowish green with a hint of orange at the base of the petals. In autumn the foliage turns wonderful shades of golden yellow. Grow the tulip tree in a large garden, where it can reach its full size unhindered, in full sun or partial shade and fertile, moist, well-drained soil.

◊ ◑ ☼ ☀ Z5–9 H9–5
‡ to 100ft (30m) ↔ to 50ft (15m)

MISCANTHUS SINENSIS *'Zebrinus'*

Perennial

Zebra grass will bring drama and height to a mixed or herbaceous border or a gravel bed. It bears tall, straplike foliage marked with horizontal yellow bands. This grass forms a large clump and produces spikes of silky maroon flowerheads in autumn. Allow the foliage and flowers to dry to a buff color during the autumn and winter, and then cut them down in early spring to make way for new growth.

◊ ◑ ☼ ☀ Z4–9 H9–1
‡ to 8ft (2.5m) ↔ to 4ft (1.2m)

ACHILLEA
'Coronation Gold'

Perennial

The bright yellow flowerheads of this
yarrow are made up of numerous tiny
flowers gathered together in broad, flat
clusters. The gray-green, deeply cut
leaves provide a perfect foil for them.
This vigorous plant tolerates a wide
range of growing conditions but does
best in a sunny situation in well-drained,
fertile soil. It is a lovely plant for a
wildflower garden. When cut and dried,
the flowerheads retain their color well.
Propagate by division in autumn.

◊ ◖ ☼ Z3–9 H9–1

‡ to 36in (90cm) ↔ to 18in (45cm)

ACHILLEA FILIPENDULINA
'Cloth of Gold'

Perennial

Although this plant grows nearly twice
the height of 'Coronation Gold', it is
actually less vigorous. It has attractive,
feathery, light green leaves and bears
large, golden yellow flowerheads, up to
5in (12cm) across, from early summer
until early autumn. It is ideal for
growing in a herbaceous border and
will thrive in any well-drained soil.
By late spring, the tall stems will need
supporting with stakes. Good for
cutting fresh or for drying.

◊ ◖ ☼ Z3–9 H9–1

‡↔ to 5ft (1.5m)

ALCHEMILLA MOLLIS

Perennial

After rain or heavy dew, the downy leaves of lady's mantle glisten with water droplets captured in the hairs on their surface. From early summer to early autumn large, airy sprays of tiny yellow-green flowers are produced, which are good for cutting. Fairly drought resistant, it is tolerant of most soil conditions, and, although it prefers full sun, it will also grow in partial shade. Plant it along the edge of a path or in a wildflower border, where it will self-seed freely.

◇ ◊ ☼ ☼ Z4–7 H7–1
‡ to 24in (60cm) ↔ to 30in (75cm)

ALLIUM FLAVUM

Bulbous perennial

A large clump of these alliums would look wonderful at the front of a border. A satisfyingly fast-growing plant, it produces stems topped with up to 60 delicately scented, bright yellow flowers. These dangle on slender stalks but turn upward when the seeds are developing. The blue-green leaves are waxy and cylindrical. Plant bulbs in autumn in a sunny position in well-drained soil.

◇ ☼ 𝆑⁄ʑ–10 H10–4
‡ to 14in (35cm) ↔ to 2in (5cm)

ALLIUM MOLY

Bulbous perennial

The golden garlic produces clusters of up to 30 golden yellow, star-shaped flowers on slender stems. Its waxy, lance-shaped leaves are usually produced in pairs. Plant in a sunny situation in fertile, well-drained soil. It often self-seeds freely and can become invasive, which, if grown in a wild garden or naturalized in woodland, is more of an asset than a problem. Plant bulbs and, if necessary, divide large clumps in autumn.

◊ ☼ Z3–9 H9–1
‡ to 10in (25cm) ↔ to 2in (5cm)

ANTHEMIS TINCTORIA
'E.C. Buxton'

Perennial

Filigree foliage and a long flowering season make the golden marguerite a great border plant. A clump-forming evergreen, it produces masses of lemon yellow, daisylike flowers with deep yellow centers. The leaves are mid-green above and a soft downy gray on the reverse. Cut back hard after flowering to reinvigorate the plant and to encourage it to produce a neat clump of leaves for next spring. Plant it in a sunny position in well-drained soil.

◊ ☼ Z3–7 H7–1
‡ to 28in (70cm) ↔ to 24in (60cm)

ARGYRANTHEMUM
'Jamaica Primrose'

Perennial

In frost-free areas, this plant will just keep on flowering; elsewhere, it is usually grown as summer bedding or in containers. Beautiful, soft yellow, daisy-like flowers and deeply divided, fern-like, midgreen leaves are a winning combination. Grow in moderately fertile, well-drained soil in full sun. Pot up the whole plant and move under cover for winter, or take stem cuttings in early autumn and grow under cover for next year. Easy to train as a standard.

◊ ☼ Z10–15 H12–1
‡ to 3½ft (1.1m) ↔ to 3ft (1m)

ASPHODELINE LUTEA
Perennial

An unusual, clump-forming plant that produces a fountain of grayish green, grasslike foliage. The tall flower spikes appear in early summer and are covered with yellow, star-shaped flowers. After flowering the plant dies down, but new leaves start to push through in autumn. It needs a well-drained, not too rich soil in full sun – a sunny bank would be ideal. Propagate by division, but take care not to damage the fleshy roots. It can also be grown from seed sown in autumn or spring.

◊ ☼ ƒZ6–9 H9–6
‡ to 5ft (1.5m) ↔ to 12in (30cm)

BIDENS FERULIFOLIA

Perennial

The trailing stems of this plant can be best appreciated when tumbling over the edges of a windowbox or used to plump up the planting in a hanging basket. It has large, daisylike, golden yellow flowers and bright green, filigree foliage and stems. A short-lived perennial, it is usually grown as an annual and is best propagated by taking cuttings at the end of the year. It needs moist but well-drained, fertile soil. Plants grown in a conservatory or heated greenhouse may flower until winter.

◊ ☼ Z8–10 H12–8
‡ to 12in (30cm) ↔ indefinite

BRACHYGLOTTIS
'Sunshine'

Evergreen shrub

A free-flowering habit and attractive silvery gray, slightly woolly foliage make this mound-forming plant a useful addition to any shrub border. From early to midsummer it produces a profusion of bright yellow, daisylike flowers. Plant it in a sunny situation in well-drained, fertile soil. It does well in coastal areas but needs to be protected from strong, cold winds. Prune in early spring to keep the bush well shaped.

◊ ☼ Z9–10 H10–8
‡ to 5ft (1.5m) ↔ to 6ft (2m)

BUPHTHALMUM SALICIFOLIUM

Perennial

Yellow ox eye has dark green, narrow
leaves and deep yellow, daisylike
flowers held on long, willowy stems.
In late spring, insert supports so they
are in place before the flowers open.
The flowers are long lasting when cut.
It is best grown in full sun in well-
drained, poor soil. If given richer soil
it may become invasive; in which case,
divide plants regularly to keep them in
check. In certain situations, however,
its spreading habit would be useful,
such as on a bank or in a wild garden.

○ ☼ Z3–7 H7–1
‡ to 24in (60cm) ↔ to 18in (45cm)

CALCEOLARIA
'John Innes'

Perennial

Curiously pouch-shaped and often
beautifully marked, the flowers of the
slipper flower are a delight. 'John Innes'
has intense yellow flowers with red-
brown spots. It is a vigorous, clump-
forming plant that needs a well-drained,
moderately fertile, acidic soil in sun or
partial shade. Wher marginally hardy,
pot up and take under cover in winter,
or take softwood cuttings in summer
and keep the plants in a cold frame
during winter as an insurance policy.

○ ☼ ☀ Z8–9 H6–1
‡ to 8in (20cm) ↔ to 12in (30cm)

Callistemon pallidus

Evergreen shrub

Aptly named, the yellow bottlebrush bristles with stiff-stemmed, greenish yellow flowers. Its graceful, arching branches are covered with grayish green leaves that are tinged with pink when they are young. Plant in full sun in well-drained, neutral to acidic soil. Wher marginally hardy, give it a sheltered spot against a south- or west-facing wall. Alternatively, plant it in a container of soil-based potting mix and overwinter in a cool greenhouse.

◊ ☼ Z10–15 H12–10
‡↔ to 12ft (4m)

Carex elata
'Aurea'

Perennial

A vibrantly colored, ornamental plant, Bowles' golden sedge is an evergreen that is grown for its gently arching, green-margined, bright yellow leaves. It may send up long, brown, male flower spikes. It requires a site in full sun in a fertile, moist but well-drained soil. To keep the tufts neat, cut out dead leaves in summer. Plant in a container or in groups near water or in a herbaceous or mixed border.

◊ ◕ ☼ ☼ Z5–9 H9–3
‡ to 28in (70cm) ↔ to 18in (45cm)

CENTAUREA MACROCEPHALA

Perennial

An imposing ornamental for the back of
a herbaceous border, this thistlelike
plant has deeply cut, lance-shaped,
slightly hairy leaves. The rounded
flowerheads, which are good for cutting
and drying, are enclosed in papery
bracts that split open to reveal a sunny
burst of bright yellow petals. Grow in
moist but well-drained soil in full sun
or light shade.

◊ ◊ ☼ ☼ Z3–7 H7–1
‡ to 5ft (1.5m) ↔ to 24in (60cm)

COREOPSIS GRANDIFLORA
'Badengold'

Perennial

Bees love the daisylike flowers of
tickseeds, as do flower arrangers, who
value them for their long life after
cutting. 'Badengold' is a short-lived
perennial that may be grown as an
annual. Sow seed *in situ* from early
spring to early summer. Its orange-
centered yellow blooms are held aloft
on tall stems above bright green, lance-
shaped leaves. It needs a sunny spot in
well-drained, fertile soil. Deadheading
helps prolong flowering.

◊ ☼ Z4–9 H9–1
‡ to 30in (75cm) ↔ to 24in (60cm)

COREOPSIS VERTICILLATA *'Grandiflora'*

Perennial

A good choice for a sunny herbaceous border, this cheerful tickseed bears masses of single yellow flowers. Deadheading helps prolong the flowering period. Plants raised from seed sown in early to midspring in a prepared seedbed will flower the same year, while the feathery, midgreen leaves quickly knit together to form a good-sized clump. Plant in fertile, well-drained soil in full sun or light shade. A good cut flower and bee plant.

◊ ☼ Z4–9 H12–1
‡ to 24in (60cm) ↔ to 12in (30cm)

CYTISUS BATTANDIERI

Deciduous shrub

The pineapple broom produces tight clusters of fruit-scented, bright yellow, lupinelike flowers. Its silvery green leaves are carried on arching, spreading branches, giving the bush an open shape. Where marginally hardy, it should overwinter successfully if it is planted in a sunny, sheltered spot by a wall in well-drained, sandy, moderately fertile soil. Other than to remove shoots that spoil the symmetry of the bush – do this in early spring – it does not need much pruning.

◊ ☼ ƒZ7–9 H9–7
‡↔ to 15ft (5m)

DELPHINIUM
'Sungleam'

Perennial

This stunning delphinium sends up
tall, tapering spires of creamy yellow
flowers with strong yellow eyes.
A second flush of flowers can be
encouraged by cutting down the flower
spikes as soon as they fade. Plant it in
groups in a sunny position in well-
drained, organic, fertile soil. To prevent
wind damage, especially on exposed
sites, insert strong stakes when planting,
and periodically tie in the flower stems
as they grow.

◊ ☼ Z3–7 H7–1
‡ to 5ft (1.5m) ↔ to 36in (90cm)

DIGITALIS GRANDIFLORA

Perennial

Overwintering as a rosette of deep
green leaves, the yellow foxglove is
an upright, short-lived perennial that
produces its spikes of pale lemon,
tubular flowers in early summer. It
prefers a semi-shaded situation and
damp, well-drained soil, where it will
happily self-seed. Deadheading after
flowering will check its spread. Grow
the slightly smaller *D. lutea* if you have
an alkaline soil. Both varieties do well
in a wild garden or a less-than-formal
herbaceous or mixed border.

◊ ◊ ☼ Z3–8 H8–1
‡ to 3ft (1m) ↔ to 18in (45cm)

EREMURUS STENOPHYLLUS

Perennial

The foxtail lily produces canary yellow flowers fading to copper on spikes that soar above other early summer border plants. They start to grow early in the season, so the young buds are prone to frost damage. Cover the crowns in winter and spring with row cover or straw to protect the emerging shoots. The bent, strappy leaves will die down when the flower spike starts to emerge. Plant in very well-drained, sandy soil in full sun. A superb cut flower.

◊ ☼ Z7–9 H8–1
‡ to 3ft (1m) ↔ to 24in (60cm)

ERIOPHYLLUM LANATUM

Perennial

The woolly sunflower has silvery green, slightly furry, deeply divided leaves that knit together to form a dense mat. The deep yellow, daisylike flowers are produced through summer. Plant in full sun in well-drained, light soil. Fairly drought tolerant, it is a good plant for rock gardens and crevices in walls and paving. To keep it compact, trim back after flowering has finished. Divide plants in spring.

◊ ☼ Z5–8 H8–5
‡↔ to 24in (60cm)

EUPHORBIA PALUSTRIS

Perennial

Needing soil that is permanently moist, this spurge would make an unusual waterside plant for an informal pond. The strong stems are covered with narrow, lime green leaves topped by clusters of green-yellow flowers. In autumn, the leaves turn various shades of yellow and orange. Choose a site in full sun. Avoid skin or eye contact with the milky sap.

◊ ☼ Z5–8 H8–5
‡↔ to 36in (90cm)

GAZANIA
'Talent Yellow'

Perennial

A superb plant for providing a splash of color in patio containers and as summer bedding, this tender perennial is grown as an annual where not hardy. It has grayish green, felted leaves and open yellow flowers, which are produced over a long period. It must be planted in full sun. A quirk of gazanias is that the flowers close on dull or cool days. Best planted in light, sandy, well-drained soil. Tolerant of coastal conditions.

◊ ☼ Z8–11 H12–1
‡↔ to 10in (25cm)

GENISTA AETNENSIS

Deciduous tree

The Mount Etna broom forms a large shrub or medium-sized tree with arching, almost leafless green branches. In summer it explodes into color, producing masses of fragrant, pealike yellow flowers. It makes a spectacular specimen tree for a sunny situation, with a canopy that is light enough to allow underplanting. Pruning is unnecessary, except to remove damaged stems. Plant in well-drained, light, poor to moderately fertile soil.

◊ ☼ *f* Z9–10 H10–9
‡↔ to 25ft (8m)

GENISTA LYDIA

Deciduous shrub

Ideally suited to the well-drained conditions of a rock garden or raised bed, this dome-shaped, low-growing shrub will trail over sunny walls and rocks. Its prickle-tipped, gray-green, arching branches are covered in bright yellow, pealike flowers. It prefers hot sites in poor, light soils that have not been enriched. Take semi-ripe cuttings in summer, or sow seed in autumn. Pruning is unnecessary, and straggly plants are best replaced.

◊ ☼ Z6–9 H9–6
‡ to 24in (60cm) ↔ to 3ft (1m)

GEUM
'Lady Stratheden'

Perennial

Geums are especially suitable for the
front of a herbaceous border. They
form clumps of arching, kidney-shaped
leaves that have a covering of fine
hairs. The cup-shaped, semidouble,
golden yellow flowers are carried on
branching stems. Plant in full sun in
moist but well-drained, soil. Divide
large clumps in autumn. Unlike many
geums, 'Lady Stratheden' will come
true from seed.

○ ◑ ☼ Z5–9 H9–5
‡ ↔ to 24in (60cm)

HELIANTHUS ANNUUS

Annual

A fast-growing, unfussy flower that is a
favorite with children. The growth spurt
of some of the giant sunflowers is
spectacular – in one season they can
reach 3m (10ft). The large, daisylike
flowers have long yellow petals and a
dark purple-brown center. If left to dry,
the seedhead will provide valuable food
for the birds over winter. Sunflowers
need a sunny position in well-drained,
fertile soil. Sow seed *in situ* in spring.
Tall-growing plants will need staking
and a sheltered site.

○ ☼ Z0 H12–1
‡ to 10ft (3m) ↔ to 24in (60cm)

HELICHRYSUM ITALICUM
SUBSP. SEROTINUM

Perennial

The curry plant is grown for its aromatic, evergreen, sage green foliage and clusters of yellow flowers. Despite its common name, the leaves of this plant are not used in curry powder; however, they are edible, and their savory tang can be used to enliven cream cheese or egg and chicken dishes. It can suffer during wet winters and should be planted in a raised bed or open, sunny situation in very well-drained soil.

◌ ☼ *f*Z7–10 H10–7
‡ to 16in (40cm) ↔ to 30in (75cm)

HEMEROCALLIS
LILIOASPHODELUS

Perennial

There are thousands of daylilies to choose from, but this species is right up there with the best of them. It is vigorous and easy to grow, with funnel-shaped, fragrant flowers that last for only a day but are soon replaced. They open in the afternoon and last through the night, so plant a clump close to the patio or other area in the garden that you use in the evening. Plant in full sun in moist but well-drained soil. Divide large clumps in spring.

◌ ◑ ☼ *f*Z4–11 H12–1
‡↔ to 3ft (1m)

HEMEROCALLIS
'Stella de Oro'

Perennial

Daylilies are perfect herbaceous border
plants. Their narrow, arching leaves
quickly form an attractive clump, and
while their colorful flowers last only a
day, they appear in rapid succession
over several weeks. Happiest in full sun
in moist but well-drained soil, daylilies
will tolerate the damp margins of a
pond. 'Stella de Oro' is a compact form
that is very free-flowering over a very
long season. Propagate by division in
spring or late summer.

◊ ◊ ☼ ƒ Z4–11 H12–1
↕ to 12in (30cm) ↔ to 18in (45cm)

HUMULUS LUPULUS
'Aureus'

Climber

Hops, a herbaceous climber, will quickly
clothe a pergola or fence. Male and
female flowers grow on separate plants,
with the female producing the hops.
The yellow color of 'Aureus' is
transitory, with the leaves turning green
later in the season. Grow in moist but
well-drained soil; full sun will enhance
leaf color. Remove remains of old
growth in early spring.

◊ ◊ ☼ Z4–8 H8–1
↕ to 20ft (6m)

IRIS
'Brown Lasso'

Perennial

Bearded irises come in a huge range of colors. 'Brown Lasso' is a lovely combination of yellow upper petals and lilac lower petals edged with butterscotch. Each stem carries 6–10 of these three-toned flowers. Plant in fertile, well-drained, neutral to acidic soil in full sun. Divide clumps when they become congested, usually after 3 years. The upright, sword-shaped leaves remain after the flowers have faded to add form to the herbaceous border.

◊ ☼ Z3–9 H9–1
‡ to 22in (55cm) ↔ indefinite

IRIS INNOMINATA

Perennial

This attractive Pacific Coast iris has pale yellow to cream flowers with bold brown veining. Other colors include purple and pale lavender. It is quite a small plant, rarely exceeding a height of 10in (25cm), with narrow, dark green, evergreen leaves that are flushed purple at the base. Easily swamped in a border, it is best appreciated in a raised bed or trough. Plant in full sun or partial shade in neutral or slightly acidic soil.

◊ ☼ ◐ Z7–9 H9–7
‡ to 10in (25cm) ↔ to 12in (30cm)

KNIPHOFIA
'Wrexham Buttercup'

Perennial

A yellow red-hot poker, 'Wrexham Buttercup' bears tapering spikes of tubular flowers lightly tipped with orange. It is similar to, but rather larger than, 'Buttercup' (see below). Grow in full sun or light shade in fertile, moist but well-drained soil. Red-hot pokers are showy herbaceous border plants and a favorite of bees. Leave remains of old foliage in place over winter for protection and remove in spring, when large clumps can also be divided.

○ ◐ ☼ ☀ Z6–9 H9–6
‡ to 4ft (1.2m) ↔ to 24in (60cm)

KNIPHOFIA
'Buttercup'

Perennial

A robust red-hot poker, 'Buttercup' will hold its own in a busy herbaceous border. It forms a large clump of narrow, strappy leaves and tall spikes of clear yellow flowers that open from green buds. They are very attractive to bees. For best results, plant in full sun or light shade in fertile, moist but well-drained soil. Old foliage offers protection over winter; remove it in spring and divide large clumps.

○ ◐ ☼ ☀ Z6–9 H9–6
‡↔ to 30in (75cm)

LIGULARIA PRZEWALSKII

Perennial

Tall, narrow spikes of yellow flowers on purple-green stems rise in stately fashion above a robust clump of deeply divided leaves. A lover of deep, moist soil, this plant looks striking beside a large pond or tucked toward the back of a permanently moist mixed or herbaceous border where, sheltered among other plants, it is less vulnerable to strong winds. Although it is happy in full sun, light shade during the middle of the day is ideal.

◊ ♦ ☼ ☼ Z4–8 H8–1
↕ to 6ft (2m) ↔ to 3ft (1m)

LIMNANTHES DOUGLASII

Annual

The two-tone petals of this fast-growing annual inspired its common name of poached-egg plant. It has deeply divided, slightly succulent, glossy green leaves and stays in flower over a long period through summer. Sow seed *in situ* during spring or late summer in moist but well-drained fertile soil. Use it to edge a path or dot it among rows of vegetables, where it will attract hoverflies, which help control aphids.

◊ ☼ Z0 H9–1
↕↔ to 6in (15cm)

LONICERA PERICLYMENUM
'Graham Thomas'

Climber

This vigorous climber has white flowers that turn yellow with age and are followed by glossy red berries. Grow it through trees and over pergolas or a trellis, or it can be used as a ground-cover. The flowers are highly fragrant and attract night-flying moths and insects. Bear this in mind if you are considering planting it near the house. Plant in sun or partial shade in any reasonable soil. Cut established plants back by up to a third after flowering.

◊ ◊ ☼ ☀ *f* Z5–9 H9–5
‡ to 22ft (7m)

LUPINUS ARBOREUS

Evergreen shrub

Tree lupines are strong shrubs, evergreen in mild winters, with sprawling branches of grayish green leaves. They make wonderful specimen plants in a hot, dry border. The species has fragrant, sulfur yellow flowers, but there are also lavender and white forms. Where marginally hardy, plant it in a sunny position in sandy, well-drained soil. It grows very well in coastal conditions. Propagate by seed in spring.

◊ ☼ *f* Z8–9 H9–8
‡↔ to 6ft (2m)

MIMULUS GUTTATUS

Perennial

The monkey flower is at home in the deep, moist soil beside a stream or pond, where it forms a spreading mat of toothed, midgreen leaves. Through summer until autumn it produces tall, narrow spikes of deep yellow flowers, which are often freckled with reddish brown spots. Their shape resembles the intricate flowers of the snapdragon (*Antirrhinum*). Plant in full sun or in dappled shade. Monkey flowers tend to be shortlived, so propagate plants by dividing them in spring.

◊ ◭ ☼ ☼ Z6–9 H9–6
‡ to 12in (30cm) ↔ to 24in (60cm)

OENOTHERA FRUTICOSA
'Fyrverkeri'

Perennial

The scented, deep yellow flowers of the evening primrose open at dusk and are pollinated by night-flying insects. While they may last only a day or so, the flowers are produced in abundance all summer long. The plant has striking red stems and, when young, the lance-shaped leaves are flushed red, too. It is a good plant for a raised bed, gravel garden, or the front of a herbaceous border. Grow it in full sun or partial shade in well-drained, sandy soil.

◊ ☼ ☼ ƒ Z4–8 H8–1
‡ to 3ft (1m) ↔ to 12in (30cm)

PHLOMIS FRUTICOSA

Evergreen shrub

Jerusalem sage forms a mound of aromatic, felted, gray-green leaves. From early to midsummer, short stems of golden yellow, hooded flowers are produced in bunches. A mass planting would be a highlight a sunny border or a gravel garden with well-drained, light soil. Propagate by taking cuttings in summer.

◊ ☼ *f* Z8–9 H9–8
‡ to 3ft (1m) ↔ to 5ft (1.5m)

PRIMULA FLORINDAE

Perennial

The giant Himalayan cowslip is one of the largest primroses, with a handsome basal rosette of midgreen, toothed leaves. The freshly fragrant, sulfur yellow, bell-shaped flowers are borne on tall stems up to 4ft (1.2m) high. It should be planted in full sun or partial shade in moist, organic, neutral or slightly acidic soil. Plant in drifts along a stream bank, in large groups in a bog or woodland garden, or around the margins of a pond.

◊ ☼ ☼ *f* Z4–8 H8–1
‡ to 4ft (1.2m) ↔ to 36in (90cm)

RANUNCULUS CONSTANTINOPOLITANUS *'Plenus'*

Perennial

This cultivated buttercup has neat, double, yellow-green pompon flowers. It has deeply divided leaves that are often dotted with grayish white spots. It is a well-behaved plant that looks attractive in a rock garden or mixed border. Plant it in full sun in moist but well-drained, soil. Propagate by dividing the woody roots after flowering has finished.

◊ ◑ ☼ Z7–8 H8–7
↕ to 20in (50cm) ↔ to 12in (30cm)

RHODIOLA ROSEA

Perennial

The waxy-covered, triangular-shaped leaves of roseroot clump together to form a neat mound of stiffly erect stems. It produces large heads of pink buds that open to greenish yellow, star-shaped flowers. Give it a sunny spot in well-drained, moderately fertile soil in a rock garden, dry wall, or at the front of a raised bed or herbaceous border.

◊ ☼ Z1–6 H6–1
↕↔ to 12in (30cm)

ROSA
Graham Thomas

Deciduous shrub

This superb modern shrub rose forms
a nicely rounded bush. It never gets out
of hand and is one of the best yellow
roses available. All through summer
until autumn it bears deep golden
yellow, cup-shaped, fragrant flowers.
If space allows, plant in a group of 3–5
in full sun in well-drained, organic,
fertile soil. Shrub roses are suitable for
growing in mixed borders and need
less rich growing conditions than bush
roses such as Mountbatten.

◊ ☼ Z5–9 H9–5
‡ to 4ft (1.2m) ↔ to 5ft (1.5m)

ROSA
Mountbatten

Deciduous shrub

A very vigorous, repeat-flowering
floribunda rose with double, fragrant,
deep yellow flowers. It forms a nice bush
with plenty of glossy green foliage. Plant
it in a sunny position in well-drained soil
enriched with plenty of organic matter.
Remove dead flowers to encourage the
production of new buds. Prune main
stems to about 12in (30cm) above the
ground in early spring, then apply a
balanced fertilizer and a thick mulch of
well-rotted manure.

◊ ☼ *f* Z5–9 H9–5
‡ to 4ft (1.2m) ↔ to 30in (75cm)

ROSA XANTHINA
'Canary Bird'

Deciduous shrub

This is a very decorative but rather
large shrub rose suitable for a wild
garden, since it needs a lot of space to
perform well. It produces long, arching
branches covered with single, saucer-
shaped, lightly fragrant, deep yellow
flowers. A smattering of flowers may
appear until autumn. In exposed areas
it is vulnerable to late frost, and the
young buds may be damaged by cold
winds. Grow in moist but well-drained,
fertile soil in full sun.

◊ ☼ ƒZ5–9 H9–5
‡ to 10ft (3m) ↔ to 12ft (4m)

SEDUM ACRE
'Aureum'

Perennial

This mat-forming plant has upright or
sprawling stems that are covered with
small, fleshy green leaves with yellow-
variegated tips. The bright yellow, star-
shaped flowers are borne throughout
the summer. Given the right conditions
– full sun and a very well-drained soil –
it may become invasive, but it is easily
controlled. It makes a colorful plant
for a trough filled with gritty soil mix,
a raised bed, or a rock garden.
Take cuttings in spring or late summer.

◊ ☼ Z4–9 H9–1
‡ to 2in (5cm) ↔ to 24in (60cm)

THERMOPSIS RHOMBIFOLIA VAR. MONTANA

Perennial

An upright plant with divided leaves and tall spikes of bright yellow, pealike flowers that are attractive to bees. Although tolerant of a wide range of conditions, it prefers a sunny spot in fertile, light, sandy soil. Often used to provide vertical accents in a herbaceous border, it is perhaps best suited to an informal wildlife garden, where its invasive tendencies are more easily accommodated. Propagate by division in spring, or sow seed in autumn.

○ ◐ ☼ ☀ Z4–9 H9–1
‡ to 36in (90cm) ↔ to 24in (60cm)

VERBASCUM '*Gainsborough*'

Perennial

This mullein is one of the Cotswold hybrids and overwinters as a large rosette of downy, grayish green leaves. In early summer it springs into action and produces a stately spire of saucer-shaped, pale yellow flowers. Further flowers often appear on side branches. A long-flowering plant for a herbaceous border it is, sadly, rather short-lived. Plant in a sunny position in well-drained fertile soil.

○ ☼ Z5–9 H9–5
‡ to 4ft (1.2m) ↔ to 12in (30cm)

BEGONIA
'City of Ballarat'

Perennial

Bright orange flowers up to 7in (18cm) across adorn this tuberous begonia. Grow it in containers of soil-based mix as a houseplant, and move it outside in summer. It can be used as bedding if the tubers are lifted in autumn before the first frost and stored in trays of dry sand in a cool place. In early spring, moisten the trays of tubers and move them to a warm place. Plant out in late spring in moist but well drained soil in partial shade.

◊ ☼ Z13 H12–10
‡ to 24in (60cm) ↔ to 18in (45cm)

BUDDLEJA GLOBOSA

Deciduous shrub

The orange ball tree forms a large shrub or small tree with spherical clusters of dark orange or yellow, fragrant flowers It has lance-shaped leaves, which may be semi-evergreen in sheltered areas. It can be used in a shrub border or as a specimen plant, although it tends to get leggy with age. It prefers a sunny site in well-drained, preferably alkaline soil. Pruning is rarely necessary.

◊ ☼ *f*Z7–9 H9–7
‡↔ to 15ft (5m)

EREMURUS × ISABELLINUS
'Cleopatra'

Perennial

This is a dramatic foxtail lily with tall, stately spikes of deep orange flowers held above midgreen, lance-shaped leaves. It needs to be grown in very well-drained, fertile, sandy soil in full sun. The fleshy roots will quickly rot if the soil becomes too wet, so it is advisable to plant it in a raised bed, where any excess water will quickly drain away. Mulch them over in winter with straw or loose leaves to protect the emerging shoots.

◊ ☼ Z5–8 H8–5
‡ to 5ft (1.5m) ↔ to 36in (90cm)

ESCHSCHOLZIA CALIFORNICA

Annual

Perfect for a sun-drenched situation in a Mediterranean-style or gravel garden, the California poppy has decorative, finely divided, feathery, blue-green foliage and bright yellow-orange, cup-shaped flowers. The blooms open in full sun and close as the light dims at the end of the day, appearing from early to midsummer. Sow them *in situ* in spring (or autumn where winters are mild) in poor, freely draining soil.

◊ ☼ Z0 H9–1
‡ to 12in (30cm) ↔ to 6in (15cm)

GLADIOLUS
'Peter Pears'

Cormous perennial

The green, sword-shaped leaves of this
gladiolus beautifully set off the spikes
of apricot flowers. In a border, plant
corms in spring in groups of 5–10. The
flower stems will need to be supported
to prevent them from blowing over.
Like other gladioli, it makes a good
cut flower. Grow it in full sun in fertile,
well-drained soil with added organic
matter. In autumn, lift the corms, dry
them, and then overwinter in a frost-
free place until mid- to late spring.

◊ ☼ Z8–11 H12–1
↕ to 5½ft (1.7m) ↔ to 14in (35cm)

HEMEROCALLIS FULVA
'Flore Pleno'

Perennial

This vigorous daylily forms large clumps
of midgreen, strap-shaped foliage. In
summer it bears double, brownish
orange flowers with darker stripes inside.
It needs to be planted
in full sun in moist, well-drained soil.
Shade or very dry conditions will reduce
the number of flowers produced. Use
this daylily in a mixed or herbaceous
border, or in a gravel bed. It could also
be planted in
a container if kept well watered.

◊ ◑ ☼ ◐ Z4–11 H12–1
↕ to 30in (75cm) ↔ to 36in (90cm)

IRIS
'Blue Eyed Brunette'

Perennial

The name of this bearded iris accurately brings to mind the color of its distinctive flowers. The petals are tinted orange-brown, with the lower set highlighted with a bright lilac spot surmounted by a golden yellow beard. Use it in a mixed or herbaceous border, and combine it with bronze grasses, such as *Carex flagellifera*, to create an unusual color theme. Plant in a sunny situation in well-drained, fertile, neutral to acidic soil (see 'Bold Print' p.159).

◊ ☼ Z3–9 H9–1
‡ to 36in (90cm) ↔ indefinite

KNIPHOFIA
'Bees' Sunset'

Perennial

A beautiful red-hot poker, 'Bees' Sunset' produces tall spikes of pale orange, tubular flowers over a long period from early summer. Grow it in groups in a fiery color-themed border or gravel garden. It complements pale yellow and bright red flowers, such as dahlias. Plant it in moist, well-drained soil in full sun or partial shade. Leave the remains of the old foliage over winter for protection then remove it in spring, when large clumps can also be divided.

◊ ◊ ☼ ☼ Z6–9 H9–6
‡ to 36in (90cm) ↔ to 24in (60cm)

PAPAVER
'Fireball'

Perennial

This low-growing poppy has cheerful, bright orange flowers that open from bristly buds. The foliage is very hairy and makes a good groundcover. Grow it toward the front of a border or in a gravel garden; it spreads by running stems but is not difficult to keep within bounds. Choose a position in full sun in any reasonably fertile, well-drained soil. Deadhead regularly to keep the flowers coming. Large clumps can be divided in spring.

◊ ☼ Z4–9 H9–1

↕ to 16in (40cm) ↔ to 12in (30cm) or more

ROSA
'Just Joey'

Deciduous shrub

A hybrid tea rose with large, pinkish orange, slightly fragrant blooms that will appear throughout summer with regular deadheading. It grows to form a medium-sized bush with dark green leaves. It can be used in a border, but it is best grown *en masse* in a rose bed and is very good for cutting. Plant it in sun in fertile, moist, well-drained soil, perferably neutral or slightly acidic and enriched with organic matter. For further care see *Rosa* 'Blessings' (p.195).

◊ ◊ ☼ ƒZ5–9 H9–5

↕ to 30in (75cm) ↔ to 28in (70cm)

TAGETES
'Tangerine Gem'

Annual

This upright Signet marigold has ferny, dark green leaves. It is very free flowering, producing vast numbers of single orange flowers throughout summer. These marigolds make excellent edging and bedding plants, or use them in hanging baskets and containers. Plant them in full sun in fertile, well-drained soil, and deadhead regularly. They are easily rasied from seed sown in early spring in pots on a windowsill or under cover.

◊ ☼ Z0 H12–1
‡ to 8in (20cm) ↔ to 12in (30cm)

TROPAEOLUM MAJUS

Climber

Nasturtiums are colorful annuals with rounded, pale green leaves held on climbing or scrambling stems. They are very free flowering and bear orange, yellow, and red long-spurred flowers. Plant nasturtiums in containers and hanging baskets or grow them trained up a tripod in an annual or herbaceous border. They prefer a sunny situation and moist, well-drained soil. Check plants regularly for caterpillars and black aphids, and control them before the plants become infested.

◊ ◊ ☼ Z0 H12–1
‡ to 12in (30cm)

LATE SUMMER

MANY OF THE PLANTS that bless the hottest and driest time of year are annuals. Zinnias, sunflowers, marigolds, clarkia, and nasturtiums are just a few that can make a cheerful show in a border. Other plants used as annuals can join them, such as salvias and *Ricinus communis* 'Carmencita'. Unlike most annuals, which are sun-lovers, flowering tobacco (*Nicotiana*) also thrives in shade, where their pastels and lime greens glow alluringly. Note: not all are scented, so check the variety if fragrance is desired.

In favorable climates, fuchsias bloom continuously; many are favorites for hanging baskets and pots, along with geraniums. As temperatures soar, water containers on a daily basis. It is also vital to water new plants in dry periods. Give priority to trees, shrubs, and climbers planted less than a year ago, and water generously so that moisture penetrates deep below the soil surface.

Borders and gravel gardens are aglow with coneflowers (*Echinacea* and *Rudbeckia*) and red-hot pokers (*Kniphofia*), but for sheer elegance, a white color theme is hard to beat. Combine *Anemone* x *hybrida* 'Honorine Jobert', *Epilobium angustifolium* var. *album,* and tall white dahlias, hollyhocks, and lilies for a display that takes on a luminous quality at dusk. To extend the show into autumn, keep deadheading, and fill any gaps with fast growers, such as salvias and petunias.

HOT TROPICAL STYLE

Mirror the heat of summer days with combinations of red and orange flowers. *Phygelius* x *rectus* 'African Queen' and dahlias like 'Bishop of Llandaff' and 'Wootton Impact' will set the garden afire. Punctuate them with red-hot pokers, and include *Ensete ventricosum*, cannas, agaves, and yuccas to increase the tropical flavor with their flamboyant foliage.

ABELIA × GRANDIFLORA

Evergreen shrub

This large, rounded plant has arching branches and glossy, dark green leaves. It flowers from mid- to late summer and produces fragrant, funnel-shaped, pink-flushed white flowers. Plant in a sunny site or against a wall where it can be protected from cold, damaging winds. Grow it in fertile, well-drained soil, and to rejuvenate established plants, cut out some of the older stems after flowering.

◊ ☼ *f* Z6–9 H9–6
‡ to 10ft (3m) ↔ to 12ft (4m)

ACTAEA ALBA

Perennial

The white baneberry forms a clump of toothed leaves divided into egg-shaped leaflets. In late spring or early summer it produces spikes of small white flowers, followed in late summer by toxic, shiny, round white berries held on red stems. It grows best in a shady situation in deep, moist soil, which should be watered during summer to prevent it from drying out.

◊ ☀ Z4–9 H9–1
‡ to 3ft (1m) ↔ to 20in (50cm)

AESCULUS PARVIFLORA

Deciduous shrub

A close relative of the horsechestnut, the bottlebrush buckeye has similar leaves that are divided into several long, slightly waxy, bronze-green leaflets. In midsummer it produces tall spikes of white flowers. In autumn the leaves turn bright yellow. It is a very tolerant plant and can be grown in full sun or partial shade, preferring fertile, slightly moist but well-drained soil. The bush spreads by suckers, which can be separated and replanted or removed to control the spread.

◊ ◊ ☼ ☀ Z5–9 H9–5
↕ to 10ft (3m) ↔ to 15ft (5m)

ANEMONE × HYBRIDA
'Honorine Jobert'

Perennial

The Japanese anemone is a popular late-flowering plant, perfect for growing in a summer or autumn herbaceous border. It is also good for cutting. This is one of the prettiest varieties, bearing single, pure white flowers with bright green centers surrounded by golden yellow stamens. Plant it in sun or light shade in moist, fertile, well-drained soil. It spreads quickly to form large clumps, but it can be invasive. Divide the plants in early spring.

◊ ◊ ☼ ☀ Z4–8 H8–1
↕ to 5ft (1.5m) ↔ indefinite

CAMPANULA ALLIARIIFOLIA

Perennial

Ivory bells is an elegant herbaceous plant that forms clumps of grayish green, hairy, heart-shaped leaves. The white, bell-shaped, pendent flowers are held on branched, wiry stems. It prefers a slightly shaded situation and is ideal for planting beneath a light canopy of deciduous trees or shrubs in a mixed border. It blooms from summer to early autumn. Cut it to the ground after flowering to prevent self-seeding. Grow it in moist, well-drained, fertile, neutral or alkaline soil.

◊ ◑ ☼ ☀ Z3–7 H7–1
‡ to 24in (60cm) ↔ to 20in (50cm)

CLERODENDRUM TRICHOTOMUM *VAR.* FARGESII

Deciduous shrub

This upright, large shrub or small tree produces clusters of very fragrant white flowers with persistent green sepals. The flowers are followed later in the year by bright blue berries. The young leaves are also a feature, opening bronze before turning green. Where marginally hardy, plant it against a west- or south-facing wall in moist, well-drained, fertile soil. Pruning is rarely required, except to remove crossing or damaged branches.

◊ ◑ ☼ *f*Z7–9 H9–7
‡ to 20ft (6m) ↔ to 20ft (6m)

DAHLIA
'Angora'

Perennial

This dahlia has double white flowers
and creates a stunning display when
planted in front of a dark background
or in a white border. The blooms also
make excellent cut flowers. Dahlias
need a sunny position in fertile, moist,
well-drained soil. Plant in spring, and
insert a sturdy stake when planting.
Lift the tubers after the first frost, allow
them to dry, and then store them in
boxes of dry sand or compost in a
frost-free, cool place.

○ ◑ ☼ Z8–11 H12–1
‡ to 36in (1m) ↔ to 24in (60cm)

ECHINACEA PURPUREA
'White Swan'

Perennial

Coneflowers originate from the prairies
of North America and have daisylike
flowers with raised, conelike centers.
The flowers of 'White Swan' are borne
on tall, erect stems above lance-shaped
leaves and are composed of white
petals with an orange-brown cone.
Plant it in a sunny site in a herbaceous
border in deep, well-drained soil. It will
also tolerate a little shade. Cut the stems
back after flowering to encourage
a second flush of blooms.

○ ☼ Z3–9 H9–1
‡ to 24in (60cm) ↔ to 18in (45cm)

EPILOBIUM ANGUSTIFOLIUM VAR. ALBUM

Perennial

The purple-pink rosebay willowherb is an invasive thug of a plant and is not suitable for growing in the garden. However, this beautiful white form is less aggressive and perfect for a wild area of the garden or the herbaceous border. Narrow, lance-shaped leaves provide a foil for the tall spikes of white flowers. It is not fussy about soil conditions and will grow in full sun or partial shade. It self-seeds, so deadhead it after flowering.

◊ ◊ ◙ ◙ ☼ ☼ Z3–7 H7–1
‡ to 5ft (1.5m) ↔ to 3ft (1m)

ERICA TETRALIX 'Alba Mollis'

Evergreen shrub

The cross-leaved heath is a spreading bush with small, silvery gray leaves, which are arranged in the shape of a cross. It is covered with small, bell-shaped white flowers. It needs damper soil conditions than other species of heather. It also requires an acidic soil and should be grown in full sun for the best results. Cut the plant back in spring to keep it neat.

◙ ☼ Z5–7 H7–5
‡ to 8in (20cm) ↔ to 12in (30cm)

EUCOMIS BICOLOR

Bulbous perennial

An exotic-looking bulb, the pineapple lily has large, straplike, light green leaves and purple-spotted flower stems. It bears dense spikes of purple-edged white flowers topped by a rosette of small leaves that inspired its common name. Plant bulbs about 6in (15cm) deep in full sun in fertile, well-drained soil. Where not hardy, lift the bulbs and store them in a frost-free place for replanting in spring. Alternatively, grow them in pots.

◊ ☼ Z8–10 H10–8
‡ to 20in (50cm) ↔ to 8in (20cm)

FALLOPIA BALDSCHUANICA

Climber

The "mile-a-minute plant," or Russian vine, is a rampant climber that grows rapidly up to a height of 40ft (12m). It has woody, twining stems covered with heart-shaped, pale green leaves. It bears masses of small, pink-flushed, creamy white flowers. Although unsuitable for a small garden, it is useful for covering an ugly wall or a dead tree. Grow it in full sun or partial shade in poor or slightly fertile, well-drained soil. Don't be afraid to cut it back very hard in spring.

◊ ☼ ☀ Z5–9 H9–5
‡ to 40ft (12m)

FUCHSIA
'Annabel'

Evergreen shrub

'Annabel' is a free-flowering, trailing fuchsia that produces delicate white flowers and is perfect for hanging baskets and tall containers. It can also be trained as a standard, if provided with a permanent supporting stake. Fertilize it regularly throughout the growing season. Where not hardy, move it indoors for the winter into a frost-free greenhouse. To propagate it, take softwood cuttings in spring.

◊ ◊ ☼ ☼ Z8–11 H12–1
‡ to 24in (60cm) ↔ to 24in (60cm)

GALTONIA CANDICANS

Bulbous perennial

Valued for its late summer blooms, this bulbous plant has long, grayish green, straplike leaves and white, pendent, slightly fragrant, tubular flowers that are produced on tall spikes. Where not hardy, the bulbs must be dug up in autumn and stored in a frost-free place, or covered with a deep mulch where marginally hardy. Plant the bulbs in spring in full sun and fertile, moist soil that never dries out.

◊ ☼ *f* Z7–10 H10–7
‡ to 4ft (1.2m) ↔ to 9in (23cm)

HELIANTHUS DEBILIS
'Italian White'

Annual

The flowerheads of this pale sunflower can measure up to 4in (10cm) across. It also has slightly hairy leaves, and the tall stems may need support in exposed gardens. Plant it in full sun in slightly fertile, well-drained soil. Raise this annual from seed under cover in early to midspring, or sow *in situ* from mid- to late spring.

◊ ☼ Z0 H12–1
‡ to 4ft (1.2m) ↔ to 24in (60cm)

HYDRANGEA MACROPHYLLA
'Veitchii'

Deciduous shrub

Lacecap hydrangeas have flat-topped flowerheads composed of small fertile blooms surrounded by larger sterile flowers. 'Veitchii' has white sterile flowers that turn pink and forms a mound of dark green foliage. The flowerheads can be cut and dried or left over winter and removed in spring, when a few of the oldest stems should be pruned to the ground. Plant in sun or partial shade in moist, well-drained, fertile soil.

◊ ◐ ☼ ◑ Z6–9 H9–6
‡ to 6ft (2m) ↔ to 8ft (2.5m)

HYDRANGEA PANICULATA *'Grandiflora'*

Deciduous shrub

This is a large beautiful plant, perfect for a mixed border or a specimen. In late summer it produces large, conical clusters of creamy white, sterile flowers that turn a delicate shade of pink as they age. Plant it in a sheltered area in moist, well-drained, fertile soil in sun or partial shade. Pruning is not essential, but for the best display of flowers, cut it back annually in early spring to a pair of buds beyond a framework of permanent branches.

◊ ◊ ☼ ☼ ☼ Z4–8 H8–1
↕ to 22ft (7m) ↔ to 8ft (2.5m)

LATHYRUS LATIFOLIUS *'Albus'*

Climber

The everlasting pea is a herbaceous perennial that can be used to climb up a support or as a groundcover. 'Albus' produces white to creamy white flowers that appear from summer to early autumn. It grows well in full sun or light shade in well-drained, fertile soil that has been enriched with well-rotted manure. Cut back any dead stems in spring, but otherwise you can leave it undisturbed.

◊ ☼ ☼ Z5–9 H9–5
↕ to 6ft (2m) or more

LILIUM AURATUM
VAR. PLATYPHYLLUM

Bulbous perennial

The golden-rayed lily originates from
Japan and bears lance-shaped, dark
green leaves. A crown of sweetly
scented white flowers with yellow
stripes down the center of the petals
are borne on stiff stems. This lily is
often short-lived and requires an acidic,
well-drained soil. Plant the bulbs in
autumn or spring in full sun, and mulch
well with leaf mold. They can also be
grown in pots of acidic soil mix, with
stakes to support the stems.

◊ ☼ *f* Z5–8 H8–5
‡ to 5ft (1.5m)

LILIUM REGALE

Bulbous perennial

One of the best lilies for fragrance, the
regal lily is a vigorous plant with erect
or arching stems clothed with shiny,
grayish green leaves. In midsummer it
produces up to 25 intensely fragrant,
trumpet-shaped white flowers. The
petals have purple streaks on the back
and golden yellow throats. Regal lilies
grow well in containers, although they
need the support of strong stakes. Plant
them in well-drained, fertile soil in full
sun, with the lower part of the plant
shaded by other planting.

◊ ☼ *f* Z4–7 H7–1
‡ to 6ft (2m) ↔ to 6ft (2m)

LOBULARIA MARITIMA
'Little Dorrit'

Annual

Also known as *Alyssum maritimum*, this pretty plant is usually grown as an annual, although it can also be a short-lived perennial. It forms a mound of narrow, grayish green leaves and bears rounded clusters of tiny, scented white flowers ifrom summer into autumn. For the best effect, plant 'Little Dorrit' in groups to form a carpet at the front of a border, or use it in bedding displays or in containers. Plant it in well-drained soil in full sun.

◊ ☀ *f* Z0 H9–1
‡ to 4in (10cm) ↔ to 4in (10cm)

MAGNOLIA GRANDIFLORA

Evergreen tree

The bull bay eventually makes a large, imposing tree with glossy, leathery, dark green leaves. From early to late summer, but most abundantly in midsummer, it bears large, creamy white flowers up to 10in (25cm) across. It should be grown in moist, well-drained soil in full sun or partial shade; where marginally hardy, site it against a west- or south-facing wall.

◊ ◐ ☀ ◗ *f* Z7–9 H10–7
‡ to 60ft (18m) ↔ to 50ft (15m)

MYRTUS COMMUNIS

Evergreen shrub

Myrtle has an upright habit and bears rounded, glossy, dark green, aromatic leaves. The attractive, fragrant white flowers have frothy centers created by long white stamens. It blooms from the middle of summer to the beginning of autumn. Where marginally hardy, myrtle is more likely to survive cold winters if planted against a sunny wall. Grow it in slightly fertile, moist, well-drained soil.

◊ ◑ ☼ *f* Z8–9 H9–8
‡ to 10ft (3m) ↔ to 10ft (3m)

NICOTIANA SYLVESTRIS

Perennial

Vigorous, short-lived perennials, flowering tobaccos are generally grown as an annual in colder areas. The flowers of this species are borne on long stems above a rosette of elliptic, dark green, sticky leaves. The long, highly fragrant white flowers resemble shooting stars and are produced from midsummer. It is easily damaged by cold, but it may survive a mild winter if protected by a thick layer of mulch. Plant it in a sunny or partially shaded site in moist, well-drained soil.

◊ ◑ ☼ ☼ *f* Z10–11 H12–1
‡ to 5ft (1.5m) ↔ to 2ft (60cm)

RESEDA ODORATA

Annual

The common mignonette is an erect or slightly spreading plant with ribbed stems and lance-shaped leaves. In summer and early autumn it produces rounded heads of small, star-shaped white or greenish white flowers with a sweet fragrance. It has been grown for centuries, because the flowers keep their fragrance even when they have been cut and dried. Plant it in well-drained soil in full sun or partial shade.

○ ☼ ☀ *f* Z0 H9–1
‡ to 24in (60cm) ↔ to 12in (30cm)

SCHIZOPHRAGMA INTEGRIFOLIUM

Climber

This is a vigorous, self-clinging climber. It bears flat-topped clusters of small, lightly scented, creamy white flowers surrounded by large, sterile, bractlike flowers that appear among the dark green leaves from midsummer. Grow it against a wall or up a large tree, in deep, fertile, moist but well-drained soil. Happy in full sun or partial shade, it can grow to a height of 40ft (12m), but it can be slow to get started.

○ ◑ ☼ *f* Z5–9 H9–5
‡ to 40ft (12m)

SENECIO CINERARIA
'Silver Dust'

Evergreen shrub

This attractive shrub has deeply divided leaves that are covered with grayish white felt. It produces mustard yellow, daisylike flowers in summer, although these should be removed before they open to maintain its foliage effect. Plant it in full sun and slightly fertile, well-drained soil. It dislikes excessive winter moisture; semi-ripe cuttings can be taken at the end of summer to produce "insurance" plants for next year.

◊ ☼ Z9–11 H12–6
‡ to 12in (30cm) ↔ to 12in (30cm)

YUCCA FILAMENTOSA
Evergreen shrub

The Spanish dagger is an architectural plant bearing stiff, lance-shaped, spiky leaves with razor-sharp points. Cut off these points if growing yuccas in gardens used by children. In late summer it produces a tall spike of bell-shaped, creamy white flowers. Plant it in well-drained soil in a sunny position, such as in a gravel garden, where it has space to grow to its full size. Protect young plants during their first winter with a loose, light mulch.

◊ ☼ Z5–10 H10–5
‡ to 6ft (2m) ↔ to 5ft (1.5m)

AGROSTEMMA GITHAGO
'Milas'

Annual

Corn cockle used to be a common grainfield weed in Europe, but the widespread use of herbicides has made it a much rarer plant. It has lance-shaped, grayish green leaves, and in summer 'Milas' has vibrant plum-pink flowers with white centers. Plant corn cockles in full sun in poor, well-drained soil. They can be grown in a cottage-style garden, in containers, or planted in a summer flower meadow. The species self-seeds freely.

◊ ☼ Z0 H9–1
‡ to 36in (90cm) ↔ to 12in (30cm)

ALCEA ROSEA

Perennial

Hollyhocks are tall, vigorous plants with rounded, slightly hairy leaves. In summer they produce a long spike of funnel-shaped pink, white, purple, or creamy yellow flowers. 'Chater's Double' is a beautiful double form. Hollyhocks need a sunny position and well-drained, fertile soil. They look good grown by a wall. Rust can be a problem, so look for resistant types. Hollyhocks are often grown as biennials to reduce the effects of rust. They often need staking in open positions.

◊ ☼ Z3–9 H9–1
‡ to 6ft (2m) ↔ to 24in (60cm)

ANEMONE HUPEHENSIS
'Hadspen Abundance'

Perennial

This late-flowering anemone produces
deep pink flowers, good for cutting,
over a long period. The edges of the
petals fade to white as the flower ages.
The long-stalked leaves have three
leaflets. This anemone enjoys a sunny
or partially shaded site. Plant it in moist
soil in a herbaceous border.

◐ ☼ ☀ Z4–8 H8–1
‡ to 36in (90cm) ↔ to 16in (40cm)

ANEMONE × HYBRIDA
'Max Vogel'

Perennial

The Japanese anemone is a vigorous
late-flowering plant with upright,
branched stems. From late summer to
midautumn, 'Max Vogel' produces
masses of beautiful single, light pink
flowers that become darker as they age.
It looks superb in a herbaceous border
and is good for cutting. It does best in
a moist, fertile soil in full sun or partial
shade. 'Margarete' has double, pale
pink flowers.

◊ ◐ ☼ ☀ Z4–8 H8–1
‡ to 5ft (1.5m) ↔ indefinite

BEGONIA
'Roy Hartley'

Perennial

The glossy leaves provide the perfect
foil for this tuberous begonia's large,
salmon-pink flowers, which are borne
from midsummer. Its upright growth
makes it an excellent bedding plant.
Tubers can be planted in the garden
when all risk of frost has passed; it
flowers better in a partially shaded site
and moist, well-drained soil. For an
indoor display, plant 'Roy Hartley' in a
container of soil-based potting mix in
bright light, away from direct sun.

◊ ◊ ☼ Z0 H7–1
‡ to 24in (60cm) ↔ to 18in (45cm)

CALLISTEPHUS CHINENSIS
Ostrich Plume Series

Annual

China aster flowers resemble
chrysanthemums with double blooms.
The Ostrich Plume Series are tall plants
with flowers in shades of pink, purple,
and red, plus white. They bloom from
late summer until the middle of
autumn. Plant them in a sunny,
sheltered site in moist, well-drained
soil. China asters make good bedding
plants and excellent cut flowers.

◊ ◊ ☼ Z0 H9–1
‡ to 24in (60cm) ↔ to 12in (30cm)

CALLUNA VULGARIS
'County Wicklow'

Evergreen shrub

There are over 500 different cultivars of ling, or heather. All are evergreen shrubs and can be used in heather gardens or as a groundcover. 'County Wicklow' is compact, with slightly prostrate stems and midgreen foliage. It bears spikes of small, double, shell pink flowers and blooms from late summer to late autumn. Plant it in full sun in well-drained, acidic soil. Cut it back in spring to keep it bushy.

◊ ☼ Z5–7 H7–5
‡ to 12in (30cm) ↔ to 14in (35cm)

CAMPANULA LACTIFLORA
'Loddon Anna'

Perennial

The milky bellflower is a tall herbaceous plant that bears large clusters of bell-shaped, lilac-pink flowers. It may need staking, since it is inclined to fall over in strong winds. It enjoys full sun or dappled shade in a fertile, neutral to alkaline, moist, well-drained soil. It self-seeds and can be divided in spring or autumn. 'Prichard's Variety' is not as tall and has violet-blue flowers.

◊ ◑ ☼ ☀ Z4–8 H8–1
‡ to 5ft (1.5m) ↔ to 24in (60cm)

CHELONE OBLIQUA

Perennial

Turtlehead bears stiff stems sparsely covered with lance-shaped, midgreen leaves. From late summer to mid-autumn it produces clusters of pink flowers that resemble the head of a turtle, hence its common name. It will perform well in a sunny border or partially shaded area in deep, fertile, moist soil. To propagate it, divide clumps in spring.

◊ ☼ ☀ Z5–9 H9–5
‡ to 24in (60cm) ↔ to 12in (30cm)

CHRYSANTHEMUM
'Clara Curtis'

Perennial

Unlike many chrysanthemums, this variety has simple, single, daisylike flowers with pale pink petals and green-yellow centers. Their fragrance comes as something of a surprise, because many chrysanthemums are unscented. Plant it in well-drained soil that has previously been enriched with well-rotted manure. Where marginally hardy, it should be dug up and overwintered in a frost-free place.

◊ ☼ *f* Z7–9 H12–1
‡ to 30in (75cm) ↔ to 18in (45cm)

CLARKIA UNGUICULATA

Annual

This is a tall, elegant, slender-stemmed annual, which from midsummer produces funnel-shaped, often frilly flowers in shades of salmon, lavender-pink, purple, and reddish purple. It makes a superb cut flower and should be grown in full sun or partial shade in moist, well-drained, slightly acidic soil. Plant seeds in autumn or early spring.

◊ ◗ ☼ Z0 H8–1
‡ to 39in (1m) ↔ to 8in (20cm)

CLEOME HASSLERIANA
'Rose Queen'

Annual

Spider flowers are tall, handsome plants with handlike leaves. They begin to flower in midsummer, producing large clusters of spidery pink, white, or purple blooms. They are ideal for the back of a herbaceous border (they do not need staking) and for filling spaces created when spring-flowering bulbs and perennials are over. Start plants in spring and plant out after all risk of frost has passed, in full sun and fertile, well-drained soil. Reseeds freely.

◊ ☼ Z0 H12–1
‡ to 5ft (1.5m) ↔ to 18in (45cm)

CRINUM × POWELLII

Bulbous perennial

From late summer to autumn, tall
stems of large, slightly fragrant, funnel-
shaped, pale pink flowers appear on
this vigorous, clump-forming perennial.
The straplike leaves can measure up
to 5ft (1.5m) in length. Where marginally hardy, protect crinums with a thick,
loose winter mulch. They should be
planted with the neck of the bulb just
above the ground in fertile, moist, well-
drained soil.

◊ ♦ ☼ *f* Z7–10 H10–7
‡ to 3ft (1m) ↔ to 2ft (60cm)

DAHLIA
'Fascination'

Perennial

Dahlias provide a late burst of color
after early-flowering perennials are past
their best. 'Fascination' is a dwarf form
with bronze-tinged leaves and purple-
pink flowers. It can be used as a
bedding plant at the front of a border,
and it makes a good cut flower. Grow it
in full sun in fertile, well-drained soil.
Dig up the tubers after the first frost,
pack them in boxes of dry sand or
compost, and overwinter them in a
frost-free place. Plant out in late spring.

◊ ☼ Z8–10 H12–1
‡ to 18in (45cm) ↔ to 12in (30cm)

DIANTHUS
GRATIANOPOLITANUS

Perennial

The Cheddar pink is a compact, low-growing evergreen that forms a carpet of waxy, narrow, gray-green leaves. In late summer, solitary, very fragrant pink or red flowers with toothed petals are borne on short stems. It will flourish in a rock garden, raised bed, or trough and should be planted in well-drained, gritty soil in full sun.

◊ ☼ *f* Z4–9 H9–1
‡ to 6in (15cm) ↔ to 12in (30cm)

DIASCIA BARBERAE
'Blackthorn Apricot'

Perennial

This mat-forming plant produces masses of apricot-pink flowers in summer and autumn and is ideal for the front of a herbaceous border or in a rock garden or container. Diascias grow well in full sun in moist, well-drained, fertile soil and need protection in cold, wet winters. Other excellent forms include 'Salmon Supreme', with larger, pale apricot flowers, and 'Ruby Field', which produces deep salmon-pink flowers.

◊ ◐ ☼ Z8–9 H9–8
‡ to 10in (25cm) ↔ to 20in (50cm)

ECHINACEA PURPUREA

Perennial

The purple coneflower has tall, erect stems that bear slightly hairy, lance-shaped leaves. In late summer and early autumn it produces large, purplish pink, daisylike flowerheads with cone-shaped centers consisting of tiny but showy orange-brown flowers. It is ideal for the middle or back of a border. Provide full sun and a deep, well-drained soil. Good for cutting.

◊ ☼ Z3–9 H9–1
↕ to 5ft (1.5m) ↔ to 18in (45cm)

ERICA CILIARIS
'Corfe Castle'

Evergreen shrub

This Dorset heath bears rose-pink flowers from midsummer to the middle of autumn. In winter the midgreen foliage has a bronze tone, and its spreading stems make a good ground-cover. *Erica ciliaris* and its cultivars should be planted in an open, sunny situation in acidic, well-drained soil. Cut back the plants in spring to keep them neat, and remove dead flowers.

◊ ☼ Z8–9 H9–8
↕ to 9in (22cm) ↔ to 14in (35cm)

ERICA CINEREA
'C.D. Eason'

Evergreen shrub

The bell heathers are grown for their
needlelike, evergreen leaves and small,
urn-shaped flowers. There are many
attractive forms, but 'C.D. Eason' is
one of the best, bearing masses of
bright magenta flowers from the middle
of summer to early autumn. It should
be planted in full sun and well-drained,
acidic soil. Cut back the plants in spring
to keep them compact, and remove
faded flowers.

◊ ☼ Z6–8 H8–6
‡ to 10in (25cm) ↔ to 20in (50cm)

ERIGERON KARVINSKIANUS

Perennial

This carpeting plant produces spreading
stems and grayish green, lance-shaped
leaves. The pretty, daisylike flowers,
which appear in summer, are solitary
or produced in groups of up to five
white or pink blooms that darken
to reddish purple as they age. It should
be planted in full sun in moist but well-
drained soil. The blooms will liven up
a rock garden or the front of a border,
and it is ideal for planting in cracks
and crevices in walls and paving.
Once established, it spreads freely.

◊ ☼ Z5–7 H7–5
‡ to 12in (30cm) ↔ to 3ft (1m)

EUPATORIUM PURPUREUM *'Atropurpureum'*

Perennial

This Joe Pye weed is an imposing plant with very strong, reddish purple stems and pointed, lance-shaped, purple-tinged green leaves. The large heads of pinkish purple flowers appear from midsummer to early autumn. It is a useful plant for the back of a large, late-summer border and blends well with grasses such as *Miscanthus*. It enjoys damp, slightly alkaline soil in full sun or partial shade.

◐ ☼ ☼ Z3–9 H9–1
‡ to 7ft (2.2m) ↔ to 3ft (1m)

FILIPENDULA RUBRA *'Venusta'*

Perennial

Queen of the prairie is a spreading perennial with architectural, deeply cut, midgreen foliage. In summer it produces branched stems bearing clusters of tiny, fragrant, deep rose-pink flowers. It is a bog plant and needs to be sited in partial shade, although it tolerates full sun in permanently moist soil. Grow close to a pond margin or in damp ground beneath deciduous trees; it will thrive in a herbaceous border only if the soil never dries out.

◐ ◑ ☼ ☼ *f* Z3–9 H9–1
‡ to 8ft (2.5m) ↔ to 4ft (1.2m)

FUCHSIA
'Leonora'

Deciduous shrub

A free-flowering, upright fuchsia that has bell-shaped, soft pink flowers with reflexed outer sepals. It is a good choice for a patio container; use soil-based potting mix, and position it in full sun or light shade. In summer, water well, and fertilize regularly with a balanced fertilizer (or use a slow-release fertilizer upon potting). Keep it frost-free over winter, moving it outside after frosts are over. New plants are easy to raise from softwood cuttings in spring.

◊ ◊ ☼ ☼ Z8–10 H8–1
↕ to 30in (75cm) ↔ to 24in (60cm)

GAURA LINDHEIMERI
'Siskiyou Pink'

Perennial

This robust plant has branched stems and forms a clump of narrow lance- or spoon-shaped leaves. The flowers of 'Siskiyou Pink' are white, heavily flushed with deep pink. They first appear in late spring but reach their peak in late summer and continue into early autumn. This long-flowering plant is perfect for the front of a sunny border and needs a fertile, moist, well-drained soil. It will tolerate partial shade and dry soil during summer.

◊ ◊ ☼ ☼ Z6–9 H9–6
↕ to 4ft (1.2m) ↔ to 3ft (1m)

HEBE
'Great Orme'

Evergreen shrub

There are over 75 species of hebe, all
suitable for coastal gardens. This one
forms a rounded bush with purple
shoots and glossy leaves. From
midsummer to midautumn it produces
spikes of pink flowers that fade to
white as they age. It is a medium-sized
shrub that can add year-round interest
to a mixed border. Plant it in a sunny
or partially shaded position in well-
drained soil. No pruning is necessary.

○ ◑ ☼ ☀ Z9–10 H10–9
↕↔ to 4ft (1.2m)

HYDRANGEA PANICULATA
Pink Diamond

Deciduous shrub

In late summer and early autumn this
spreading hydrangea bears large, cone-
shaped flowerheads that open creamy
white but then turn deep pink as they
age. It should be planted in a moist,
well-drained, fertile soil in sun or partial
shade. No pruning is necessary, but
flowering is improved by cutting back
stems in early spring to a permanent
framework of branches.

○ ◑ ☼ ☀ Z4–8 H8–1
↕ to 22ft (7m) ↔ to 8ft (2.5m)

HYDRANGEA VILLOSA

Deciduous shrub

This delightful spreading plant is much loved by garden designers for its lance-shaped, velvety, midgreen leaves and large, flat flowerheads. In summer, masses of tiny, bluish purple fertile flowers are borne, surrounded by larger, lilac-pink sterile blooms. It can be grown as a specimen plant or in a mixed border. This hydrangea will thrive when grown in sun or partial shade and moist, well-drained soil. Little pruning is needed apart from deadheading in spring.

◊ ◑ ☼ ◔ Z7–9 H9–7
↔ to 10ft (3m)

INDIGOFERA DIELSIANA

Deciduous shrub

The dark green leaves of this medium-sized bush are composed of many small, compound leaves that contrast well with the pealike, pale reddish pink flowers produced from summer to early autumn. It does well when planted in fertile, moist, well-drained soil.
The stems produce an orange-yellow latex that may irritate the skin.

◊ ☼ Z6–9 H9–6
‡↔ to 5ft (1.5m)

LATHYRUS LATIFOLIUS

Climber

The everlasting pea is a herbaceous climber with branched stems and pairs of blue-green leaflets. The leaves terminate in tendrils that enable the plant to scramble through shrubs or climb over banks. In late summer and early autumn it bears clusters of pea-like, magenta-purple flowers. Plant it in fertile, well-drained soil in full sun or partial shade, and prune it to the ground in spring to encourage new stems; otherwise, leave undisturbed. Sow seed in autumn.

◊ ☼ ☼ Z5–9 H9–5
‡ to 6ft (2m)

LATHYRUS ODORATUS
'Jayne Amanda'

Climber

'Jayne Amanda' is a superb sweet pea that can be trained up stakes or over tripods. The branched stems bear pairs of leaves and delicate tendrils. In the summer it produces an abundance of highly fragrant, deep pink flowers. Plant it in full sun or dappled shade in fertile, well-drained soil. Cut flowers regularly to prolong flowering, and deadhead when necessary. Seed can be sown under cover in autumn or spring. Plant out young plants in late spring.

◊ ◊ ☼ ☼ *f* Z5–9 H9–5
‡ to 10ft (3m)

LILIUM
Pink Perfection Group

Bulbous perennial

These lilies have large, slightly nodding, trumpet-shaped flowers held on tall, robust stems. The blooms are fragrant and have deep pinkish purple petals with swept-back tips. Plant these lilies in well-drained, fertile soil that has been enriched with leaf mold or well-rotted compost. They need a sunny position to thrive, with the base of the plant in shade. If using them as cut flowers, snip off the orange anthers, because the pollen stains badly.

◊ ☼ Z4–8 H8–1
‡ to 6ft (2m)

LONICERA PERCLYMENUM
'Serotina'

Climber

The late Dutch honeysuckle has woody, twining stems and grayish green leaves. In mid- to late summer it produces clusters of pink buds opening into highly fragrant, creamy white and purple-pink flowers. It can be grown over fences and pergolas, through trees and shrubs, or as a groundcover on a bank. Plant it in full sun or partial shade in fertile, moist but well-drained soil. Prune back after flowering to keep it within bounds.

◊ ◑ ☼ ◑ ƒ Z5–9 H9–5
‡ to 22ft (7m)

LYCHNIS CORONARIA

Biennial

The rose campion has lance-shaped, soft, downy, silver-gray leaves and stems, which in summer contrast beautifully with the bright magenta, rounded, flat-topped flowers. It self-seeds with abandon and is a welcome addition to garden beds or borders. Plant rose campion in full sun in slightly fertile, well-drained soil. Sow the seed in spring to flower the following year.

◊ ☼ Z4–8 H8–1
‡ to 32in (80cm) ↔ to 18in (45cm)

LYCHNIS FLOS-JOVIS

Perennial

The upright stems of the flower of Jove are covered with white hairs, giving them a silvery appearance, while the spoon-shaped, soft basal leaves are also silver-gray. From mid- to late summer clusters of pink, scarlet, or white flowers with deeply divided petals appear. This species is a good choice for the front of a sunny border or a gravel garden. Plant it in well-drained, slightly fertile soil. Sow seed in spring.

◊ ☼ Z6–9 H9–6
‡ to 24in (60cm) ↔ to 18in (45cm)

MACLEAYA MICROCARPA
'Kelway's Coral Plume'

Perennial

This unusual member of the poppy family is a spreading perennial with deeply lobed, grayish green leaves, the undersides of which are covered with a white felt. In late summer grayish green stems carry tall plumes of pinkish beige, feathery flowers. Plant it in the flower border or among shrubs in slightly fertile, moist, well-drained soil in full sun or light shade. Once established, it may spread vigorously

○ ◐ ☼ ☀ Z4–9 H9–1
‡ to 7ft (2.2m) ↔ to 3ft (1m)

NERIUM OLEANDER

Evergreen shrub

The oleander, or rose bay, forms an upright or rounded bush of narrow, grayish evergreen leaves. In summer it produces loose clusters of clear pink flowers (there are selections with white and red flowers as well). It is often grown in a container and moved to frost-free conditions under cover during the winter. Water it frequently during the warmer months, but keep the soil drier in winter. All parts of the plant are very toxic.

○ ☼ Z13–15 H12–1
‡↔ to 20ft (6m)

NICOTIANA
'Domino Salmon-pink'

Annual

This flowering tobacco has large, sticky basal leaves and narrow, lance-shaped stem leaves. In mid- to late summer, 'Domino Salmon-pink' is clothed with star-shaped, salmon-pink flowers that open up in the early evening and emit a delicate scent. Grow flowering tobacco in full sun or partial shade in fertile, moist, well-drained soil near a window or path where the fragrance can be enjoyed.

◊ ◑ ☼ ☀ *f* Z0 H9–1
‡ to 18in (45cm) ↔ to 16in (40cm)

ORIGANUM
'Kent Beauty'

Deciduous shrub

This semi-evergreen herb has creeping roots and a prostrate habit, and aromatic, rounded, bright green leaves. From midsummer it produces masses of small, tubular, pale-pink or mauve flowers surrounded by deep pink bracts. 'Kent Beauty' is perfect for a herb or gravel garden, patio pot, or the front of a herbaceous border. Plant it in full sun in moderately fertile, well-drained soil.

◊ ☼ *f* Z5–8 H8–5
‡ to 4in (10cm) ↔ to 8in (20cm)

PELARGONIUM
'Bird Dancer'

Perennial

This versatile geranium bears pointed
green leaves with a darker zone in the
center. The flowers are pale salmon-
pink and borne on long stems in open-
headed clusters from summer to
autumn. Its compact, neat habit makes
it ideal for a patio container or a sunny
windowbox, or train it as a mini-
standard. Grow it in fertile, well-drained
potting mix, or bed out in free-draining
garden soil. Move under cover for the
winter and keep fairly dry.

◊ ☼ ❋ Z8–11 H12–1
‡ to 8in (20cm) ↔ to 6in (15cm)

PELARGONIUM
'Clorinda'

Perennial

This vigorous scented-leaved geranium
has crinkled, evergreen foliage that
smells of cedar. Rounded clusters of
deep rose-pink flowers appear from
summer to autumn. Grow it in
containers in well-drained potting mix
in a position in sun or light shade.
Where not hardy, this geranium must
be overwintered in a frost-free
greenhouse or indoors. Alternatively,
root softwood cuttings of nonflowering
shoots from spring to autumn.

◊ ☼ ❋ ƒ Z0 H12–1
‡ to 20in (50cm) ↔ to 10in (25cm)

PENNISETUM SETACEUM *'Rubrum'*

Perennial

This beautiful grass has red leaves and feathery, purplish pink flowerheads that appear from midsummer. Plant it in a sunny border, gravel garden, or in a large container in full sun or partial shade in slightly fertile, well-drained soil. It is often best grown as an annual; raise it from small plants or seed sown in spring. Otherwise, overwinter under cover; divide the clump and plant out the following spring. 'Burgundy Giant' is a larger variety with purplish flowers.

○ ☼ Z9–11 H12–1
‡ to 3ft (1m) ↔ to 18in (45cm)

PENSTEMON *'Apple Blossom'*

Perennial

This penstemon bears spikes of elegant, tubular, light pink flowers with white throats from midsummer through autumn if the blooms are deadheaded regularly. It prefers a moist but free-draining soil in full sun or light shade and is perfect for a border with a pastel color theme. As a precaution against winter loss, take softwood cuttings in midsummer and overwinter the plants in a cold frame or cool greenhouse.

○ ☼ ◑ Z4–9 H9–1
‡ to 24in (60cm) ↔ to 24in (60cm)

PHLOX PANICULATA
'Windsor'

Perennial

The dense, conical heads of carmine-rose flowers with distinctive, deep red eyes are borne on this phlox in late summer above oval, midgreen leaves. Grow it in full sun or partial shade in well-drained, moist soil, and stake where necessary. Plant groups of this tall phlox in a herbaceous border or behind shorter plants in a gravel garden. Deadhead regularly in summer, and thin out weak shoots in spring for improved flowering.

◐ ☼ ☀ Z4–8 H8–1
↕ to 4ft (1.2m) ↔ to 36in (1m)

PHYSOSTEGIA VIRGINIANA
'Variegata'

Perennial

The obedient plant is unusual because its flower stalks are hinged, so that when the blooms are moved they stay in position. In summer, tall spikes bear small, mauve-pink, tubular flowers that will brighten up a border and are also good for cutting. The leaves are lance-shaped and midgreen, edged with white. Plant in sun or partial shade in moist soil.

◐ ☼ ☀ Z4–8 H8–1
↕ to 24in (60cm) ↔ to 12in (30cm)

RHODANTHE MANGLESII

Annual

This strawflower is a fast growing
annual ideal for cutting and drying.
It has pink, daisylike summer flowers
with papery petals and yellow centers,
and grayish green leaves. Grow it in a
sunny annual or mixed border in a
poor, well-drained soil. Sow the seed
outdoors *in situ* in midspring. To dry
the flowers, cut them as soon as the
buds begin to open, then hang them
upside down in bunches in a cool,
dry place out of the sun.

○ ☼ Z0 H8–1
‡ to 12in (30cm) ↔ to 6in (15cm)

SCHIZOSTYLIS COCCINEA *'Sunrise'*

Perennial

This kaffir lily produces tall spikes of
delicate, cup-shaped, soft pink flowers
in late summer and autumn. The
midgreen, narrow leaves are sword-
shaped, and both flowers and foliage
are excellent for indoor arrangements.
In the garden it is suited to sunny
borders and waterside plantings, or it
can be planted against sunny wall.
Grow in fertile, moist, well-drained soil
in full sun. Divide regularly in spring
to maintain the plant's vigor.

◑ ☼ Z7–9 H9–7
‡ to 24in (60cm) ↔ to 12in (30cm)

SEDUM SPECTABILE
'Brilliant'

Perennial

Excellent for the front of a sunny border, the ice plant is invaluable from late summer to autumn, when its flat heads of pink flowers open from green buds. They are attractive to bees and butterflies. The fleshy leaves are borne on upright stems and are a feature in their own right. Plant in any well-drained soil in sun. The flowerheads can be cut or left to stand over winter. Clear them in early spring, when large clumps can be divided.

◊ ☼ Z4–9 H9–1
‡↔ to 18in (45cm)

SPIRAEA JAPONICA
'Anthony Waterer'

Deciduous shrub

This medium-sized, twiggy shrub has small, lance-shaped leaves that emerge red and gradually turn dark green as they age. The foliage is occasionally tinged with cream or pink, too. The flat heads of purple buds open to frothy, dark pink flowers from mid- to late summer. Grow this spirea in a shrub or mixed border in full sun and any moderately fertile soil that does not completely dry out. Cut back lightly after flowering.

◊ ◑ ☼ Z4–9 H9–1
‡↔ to 5ft (1.5m)

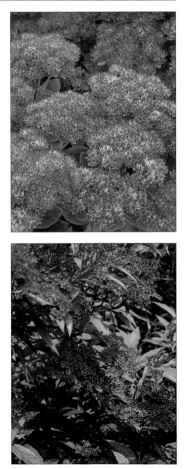

ASTER NOVAE-ANGLIAE
'Andenken an Alma Pötschke'

Perennial

New England asters are clump-forming perennials with erect, woody stems covered with midgreen, narrow, lance-shaped leaves. This variety bears dense sprays of salmon-red, daisylike flowers and is a superb plant for a late summer border. It is also good for cutting. Plant New England asters in full sun or light shade and fertile, moist, well-drained soil. They also benefit from support with twiggy sticks, or stakes and string. Divide clumps regularly in spring.

◊ ◑ ☼ ☀ Z4–8 H8–1
↕ to 4ft (1.2m) ↔ to 24in (60cm)

BEGONIA
Nonstop Series

Perennial

These compact tuberous begonias have heart-shaped, midgreen leaves and double flowers measuring up to 3in (8cm) across. They are available in a wide range of bright colors, including red, pink, yellow, and orange. Use them as bedding plants or in pots, and grow them in full sun to partial shade in fertile, moist, well-drained soil. The tubers must be dug up before the first frosts. Store them in dry sand in a cool room indoors.

◊ ◑ ☀ Z11–12 H8–1
↕ to 12in (30cm) ↔ to 12in (30cm)

BRACTEANTHA BRACTEATA

Annual

The strawflower has grayish green, lance-shaped leaves and flowers over a long period from late spring to mid-autumn. There are many good varieties available, but the Bright Bikini Series is among the best, with double flowers in a wide range of colors, including red, orange, and pink. This everlasting flower is a useful filler in a herbaceous border and is excellent for cutting or drying (cut before the flowers are fully open). Plant it in full sun and moist but well-drained soil.

◊ ◐ ☼ Z0 H8–1
↕ to 12in (30cm) ↔ to 12in (30cm)

CAMPSIS RADICANS

Climber

The common trumpet creeper has dark green leaves divided into many leaflets, and in late summer produces clusters of orange-red, trumpet-shaped flowers. It is best planted in full sun against a wall or fence, to which it will cling by aerial roots. Plant it in fertile, moist, well-drained soil. In warmer areas it will grow vigorously to cover a large area within a few seasons, and it fits in well in a tropical-style garden. Keep it clear of roofs and gutters, and prune it hard in winter to keep it in check.

◊ ◐ ☼ Z5–9 H9–5
↕ to 30ft (10m)

CANNA
'Assaut'

Perennial

Cannas are grown for their large, broad leaves and exotic-looking flowers. 'Assaut' has impressive purple-brown foliage and spikes of scarlet blooms. Cannas grow quickly and make a dramatic addition to a late summer border or tropical-style garden, or they can be grown in pots. Plant them in late spring in full sun and moist, well-drained soil. Where not hardy, the rhizomes must be overwintered in just-moist compost in a frost-free place.

◊ ◊ ☼ Z8–10 H12–1
‡ to 4ft (1.2m) ↔ to 2ft (60cm)

CHRYSANTHEMUM
'Cherry Chintz'

Perennial

'Cherry Chintz' produces huge, double blooms composed of many red petals. Plant it in a sheltered site in fertile, moist, well-drained soil, with well-rotted manure incorporated into it before planting. It is grown mostly for cutting and needs staking. Often grown in pots of soil-based mix under cover, it is also suitable for a sheltered, sunny patio or terrace. For the largest flowers, remove all but the terminal bud.

◊ ◊ ☼ Z3–9 H9–1
‡ to 4½ft (1.3m) ↔ to 30in (75cm)

CLEMATIS
'Niobe'

Climber

Possibly the best of all the red clematis, 'Niobe' has single, velvety, deep ruby red flowers with yellow stamens and blooms for a long period in summer. It will brighten up a trellis, or train it over an arch or up a post. Plant 'Niobe' in a fertile, well-drained soil in sun or partial shade, with the roots in shade. It does particularly well in alkaline soil. In early spring remove any dead or damaged growth, and cut the rest of the stems back to a strong pair of buds.

◊ ☼ ☀ Z4–9 H9–1
‡ to 10ft (3m)

COSMOS
ATROSANGUINEUS

Perennial

This Mexican plant has green, deeply lobed leaves, and from midsummer to early autumn produces masses of dark red, chocolate-scented, single flowers on reddish brown stems. Where it is marginally hardy, it should survive most winters if covered with a thick, loose layer of mulch. In very cold locations, dig up the tubers in autumn and store them during the winter in trays of slightly damp sand or compost. Plant it in full sun in moist, well-drained soil.

◊ ◊ ☼ ƒZ7–10 H10–1
‡ to 30in (75cm) ↔ to 18in (45cm)

CROCOSMIA
'Lucifer'

Perennial

This widely grown plant has dramatic midgreen leaves and from mid- to late summer produces arching stems bearing clusters of bright-red flowers. For the maximum effect, plant it in groups in a gravel garden or herbaceous border. It prefers full sun or partial shade and a moist, well-drained soil. When clumps become congested after a few years, divide them in autumn and replant the corms elsewhere. Where marginally hardy, apply a loose winter mulch.

◊ ◊◊ ☼ ☀ Z6–9 H9–6
‡ to 3ft (1m) ↔ to 10in (25cm)

DAHLIA
'Bishop of Llandaff'

Perennial

This superb dahlia is grown as much for its reddish black foliage as for its bright red, semidouble flowers, which appear from midsummer to early autumn. Plant it in full sun in fertile, moist, well-drained soil, and deadhead regularly. Dig up dahlia tubers after the first frost, and store them during the winter in dry sand in a frost-free place. Plant them out in mid- to late spring, with the top of the tuber about 3in (8cm) below the surface.

◊ ◊◊ ☼ Z8–11 H12–1
‡ to 3ft (1m) ↔ to 18in (45cm)

DAHLIA
'Hillcrest Royal'

Perennial

The red-purple, cactus-type flowers of this striking dahlia are held on strong stems and make a dramatic statement in the middle of a herbaceous border. It needs a sunny site and fertile, moist, well-drained soil. Deadhead it regularly to promote the development of more flowers, and in summer fertilize with a general-purpose fertilizer. Lift the tubers and store them over winter in a frost-free place. Plant in mid- to late spring, and insert a stake at the same time.

◊ ◊ ☼ Z8–11 H12–1
↕ to 4ft (1.2m) ↔ to 24in (60cm)

DAHLIA
'Whale's Rhonda'

Perennial

A dark purple-red pompon dahlia, the petals of 'Whales Rhonda' have silver undersides, giving them a two-tone appearance. It is often grown for cut flower arrangements or for exhibitions. Plant in full sun in a moist, well-drained soil. It can also be planted in a large container. Lift and store the tubers as described for 'Bishop of Llandaff' (see left).

◊ ☼ Z8–11 H12–1
↕ to 3ft (1m) ↔ to 24in (60cm)

FUCHSIA
'Celia Smedley'

Deciduous shrub

This upright fuchsia produces flowers
with currant red petals and pink sepals
from the middle of summer. It can be
grown outside in sun or partial shade,
after the risk of frost has passed, in a
container of soil-based potting mix.
Fertilize it every month with a balanced
liquid fertilizer, or add a slow-release
fertilizer when planting. It is also
suitable for training as a standard.
Overwinter it in a frost-free greenhouse
or conservatory.

◊ ◊ ☼ ☼ Z8–11 H8–1
‡ to 30in (75cm) ↔ to 30in (75cm)

FUCHSIA
'Golden Marinka'

Deciduous shrub

From midsummer to early autumn, this
trailing fuchsia produces bright red
flowers and yellow-variegated foliage.
Grow in full sun or partial shade. It can
be used as a groundcover or planted
in baskets of soilless potting mix or
containers of soil-based mix. In the
garden, grow it in moist, well-drained
soil. Fertilize fuchsias in containers every
two weeks with a balanced liquid
fertilizer, or mix in slow-release fertilizer
when planting.

◊ ◊ ☼ ☼ Z8–11 H8–1
‡ to 12in (30cm) ↔ to 18 in (45cm)

FUCHSIA MAGELLANICA *'Thompsonii'*

Deciduous shrub

A fuchsia with small red flowers that begin to appear in midsummer, this plant can be grown as a hedge or a shrubby specimen in a border. Where marginally hardy, mulch it for the winter. Cut out dead stems in spring, and pinch out the soft tips of the stems to encourage bushy growth. It is suitable for training as a standard, or grow it in a large pot. Plant it in a sheltered position in moist, free-draining soil in sun or partial shade.

◊ ◊ ☼ ☀ Z8–11 H8–1
‡ to 10ft (3m) ↔ to 6ft (2m)

GREVILLEA ROSMARINIFOLIA

Evergreen shrub

This shrub from Australia has ascending or arching stems covered with clusters of narrow, dark green leaves with silky hairs on the undersides. In summer it produces clusters of spiderlike red, pink, or creamy white flowers. Whre marginally hardy, plant it in a sheltered, sunny spot, such as by a wall, in free-draining neutral to acidic soil, and mulch it over winter. Alternatively, grow it in containers of gritty, acidic soil mix and bring it inside for winter.

◊ ☼ Z9–11 H12–6
‡ to 6ft (2m) ↔ to 6ft (2m)

KNAUTIA MACEDONICA

Perennial

This clump-forming, often short-lived plant forms a rosette of hairy, lobed, basal leaves, and in summer it produces branched stems that bear deeply divided leaves and small, pincushion-shaped heads of tiny, dark red flowers. Attractive to bees, it is perfect for a wild garden, herbaceous border, or cottage garden. It will flourish in full sun in a well-drained, preferably alkaline soil.

⬥ ☼ Z5–9 H9–5

‡ to 30in (75cm) ↔ to 24in (60cm)

LATHYRUS ODORATUS
'Red Ensign'

Climber

This sweet pea carries sweetly scented, scarlet-red flowers from summer to late autumn. It can be grown up a stake pyramid in a border for instant height, or train it against a trellis. Cut the flowers regularly to cause more to develop. Grow sweet peas in full sun in moist, well-drained soil with well-rotted manure incorporated into it. Sow the seeds in pots in autumn to overwinter in a cold frame for planting out in spring, or sow *in situ* in spring.

⬥ ☼ *f*Z0 H8–1

‡ to 6ft (2m)

LILIUM SPECIOSUM
VAR. RUBRUM

Bulbous perennial

This tall lily has erect, purple-flushed stems and lance-shaped, dark green leaves. In late summer it produces up to a dozen fragrant, slightly pendent, turk's-cap flowers with swept-back petals. The deep carmine-red blooms are marked with darker red spots and have very long stamens. This lily grows well in moist, well-drained, slightly acidic soil in partial shade and will thrive in a woodland garden.

◊ ◊ ☼ *f* Z4–8 H8–1
‡ to 5½ft (1.7m)

LOBELIA
'Cherry Ripe'

Perennial

'Cherry Ripe' has narrow, deep green leaves and spikes of bright cherry red flowers. It will bring a splash of color to a damp herbaceous border, woodland, or the margins of a pond. For a spectacular effect, plant a group of five or more in moist soil and full sun. Lobelias are very vulnerable to damage by slugs and snails in spring – a ring of wood ashes or diatomaceous earth around the new shoots may deter them.

◊ ☼ Z3–8 H8–1
‡ to 3ft (1m) ↔ to 9in (23cm)

LYCHNIS CHALCEDONICA

Perennial

Maltese cross forms a clump of evergreen basal leaves, above which domed heads of small scarlet flowers appear on tall, hairy flower stems. The stems of this plant are rather weak, so it will need to be staked if it is grown in an exposed site. It is ideal for a herbaceous border or a gravel or wild garden, and it should be planted in moist, well-drained soil in full sun or dappled shade.

◊ ◊ ☼ ☀ Z4–8 H8–1
‡ to 4ft (1.2m) ↔ to 12in (30cm)

PELARGONIUM
'Brockbury Scarlet'

Perennial

This erect geranium has rounded leaves zoned with darker green. It produces clusters of spiky, single scarlet flowers, which should be deadheaded regularly to keep the show going. Geraniums are widely grown in containers or used as bedding. When grown in the open garden, plant them in full sun in well-drained, fertile soil, then discard them or pot them up to overwinter in a frost-free greenhouse or on a windowsill.

☼ ◊ Z9–11 H12–1
‡ to 12in (30cm) ↔ to 8in (20cm)

PELARGONIUM
'Voodoo'

Perennial

This tall, shrubby geranium produces
clusters of single, bright red flowers with
purplish black centers in summer and
early autumn. Plant it in a container and
place it in a sheltered, sunny location on
a patio or terrace. Deadhead regularly,
and fertilize it occasionally with a tomato
fertilizer when it is in flower .

◊ ☼ Z9–11 H12–1
‡ to 24in (60cm) ↔ to 10in (25cm)

PENSTEMON
'Chester Scarlet'

Perennial

In late summer and up to the first
frosts, this beautiful penstemon
produces tall spikes of bell-shaped
scarlet flowers. It should be planted in
full sun or partial shade in fertile, well-
drained soil and is suitable for a herbaceous border. Deadhead it regularly
to prolong the flowering period. It is
easy to propagate from softwood
cuttings taken in early summer.

◊ ☼ ◐ Z6–9 H9–6
‡ to 36in (90cm) ↔ to 30in (75cm)

PHYGELIUS × RECTUS
African Queen

Evergreen shrub

In late summer, this upright plant bears tall spires of pendent, pale red flowers above lance-shaped, dark green leaves. It should be planted in fertile, free-draining soil in a border among shrubs, or against a sunny wall. Where marginally hardy, it is best to treat this frost-tender shrub as a herbaceous perennial: cover with a thick but loose mulch in autumn, then cut the stems down to the ground in spring.

◊ ◑ ☼ Z8–9 H9–8
↕ to 3ft (1m) ↔ to 4ft (1.2m)

RICINUS COMMUNIS
'Carmencita'

Annual

Castor beans are usually grown for their large, architectural, palm-shaped leaves. This variety has dark bronzy red foliage, and in late summer it produces tall spikes of small, bright red flowers. It should be planted in full sun in fertile, well-drained soil and is useful in bedding designs and tropical-style gardens. It can also be grown in a large container. All parts of this plant are highly toxic.

◊ ☼ Z0 H12–1
↕ to 5ft (1.5m) ↔ to 3ft (90cm)

SALVIA COCCINEA
'Lady in Red'

Perennial

This tender South American perennial is usually treated as an annual in colder areas. It has erect stems and oval or heart-shaped dark green leaves, and in summer and autumn it produces spikes of bright red flowers. Plant it in a sunny position in light, well-drained soil. This bushy salvia works well at the front of a herbaceous border, or use it as a bedding or container plant. Sow seeds in spring for flowers the same year.

◊ ☼ Z0 H12–1
↕ to 24in (60cm) ↔ to 12in (30cm)

SALVIA SPLENDENS
'Scarlet King'

Perennial

Scarlet sage is a perennial, but it is widely grown as an annual bedding plant. 'Scarlet King' has a compact habit and produces dense spikes of bright red flowers above slightly hairy, oval, dark green leaves. Grow it in groups in a sunny position in moist, well-drained soil or in containers. Plant out young plants in early summer after all risk of frost has passed.

◊ ◖ ☼ Z9–11 H12–1
↕ to 10in (25cm) ↔ to 14in (35cm)

SOLENOSTEMON SCUTELLARIOIDES

Perennial

Coleus is a tender plant grown primarily for its foliage. The most decorative varieties have toothed, usually variegated leaves in a range of bright colors, including red, burgundy, pink, yellow, green and near black. They bear spikes of small blue flowers, which should be removed before they open to retain the foliage effect. Plant them in light shade in pots of soil-based mix or as part of a bedding design in moist, well-drained soil.

◊ ◊ ☼ Z13–15 H12–1
‡ to 18in (45cm) ↔ to 12in (30cm)

TAGETES *'Cinnabar'*

Annual

One of many varieties of fast-growing French marigold, this has feathery, deeply divided, dark green leaves. From midsummer to early autumn it bears rusty red, single flowers with bright yellow eyes. Usually grown as an annual bedding plant or for containers, it should be planted in a sunny location in fertile, well-drained soil. Easy to raise from seed, it can be sown under cover in early spring, or *in situ* in late spring.

◊ ☼ Z0 H12–1
‡ to 12in (30cm) ↔ to 12in (30cm)

ZAUSCHNERIA CALIFORNICA
'Dublin'

Perennial

This California fuchsia forms a clump of
slightly hairy, grayish green, lance-shaped
leaves and bears large numbers of bright
red, tubular flowers on slightly arching
stems. Plant it in a gravel or rock garden,
at the front of a mixed border, or in the
gaps of a drystone wall in full sun and
reasonably fertile, well-drained soil.
It benefits from a protected site.

◊ ☼ Z8–10 H10–8
‡ to 12in (30cm) ↔ to 18in (45cm)

ZINNIA ELEGANS
'Ruffles'

Annual

A striking, upright, bushy plant with
egg- or lance-shaped, midgreen leaves,
'Ruffles' lives up to its name, bearing
frilly, pompon, fully double flowers in
a wide range of colors, including red.
Plant it in sun in any well-drained soil.
Use it as bedding, or plant it in groups
in a herbaceous border. Zinnias are
excellent for cutting.

◊ ☼ Z0 H12–1
‡ to 24in (60cm) ↔ to 12in (30cm)

ACONITUM
'Bressingham Spire'

Perennial

Monkshood is a tall, striking plant that thrives in woodland gardens and in herbaceous borders. It has glossy, dark green, deeply lobed leaves, and in late summer and early autumn it produces large spikes of deep violet-blue flowers It can be grown in full sun but will perform better in partial shade and moist soil. To maintain its vigor, dig it up and divide it after 3-4 years. All parts of this plant are very toxic.

◊ ☼ ☀ Z3–7 H7–1
‡ to 3ft (1m) ↔ to 20in (50cm)

ASTER X FRIKARTII
'Mönch'

Perennial

Considered by many people to be one of the best of the perennial asters, this form has bright lavender-blue, daisy-like flowers held on tall sturdy stems that rarely need staking. It flowers over a very long period from midsummer until the first frosts. An excellent addition to a herbaceous border, this aster needs a sunny site and well-drained, fertile soil. It can be propagated by division in spring.

◊ ☼ Z5–8 H8–5
‡ to 28in (70cm) ↔ to 16in (40cm)

ASTER NOVI-BELGII
'Chequers'

Perennial

Also known as 'Queen Charlotte', this vigorous plant will spread rapidly. The erect, branched stems bear dark green leaves; the purple, daisylike flowers with yellow eyes appear from late summer to early autumn. Plant this aster in rich, moist soil in full sun or partial shade in a border or gravel garden, and provide support from early summer with twiggy sticks, which will soon be covered by the foliage.

◊ ☼ Z4–8 H8–1
‡ to 36in (90cm) ↔ to 30in (75cm)

BUDDLEJA DAVIDII
'Dartmoor'

Deciduous shrub

This butterfly bush has long, arching branches and gray-green leaves. From mid- to late summer it produces large conical clusters of small, magenta-purple, fragrant flowers. Its flowers attract butterflies, making it is ideal for a wildlife garden; plant it close to a path or the house where the butterflies can be seen. It prefers full sun and a well-drained soil. Prune it hard in the spring to the ground or to a permanent framework.

◊ ☼ *f* Z6–9 H9–6
‡ to 10ft (3m) ↔ to 15ft (5m)

CLEMATIS
'Jackmanii'

Climber

From midsummer to the middle of autumn, this widely grown clematis bears an abundance of large, single, velvety, purple-violet flowers. Team it with roses on a pergola or arch, or train it up a trellis for late summer color. It will flourish in full sun or partial shade in fertile, moist, well-drained soil, with the roots in shade. Since it flowers on the current year's stems, it should be pruned back to about 8in (20cm) from the ground in early spring.

◊ ◊ ☼ ☀ Z4–9 H9–1
↕ to 10ft (3m)

CLEMATIS VITICELLA
'Purpurea Plena Elegans'

Climber

This variety of clematis has leathery, lobed leaves. In late summer it produces double, purplish mauve flowers with unusual ruffled petals. Plant it in full sun or partial shade in fertile, moist, well-drained soil. Train it over a pergola or arch, or grow it through a large shrub. It flowers on the current year's growth, so it should be cut back to strong buds just above the ground in early spring.

◊ ◊ ☼ ☀ Z5–9 H9–5
↕ to 12ft (4m)

DABOECIA CANTABRICA
'Bicolor'

Evergreen shrub

The leaves of the Cantabrian heath are larger than other heathers. The urn-shaped flowers are borne over a long period from summer to midautumn, and 'Bicolor' produces blooms in purple-pink, white, or striped on the same flower spike. Plant it in full sun or light shade in neutral or acidic, well-drained soil. It is suitable for a rock or heather garden and forms a colorful carpet when used as a groundcover.

◊ ☼ ☀ Z6–8 H8–6
‡ to 18in (45cm) ↔ to 24in (60cm)

FUCHSIA
'Auntie Jinks'

Deciduous shrub

From midsummer to midautumn this trailing plant produces flowers with deep pink tubes, pink-edged white sepals, and purple petals. For hanging baskets, use a soilless potting mix, while plants in containers are better grown in soil-based mix. Fertilize every two weeks with a balanced fertilizer. It is happy in full sun or partial shade. Where not hardy it must be overwintered in a bright, frost-free place. Easy to raise from softwood cuttings in spring.

◊ ◊ ☼ ☀ Z8–11 H12–1
‡ to 8in (20cm) ↔ to 16in (40cm)

FUCHSIA
'La Campanella'

Deciduous shrub

The trailing branches of this fuchsia bear midgreen leaves and masses of blooms from midsummer up to the first frosts. The semidouble flowers are pale pink and deep purple. Grow it in full sun or partial shade in hanging baskets filled with soilless potting mix; it can also be grown in a pot filled with a soil-based mix. Fertilize every other week with a balanced fertilizer.

○ ◐ ☼ ☀ Z8–11 H12–1
↕ to 12in (30cm) ↔ to 18in (45cm)

LAVANDULA ANGUSTIFOLIA
'Hidcote'

Evergreen shrub

This English lavender has narrow, silver-gray, aromatic leaves, and in mid- to late summer it produces spikes of highly fragrant, small purple flowers loved by bees. 'Hidcote' makes a good low hedge and is suitable for planting in a gravel garden. It needs a site in full sun and a slightly fertile, well-drained soil. Lavenders are easily propagated by taking semi-ripe cuttings in summer. Trim hedges in spring and also lightly after flowering to keep them bushy.

○ ☼ *f* Z5–8 H9–3
↕ to 24in (60cm) ↔ to 30in (75cm)

LAVANDULA STOECHAS

Evergreen

French lavender forms an attractive, rounded shrub with branching stems covered with narrow, grayish green, slightly fragrant leaves. It is smaller and flowers slightly earlier than English lavender, but the blooms are not as fragrant. The small purple flowers, each topped by a tuft of pink-mauve, petal-like bracts, are produced throughout the summer. Grow in slightly fertile, well-drained soil or in containers.

◊ ☼ *f* Z8–9 H12–7
‡ to 24in (60cm) ↔ to 24in (60cm)

LIATRIS SPICATA

Perennial

Gayfeather is an attractive plant from the prairies of North America. It forms a tuft of narrow leaves measuring up to 16in (40cm) in length, and in summer into early autumn it produces tall spikes of feathery, pinkish purple flowers that are attractive to bees. The flower buds at the top of the spike open before those farther down. Plant it in full sun and very well-drained, reasonably fertile soil. It is not suitable for heavy clay soils, since the roots will rot if they get too wet.

◊ ☼ Z4–9 H9–1
‡ to 24in (60cm) ↔ to 12in (30cm)

LIMONIUM PLATYPHYLLUM

Perennial

Sea lavender forms a rosette of large, elliptic- or spoon-shaped, dark green leaves, over which appear dense, wiry, branched stems covered with clusters of tiny, tubular, lavender-blue flowers. It grows well in coastal areas, but the frothy sprays of flowers are a valuable addition to any mixed or herbaceous border. Plant three or five plants together for maximum impact, and grow them in full sun and sandy, well-drained soil. The cultivar 'Violetta' has deep violet flowers.

◊ ☼ Z4–9 H9–1
‡ to 24in (60cm) ↔ to 18in (45cm)

LOBELIA ERINUS
'Cascade Blue'

Perennial

This small, trailing lobelia flowers from summer to the middle of autumn. It is grown as an annual. It produces hundreds of tiny, two-lipped, dark blue flowers; similar selections with white, pink, red, purple, and violet flowers are available. All lobelias make superb plants for hanging baskets and for trailing over the edges of pots or windowboxes. Plant them in full sun or in partial shade, in which they last longer, and do not let them dry out.

◊ ☼ ☼ Z0 H7–1
‡ ↔ to 6in (15cm)

LOBELIA × GERARDII
'Vedrariensis'
Perennial

This tall, stately plant forms a rosette of elliptic- or lance-shaped, deep green leaves. The flower spikes appear in late summer and bear small, violet-purple, tubular flowers. Position three or five plants together in a group to maximize their impact, and plant them in moist, fertile soil that does not dry out, in full sun or partial shade. This lobelia is perfect for a late-summer border or for the margins of a water garden.

◑ ☼ Z8–9 H9–1
‡ to 3ft (1m) ↔ to 12in (30cm)

LYTHRUM SALICARIA
Perennial

Purple loosestrife is a vigorous, clump forming plant with lance-shaped, soft green leaves and spikes of small, star-shaped, reddish purple flowers. It needs moist soil and a sunny situation to do well and will flourish in a bog garden, damp border, or beside water. Note: lythrums have escaped into many wetland areas of North America and pose a serious threat to the stability of those habitats. It is strongly recommended that you do not plant lythrums if you live near a wetland.

◑ ☼ Z4–9 H9–1
‡ to 36in (1m) ↔ to 18in (45cm)

PASSIFLORA
'Amethyst'

Climber

This fast-growing passionflower bears
distinctive purple-blue flowers, followed
by large, oval orange fruits. Where not
hardy, grow this climber in a warm
greenhouse or a conservatory, where it
will form a leafy canopy when trained
on wires or other support. Plant it in a
container filled with soil-based potting
mix, and water it well in summer.
Prune back the vigorous growth in
spring to keep it within bounds.

◊ ◗ ☼ Z12–15 H12–1
‡ to 12ft (4m)

PENSTEMON
'Stapleford Gem'

Perennial

The bell-shaped flowers of this lilac-
purple penstemon are suffused with
shades of mauve, pink, and purple,
giving a multicolored effect. It blooms
from midsummer to early autumn and
needs full sun and a well-drained soil.
Penstemons are wonderful plants for a
herbaceous border, and this one works
well as part of a pastel color scheme.
'Stapleford Gem' is one of the hardiest
penstemons, but it will need a sheltered
spot and winter mulch where marginal.

◊ ☼ Z6–9 H9–6
‡ to 24in (60cm) ↔ to 18in (45cm)

STACHYS OFFICINALIS

Perennial

Wood betony is an attractive perennial that produces ground-covering rosettes of deeply veined leaves with scalloped edges. From early summer to early autumn it is adorned with spikes of tubular, reddish purple flowers. Its long flowering season makes it an ideal candidate for the front of a herbaceous border, or use it in a wild garden. Easy to grow, this betony prefers a sunny or lightly shaded position in well-drained, slightly fertile soil. Divide in autumn or spring.

◊ ☼ ☀ Z5–8 H8–5
↕ to 24in (60cm) ↔ to 18in (45cm)

THALICTRUM AQUILEGIIFOLIUM *'Thundercloud'*

Perennial

Meadow rues are clump-forming plants with fernlike foliage composed of small, rounded leaflets. 'Thundercloud' has erect, waxy stems and clusters of tiny flowers. The outer part of the flower quickly falls away to leave the colorful, dark purple stamens that give the blooms a frothy appearance. It may take some time to become established, and it prefers partial shade and deep, moist soil.

◖ ☀ Z5–9 H9–5
↕ to 3ft (1m) ↔ to 18in (45cm)

TRADESCANTIA
'Purple Dome'

Perennial

This clump-forming plant belongs to
the Andersoniana group of tradescantias
and has branching stems and narrow,
strappy leaves. In summer to early
autumn it produces clusters of small,
deep purple flowers with three
triangular petals and fluffy purple
stamens. Plant it *en masse* in a mixed or
herbaceous border, in full sun or partial
shade and a moist, fertile soil. Divide
large clumps in autumn or spring.

◊ ☼ ◐ Z5–9 H9–5
‡ to 24in (60cm) ↔ to 18in (45cm)

TULBAGHIA VIOLACEA

Bulbous perennial

This South African plant forms clumps
of narrow, grayish green leaves, and
from midsummer to early autumn it
produces wiry stems that bear clusters
of fragrant, star-shaped, lilac-blue
flowers. Grow in slightly fertile, well-
drained soil; where temperatures dip
well below freezing for long periods,
grow it in a container filled with soil-
based potting mix, and overwinter it in
a cool greenhouse or conservatory.

◊ ☼ *f*Z7–11 H12–1
‡ to 24in (60cm) ↔ to 12in (30cm)

VERBENA BONARIENSIS

Perennial

The tall, airy, branched stems of this verbena hold aloft small, domed clusters of tiny, lilac-purple flowers that appear from midsummer to early autumn. Individual plants come into their own when planted in a group and can be positioned at the front, middle, or back of the border or in a gravel garden. It needs full sun and fertile, well-drained soil in a sheltered position. It can be grown as an annual, but those will flower later than established plants. Attractive to butterflies.

◊ ☼ *f*Z7–11 H12–1
‡ to 5ft (1.5m) ↔ to 2ft (60cm)

VIOLA
'Bowles' Black'

Perennial

This short-lived, clump-forming pansy is more often grown as a biennial. It is quite vigorous and produces a mat of short stems covered with lobed, oval leaves. The flowers open from spring to autumn and are a very deep shade of violet, which can appear almost black. A good plant for a rock garden, gravel garden, sunny bank, or pot, this viola needs a sunny position and a well-drained, reasonably fertile soil.

◊ ☼ Z4–8 H8–1
‡ to 6in (15cm) ↔ to 3in (8cm)

AGAPANTHUS
'Blue Giant'

Perennial

This African blue lily is impossible to
overlook in the late summer garden. It
forms a clump of arching, deep green,
strap-shaped leaves and large, spherical
flowerheads held on tall, stiff stems.
'Blue Giant' is exceptionally large, with
huge balls of deep blue, bell-shaped
flowers. It should be grown in a sunny,
sheltered position in fertile, moist, well-
drained soil. Where marginally hardy,
protect it with a loose, thick layer of
mulch in winter.

◊ ◊ ☼ Z8–11 H12–1
‡ to 4ft (1.2m) ↔ to 24in (60cm)

ASTER AMELLUS
'King George'

Perennial

This species prefers drier conditions
than the popular New England and
New York asters, and it thrives in
alkaline soil. It has small, midgreen
leaves, and from late summer to late
autumn it produces loose clusters of
light violet-blue, daisylike flowers. Plant
it in groups in a sunny herbaceous or
mixed border in reasonably fertile, well
drained soil. Divide clumps every three
to four years in spring to keep plants
growing vigorously.

◊ ☼ Z5–8 H8–5
‡ ↔ to 18in (45cm)

BRACHYSCOME IBERIDIFOLIA

Annual

The Swan River daisy is a bushy, sprawling plant with deeply divided, grayish green, ferny foliage. From mid- to late summer it produces slightly scented, daisylike blue, violet, or white flowers. An excellent plant for edging summer containers, including hanging baskets, it will also bring color to the front of a herbaceous border. The seed should be sown under cover in spring, then young plants moved out after the last frost to a sunny position and well-drained, fertile soil.

◊ ◊ ☼ ƒ Z12–13 H12–1
‡ to 18in (45cm) ↔ to 14in (35cm)

CAMPANULA COCHLEARIIFOLIA

Perennial

Known as fairies' thimbles, this dwarf campanula forms rosettes of toothed, bright green leaves, and in summer produces masses of slightly pendent, pale blue or white flowers. It will add color and interest to a rock garden or the gaps in paving or a drystone wall, flourishing in the well-drained soil both sites provide. It can be grown in full sun or partial shade, and, although it may become rather invasive, it is easy to control by pulling up surplus growth.

◊ ☼ ◑ Z5–7 H7–5
‡ to 3in (8cm) ↔ to 12in (30cm)

CARYOPTERIS X CLANDONENSIS *'Heavenly Blue'*

Deciduous shrub

This free-flowering plant with aromatic, grayish green foliage bears clusters of deep blue flowers. It provides color and form in a mixed border or gravel garden, and it needs full sun and a sheltered site in well-drained soil. Prune it back hard in spring, taking care not to cut too far into old wood, from which it may not regrow.

◊ ☼ *f* Z6–9 H9–6
‡ to 3ft (1m) ↔ to 3ft (1m)

CATANANCHE CAERULEA *'Major'*

Perennial

Cupid's dart is a short-lived perennial that is often grown as biennial. It looks like a cornflower with oblong, lilac-blue petals with serrated tips and a dark blue center. Plant it in a sunny position in well-drained soil at the front or in the middle of a herbaceous border. It does not grow very well in heavy soils, in which it may die at the end of the season.

◊ ☼ Z3–8 H8–1
‡ to 24in (60cm) ↔ to 12in (30cm)

CEANOTHUS
'Autumnal Blue'

Evergreen shrub

Although many *Ceanothus* are spring-flowering, some perform later in the year. 'Autumnal Blue' bears bright blue flowers from late summer until autumn. It is one of the hardiest evergreen ceanothus and forms a round bush that can also be wall trained, a particularly suitable way of growing it where it is marginaly hardy. It grows best in well-drained, fertile soil and sunny position, sheltered from wind. Prune in spring to keep it in shape.

◊ ☼ Z9–11 H12–1
↕↔ to 10ft (3m)

CEANOTHUS
'Burkwoodii'

Evergreen shrub

Compact clusters of tiny, bright blue flowers are borne on this medium-sized bush from late summer to early autumn. It also produces attractive oval, glossy, dark evergreen foliage. This ceanothus will thrive and grow larger than indicated when planted against a west- or south-facing wall, sheltered from cold winds. It prefers a well-drained, fertile soil and should be pruned lightly in spring to help maintain its shape.

◊ ☼ Z9–11 H12–1
↕ to 5ft (1.5m) ↔ to 6ft (2m)

EICHHORNIA CRASSIPES

Perennial

The water hyacinth is a floating aquatic plant that forms rosettes of glossy green leaves. In warm areas it will produce a spike of pale blue or violet flowers. It has become a waterway nuisance in many parts of the world, but it is safe to introduce it into ponds in areas where it is not hardy. Overwinter in an aquarium of moist soil mix at a minimum temperature of 59°F (15°C) in good light, such as a windowsill. Alternatively, buy new plants each year in late spring.

◗ ☼ Z14 H12–1
‡↔ to 45in (18cm)

FELICIA AMELLOIDES
'Santa Anita'

Evergreen shrub

The blue daisy is often grown as an annual in cooler climates. It is bushy and compact, with oval, deep green leaves. From the middle of summer to autumn it bears bright blue, daisylike flowers with yellow centers. It can be grown in containers or as summer bedding, although it may survive in sheltered areas where marginally hardy. Plant it in full sun in any well-drained soil. Pinch out the shoot tips in the spring to promote more flowers.

◊ ☼ Z13–15 H12–1
‡↔ to 12in (60cm)

FELICIA BERGERIANA

Annual

The kingfisher daisy looks like a small
aster, with its single blue flowers with
bright yellow eyes and grayish green,
lance-shaped leaves. It is an excellent
plant for summer containers or for the
front of a raised bed. Grow it in a
sunny position in any well-drained soil
or in containers filled with soil-based
potting mix.

◊ ☼ Z0 H12–1
↕↔ to 6in (15cm)

GENTIANA ASCLEPIADEA

Perennial

An erect herbaceous plant, the willow
gentian forms a clump of lance-shaped
leaves, and from late summer to early
autumn it produces clusters of beautiful
deep blue, funnel-shaped flowers.
A good plant for a lightly shaded
border, it prefers permanently moist
but well-drained soil rich in organic
matter. There is also an attractive white
form called 'Alba'. To propagate it,
divide the clumps in spring.

◑ ☼ Z6–9 H9–6
↕ to 36in (90cm) ↔ to 18in (45cm)

HIBISCUS SYRIACUS
'Oiseau Bleu'

Deciduous shrub

This rose of Sharon makes a cheerful
addition to a shrub or mixed border.
It has upright to arching branches and
toothed, lobed, midgreen leaves that
appear late in spring. From midsummer
to frost it produces deep blue, trumpet-
shaped flowers. Plant it in full sun
and moist, well-drained, reasonably
fertile soil.

◊ ◊ ☼ Z5–9 H9–5
↕ to 10ft (3m) ↔ to 6ft (2m)

HYDRANGEA MACROPHYLLA
'Blue Wave'

Deciduous shrub

This lacecap hydrangea makes a
rounded shrub with large green leaves
and flat flowerheads that appear from
mid- to late summer. The blooms are
made up of small, dark blue fertile
flowers surrounded by large, pale blue
sterile flowers. In acidic soil the flowers
turn a rich shade of gentian blue, but in
alkaline soil they are mauve-pink. Plant
it in full sun or partial shade in moist,
well-drained, fertile soil rich in organic
matter. Suitable for coastal gardens.

◊ ◊ ☼ ☀ Z6–9 H9–6
↕ to 6ft (2m) ↔ to 8ft (2.5m)

HYDRANGEA SERRATA
'Bluebird'

Deciduous shrub

This compact hydrangea has bright
green leaves. From late summer to early
autumn it bears large, flat flowerheads
of tiny, deep blue fertile flowers
surrounded by larger, pale blue infertile
flowers, which may be pink in alkaline
soil. Ideal for a shrub or mixed border
in a small garden, it grows well in full
sun or partial shade and moist but well-
drained, fertile soil, preferably neutral
or slightly acidic for the best blue
flower color.

◊ ◊ ☼ ☼ Z6–9 H9–6
‡↔ to 4ft (1.2m)

HYSSOPUS OFFICINALIS

Evergreen shrub

Hyssop is a small, bushy herb with
narrow, midgreen, aromatic leaves and
deep blue flowers arranged on a spike;
they appear from late summer to early
autumn. Hyssop makes a superb plant
for an herb, gravel, rock, or wild
garden, where it will attract bees and
other nectar-seeking insects. It thrives in
full sun and fertile, well-drained neutral
or alkaline soil. Prune it lightly after
flowering to keep it neat. There are
also forms with white or pink flowers.

◊ ☼ *f* Z6–9 H9–6
‡ to 2ft (60cm) ↔ to 3ft (1m)

IPOMOEA
'Heavenly Blue'

Climber

This popular morning glory has fast-growing twining stems, heart-shaped, light green leaves, and large, funnel-shaped, sky blue flowers with white throats. Sow seeds of this eye-catching annual climber outside in mid- to late spring in full sun and well-drained soil. Provide support in the form of a tripod or use it to clothe an arch or a trellis, or grow it in a large container.

◊ ☼ Z0 H12–1
↕ to 12ft (4m)

LATHYRUS NERVOSUS

Climber

Lord Anson's blue pea, a perennial, is often grown as an annual. In late summer it bears fragrant, indigo blue flowers. Each leaf is split into a pair of grayish green leaflets. It will quickly ascend a support when grown in full sun and a well-drained, fertile soil. Sow seeds in early spring, and plant it out in late spring or early in summer.

◊ ☼ *f* Z3–10 H10–1
↕ to 15ft (5m)

LATHYRUS ODORATUS
'Noel Sutton'

Annual

'Noel Sutton' is a vigorous sweet pea that can be grown up supporting stakes or a trellis. If shoot tips are pinched out while the plant is young, it will form a much smaller bush suitable for a container. In summer the stems are covered with sweetly fragrant, mauve-blue flowers, which should be picked regularly to promote new blooms. Plant it in sun or light shade in moist, well-drained soil rich in organic matter.

◊ ◐ ☼ ☽ *f* Z0   H8–1
‡ to 8ft (2.5m)

LOBELIA SIPHILITICA

Perennial

The blue cardinal flower forms a rosette of egg-shaped, light green leaves. In summer it produces tall stems that bear tubular, bright blue blooms with double lips. It needs permanently moist, fertile soil and is happy in full sun or partial shade. It adds grace and elegance to a damp border or an area beneath deciduous trees, or grow it beside a pond. Divide it in spring.

◐ ☼ ☽ Z5–9   H9–5
‡ to 48in (120cm) ↔ to 12in (30cm)

NEMESIA STRUMOSA
'Blue Gem'

Annual

This vigorous, compact, bushy annual has spoon- or lance-shaped, toothed, slightly hairy leaves. In late summer it bears masses of small, bright blue flowers, making it a colorful bedding or container plant. It needs a site in full sun and moist, well-drained soil. It must be watered regularly during the summer if it is to produce a good display of flowers. Nemesias come in other colors, including red, yellow, and pink.

◊ ◊ ☼ Z0 H8–1
‡ to 12in (30cm) ↔ to 6in (15cm)

NEPETA SIBIRICA

Perennial

This relative of catmint is a vigorous plant with branched, upright stems and dark green, lance-shaped, toothed, aromatic foliage. Lavender-blue flowers appear on tall spikes and make a bold statement in a gravel garden or a herbaceous bed. As its name suggests, this plant comes from Siberia. It should be planted in spring in a sunny position and well-drained soil. Divide it in spring as well.

◊ ☼ Z3–8 H8–1
‡ to 36in (90cm) ↔ to 18in (45cm)

PEROVSKIA
'Blue Spire'

Deciduous shrub

This is an attractive, late flowering
subshrub with tall stems and silvery,
deeply dissected, aromatic foliage.
It produces branched spikes of small
lavender-blue flowers. It prefers a
sunny position and should be planted
in very well-drained soil in a gravel bed
or a herbaceous border, or use it in a
low hedge to edge a path. To keep it
bushy, cut back new growth in late
spring. It will tolerate alkaline soil and
coastal conditions.

◊ ☼ Z6–9 H9–6
↕ to 4ft (1.2m) ↔ to 3ft (1m)

PLATYCODON
GRANDIFLORUS

Perennial

The balloon flower is often mistaken
for a campanula, to which it is related.
The new shoots appear late in spring,
forming a clump of toothed, blue-green
foliage. Bell-shaped, purplish blue
flowers open from balloon-shaped
buds. Ideal for a rock garden or the
front of a border, it does not like to be
disturbed and should not be divided.
Plant it in full sun or partial shade in
moist, well-drained soil.

◊ ◐ ☼ ◑ Z4–9 H9–1
↕ to 24in (60cm) ↔ to 12in (30cm)

SALVIA FARINACEA 'Victoria'

Perennial

Although mealy sage is perennial, it is usually grown as an annual bedding plant. This erect, bushy plant has glossy, lance-shaped leaves that are white beneath, and attractive stems dusted white. It blooms from summer to autumn and bears spikes of deep blue flowers. Plant after danger of frost is past in a sunny border, or use as bedding in well-drained, moist soil. Mealy sage is best grown from seed each year.

◊ ◊ ◊ ☼ Z9–10 H10–9
‡ to 18in (45cm) ↔ to 12in (30cm)

SALVIA GUARANITICA 'Blue Enigma'

Perennial

This sage is usually grown as a tender perennial but will survive mild winters and grow to form a substantial clump of broad, lance-shaped leaves that smell of anise if crushed. From late summer the tall stems of 'Blue Enigma' bear spikes of tubular, deep blue flowers. When grown in large groups, it makes a spectacular display at the back of a border. Plant it in moist, well-drained soil in sun or light shade.

◊ ◊ ◊ ☼ ◑ Z5–8 H8–5
‡ to 5ft (1.5m) ↔ to 36in (90cm)

SALVIA ULIGINOSA

Perennial

The bog sage forms a clump of lance-shaped, midgreen leaves, above which tall, often floppy flower spikes bear clusters of pale blue flowers. A different source of color for the back of a moist border, it should be planted in full sun and moist soil.

◑ ☼ Z8–10 H10–8
↕ to 6ft (2m) ↔ to 36in (90cm)

SOLANUM RANTONNETII
'Royal Robe'

Evergreen shrub

The blue potato bush has wavy-edged, deep green leaves and clusters of large, violet-blue flowers with a bright yellow star in the center. The blooms are followed by red fruits in autumn. It is a tender plant but offers late-summer color when grown in a large container and moved out on to the patio. Plant it in soil-based potting mix and position it in bright, indirect light, because strong, full sun may scorch it.

◌ ☼ Z12–15 H12–1
↕ to 6ft (2m) ↔ to 6ft (2m)

STOKESIA LAEVIS
Evergreen perennial

Stokes' aster is an evergreen, clump-forming plant with long, lance-shaped leaves with a distinctive pale green midrib. From midsummer to early autumn it bears solitary cornflower-like blooms on sturdy stems. The outer petals are purplish blue, pink, or white; the pale varieties exhibit a darker center, while the dark forms have pale centers. 'Blue Star' has deep blue petals and a pale blue eye. Plant Stokes' asters in a sunny border in well-drained soil.

◊ ☼ Z5–9 H9–5
‡↔ to 18in (45cm)

TRADESCANTIA
'*J. C. Weguelin*'
Perennial

This clump-forming plant has narrow, lance-shaped, midgreen leaves held on branching stems. The blooms are composed of pale blue petals that surround fluffy stamens. It can be used at the front of a mixed or herbaceous border and should be planted in full sun or partial shade in moist, well-drained, fertile soil. It can be divided in spring or autumn.

◊ ☼ ☼ Z5–9 H9–5
‡ to 24in (60cm) ↔ to 18in (45cm)

VERONICA PROSTRATA

Perennial

The prostrate speedwell forms a low-
growing mat of small, toothed leaves
and short, upright stems clothed with
tiny, pale or deep blue blooms. It is
ideal for a rock garden or raised bed,
but it will also add interest to a gravel
garden or a drystone wall. Plant it in
full sun in slightly fertile, well-drained
soil. To propagate it, divide it in
autumn or spring.

◊ ☼ Z5–8 H8–5
‡ to 6in (15cm) ↔ to 16in (40cm)

VERONICA SPICATA

Perennial

This mat-forming plant has spreading
stems that root when they touch
the soil. It soon makes a dense clump
of linear, toothed leaves, and in late
summer it bears upright stems of small,
bright blue flowers with purple
stamens. Plant this veronica at the
front of a herbaceous border or in a
gravel garden in full sun or partial
shade and slightly fertile, moist,
well-drained soil. 'Rotfuchs' has
spikes of deep pink flowers.

◊ ◐ ☼ ◑ Z3–8 H8–1
‡ to 14in (40cm) ↔ to 18in (45cm)

AGAVE AMERICANA 'Variegata'

Perennial

This plant, ideal for a patio or tropical-style garden, forms a basal rosette of fleshy, lance-shaped, cream-edged leaves with spiny margins and pointed tips. The leaves grow upright, arch over, and finally lie flat on the ground. Plant in a large container of soil-based potting mix. Place it outside in summer, and move it indoors in winter. In the ground, provide well-drained, average soil in full sun.

○ ☼ Z12–15 H12–1
↕↔ to 5ft (1.5m)

DESCHAMPSIA CESPITOSA 'Goldtau'

Perennial grass

Tussock grass is a robust, evergreen plant with rigid, rough-edged green leaves. 'Goldtau' bears arching stems of yellow-green that turn golden brown as they age. This form is much more compact than other tussock grasses and is perfect for a herbaceous or wildflower garden. It is happy in full sun or partial shade and a moist or well-drained soil. Leave the dried flowerheads to decorate a winter garden, but remove them in spring.

○ ◐ ☼ ◑ Z5–9 H9–5
↕↔ to 30in (75cm)

ENSETE VENTRICOSUM

Perennial

The Ethiopian banana is a tender plant that bears huge, paddle-shaped leaves. It will insert an exotic look into a late summer border or tropical-style garden, placed in full sun or light shade. Fertilize and water it regularly when in growth. Where not hardy, grow it in a large pot of soil-based potting mix; it must be moved indoors and over-wintered in a heated greenhouse or conservatory with a minimum temperature of 45°F (7°C).

◊ ◊ ☼ ☀ Z11 H12–1
‡ to 20ft (6m) ↔ to 10ft (3m)

MELIANTHUS MAJOR

Evergreen shrub

The honey bush is usually treated as a herbaceous perennial or container plant. Grown for its foliage, it has beautiful, bluish green, featherlike leaves that are divided into several sharply toothed leaflets. The brown flowers are rather uninspiring. Plant it in a sunny position in moist, well-drained, fertile soil. Where marginally hardy, the top-growth usually dies back over winter, but if it is protected during winter with a thick, loose mulch it should resprout again in spring.

◊ ◊ ☼ Z8–10 H10–8
‡ ↔ to 10ft (3m)

MOLUCCELLA LAEVIS

Annual

Bells of Ireland bears deeply veined,
rounded, pale green leaves, and from
summer to autumn it produces stems of
tiny white flowers surrounded by large,
pale green cups. Its architectural flower
spikes make a dramatic statement in a
herbaceous border and are very useful
in flower arrangements, fresh or dried.
Plant it in full sun in fertile, moist, well-
drained soil. Sow seeds in spring.

◊ ◊ ☼ *f* Z0 H8–1
‡ to 36in (90cm) ↔ 9in (23cm)

NICOTIANA LANGSDORFFII

Annual

This flowering tobacco forms a rosette
of large, egg-shaped leaves at the base,
and in summer it produces apple green
flowers that dangle like slender bells
from the tall, branched, sticky stems.
It adds interest to the middle of a
herbaceous border and is ideal for
disguising the space left by spring
bulbs. Plant it in a sunny or lightly
shaded position in fertile, moist, well-
drained soil, and stake if necessary.

◊ ◊ ☼ ☼ Z0 H12–1
‡ to 5ft (1.5m) ↔ to 24in (60cm)

OSMANTHUS HETEROPHYLLUS *'Aureomarginatus'*

Evergreen shrub

This plant has spiny, toothed leaves that resemble those of a holly, making it an attractive choice for a hedge. 'Aureomarginatus' has glossy, bright green, mottled foliage edged in golden yellow. It bears small clusters of highly fragrant, tubular, small white flowers. Grow in full sun or partial shade in a sheltered position in fertile, well-drained soil.

◊ ☼ ☀ *f* Z7–9 H9–7
↕ to 15ft (5m) ↔ to 15ft (5m)

ZINNIA ELEGANS *'Envy'*

Annual

Most zinnias stand out because of their brightly colored flowers, but 'Envy' is more subtle, with semidouble, yellow-green blooms. It makes a good bedding or container plant and will perform well when grown in a sunny or lightly shaded position and fertile, moist, well-drained soil. The seed should be sown indoors in early spring, or *in situ* outside in late spring. Useful in flower arrangements because of its unusual color.

◊ ☼ ☀ Z0 H12–1
↕ to 24in (60cm) ↔ to 12in (30cm)

ARGEMONE MEXICANA

Annual

The prickly poppy is a tall, architectural annual with beautiful thistlelike, spiky, lobed foliage with silver veins. In late summer and early autumn pale or deep yellow poppylike flowers appear, their delicate petals contrasting well with the thorny leaves. The flowers are followed by attractive prickly seedheads that hold the highly toxic seeds. Grow this annual from seed in spring, and plant it in a sunny location in poor, dry soil. This poppy will add interest to a hot, dry gravel garden or herbaceous border.

◊ ☼ Z0 H9–1
‡ to 36in (1m) ↔ to 16in (40cm)

CANNA
'King Midas'

Perennial

Cannas hint at the exotic in a tropical-style garden or late summer border with their huge, paddle-shaped leaves and gladiolus-like flowers. 'King Midas' has dark green foliage that provides a foil for the clusters of large, golden yellow blooms. Plant out the rhizomes in late spring or early summer in full sun and moist, well-drained soil. In autumn, cut off the stems, dig up the rhizomes, and store them in trays of slightly damp compost or sand in a frost-free place.

◊ ♦ ☼ Z8–11 H12–1
‡ to 5ft (1.5m) ↔ to 20in (50cm)

CATALPA BIGNONIOIDES
'Aurea'

Deciduous tree

The golden form of the Indian bean
tree has spreading branches and large,
heart-shaped leaves. The young foliage
is bronze in spring but turns golden
yellow by the time the flowers appear
in midsummer. The candle-shaped
spikes of fragrant white flowers with
yellow and purple marks are followed
by dangling pods that last through
winter and give this tree its name. Plant
it in full sun, away from strong winds,
in deep, fertile, moist, well-drained soil.

◊ ◊ ☼ *f* Z5–9 H9–5
‡ to 30ft (10m) ↔ to 30ft (10m)

CEPHALARIA GIGANTEA

Perennial

The giant scabious is a clump-forming
perennial with large green leaves that
are divided into many small lance-
shaped leaflets. In summer it produces
tall, branched, erect stems that hold
large, primrose yellow flowers, the
outer petals of which surround a pincushion of smaller blooms. Plant it in
full sun and fertile, moist, well-drained
soil. It makes a superb, eyecatching
plant for the back of a herbaceous
border, needing plenty of space to
grow to its full potential.

◊ ◊ ☼ Z3–7 H7–1
‡ to 8ft (2.5m) ↔ to 24in (60cm)

CHRYSANTHEMUM
'Mary Stoker'

Perennial

In late summer and early autumn this hardy chrysanthemum bears single, apricot-yellow, daisylike flowers with green centers that turn yellow as they mature. The flowers are set off by the lobed, deep green leaves that have a slight silvery sheen. Plant it in a sunny, sheltered herbaceous or mixed border in well-drained soil. It often benefits from a thick, loose mulch in winter.

◊ ☼ Z7–9 H12–1
‡ to 4ft (1.2m) ↔ to 30in (75cm)

CROCOSMIA
'Citronella'

Cormous perennial

The clumps of sword-shaped leaves and arching spikes of lemon yellow flowers make this a perfect plant for a late-summer border or gravel garden. It prefers a sunny or partially shaded situation and fertile, moist, well-drained soil. Provide a light, loose winter mulch where marginally hardy. To maintain vigor, divide and lift the corms every three or four years in spring.

◊ ◊ ☼ ☀ Z6–9 H9–6
‡ to 30in (75cm) ↔ to 3in (8cm)

CROCOSMIA X CROCOSMIIFLORA *'Solfatare'*

Cormous perennial

The bronzy green leaves and clusters of apricot-yellow flowers that appear on slender, arching stems make this a very desirable plant for a border or gravel garden. It will grow well in full sun or partial shade and prefers moist, well-drained soil. The individual plants are quite small and are best planted in groups of three or five. Provide a loose, thick winter mulch where marginally hardy.

◊ ◊ ☼ ☀ Z6–9 H9–6
↕ to 28in (70cm) ↔ to 3in (8cm)

DAHLIA *'Yellow Hammer'*

Perennial

This tender perennial is usually grown as an annual bedding plant for its bronze-green leaves and clear yellow flowers. For a dazzling bedding display, plant it with other dwarf dahlias, or grow it in a herbaceous border or in containers. Providing it is deadheaded regularly, 'Yellow Hammer' will flower continuously up to the first frosts. Plant it in full sun in fertile, well-drained soil or soil-based potting mix.

◊ ☼ Z8–11 H12–1
↕ to 24in (60cm) ↔ to 18in (45cm)

GENTIANA LUTEA

Perennial

As implausible as it may seem, the dainty blue gentian is a relative of this tall, imposing plant. The yellow gentian is a herbaceous, clump-forming perennial with pleated, elliptic, bluish green leaves. Starry yellow flowers are borne in clusters on a tall, sturdy stem. Found growing wild in the dappled shade of deciduous woodland or beside a stream, this gentian needs a light soil that is moist but well-drained and neutral to acidic. It mixes well with ferns in a partially shaded border.

◊ ◊ ☀ Z7–8 H8–7
‡ to 5ft (1.5m) ↔ to 24in (60cm)

HEDYCHIUM GARDNERIANUM

Perennial

From the imposing spikes of fragrant flowers with their long red stamens to the lance-shaped, bluish green leaves, the Kahili ginger is every inch an exotic. It could be the star turn in a "hot" border or the main focus of planting around an ornamental pond. For best effect, grow it in groups. It needs the protection of a warm greenhouse during winter and should not be planted out until all danger of frost is past. Choose a sunny spot in moist but well-drained soil, or grow it in pots of soil-based mix.

◊ ◊ ☀ ƒ Z9–10 H10–9
‡ to 7ft (2.2m) ↔ to 3ft (1m)

HELENIUM
'Butterpat'

Perennial

Unlike many heleniums, which tend to
have muddy-colored flowers, those of
'Butterpat' are a clear, bright yellow.
Very free flowering, it is a good clump-
forming plant for a herbaceous border.
The blooms, which are usually crowded
with bees, are held on tall stems and
make excellent cut flowers. Remove the
dead heads to encourage more blooms.
Grow it in sun in moist, well-drained,
fertile soil, and divide it in early spring
every 2–3 years to maintain its vigor.

◊ ◑ ☼ Z4–8 H8–1
‡ to 36in (90cm) ↔ to 24in (60cm)

HELIANTHUS
'Lemon Queen'

Perennial

In late summer 'Lemon Queen' bears
large quantities of acid yellow, daisylike flowers with darker centers. This is
a vigorous, herbaceous perennial with
erect stems and slightly hairy, lance-
shaped, dark green leaves. Plant it in
a sunny position in fertile, moist but
well-drained, neutral or alkaline soil. A
good plant for cutting, it also combines
well with other plants in a herbaceous
border. To maintain its vigor, divide
plants every 2–3 years in early spring.

◊ ◑ ☼ Z5–9 H9–5
‡ to 5½ft (1.7m) ↔ to 4ft (1.2m)

HELIANTHUS
'Monarch'

Perennial

This sunflower bears large, semidouble,
daisylike flowers with golden yellow
petals and yellowish brown centers.
If the side buds are removed in spring,
the flowers will grow to 6in (15cm)
across, and they are good for cutting.
The leaves are toothed and lance-
shaped. It is a tall plant ideal for the
back of the border, but it will need
supporting, so insert stakes early in
summer. Give it a spot in full sun in
well-drained, fertile soil.

◊ ☼ Z5–9 H9–5
‡ to 6ft (2m) ↔ to 4ft (1.2m)

HELICHRYSUM
'Schwefellicht'

Perennial

Clusters of small, fluffy, sulfur yellow
flowers, which turn orange-yellow as
summer progresses, make this an
interesting plant for a well-drained rock,
gravel or scree garden. Its spreading
stems, covered with white hairs and
narrow, silvery white leaves, form an
attractive, weed-suppressing mound.
Plant it in a sunny situation in
reasonably fertile, well-drained,
neutral to acidic soil.

◊ ☼ Z9–10 H10–9
‡ to 16in (40cm) ↔ to 12in (30cm)

HELIOPSIS HELIANTHOIDES
'Sommersonne'

Perennial

A superb plant for the herbaceous
border, the ox eye is a clump-forming
perennial with erect, branched stems
and egg- or lance-shaped, midgreen
leaves. In late summer it produces
semidouble flowerheads, which look
rather like small sunflowers, with deep
golden petals and a brownish center.
Grow it in full sun in fertile, moist but
well-drained soil. Established clumps
need dividing in early spring every 2–3
years to maintain vigor.

◊ ◊ ☼ Z4–9 H9–1
‡ to 36in (90cm) ↔ to 24in (60cm)

HEMEROCALLIS
'Corky'

Perennial

One of the more compact daylilies,
'Corky' is suitable for planting in a
small garden or in containers. Clusters
of reddish brown buds appear on long,
erect stems among the evergreen, midgreen leaves. These buds open one
or two at a time into bright yellow
flowers. Although each flower lasts only
for one day, they are quickly replaced.
Plant it in full sun in fertile, moist but
well-drained soil. Propagate daylilies
by dividing in spring or late summer.

◊ ◊ ☼ ☀ Z4–11 H12–1
‡ to 28in (70cm) ↔ to 16in (40cm)

HYPERICUM CALYCINUM

Evergreen shrub

Through summer to midautumn, this St. Johns wort produces cup-shaped yellow flowers with showy stamens. It is a low-growing shrub that quickly spreads by means of trailing stems. It is unfussy and makes an excellent groundcover for a bank or area where little else will grow. It can become invasive; to keep it neat and bushy, cut it back to the ground in spring. Plant in full sun or partial shade, in any well-drained soil. It is easily propagated by division in spring.

◊ ◑ ☀ ☼ Z5–9 H9–5
↕ to 24in (60cm) ↔ indefinite

HYPERICUM 'Hidcote'

Evergreen shrub

The arching, spreading branches of 'Hidcote' are covered with handsome, lance-shaped, dark green leaves. Through summer to early autumn clusters of bright golden yellow flowers, up to 2½in (6cm) across, are produced in profusion. Plant in a reasonably fertile, moist but well-drained soil in full sun. This is a good choice for a shrub or mixed border.

◊ ◑ ☀ Z6–9 H9–6
↕ to 4ft (1.2m) ↔ to 5ft (1.5m)

INULA HOOKERI

Perennial

A superb plant for a shady border, this
perennial from the Himalayas will soon
form large clumps where conditions
suit. It has slender, erect, softly hairy
stems and lance-shaped, midgreen
leaves. From late summer to autumn
it produces clusters of pale yellow
flowers with a darker, brownish yellow
center. Plant it in partial shade in fertile,
moist but well-drained soil. To propagate it, divide established clumps in
spring or autumn.

◊ ◊ ☼ Z4–8 H8–1
‡ to 30in (75cm) ↔ to 24in (60cm)

IRIS PSEUDACORUS

Perennial

The yellow flag is a vigorous aquatic
plant ideal for a large wildlife pond, but
in a small pond you will need to thin it
out unless you contain it in a planting
basket. It has upright, sword-shaped
leaves that are a soft gray-green color.
Choose 'Variegata' for yellowish white-
striped foliage. Full sun and wet soil is
the yellow flag's first choice, but it is
unfussy and adaptable. In early spring,
propagate by division or sow seed in
pots, and keep the soil wet. 'Golden
Fleece' has deeper yellow blooms.

◊ ● ☼ ☼ Z5–8 H8–5
‡ to 6ft (2m) ↔ indefinite

KNIPHOFIA
'Royal Standard'

Perennial

Although 'Royal Standard' has been around for a long time, it is still one of the best red-hot pokers for the herbaceous border. Strappy green leaves form a large clump, from which rise tall, robust flower spikes. These are studded with scarlet buds that open to bright yellow, tubular flowers. Kniphofias are a favorite of bees. Plant them in fertile, moist but well-drained soil in sun.

◊ ◑ ☼ Z6–9 H9–6
↕ to 3ft (1m) ↔ to 24in (60cm)

KOELREUTERIA
PANICULATA

Deciduous tree

The golden-rain tree deserves a rest over winter, because for the other three seasons it puts on an amazing show. This wonderful specimen tree produces spikes of small yellow flowers, followed in autumn by pink to red seed capsules. Early spring foliage is a bright pinkish red becoming mid- to dark green in summer, then turning a rich golden or buttery yellow in early autumn. Plant it in full sun in fertile, well-drained soil. Little pruning is needed.

◊ ☼ Z6–9 H9–6
↕↔ to 30ft (10m)

LIGULARIA
'Gregynog Gold'

Perennial

From a base of large, heart-shaped
leaves, 'Gregynog Gold' sends up
pyramids of daisylike golden flowers
on very tall, stiff stems. Each flower is
delicately flecked with chocolate brown
filaments. Choose a site where the soil
is moderately fertile and permanently
moist – around the margins of a pond
would be ideal – in full sun or (better)
partial shade.

◊ ◆ ☼ ☀ Z4–8 H8–1
↕ to 6ft (1.8m) ↔ to 3ft (1m)

LILIUM PYRENAICUM

Bulbous perennial

In summer this clump-forming lily
produces a dozen or so yellow to
greenish yellow blooms with maroon
throats. They are produced on stiff
stems clothed with lance-shaped, dark
green leaves. However, these stylish
flowers are best enjoyed in the border
rather than a vase, because they have a
rather unpleasant smell. Plant preferably
in early autumn or spring in neutral
or slightly alkaline, well-drained soil
in full sun or partial shade.

◊ ☼ ☀ Z4–7 H7–1
↕ to 39in (100cm)

LINARIA DALMATICA

Perennial

The bright yellow, spurred flowers of
this toadflax bear more than a passing
resemblance to those of the snapdragon
(*Antirrhinum*). The slightly erect, lance-
shaped, waxy green leaves grow up to
7in (18cm) long. Plant it in full sun in
a light, preferably sandy, fertile, well-
drained soil. Its upright stature will
ensure it stands out in the middle of a
busy herbaceous border; it would also
do well in a gravel garden.

◊ ☼ Z5–8 H8–5
↕ to 3ft (1m) ↔ to 24in (60cm)

LYSIMACHIA NUMMULARIA
'Aurea'

Perennial

The golden form of creeping Jenny is
a vigorous evergreen that readily roots
when its stems touch the soil. It can
become rampant and may need to be
controlled by weeding. The leaves are
a bright yellow (lime green in partial
shade), and during summer it has small
yellow, upright, cup-shaped flowers.
Choose a spot in full sun or partial
shade in a moist, well-drained soil that
won't dry out during summer. Propagate by division in spring or autumn.

◊ ☼ ☀ Z4–8 H8–1
↕ to 2in (5cm) ↔ indefinite

LYSIMACHIA PUNCTATA

Perennial

This is an extremely vigorous perennial that quickly spreads by means of underground rhizomes. The upright stems have tiers of lance-shaped leaves and numerous bright yellow, cup-shaped flowers. It makes an attractive plant for a moist border, but take care, because it can become invasive. It grows best in partial shade but will tolerate full sun. Plant it in fertile, moist but well-drained soil.

◇ ◊ ☼ ☀ Z4–8 H8–1
↕ to 3ft (1m) ↔ to 24in (60cm)

OSTEOSPERMUM
'Buttermilk'

Perennial

This tender subshrub starts flowering in spring and keeps on going right through to autumn. The single flowers are primrose yellow with a dark mauve center. An upright, perky plant for a gravel garden, a border, or in a container, it has handsome, toothed, midgreen leaves. Where not hardy, overwinter in pots under cover or take semi-ripe cuttings in late summer. Plant in full sun in very well-drained soil.

◇ ☼ Z10–11 H9–1
↕ ↔ to 24in (60cm)

ROBINIA PSEUDOACACIA *'Frisia'*

Deciduous tree

Dramatic leaf color makes this fast-growing, spreading tree special: in spring, the leaves are bright yellow; in early summer, they take on a dash of lime; then, in late summer, they turn a rich orange-yellow. The tree has fragrant white flowers in spring on spiny branches. A wonderful specimen tree, with a canopy light enough for underplanting. Give it a spot in full sun in fertile, moist but well-drained soil. Little pruning is required.

○ ◊ ☼ *f* Z4–9 H9–1
‡ to 50ft (15m) ↔ to 25ft (8m)

RUDBECKIA *'Herbstsonne'*

Perennial

This cheerful coneflower is one of the mainstays of the late-summer garden. 'Herbstsonne' has yellow, daisylike flowers with conical, green-brown centers that are carried aloft on tall, upright stems. The glossy green leaves are deeply veined. It does best in fertile, moist but well-drained soil, including clay. This clump-forming plant is perfect for the back of a herbaceous border, where it will act as a foil for smaller plants. Good for cutting.

○ ◊ ☼ ☼ Z3–9 H9–1
‡ to 6ft (2m) ↔ to 36in (90cm)

RUDBECKIA FULGIDA
'Goldsturm'

Perennial

The dark-centered flowers of this black-eyed Susan are produced in abundance from late summer to midautumn. The deep green leaves are lance-shaped. It will grow in any reasonably fertile, well-drained soil as long as it does not dry out in summer; it also does well in heavy clay soil. A good mixer in a herbaceous or woodland border, it is also perfect for naturalistic plantings with ornamental grasses.

○ ◑ ☼ ☀ Z4–9 H9–1
‡ to 24in (60cm) ↔ to 18in (45cm)

SILPHIUM PERFOLIATUM

Perennial

From mid-to late summer, the upright, branching stems of the cup plant are crowned with sunny yellow, daisylike flowers. Its deeply cut leaves are attractive, too, and quite bristly to touch. This clump-forming herbaceous perennial prefers a rather heavy, neutral or alkaline soil, including clay, that is moist but well-drained. It would be at home in a prairie or similar wild garden.

○ ◑ ☼ ☀ Z5–9 H9–5
‡ to 8ft (2.5m) ↔ to 3ft (1m)

SOLIDAGO
'Goldenmosa'

Perennial

With its upright, yellow-stalked golden flowerheads and wrinkled, midgreen leaves, this is a select form of goldenrod. Compact and bushy, it is much less invasive than others. Plant it in a late-summer border in full sun and well-drained, slightly fertile, sandy soil. It is an ideal plant for a wild garden and is also good for cutting.

◊ ☼ Z5–9 H9–5
↕ to 30in (75cm) ↔ to 18in (45cm)

SPARTIUM JUNCEUM

Deciduous shrub

When broom comes into bloom, the profusion of fragrant, golden yellow, pea-shaped flowers really brightens up a garden. In autumn, long brown seed-pods are borne. Its green, upright stems are sparsely covered in narrow leaves. A Mediterranean natve, it will grow in any well-drained soil in full sun. Grow it against a wall or in a shrub border. It will also thrive on alkaline soils and by the coast. Trim back after flowering, but do not cut back into the old wood; it will not reshoot.

◊ ☼ *f* Z8–10 H10–8
↕↔ to 4ft (3m)

TROPAEOLUM PEREGRINUM

Climber

The Canary creeper is a vigorous annual climber with deeply lobed, gray-green leaves. In summer it produces clusters of bright yellow flowers. These have three small lower petals and two larger, deeply fringed upper petals, which give it a birdlike appearance. Plant it in a sunny position in moist but well-drained, slightly fertile soil. Canary creeper is ideal for growing on a trellis, over a fence or pergola, or through a tree. Sow seed *in situ* in early spring.

◊ ◑ ☼ Z9–10 H10–1
‡ to 12ft (4m)

VERBASCUM NIGRUM

Perennial

The elegant dark mullein bears 20in (50cm) tall flower spikes dotted with yellow, saucer-shaped blooms that have purple filament hairs. The heart-shaped leaves are fuzzy and gray beneath and form a rosette at the base, gradually becoming smaller as they go up the stem. Grow in poor, well-drained, alkaline soils; in richer soils the plant grows larger and needs staking. Ideal for planting in gravel or naturalizing in a wild garden, this mullein also mixes well in a sunny herbaceous border.

◊ ☼ Z3–8 H8–1
‡ to 36in (90cm) ↔ to 24in (60cm)

ANTIRRHINUM MAJUS
'Trumpet Serenade'

Perennial

In a range of cheerful colors, including this rich gold, the freesia-like blooms of 'Trumpet Serenade' are very different from the usual "squeeze-open, snap-shut" flowers of most snapdragons As short-lived, tender perennials, they are usually grown as annual bedding plants, filling gaps at the front of a herbaceous border or used as a cut flower. Plant in full sun in fertile, preferably sandy soil. Avoid wet soil since it encourages rust, although this is a resistant variety.

◊ ☼ Z7–11 H12–1
‡↔ to 12in (30cm)

ARCTOTIS FASTUOSA

Perennial

The deeply lobed leaves of the African daisy are silvery white and covered with hairs. It bears orange, daisylike flowers with a black or dark maroon center. A tender perennial, it is usually treated as an annual used in bedding, gravel gardens, and containers. Outside it needs a moist but very well-drained soil in an open, sunny site. It can be grown in a pot of gritty, well-drained soil mix and overwintered under cover.

◊ ☼ Z12–15 H12–1
‡ to 24in (60cm) ↔ to 12in (30cm)

CALENDULA OFFICINALIS

Annual

An old favorite, the pot marigold is a
vigorous, erect plant with hairy, aromatic,
spoon-shaped leaves. The bright orange-
yellow, daisylike flowers are produced
from early summer to autumn. Superb
as bedding, it can also be used in pots
or as a cut flower. Plant in sun in well-
drained, fertile soil. Sow seed *in situ*
in spring. For strong orange shades
choose 'Fiesta Gitana' (a dwarf cultivar),
'Orange King' (double blooms)
or 'Indian Prince' (reddish flowers).
Deadhead to keep the show going.

◊ ☼ Z0 H9–1
‡ to 30in (75cm) ↔ to 18in (45cm)

CAMPSIS X TAGLIABUANA
'Madame Galen'

Climber

The trumpet creeper is a vigorous, self-
clinging climber with long, divided
leaves. From late summer to autumn
it produces clusters of orange-red,
trumpet-shaped flowers. It can quickly
cover a trellis or clamber through an
old tree. Keep it clear of the roof and
gutters, and prune it hard in winter to
keep it within bounds. The soil should
be fertile and moist but well drained.

◊ ◊ ☼ Z5–9 H9–5
‡ to 30ft (10m)

CANNA
'Striata'

Perennial

This striking plant pushes up tall spikes of gladiolus-like orange flowers. The real scene-stealer, though, is the flamboyant foliage marked with green and yellow stripes. It makes a superb plant for a border among other red or orange flowers, or it can be grown in pots. Plant out in late spring in sun and well-drained soil. It is tender, so lift rhizomes before the first frosts, place in a tray of moist compost, and overwinter under cover.

◊ ☼ Z8–11 H12–1
‡ to 5ft (1.5m) ↔ to 20in (50cm)

CROCOSMIA
'Star of the East'

Cormous perennial

With its large orange flowers, 'Star of the East' is a particularly attractive crocosmia. A vigorous plant with erect, sword-shaped, deep green leaves, it looks wonderful planted among shrubs or with other late-flowering perennials. If the corms become overcrowded they will lose their vigor, so dig them up in spring and replant them on a fresh site. Crocosmias prefer a spot in full sun in fertile, moist but well-drained soil.

◊ ◑ ☼ Z6–9 H9–6
‡ to 28in (70cm) ↔ to 3in (8cm)

DAHLIA
'Hamari Gold'

Perennial

Golden yellow blooms and deeply divided, dark green leaves make this an attractive border plant. Where not hardy, after the foliage has been blackened by the first frosts, dig up the tubers and store them in dry compost over winter. Wait until all risk of frost has past before replanting in full sun in well-drained soil. It benefits from a stake being inserted at planting time to avoid damaging the tubers. Fertilize and water regularly in the growing season.

◊ ☼ Z8–11 H12–1
↕ to 4ft (1.2m) ↔ to 24in (60cm)

DAHLIA
'Wootton Impact'

Perennial

This attractive semi-cactus dahlia is ideal for a sunny border where space is limited. Strong stems of medium-sized, bronze-colored flowers, which are good for cutting, are held well above the main body of the plant. They need early staking. Like all dahlias, it requires a sunny spot in fertile, well-drained soil, and for winter the tubers need to be lifted and stored (see 'Hamari Gold', above).

◊ ☼ Z8–11 H12–1
↕ to 4ft (1.2m) ↔ to 24in (60cm)

FUCHSIA
'Coralle'

Deciduous shrub

The tubular bells of 'Coralle', which are
borne in tight clusters, will appeal to
those who prefer less artificial-looking
fuchsias. Upright in habit, this shrub has
strong stems with velvety, olive green
leaves. It is superb for growing in a
container: use a soil-based pottng mix,
and choose a spot in full sun or light
shade. Fertilize regularly throughout
summer with a balanced fertilizer,
and move it under cover during winter
in areas where it is not hardy.

◊ ◓ ☼ ◑ Z0 H9–1
↕ to 36in (90cm) ↔ to 24in (60cm)

HELENIUM
'Septemberfuchs'

Perennial

Heleniums are invaluable for providing
areas of warm color in the late-summer
border. This particularly tall variety
benefits from early staking. It has dark
green leaves and burnt orange flowers
streaked with yellow. Bees find the
domed centers irresistible. For best
effect, plant them in groups of three or
more in a sunny position in moist but
well-drained fertile soil. Established
clumps need dividing every few years.

◊ ◓ ☼ Z4–8 H8–1
↕ to 5ft (1.5m) ↔ to 24in (60cm)

HELIANTHUS ANNUUS
'Music Box'

Annual

From late summer this small sunflower
produces an abundance of bright
orange, yellow, or red flowers, each
bloom measuring up to 5in (12cm)
across. The markings on the petals
subtly darken toward the black central
disk. Wonderful as cut flowers and
short enough to grow in a pot, they
also blend well among other plants in
a sunny herbaceous or annual border.
Sow the seed *in situ* in spring in fertile,
moist but well-drained soil.

◊ ◊ ☼ Z0 H12–1
‡ to 28in (70cm) ↔ to 24in (60cm)

KNIPHOFIA ROOPERI

Perennial

Living up to its common name of red-
hot poker and torch lily, this dazzling
plant is guaranteed to brighten up the
herbaceous border or gravel garden. Its
globe-shaped spikes of reddish orange
flowers turn a golden color as they
mature. It is a very robust, clump-
forming plant with shapely, pointed,
evergreen leaves. Plant it in late spring
in full sun or partial shade in fertile,
well-drained, preferably sandy soil.
Mulch over winter the first year.
Divide large clumps in spring.

◊ ☼ ☀ Z6–9 H9–6
‡ to 4ft (1.2m) ↔ to 2ft (60cm)

LILIUM HENRYI

Bulbous perennial

Vigorous and clump-forming, this tall lily has erect stems and narrow, dark green, lance-shaped leaves. In late summer it produces clusters of ten or more delicately scented flowers with black-spotted, swept-back petals. It is happiest in partial shade in neutral or slightly alkaline, well-drained soil. Tall lilies like this one are ideal for brightening up the back of a shrub or herbaceous border.

◊ ☼ ƒ Z3–8 H8–1
‡ to 10ft (3m)

LONICERA X HECKROTTII

Climber

The twining stems of this pretty hybrid honeysuckle make it ideal for growing through a small tree or against a wall or trellis. Its fragrant, orange-yellow, tubular flowers are followed in autumn by bright red berries. The lush, dark green leaves are deciduous or semi-evergreen, depending on conditions. Look for the cultivar 'Gold Flame', which is more vigorous and has even brighter flowers. Honeysuckles need moist but well-drained, fertile soil. They grow well in sun or light shade.

◊ ◖ ☼ ☼ ƒ Z6–9 H9–6
‡ to 15ft (5m)

MIMULUS AURANTIACUS

Evergreen shrub

This shrubby monkeyflower is an attractive, small plant for a warm, sunny border. The dark green, sticky, lance-shaped leaves are the perfect foil for the orange, trumpet-shaped flowers, which appear from late summer to autumn. Plant it in fertile, well-drained soil in full sun. It is best grown under cover where not hardy.

◊ ☼ Z7–10 H10–7
↕ ↔ to 3ft (1m)

XEROCHRYSUM BRACTEATUM
Monstrosum Series

Annual

Strawflowers are erect annuals with grayish green, lance-shaped leaves. The Monstrosum Series has vibrant orange, double flowers that measure 3in (8cm) across. Other colors are available, including yellows and reds, plus white. Use it to fill spaces in a herbaceous border, or line it out in a cut-flower garden. Plant in full sun in slightly fertile, moist but well-drained soil. Strawflowers dry well and retain their color for a long time.

◊ ◐ ☼ Z0 H12–1
↕ to 36in (90cm) ↔ to 12in (30cm)

AUTUMN

As the days begin to shorten and night temperatures fall, many plants have completed their annual cycles and will soon retreat underground. The end of the growing season is signaled by the brilliant color displays of deciduous trees before they drop their leaves and enter their dormancy. The vibrance of the show varies each year, but most of the maples (*Acer*) give rich, reliable autumnal colors. In gardens that are too small for large trees, there are plenty of shrubs, such as *Euonymus alatus* and the stag-horn sumac (*Rhus typhina*), that can provide dramatic foliage displays of crimson, scarlet, and gold.

Ornamental grapes *Vitis* 'Brant' and *V. coignetiae* are among the climbers with bright red foliage in autumn, and vigorous Boston ivy, *Parthenocissus tricuspidata*, transforms the appearance of walls as it turns from shiny green to a glowing sheet of scarlet.

FRUIT AND FLOWERS

Decorative fruits are much in evidence now, and some of the best crops are provided by cotoneasters, viburnums, and crabapples (*Malus*). And there are shrub roses, such as *Rosa rugosa*, that produce masses of shining scarlet hips.

Although the annual border has been cleared and many perennials have begun to die down, some flowering plants come into their own at this time, notably autumn crocuses and colchicums. Monkshood (*Aconitum*), many asters, and chrysanthemums of nearly every color will continue to flower as long as the weather permits. Do not be in too much of a hurry to clear away all remnants of summer; decorati seedheads can stay until the collapse, and allow the gr flowerheads and foliag ornamental grasses t through winter, no can enjoy them, protection it o

ANAPHALIS TRIPLINERVIS

Perennial

Pearly everlasting is an easily grown perennial from the Himalayas and SW China. It is a good groundcover plant, forming dense clumps of soft, silvery green, spear-shaped leaves. From midsummer well until into autumn, the clumps are topped by clusters of papery, daisylike white flowers. The flowers can be dried for indoor display by hanging them upside down in bunches in a light, airy place. Grow in well-drained, moisture-retentive soil in sun or partial shade.

◊ ◑ ☼ ☀ Z3–8 H8–1
‡ to 36in (90cm) ↔ to 24in (60cm)

ARALIA ELATA
'Variegata'

Deciduous tree

The Japanese angelica tree is upright in habit with a few thick, thorny branches bearing large, compound leaves. In warmer areas it forms a small tree, but elsewhere may be only a large shrub up to 10ft (3m) tall. The leaflets, which are edged with creamy white, turn gold in autumn. Abundant clusters of small white flowers are borne in late summer and early autumn. It prefers fertile, moist but well-drained soil in sun but tolerates light, dappled shade.

◊ ◑ ☼ ☀ Z4–9 H9–1
‡↔ to 30ft (10m)

ARBUTUS × ANDRACHNOIDES

Evergreen tree

The Grecian strawberry tree is a shrubby, spreading evergreen with peeling, red-brown bark and oval, glossy, dark green leaves. From autumn through to spring it bears hanging clusters of small, almost spherical white flowers; occasionally it produces small, bright red fruits at the same time. Grow it in a sheltered site in full sun in organic, well-drained soil. It tolerates alkaline soils so long as they are deep and rich in organic matter.

◊ ☼ Z8–9 H9–8
‡↔ to 25ft (8m)

ASTER ERICOIDES
'White Heather'

Perennial

Asters are invaluable for autumn color in herbaceous and mixed borders. This bushy perennial has wiry, upright stems smothered in tiny, long-lasting white daisies from late summer to late autumn. The slender stems need staking. Grow in sun or partial shade in fertile, well-drained soil that does not dry out during the growing season; moisture helps reduce the risk of mildew, although this variety shows some resistance to the disease.

◊ ◑ ☼ ☼ Z5–8 H8–5
‡ to 3ft (1m) ↔ to 12in (30cm)

CIMICIFUGA SIMPLEX

Perennial

The tiny, star-shaped autumn flowers of this herbaceous perennial, also known as *Actea simplex*, appear brilliant white against their dark stems. The tall, arching flower spikes are seen at their best if the stems are supported by an unobtrusive, grow-through support, best positioned in spring. The leaves are glossy, finely divided, and fresh green. Good for late color in a woodland garden or shady border. Grow in moist, organic soil in light shade to prevent the sun from scorching the delicate leaves.

◐ ☼ Z4–8 H8–1
↕ to 4ft (1.2m) ↔ to 24in (60cm)

CORTADERIA RICHARDII

Perennial

Commonly known as toe toe, *Cortaderia richardii* is native to New Zealand. The arching, fluffy flowerheads, up to 2ft (60cm) long, first appear in summer, high above the tussocks of long, narrow, olive green leaves. If left on the plant, the slender, creamy white plumes will persist through autumn and winter. They can also be cut for fresh or dried-flower arrangements. Grow in well-drained soil in sun. Cut out the dead foliage and flowerheads in early spring – protect your hands with gloves.

○ ☼ Z7–10 H10–7
↕ to 9ft (2.5m) ↔ to 6ft (1.8m)

CORTADERIA SELLOANA
'Sunningdale Silver'

Perennial

Large, dense, evergreen tussocks of sharp-edged, deep grayish green leaves are topped by tall upright stems of long-lasting, silvery white flowerheads in late summer and autumn. It makes an impressive specimen plant where space is available. Leave dead foliage in place over winter to protect the crown,then, wearing thick gloves, cut and comb it out in spring. Grow in sun in well-drained soil. Divide it every two or three years in spring to rejuvenate it.

○ ☼ Z7–10 H10–7
‡ tn 10ft (3m) or more ↔ 8ft (2.5m)

CROCUS OCHROLEUCUS

Cormous perennial

This crocus bears slender, creamy white flowers with yellow throats in late autumn, when most other autumn-flowering crocus are over. The leaves usually emerge with or just after the flowers and are green with a central white stripe. It is very easy to grow in well-drained soil in sun, and it will naturalize if planted in drifts in short grass. Overcrowded clumps can be divided after flowering. Plant corms in late summer.

○ ☼ Z5–8 H8–5
‡ to 2in (5cm) ↔ 1in (2.5cm)

GALANTHUS REGINAE-OLGAE

Bulbous perennial

This snowdrop flowers from midautumn to early winter, with petals up
to 1in (2.5cm) long. The narrow leaves
appear after flowering and are dark
green with a central gray stripe.
Grow in sun or dappled shade in
well-drained, neutral to alkaline soil.
It prefers drier soils and more sun than
other snowdrops. Overcrowded clumps
can be divided as the leaves start to
wither. Plant bulbs in autumn.

◊ ☼ ☼ Z7–9 H9–7
‡ to 8in (20cm) ↔ to 2in (5cm)

JASMINUM POLYANTHUM

Climber

Grown for its beautiful and abundant,
highly scented flowers, this vigorous
climber bears large clusters of tubular
white blooms that open from pink buds
between late summer and winter.
The foliage is evergreen, or almost so,
and the dark green leaves are made up
of several leaflets. Overwinter a
container-grown plant in a greenhouse
or conservatory where not hardy.
It grows best in full sun in well-drained,
fertile soil, although it will tolerate
light shade.

◊ ☼ ☼ ƒ Z9–10 H10–9
‡ to 10ft (3m)

Leucojum autumnale

Bulbous perennial

The autumn snowflake is a beautiful plant with narrow, dark green, grass-like leaves. The nodding white flowers, tinged with pink at the base, are borne on slender stems in late summer and early autumn. A native of the stony slopes of the western Mediterranean, it prefers a warm, sunny spot in light, free-draining soil. It is ideal for rock gardens, sunny banks, and terraces. Plant bulbs in late summer.

◊ ☼ Z5–9 H9–5
‡ to 6in (15cm) ↔ to 2in (5cm)

Sorbus cashmiriana

Deciduous tree

The Kashmir mountain ash forms a spreading, open-branched small tree. The white or blush pink flowers open in late spring or early summer. The divided, rich green leaves turn gold and russet in autumn, forming a backdrop for the clusters of marble-sized white berries that appear from late summer and early autumn onward. Grow in sun or dappled shade in fertile, well-drained but moisture-retentive soil. It is most easily propagated by seed sown as soon as it is ripe in autumn.

◊ ◗ ☼ ☼ Z5–7 H7–5
‡ to 25ft (8m) ↔ to 22ft (7m)

Amaryllis belladonna

Bulbous perennial

This South African bulb is grown for its late-summer and early-autumn flowers. The fragrant, trumpet-shaped pink blooms are borne in clusters on long, purple-tinted stems. The dark green, straplike leaves appear after the flowers and last until the following summer if winter is not too harsh. Grow in a sunny to partially shaded site in very well-drained soil enriched with organic matter. Plant in summer, with the tip of the bulb just below the soil surface.

◊ ☼ *f*Z7–10 H10–7
‡ to 32in (80cm) ↔ to 18in (45cm)

Androsace lanuginosa

Perennial

The fine, silky hairs that clothe the evergreen leaves of this low-growing perennial give the plant a soft-textured appearance. The primroselike pink flowers appear in mid- to late summer or early autumn. Rosettes of tiny, deep gray-green leaves are arranged along the length of the trailing stems. It needs a sunny position and very well-drained soil. Add plenty of coarse sand to heavy clay soils to improve drainage. Good for a rock garden, trough, or along the top of a drystone wall.

◊ ☼ Z5–7 H7–5
‡ to 4in (10cm) ↔ to 12in (30cm)

CHRYSANTHEMUM
'Rose Yvonne Arnaud'

Perennial

The fully double flowers of this florist's chrysanthemum are produced in abundance in late summer and autumn. The deep rose-pink petals are neatly backswept. The plant should be lifted in autumn after flowering and over-wintered in frost-free conditions. New shoots can be planted out after the last frost or used for basal cuttings in early spring to produce new plants. Grow in fertile, well-drained soil in full sun.

◊ ☼ Z3–9 H9–1
‡ to 4ft (1.2m) ↔ to 30in (75cm)

CLERODENDRUM BUNGEI

Deciduous shrub

Where marginally hardy, the woody stems of this shrub die back in cold winters, but the plant should sprout again from the base in spring if given a deep, loose winter mulch. The fragrant flowers are deep pink and, although tiny, are borne in large clusters throughout late summer and early autumn. The large, heart-shaped, serrated-edged leaves emit a pungent odor when brushed against. Grow in a warm, sunny, sheltered site in organic, well-drained soil.

◊ ☼ ƒ Z8–10 H10–8
‡↔ to 6ft (2m)

COLCHICUM BYZANTINUM

Cormous perennial

C. byzantinum produces up to 20 large, funnel-shaped, pale mauve-pink flowers in autumn. The broad leaves, which are ribbed or pleated, appear in spring and last until early summer. As they fade they can look rather messy, so hide the foliage by growing them among other plants. Plant the corms, which resemble a tiny clenched fist, in late summer in a sunny position in soil that is moist but free draining. This colchicum establishes quickly and will spread where the conditions are favorable.

◊ ◊ ☼ Z4–9 H9–1
‡ to 5in (12cm) ↔ to 4in (10cm)

COLCHICUM *'The Giant'*

Cormous perennial

The flowers of this autumn-flowering corm are very large. Mauve-pink with white throats, they are lightly checkered and crocuslike. This is one of the easiest colchicums to grow, and it will increase rapidly. Broad leaves appear in winter and die back in summer, so they are best grown among other plants to conceal the leaves. Plant the corms in late summer in fertile, free-draining soil in sun. Plants tolerate light shade.

◊ ☼ Z4–9 H9–1
‡↔ to 8in (20cm)

CROCUS KOTSCHYANUS
Cormous perennial

In autumn, this crocus bears delicate, lilac-pink flowers with yellow centers and white stamens. The flowers open out fully in sun to display the glossy surface of the petals. They are followed in winter through to spring by narrow, semi-erect leaves with white lines along the center. It is ideal for naturalizing in drifts in well-drained soil in a warm, sunny position. Overcrowded clumps can be divided after flowering. Plant corms in late summer.

◊ ☼ Z3–8 H8–1
‡ to 3in (8cm) ↔ to 2in (5cm)

CYCLAMEN HEDERIFOLIUM
Perennial

This small cyclamen has ivy-shaped leaves that are intricately patterned in shades of gray-green. Appearing after the flowers in autumn, they can provide a foil for other plants until they fade by early summer. The pink flowers appear from late summer to autumn. Grow in light shade in a well-drained, organic soil. Plant tubers in late summer about 1in (2.5cm) deep. Clumps are best left undisturbed, but self-sown seedlings can be lifted and moved.

◊ ☼ ◐ Z8–9 H9–8
‡ to 5in (13cm) ↔ to 6in (15cm)

HYDRANGEA MACROPHYLLA *'Hamburg'*

Deciduous shrub

Long-lasting "mopheads" of flowers appear on this vigorous, deciduous shrub from summer and into autumn. They are a deep rose-pink on neutral to alkaline soils, and deep blue on acidic soils. The leaves are deep green, oval, and pointed. Position in full sun or light shade in a fertile, moist but well-drained soil. The flowerheads can be cut and dried for winter arrangements.

◊ ◑ ☼ ☼ Z6–9 H9–6
‡ to 3ft (1m) ↔ to 5ft (1.5m)

NERINE BOWDENII

Bulbous perennial

Sturdy stems bear umbrella-like clusters of rose-pink flowers with wavy-edged petals from early to midautumn. The strap-shaped leaves appear with, or just after, the flowers. Grow in sun in very free-draining soil; they thrive at the foot of a sunny wall if left to multiply undisturbed. Plant in spring with the tip of the bulb at, or just below, the soil surface. Where marginally hardy, provide a loose, thick winter mulch.

◊ ☼ Z8–10 H10–8
‡ to 18in (45cm) ↔ to 6in (15cm)

PHYSOSTEGIA VIRGINIANA *'Vivid'*

Perennial

Commonly known as the obedient plant because the flowers will remain in position after they are moved on their stalks. Tall spikes of small, tubular, vivid purple-pink flowers appear from midsummer to autumn and are ideal for cutting. The midgreen leaves are lance-shaped and toothed and form dense clumps. Grow in full sun in well-drained, moisture-retentive soil. Overcrowded clumps can be divided in spring.

○ ◐ ☼ Z4–8 H8–1
↕ to 24in (60cm) ↔ to 12in (30cm)

SCHIZOSTYLIS COCCINEA *'Viscountess Byng'*

Perennial

Kaffir lilies originate from South Africa, where they grow beside streams and in moist meadows. They have narrow, bright green leaves and spread gradually to form clumps. 'Viscountess Byng' is a delicate variety, and its flowers can be damaged by cold. However, it is good for cutting and in late autumn produces masses of pink flowers measuring up to 1¼in (3cm) across. Plant it in full sun in moist soil, and mulch it for winter where marginally hardy.

◐ ☼ Z7–9 H9–7
↕ to 24in (60cm) ↔ to 12in (30cm)

SEDUM SPECTABILE

Perennial

The ice plant is deservedly popular, flowering over long periods from late summer to autumn. It is ideal for the front of a sunny border, where its densely packed, flat heads of tiny star-shaped, soft pink flowers will attract butterflies and bees. The leaves are fleshy and pale gray-green. Grow in any well-drained soil in full sun. The flowerheads can be cut and dried or left to stand over winter, adding interest to the border.

◊ ☼ Z4–9 H9–1
↕↔ to 18in (45cm)

SORBUS HUPEHENSIS
VAR. OBTUSA

Deciduous tree

This mountain ash has a narrow, compact habit. The young foliage is followed by clusters of white flowers in late spring and early summer. Pink fruits form during late summer and become deeper pink as they mature. The leaves are divided into many leaflets that turn fiery orange and red in autumn. The fruits remain long after the leaves have fallen. Grow in moisture-retentive, well-drained neutral or slightly acidic soil in sun or light shade.

◊ ◊ ☼ ◑ Z6–8 H8–6
↕ to 40ft (12m) ↔ to 25ft (8m)

SORBUS VILMORINII

Deciduous tree

The delicate-looking, fernlike leaves of
Vilmorin's mountain ash are dark green,
turning shades of orange to bronze-red
in autumn. This large shrub or small
tree has a rounded crown with slender,
arching branches and is suitable for a
small garden. White flowers in late spring
are followed by fruits in autumn, which
ripen through shades of deep red-pink
to white flushed with pink. Plant in
moisture-retentive but well-drained
neutral or slightly acidic soil in full sun
or light shade.

○ ◐ ☼ ❀ Z6–8 H8–6
↕↔ to 15ft (5m)

ZEPHYRANTHES GRANDIFLORA

Bulbous perennial

Soft pink, funnel-shaped flowers open
to a starry shape between late summer
and early autumn above clumps of very
slender leaves. Plant bulbs 4in (10cm)
deep in spring in a sheltered, sunny site
in well-drained, moisture-retentive soil.
Where not hardy, lift after flowering
and overwinter in a frost-free place.
It can also be grown in containers of
gritty potting mix and moved under
glass in winter, or grown permanently
in the greenhouse or conservatory.

○ ◐ ☼ Z8–11 H12–9
↕ to 30cm (12in) ↔ to 10cm (4in)

ACER PALMATUM *Dissectum Atropurpureum Group*

Deciduous tree

This small tree is one of the most popular forms of Japanese maple. It has wide-spreading branches clothed with ferny, deeply divided, red-purple leaves that turn red in autumn. Grow in full sun or partial shade in fertile, moist but well-drained soil in a sheltered position; the leaves may be damaged by frosts and cold or dry winds. Grow it with other Japanese maples or in a large container of soil-based mix.

○ ◊ ☼ ◑ Z6–8 H8–6
‡ to 5ft (1.5m) ↔ to 3ft (1m)

ACER PALMATUM '*Ôsakazuki*'

Deciduous tree

This Japanese maple has large, bright green leaves that are divided into seven lobes, each drawn out into a finely tapered tip. In autumn they turn a vivid scarlet. Plant it in full sun or partial shade in fertile, moist but well-drained soil with shelter from wind. To fully appreciate its autumn foliage, it is best grown as a specimen tree.

○ ◊ ☼ ◑ Z6–8 H8–6
‡↔ to 20ft (6m)

ACER RUBRUM
'October Glory'

Deciduous tree

This red maple dons its bright red autumn colors late in the season and retains its leaves for a long time, even in windy weather. The dark green leaves will develop their most vibrant colors if the tree is grown in acidic soil. Plant it in full sun or partial shade in fertile, moist but well-drained soil. This tree has a spreading habit.

○ ◊ ☼ ◐ Z3–9 H9–1
‡ to 70ft (20m) ↔ to 30ft (10m)

ACER RUBRUM
'Scanlon'

Deciduous tree

There are few trees that color up as vividly in autumn as this one – the dark green leaves turn a vivid shade of deep reddish orange. Plant it in full sun in moist but well-drained, fertile soil. The best autumn colors appear when grown in acidic soil. This tree has a narrow columnar form, making it more suitable for smaller gardens than 'October Glory'.

○ ◊ ☼ Z3–9 H9–1
‡ to 50ft (15m) ↔ to 15ft (5m)

AMELANCHIER LAMARCKII

Deciduous tree

Often shrubby, this attractive small tree has upright branches and downy young shoots. It bears hanging clusters of white flowers in midspring that are followed by edible, purplish black fruit in summer. The leaves are flushed bronze as they emerge in spring, then they turn dark green before becoming orange and finally red in autumn. Plant it full sun or partial shade in acidic, fertile, moist but well-drained soil. Thin out main stems if necessary to improve the appearance.

◊ ◊ ☼ ☀ Z5–9 H9–5
↕ to 30ft (10m) ↔ to 40ft (12m)

ARBUTUS UNEDO

Evergreen tree

The strawberry tree has a bushy, spreading habit and attractive, peeling, reddish brown bark. The oval leaves are dark green and glossy. From late autumn to spring it bears hanging sprays of small, waxy-textured white flowers that are accompanied by small, strawberry-like red fruits – these result from the previous year's flowers. Grow in full sun in a fertile, well-drained soil enriched with organic matter. It is best in a sheltered spot that provides protection from wind.

◊ ☼ Z7–9 H9–7
↕↔ to 25ft (8m)

BERBERIS THUNBERGII
'Rose Glow'

Deciduous shrub

This is a vigorous, dense, spiny shrub
with small, rounded, reddish purple
leaves. Later in autumn, white and pink
flecks appear on the leaves, spreading
so the outer leaves become variegated.
In autumn the leaves turn orange and
red. In late spring it bears small clusters
of red-tinged yellow flowers. It makes a
dense hedge that grows to medium
height; pruning should be delayed until
after flowering. Plant in full sun or
partial shade in well-drained soil.

◊ ☼ ☀ Z5–8 H8–5
‡↔ to 6ft (2m)

BERBERIS WILSONIAE

Deciduous shrub

This is a very dense shrub with spiny,
spreading, gracefully arching branches.
It has glossy, grayish green leaves that
turn intense shades of bright orange
and red in autumn. In summer, it
produces small clusters of pale yellow
flowers that are followed by tight
bunches of gleaming coral-red fruit in
autumn. Plant it in full sun or partial
shade in any well-drained soil. Good
for a shrub border or as a specimen.

◊ ☼ ☀ Z6–9 H9–6
‡ to 3ft (1m) ↔ to 6ft (2m)

CERCIDIPHYLLUM JAPONICUM

Deciduous tree

The Katsura tree is pyramid-shaped when young, becoming more rounded with maturity. It has rounded, fresh green leaves that turn yellow, orange, and red in autumn, with a scent like burnt sugar when they fall. It makes a beautiful specimen tree. Plant it in full sun or partial shade in organic, moist but well-drained, neutral to acidic soil. The best autumn color is obtained when it is planted in acidic soil.

◊ ◊ ☼ ☀ *f* Z4–8 H8–1
‡ to 70ft (20m) ↔ to 50ft (15m)

CHRYSANTHEMUM '*George Griffiths*'

Perennial

Chrysanthemums should be planted in in a sheltered position in full sun. They need a fertile, moist but well-drained soil that is enriched with well-rotted manure. The flowerheads of 'George Griffiths' are heavy, so the stems should be tied in to a stake for support. Lift plants after flowering, then overwinter in frost-free conditions. Plant out in spring after the final frost, or raise new plants from basal cuttings. This "mum" is often grown for exhibition.

◊ ◊ ☼ Z3–9 H9–1
‡ to 5ft (1.5m) ↔ to 30in (75cm)

COTINUS
'Grace'

Deciduous shrub

This is an extremely beautiful form of
smoke bush, with rich purple, oval
leaves. In summer it bears plumes of
small flowers that are followed by sprays
of tiny purplish pink fruits. In autumn,
the leaves turn a vivid shade of scarlet.
Plant it in full sun or light shade in
moisture-retentive but well-drained soil.
To obtain the best autumn color, do not
plant it in too rich a soil and choose
a sunny position; it does not color as
well in shade.

◊ ◊ ☼ ☀ Z5–8 H8–4
‡ to 20ft (6m) ↔ to 15ft (5m)

COTONEASTER FRIGIDUS
'Cornubia'

Semi-evergreen shrub

This vigorous shrub or small tree has
arching branches clothed in dark green
leaves; some of them turn bronze in
autumn. It is one of the tallest of the
cotoneasters. The clusters of small
white spring flowers produce an
abundance of bright red fruits in
autumn. Plant it in full sun or partial
shade in moisture-retentive but well-
drained soil. It can be planted as a
screen or in a large shrub border, or it
can be trained to form a standard tree.

◊ ◊ ☼ ☀ Z7–8 H8–7
‡ ↔ to 30ft (10m)

COTONEASTER HORIZONTALIS

Deciduous shrub

A low-growing shrub with flattened, wide-spreading branches covered with small, oval, dark green leaves. The branches are arranged in a distinctive herringbone pattern. Small white, pink-flushed flowers appear in spring and are followed in autumn by bright scarlet-red fruit. The leaves also turn red in autumn, creating an outstanding display. Grow it against a wall or use it as a groundcover. Plant it in full sun in any moderately fertile, well-drained soil.

◊ ☼ Z5–7 H7–5
‡↔ to 3ft (1m)

EUONYMUS ALATUS

Deciduous shrub

There are few plants that can compete with the burning bush for dramatic autumn color. It has dark green leaves that are borne on curious, corky-winged shoots. In autumn the leaves turn a brilliant crimson-red. The purple-red autumn fruits open to reveal seeds with bright orange coats. Plant it in full sun or light shade in any well-drained soil. It can be grown in a shrub border, but it also makes a beautiful specimen, planted alone so that its beauty can be fully appreciated.

◊ ☼ ☀ Z4–9 H9–1
‡ to 6ft (2m) ↔ to 10ft (3m)

EUPHORBIA DULCIS

Perennial

This spreading perennial has upright stems with oblong green leaves. The upper part of the stem is branched and covered with triangular leaves. In autumn, the stems turn purple and the leaves take on various shades of red, yellow, and orange. Yellow-green flowerheads are produced in late spring. It is best in a moist, organic soil in light shade, but it does tolerate drier soils. It self-seeds freely. Good for a shady border and excellent for a woodland garden.

◊ ◊ ☼ Z4–9 H9–1
‡↔ to 12in (30cm)

FOTHERGILLA GARDENII

Deciduous shrub

The witch alder is a small, bushy shrub with dark green, oval leaves. In late spring it produces cylindrical spikes of small white flowers. It is also grown for its autumn display, in which the leaves become infused with intense shades of red, yellow, and orange. It should be grown in a sunny position in moisture-retentive but well-drained, organic, acidic soil. It can be grown in partial shade, but the color of the autumn foliage will be less vibrant.

◊ ◊ ☼ ƒ Z5–9 H9–5
‡↔ to 3ft (1m)

GAULTHERIA TASMANICA

Evergreen shrub

Originating in Tasmania, this is a dwarf, mat-forming shrub with small, glossy, dark green leaves. In spring it produces bell-shaped white flowers that are followed in autumn by bright red fruits. It is best planted in partial shade in moist, neutral or acidic soil, but it will tolerate some sun if the soil does not dry out. It is suitable for the front of a shady border or a woodland garden. It can also be planted in containers; use acidic soil mix, and do not let it dry out.

◐ ☼ Z8–9 H9–8
‡ to 3in (7cm) ↔ to 10in (25cm)

HAKONECHLOA MACRA
'Aureola'

Perennial

This clump-forming Japanese grass has arching, slender, bright yellow leaves that are narrowly striped with green. They become red-tinted in autumn. In late summer and early autumn it bears spiky flowerheads. Plant it in partial shade in fertile, moist but well-drained, organic soil. It is ideal for a woodland garden or for planting at the front of a mixed or herbaceous border. It also looks good in containers.

○ ◐ ☼ Z5–9 H9–5
‡ to 14in (35cm) ↔ to 16in (40cm)

HELENIUM
'Bruno'

Perennial

This upright perennial forms dense
clumps of midgreen leaves. From late
summer to autumn it produces
abundant heads of deep red-crimson,
daisylike flowers with chocolate brown
centers. Although the flower stems are
sturdy, they may need staking in
exposed sites. Grow it in a sunny
border in any moisture-retentive but
well-drained fertile soil. To keep
clumps vigorous and productive,
divide them every two or three years.

◊ ◑ ☼ Z4–8 H8–1
‡ to 4ft (1.2m) ↔ to 24in (60cm)

HYDRANGEA
QUERCIFOLIA

Deciduous shrub

The oak-leaved hydrangea is a mound-
forming shrub with deeply lobed green
leaves that flush to deep red and
bronze-purple in autumn. From late
summer to autumn it bears tall, cone-
shaped spikes of white flowers that
become flushed with pink as they age.
It should be planted in full sun or
partial shade in moist but well-drained,
organic, moderately fertile soil.
It is suitable for a shrub border or
a woodland garden.

◊ ◑ ☼ ◐ Z5–8 H8–5
‡ to 6ft (2m) ↔ to 8ft (2.5m)

IMPERATA CYLINDRICA *'Rubra'*

Perennial

Japanese blood grass forms clumps of narrow green leaves that turn wine red as the season progresses. By autumn, when fluffy, silvery flowerheads appear, the leaves have become crimson-scarlet. Grow in full sun or light shade in organic, moist but well-drained soil. Protect young plants with a winter mulch. Overcrowded clumps can be divided in early spring. It is a good plant for woodland gardens, herbaceous borders, or containers.

◊ ◊ ☼ ☀ Z4–9 H9–1
‡ to 16in (40cm) ↔ to 12in (30cm)

LONICERA PERICLYMENUM *'Belgica'*

Climber

Early Dutch honeysuckle is a vigorous climber with bright red berries for autumn interest. It has midgreen leaves and flowers in spring and again in late summer. The tubular flowers, white on the inside and red outside, are highly scented. It is ideal for growing through a tree or over a trellis. If given space to scramble, it will seldom need pruning. Grow it in full sun or partial shade in organic, moist but well-drained soil.

◊ ◊ ☼ ☀ ƒ Z5–9 H9–5
‡ to 22ft (7m)

MALUS × SCHIEDECKERI
'Red Jade'

Deciduous tree

An attractive small tree with weeping branches, 'Red Jade' has bright pink buds that open in the spring to semi-double, pink-flushed white flowers. These are followed in autumn by a profusion of bright red, cherry-sized fruit. The leaves are bright green and glossy. Grow it in full sun in moist but well-drained, moderately fertile soil. It makes a beautiful specimen tree that is suitable for small gardens.

○ ◐ ☼ Z5–8 H8–5
↕ to 12ft (4m) ↔ to 20ft (6m)

NYSSA SYLVATICA

Deciduous tree

The tupelo is a broad, cone-shaped tree with slightly drooping lower branches, an interestingly textured bark, and exuberant autumn color. The dark green leaves turn vibrant yellow, orange, and finally red-crimson shades in mid- to late autumn. Plant it in a sheltered site in full sun or partial shade in neutral to slightly acidic soil that is fertile and moisture retentive but well drained. It makes a glorious specimen tree for larger gardens.

○ ◐ ☼ ◑ Z5–9 H9–5
↕ to 70ft (20m) ↔ to 30ft (10m)

PARROTIA PERSICA

Deciduous tree

The Persian ironwood is a shrubby tree with peeling gray and brown bark. The large, glossy leaves put on a glorious autumn display in shades of red, orange, and yellow. In late winter or early spring small, spidery red flowers appear on the bare branches. Plant in full sun or partial shade in a good depth of fertile, moist but well-drained soil. The best autumn color occurs on acidic soil, but it also tolerates alkaline conditions. A fine specimen tree, it develops great character with age.

◊ ◑ ☼ ☀ Z4–7 H7–1
↕ to 25ft (8m) ↔ to 30ft (10m)

PARTHENOCISSUS TRICUSPIDATA

Climber

Boston ivy is a vigorous woody climber with glossy, dark green leaves that are toothed and divided into three lobes. In autumn these turn gold, brilliant red, and purple before falling. It is superb for covering a large, unattractive, or featureless wall or for growing through a tall, sturdy tree. Grow it in full sun or shade in fertile, organic, well-drained soil. Provide young plants with support until they are established.

◊ ◑ ☼ ☀ Z4–8 H8–1
↕ to 70ft (20m)

PRUNUS AVIUM

Deciduous tree

The European wild cherry, or gean, is a large, spreading tree with dark green leaves that are tinted bronze in spring and turn red and gold in autumn. In the middle of spring it bears clusters of white flowers, followed in late summer and autumn by small, dark red fruit that birds love to eat. Plant it in full sun or partial shade in fertile, moist but well-drained soil. It is a fine specimen tree and is also useful in a larger garden for attracting wildlife.

○ ◑ ☼ ☀ Z4–8 H8–1
‡ to 70ft (20m) ↔ to 30ft (10m)

RHUS TYPHINA
'Dissecta'

Deciduous tree

The staghorn sumac gets its common name from the upright, velvet-covered branch tips that resemble antlers. In summer, upright spikes of small, yellow-green flowers turn dark crimson as they become fruit. The ferny leaves turn shades of brilliant red, gold, and orange in autumn. Plant in full sun in fertile, moist but well-drained soil. If its spreading suckers are a nuisance, they can be dug out in late autumn or early spring, when the plant is dormant.

○ ◑ ☼ Z3–8 H8–1
‡ to 6ft (2m) ↔ to 10ft (3m)

ROSA MOYESII
'Geranium'

Deciduous shrub

'Geranium' is a more compact form of a rather vigorous species. It has strong, arching stems and delicately divided green leaves. In summer it bears single, cup-shaped, sealing-wax-red flowers that are followed by spectacular bright orange-red, flask-shaped hips (fruit) in autumn. It is good for a sunny mixed border or wild garden. Plant it in fertile, organic, moist but well-drained soil. To keep it compact, shorten the main stems by up to a third after flowering.

◊ ◖ ☼ Z4–9 H9–1
↕ to 12ft (4m) ↔ to 10ft (3m)

ROSA × ODORATA
'Mutabilis'

Deciduous shrub

This slender shrub has purple-red stems and purple-flushed, dark green leaves. The single, cup-shaped flowers open pale yellow, then turn pink and then finally carmine-red; they are borne over a long period from summer to autumn and have a wonderful fragrance. Plant it in a sheltered position in fertile, organic, moist but well-drained soil. It is often grown as a shrub rose but will also climb if it is provided with some support.

◊ ◖ ☼ *f*Z7–9 H9–7
↕↔ to 6ft (2m)

ROSA RUGOSA

Deciduous shrub

Easy-going and vigorous, this repeat-flowering rose has robust, prickly stems and wrinkled, bright green leaves that turn yellow in autumn. The single, fragrant, carmine-red flowers are borne from early summer to autumn. From late summer they are accompanied by large, spherical, orange-red hips. Tolerant of a wide range of conditions, it prefers full sun or light shade and a moist but well-drained soil. It makes a superb, intruder-proof hedge. Trim or prune to shape in late winter or early spring.

◊ ◊ ☼ ☀ *f* Z2–9 H9–1
‡↔ to 2m (6ft)

RUSCUS ACULEATUS

Evergreen shrub

Butcher's broom is a clump-forming plant with upright stems that bear very tough, spine-tipped, leaflike modified stems. From late summer to winter, female plants produce small, round, bright red berries. Male and female or hermaphrodite plants are needed to ensure fruiting. It grows in sun to deep shade and in any but waterlogged soil; it also tolerates dry soil. The cut stems can be used in flower arrangements.

◊ ◊ ☼ ☀ Z7–9 H9–7
‡ to 75cm (2½ft) ↔ to 1m (3ft)

SCHIZOSTYLIS COCCINEA

Perennial

From late summer to autumn, the Kaffir lily produces shiny, bright red flowers on strong but slender stems that are held above green, strap-shaped, almost evergreen leaves. Remove flowers as they fade. Grow in a sunny, sheltered position in fertile, moist soil, and protect the crowns with a mulch in winter where marginally hardy. It spreads freely; divide overcrowded clumps in spring. Plant it in a herbaceous border or beside water. It is also good for cutting.

◊ ☼ Z7–9 H9–7
‡ to 20in (50cm) ↔ to 12in (30cm)

SORBUS AUCUPARIA

Deciduous tree

The European mountain ash is a small or medium-sized tree with midgreen leaves divided into small leaflets. In spring it bears clusters of creamy white flowers that are followed by bright red berries in autumn. They are very attractive to birds. The foliage turns red or yellow in autumn. Plant in full sun or partial shade in moderately fertile, organic, well-drained soil. It is tolerant of a wide range of conditions and will grow happily on both acidic and slightly alkaline soils.

◊ ☼ ☀ Z4–7 H7–1
‡ to 50ft (15m) ↔ to 22ft (7m)

SORBUS COMMIXTA

Deciduous tree

Slightly smaller than *Sorbus aucuparia*, this tree has dark green leaves divided into many small, lance-shaped leaflets. The autumn color is outstanding as the leaves become infused with brilliant shades of vivid red, yellow, and purple. In late spring it bears clusters of white flowers that are followed by bright orange-red or red autumn fruits. It should be planted in full sun or dappled shade in moderately fertile, organic, moist but well-drained soil.

◊ ◊ ☼ ☀ Z6–8 H8–6
‡ to 30ft (10m) ↔ to 27ft (7m)

SORBUS SARGENTIANA

Deciduous tree

The large leaves of this slow-growing tree are divided into lance-shaped green leaflets that take on brilliant shades of red and orange in autumn. In winter, distinctive, bright red, sticky buds form. In early summer it produces clusters of white flowers, followed by broad bunches of small scarlet fruits in autumn. Plant it in a sunny position in organic, fertile, moist but well-drained soil. It makes a beautiful specimen tree and, like other mountain ashes, has several seasons of interest.

◊ ◊ ☼ Z5–7 H7–5
‡↔ to 30ft (10m)

TIGRIDIA PAVONIA

Bulbous perennial

The tiger flower bears unusual flowers in succession during late summer to early autumn. The flowers, up to 6in (15cm) across, are bright red and marked at the base with dark red or brown spots. Pink, white, or yellow varieties are also available. It can be grown in sunny borders in light sandy soil. Where not hardy, it must be lifted before winter. Store bulbs dry in a frost-free place and replant in spring, or grow in deep pots of sandy, soil-based potting mix.

◊ ☼ Z13–15 H12–7
‡ to 5ft (1.5m) ↔ to 4in (10cm)

TITHONIA ROTUNDIFOLIA
'Torch'

Annual

The Mexican sunflower is a robust annual with large, three-lobed leaves. It flowers from late summer to early autumn and has large, dahlia-like flowers on tall, sturdy stems. The petals are bright red or orange-red and surround a raised yellow center. Plant out after the last frosts. Grow in full sun in fertile, well-drained soil. Provide a spot that is sheltered from strong winds, and support the tall stems by tying them in to sturdy stakes as they grow.

◊ ☼ Z0 H12–6
‡ to 6ft (2m) ↔ to 12in (30cm)

VITIS
'Brant'

Climber

This vigorous, woody-stemmed grape is
grown for its autumn color and edible,
blue-black fruit that ripen in autumn.
The deeply lobed leaves are green
throughout summer, but in autumn they
take on vibrant shades of deep red and
purple, with yellow veins. It can be
trained against a wall on supporting
wires and is excellent on a pergola.
Grow it in a warm, sheltered spot in
full sun in well-drained, preferably
neutral to alkaline soil.

◊ ☼ Z5–9 H9–5
‡ to 22ft (7m)

VITIS COIGNETIAE

Climber

One of the best climbers for autumn
color, this rampant grape has large,
heart-shaped green leaves that turn
vivid shades of bright red and crimson
in autumn. It is ideal for clothing a
pergola, growing through a big tree,
or for disguising a large, featureless wall.
Plant it in full sun or partial shade in
well-drained, neutral to alkaline soil.
If it gets too large, prune it back to
strong buds in winter to within 2in
(5cm) of the previous year's growth.

◊ ☼ ☼ Z5–9 H9–5
‡ to 50ft (15m)

ASTER NOVI-BELGII
'Peace'

Perennial

This vigorous New York aster produces large, mauve-purple flowerheads from late summer to autumn. It is best planted at the back or middle of the herbaceous border in full sun and in fertile, moist soil. It has strong stems, so supports are not essential. Divide every two or three years in spring.

◑ ☼ Z4–8 H8–1
‡ to 36in (90cm) ↔ to 30in (75cm)

ASTER NOVI-BELGII
'Jenny'

Perennial

Late-flowering New York asters come in shades of pink, purple, or blue. 'Jenny' has yellow-centered, double, red-purple, daisylike flowerheads. It is best planted in a herbaceous border in full sun or light shade and in fertile, moist soil with twiggy sticks or stakes for support. Divide every second or third year in spring to maintain vigor.

◑ ☼ ☀ Z4–8 H8–1
‡ to 5ft (1.5m) ↔ to 24in (60cm)

BILLARDIERA LONGIFLORA

Climber

The climbing blueberry has rather wiry stems that will climb over any suitable support. It has narrow, lance-shaped, dark green leaves. The green, bell-shaped flowers of summer are followed by purplish blue, egg-shaped fruit in autumn; some plants bear pink, red, or white fruit. Grow in full sun or light shade in organic, neutral to acidic soil. Where not hardy, grow in a greenhouse in a container of acidic soil mix.

◊ ☼ ☀ Z8–9 H9–8
‡ to 10ft (3m)

BUDDLEJA CRISPA

Deciduous shrub

The arching stems of this attractive, late-flowering shrub are clothed in toothed, white-felted leaves. From midsummer to early autumn it produces large, fragrant, clustered spikes of lilac flowers. It is very attractive to beneficial insects and butterflies. Grow in a mixed border or in a shrub border. Plant it in full sun in fertile, well-drained soil.

◊ ☼ ƒ Z8–9 H9–8
‡↔ to 10ft (3m)

CALLICARPA BODINIERI
'Profusion'

Deciduous shrub

This beautyberry is a striking shrub with upright branches and large, pale green leaves that are tinted bronze in spring. It produces pale pink flowers in midsummer but is grown mainly for its colorful fruit that look just like clusters of shining, bright violet beads. These are retained on the bare branches after leaf fall. Grow in full sun or light, dappled shade in well-drained, fertile soil. Planting in groups will maximize fruiting.

◊ ☼ ☀ Z6–8 H8–6
‡ to 10ft (3m) ↔ to 8ft (2.5m)

CALLUNA VULGARIS
'Silver Queen'

Evergreen shrub

Heathers are invaluable for providing color at the end of summer. 'Silver Queen' is grown for the year-round interest of its attractive, downy, silver-gray leaves and for the display of tiny, bell-shaped mauve flowers from midsummer to autumn. The flowers are very attractive to bees. Plant it in full sun in an open site in organic, well-drained, acidic soil. Trim plants in spring to keep them compact.

◊ ☼ Z5–7 H7–5
‡ to 16in (40cm) ↔ to 22in (55cm)

COLCHICUM AGRIPPINUM

Cormous perennial

This autumn crocus has funnel-shaped, purplish pink flowers that are marked with a conspicuous checkerboard pattern. It has upright, slightly wavy, strap-shaped leaves that appear in early spring but disappear by summer. The corms should be planted 10cm (4in) deep in summer or early autumn. Grow in an open situation in full sun in deep, fertile, well-drained soil. It is suitable for a rock garden or trough or can be grown in a container.

◊ ☼ Z4–9 H9–1
‡ to 4in (10cm) ↔ to 3in (8cm)

CROCUS MEDIUS

Cormous perennial

This is an attractive dwarf crocus with funnel-shaped, bright purple flowers in late autumn. The narrow leaves, which are green with a silvery white line down the center, appear with or just after the flowers. It is suitable for naturalizing in grass or for planting in a rock garden. Grow it in full sun in gritty, very well-drained, poor to moderately fertile soil. It prefers dry conditions during summer, when it is dormant.

◊ ☼ Z3–8 H8–1
‡ to 3in (8cm) ↔ to 1in (2.5cm)

GAULTHERIA MUCRONATA
'Mulberry Wine'

Evergreen shrub

This bushy shrub has shining, spine-tipped, dark green leaves. In late spring and summer it bears small white flowers that are followed in autumn by glossy fruits that ripen to dark purple. Grow in partial shade, in acidic, organic, moist soil. Grow male and female plants together to ensure fruiting. Gaultherias associate well with heathers and are suitable for woodland gardens. There are also varieties with pink, red, or white fruits.

◊ ☼ Z8–9 H9–8
↕ ↔ to 4ft (1.2m)

LIRIOPE MUSCARI

Perennial

The big blue lilyturf is a densely clump-forming, evergreen perennial with narrow, strap-shaped, dark green leaves. In late summer and early autumn it produces long, slender spikes of small violet-mauve flowers. Plant it in partial or full shade in acidic to neutral, preferably moist but well-drained soil. It will tolerate dry, shady conditions. Use it as a groundcover, in a woodland garden, or for planting toward the front of a border. Overcrowded clumps can be divided in spring.

◊ ◊ ☼ ☼ Z6–10 H10–6
↕ to 12in (30cm) ↔ to 18in (45cm)

SORBUS REDUCTA

Deciduous shrub

The upright, suckering stems of this unusual shrubby mountain ash spread to form a dense, low thicket. The finely divided leaves turn red and purple in autumn. In spring it bears clusters of small white flowers, followed by pink-flushed white berries. Plant in an open site in full sun in organic, moderately fertile, well-drained soil. It is good for small urban gardens and roadside situations, since it tolerates pollution. Pull out unwanted stems when still young and soft.

◊ ☼ Z5–8 H8–5
‡ to 5ft (1.5m) ↔ to 6ft (2m)

TRICYRTIS FORMOSANA

Perennial

This vigorous perennial spreads by means of underground stems. In autumn it produces small, pinkish purple flowers patterned with purple spots. It has slightly hairy, branched stems and glossy, dark green leaves. Plant it in a sheltered, shady situation, in moist but well-drained, organic soil. It is an excellent plant for a damp woodland garden or a shady border.

◊ ◊ ☼ ☀ Z6–9 H9–6
‡ to 32in (80cm) ↔ to 18in (45cm)

ACONITUM CARMICHAELII *'Arendsii'*

Perennial

This monkshood makes a striking display with its tall spikes of deep blue flowers that appear from early to midautumn. An upright plant with deeply lobed, dark green leaves, it is suitable for a woodland garden and is also successful in a shaded mixed or herbaceous border. Plant in partial shade and in moist, fertile soil. It is best in a site sheltered from strong winds; support the stems with stakes. All parts of this plant are toxic.

◊ ♦ ☼ Z3–7 H7–1
‡ to 5ft (1.5m) ↔ to 12in (30cm)

AMPELOPSIS GLANDULOSA *VAR.* BREVIPEDUNCULATA

Climber

The leaves of this vigorous climber are divided into three or five lobes and color well in autumn. It is grown for its attractive fruit, which change color from green to pinkish purple to greenish blue and deep blue. Plant it against a wall or fence or on a pergola. Choose a position in full sun with fertile, moist but well-drained soil. It tolerates partial shade but fruits more freely in sun.

◊ ♦ ☼ ☼ Z5–8 H8–5
‡ to 15ft (5m)

ASTER NOVI-BELGII
'Professor Anton Kippenburg'

Perennial

This is one of the best New York asters
for the small garden. From late summer
to midautumn it bears pale, clear blue,
daisylike flowerheads with yellow
centers. The leaves are dark green and
lance shaped. It is very vigorous, but
because it is relatively short-growing,
it does not require staking. Plant it in
full sun or partial shade in fertile, moist
soil. Cut back and mulch after flowering.
It should be divided every two or
three years in spring.

◊ ☼ ☼ Z4–8 H8–1
‡ to 14in (35cm) ↔ to 18in (45cm)

ASTER × FRIKARTII
'Wunder von Stäfa'

Perennial

A superb plant for the middle of a
border, this tall aster has dark green
leaves and stiffly upright stems. Bright
blue flowers with yellow centers are
produced from late summer until early
autumn. Plant in moderately fertile, well-
drained, preferably alkaline soil in full
sun. After flowering, cut stems back to
the ground and apply a layer of mulch.
It can be increased quickly by division
in spring.

◊ ☼ Z5–8 H8–5
‡ to 28in (70cm) ↔ to 16in (40cm)

CEANOTHUS
'Autumnal Blue'

Evergreen shrub

The majority of California lilacs flower
during spring or early summer, but this
one produces clusters of small, vivid
blue flowers in late summer to early
autumn. It has broadly oval, glossy,
dark green leaves. Plant it in full sun,
with some protection from wind, in
fertile, well-drained soil. It rarely needs
pruning, but if wayward shoots spoil
the symmetry of the shrub, they should
be removed when flowering is over.

○ ☼ Z9–10 H10–9
↕↔ to 10ft (3m)

CERATOSTIGMA
WILLMOTTIANUM

Deciduous shrub

This is an attractive, spreading shrub
with small, lance-shaped green leaves.
In late summer and early autumn it
bears pale blue flowers – the later ones
among red-tinted autumn leaves. Grow
in full sun in moderately fertile, moist
but well-drained soil. Where marginally
hardy the shoots may be killed by
winter cold, but if mulched for winter,
the plant should produce new shoots
from the base in spring.

○ ◐ ☼ Z6–9 H9–6
↕ to 3ft (1m) ↔ to 5ft (1.5m)

GENTIANA SINO-ORNATA

Perennial

This beautiful autumn gentian
overwinters as a rosette of glossy, dark
green leaves. Low, spreading shoots
appear in spring, each developing at its
tip an upward-pointing, deep blue
flower in autumn. The base of the
flower's throat is greenish white marked
with distinct purplish blue lines radiating
from the center. Plant it in organic,
moist but well-drained, acidic or neutral
soil with some shade from strong
summer sun. It is suitable for
a rock garden or trough.

◊ ◊ ☼ Z5–7 H7–5
‡ to 3in (7cm) ↔ to 12in (30cm)

HEBE
'Autumn Glory'

Evergreen shrub

Among the prettiest of the autumn-
flowering hebes, this shrub forms a
spreading mound of purple-tinted, dark
green, broadly oval leaves. The spikes
of small, violet-blue flowers open in the
middle of summer and continue to be
produced until the first frosts. Plant in
full sun or light shade in moist but
well-drained, fertile, neutral to slightly
alkaline soil.

◊ ◊ ☼ ☼ Z9–10 H10–9
‡ to 24in (60cm) ↔ to 36in (90cm)

Hordeum jubatum

Perennial

The squirrel-tail grass is a tufted grass with arching, narrow green leaves. The attractive, nodding flowerheads with long, feathery bristles appear in summer. They are green when young, turning pale buff-beige in autumn. Plant in full sun in well-drained, moderately fertile soil in a herbaceous border or wild garden. The heads may be cut and dried upside down for use in winter flower arrangements

◊ ☼ Z4–8 H8–1
↕ to 24in (60cm) ↔ to 12in (30cm)

Kniphofia
'Percy's Pride'

Perennial

This red-hot poker forms clumps of tough, slender, arching leaves and bears heads of tubular flowers in late summer and early autumn. Green in bud, the flowers open greenish yellow and become cream with age. Grow in a sunny or partially shaded site in deep, fertile, moist but well-drained soil. Cover young plants with a protective mulch for their first winter, and cut back old growth in spring.

◊ ◑ ☼ ☼ Z6–9 H9–6
↕ to 4ft (1.2m) ↔ to 24in (60cm)

MATTEUCCIA STRUTHIOPTERIS

Perennial

In spring, the ostrich fern produces a cluster of brilliant green fronds arranged in a tight funnel. In late summer, dark brown fertile fronds appear at the center of the plant. Plant in partial shade in moist, neutral to acidic, organic soil, particularly in a woodland or near water. It spreads by underground stems to form large colonies. It can be increased by lifting and separating young plants from the parent plant in spring.

◊ ☼ Z3–8 H8–1
‡ to 5ft (1.5m) ↔ to 30in (75cm)

MISCANTHUS SINENSIS *'Silberfeder'*

Perennial

This tall grass forms a large clump of arching, midgreen leaves and, in early and midautumn, upright stems bearing silvery buff flowerheads. Suitable for most soils, it grows best in full sun in moderately fertile, moist but well-drained soil. The flowerheads can be left in place during winter but should be cut down to the ground, together with all dead growth, in early spring. This grass is easily increased by dividing established clumps in spring.

◊ ◊ ☼ Z4–9 H9–1
‡ to 8ft (2.5m) ↔ to 4ft (1.2m)

OSMUNDA REGALIS

Perennial

The elegant royal fern forms a
substantial clump of upright, finely
divided, bright green fronds that turn
shades of apricot-yellow before they
die down. In summer, distinctive rusty
brown, tassel-like fronds rise from the
center of the clump. Grow in partial
shade in moist, organic, preferably
acidic soil. It can be planted in full sun
in permanently damp soils. The royal
fern makes a beautiful specimen in
damp woodland or beside a stream
or pond.

◊ ◐ ☼ Z4–9 H9–1
‡ to 6ft (2m) ↔ to 12ft (4m)

PANICUM VIRGATUM
'Heavy Metal'

Perennial

This is a particularly upright-growing
switch grass. In late summer it produces
beautiful, nodding spikes of small,
purple-green flowers. The metallic,
bluish green leaves turn golden yellow
in late autumn and finally light brown
in winter. It has a beautiful winter
presence in the garden, especially when
the flowerheads are left in place. Grow
in a sunny site in well-drained,
moderately fertile soil. Cut back before
growth begins in early spring.

◊ ☼ Z5–9 H9–5
‡ to 3ft (1m) ↔ to 30in (75cm)

PENNISETUM ALOPECUROIDES
'Hameln'

Perennial

Fountain grass is a clump-forming plant with flat, pointed, dark green evergreen leaves. 'Hameln' is compact and, in summer and early autumn, it bears long, arching spikes of pale green flowers. The leaves turn yellow before they die, and the flowers age to a warm, light gray-brown. Grow in full sun in moderately fertile, well-drained soil. Provide a winter mulch where marginally hardy, or grow in containers. Cut back in spring before growth begins.

◊ ☼ Z6–9 H9–6
↕ to 5ft (1.5m) ↔ to 4ft (1.2m)

THELYPTERIS PALUSTRIS

Perennial

The marsh fern has attractive, long-stalked, lacy, pale green fronds. It is suitable for growing in a damp border and is perfectly at home on the banks of a stream or pool, especially in a wild garden. Grow it in full sun or partial shade in permanently moist, moderately fertile soil. Spreading by means of creeping, underground stems, it can become rather invasive; chop out unwanted clumps with a sharp spade.

◊ ◊◊ ☼ ☼ Z5–8 H8–5
↕ to 24in (60cm) ↔ to 3ft (1m)

ASTER LINOSYRIS

Perennial

Goldilocks is an upright, slender,
herbaceous perennial with stems
clothed in narrow, midgreen leaves.
In late summer and early autumn
it produces dense heads of many tiny,
fluffy, bright yellow flowers. Grow
in well-drained, moderately fertile,
preferably alkaline soil in a sunny site.
It can be grown on a rock garden,
at the front of a border, or in a wild
garden. It is attractive to late-flying
beneficial insects.

◊ ☼ Z3–8 H8–1
‡ to 24in (60cm) ↔ to 12in (30cm)

BETULA PENDULA
'Tristis'

Deciduous tree

This elegant, fast-growing tree has
white bark and cascading branches
bearing diamond-shaped, dark green
leaves that turn bright golden yellow
in autumn. It bears long, hanging
yellow catkins in early spring. Its
narrow crown casts little shade, making
it ideal for a small garden. Plant it as a
specimen tree or in a group in full sun
or light, dappled shade. It tolerates a
range of soils but prefers moist but well
drained and moderately fertile ones.

◊ ◊ ☼ ☀ Z2–7 H7–1
‡ to 80ft (25m) ↔ to 30ft (10m)

CALLUNA VULGARIS
'Robert Chapman'

Evergreen shrub

This heather has dense, golden yellow
foliage and bears spikes of purple-pink
flowers in late summer. In winter the
leaves take on orange and red shades,
retaining the color until the new growth
emerges the following spring. Plant in
a group to maximize its effect; it
associates well with other heathers with
different foliage tints. Grow in sun,
in well-drained, organic, acidic soil.
Shear off flowered shoots in spring
to keep it compact.

○ ☼ Z5–7 H7–5
‡ to 10in (25cm) ↔ to 26in (65cm)

CHRYSANTHEMUM
'Pennine Alfie'

Perennial

In early autumn this chrysanthemum
has bright yellow, semidouble flowers
with spoon-shaped petals and bright
red bases. Plant it in a sunny border
in fertile, moist but well-drained soil.
Support the stems with stakes. Lift
plants after flowering, and overwinter
in frost-free conditions. Plant out in
spring after the last frost or raise
new plants from basal cuttings.

○ ◑ ☼ Z3–9 H9–1
‡ to 4ft (1.2m) ↔ to 30in (75cm)

CHRYSANTHEMUM
'Wendy'

Perennial

A spray chrysanthemum with light bronze, double flowers in early autumn. The outer petals point downward, rather like an umbrella. For extra-large flowers, remove all but four of the buds. Support stems with stakes. Lift plants after flowering, then overwinter in frost-free conditions. Plant out in spring once frost is over, or raise new plants from basal cuttings taken in winter. Grow in reasonably fertile, moist but well-drained soil in a sunny position.

◊ ◊ ☼ Z3–9 H9–1
‡ to 4ft (1.2m) ↔ to 30in (75cm)

CLEMATIS
'Bill MacKenzie'

Climber

In late summer and early autumn, this vigorous climber produces hanging, bell-shaped flowers up to 3in (8cm) across. The blooms are yellow with red anthers and are followed by feathery, silvery seedheads. Plant in fertile, organic, moist but well-drained soil, with the plant's base in shade and the upper growth in sun or light shade. Provide support. In spring, cut back the previous year's growth to a pair of strong buds about 8in (20cm) from the base.

◊ ◊ ☼ ☼ Z6–9 H9–6
‡ to 22in (7m)

CLEMATIS TANGUTICA

Climber

This late-flowering clematis has bluish green, divided leaves and from midsummer to autumn produces large numbers of hanging, bell-shaped, bright yellow flowers. They are followed by silky seedheads that last into winter. Grow it up a trellis or through a small tree, or allow it to scramble over a bank as a groundcover. Plant in fertile, organic, moist but well-drained soil in full sun or partial shade with the roots in cool shade. Cut back hard in spring to within 8in (20cm) of the base.

◊ ◖ ☼ ☀ Z6–9 H9–6
‡ to 20ft (6m)

CLEMATIS REHDERIANA

Climber

One of the more unusual species of clematis, with clusters of small, nodding, primrose yellow flowers that smell like cowslips. It flowers from the middle of summer to autumn. Plant in fertile, organic, moist but well-drained soil in full sun or partial shade, but with the roots shaded and kept cool with a gravel mulch. Grow it on supports against a fence or wall, over a pergola, or into a tree. Cut back hard in spring, cutting strong shoots to a pair of strong buds 8in (20cm) from the base.

◊ ◖ ☼ ☀ ƒ Z6–9 H9–6
‡ to 22ft (7m)

COTONEASTER FRIGIDUS
'Fructu Luteo'

Deciduous shrub

The upright stems of this shrubby or
treelike cotoneaster arch gracefully as
it matures. The narrow leaves are dull
green but develop golden tints in
autumn. In summer the branches are
wreathed with white flowers that give
rise to creamy yellow fruit in autumn.
Grow in sun or dappled shade in any
well-drained, moderately fertile soil.
Use as an ornamental screen, at the
back of a shrub border, or as a specimen.

◊ ☼ ◐ Z7–8 H8–7
↕↔ to 30ft (10m)

COTONEASTER SALICIFOLIUS
'Rothschildianus'

Evergreen shrub

This vigorous, spreading shrub has
narrow, pale green leaves and clusters
of white flowers along the arching
branches in early summer. In autumn
it produces clusters of attractive golden
yellow fruit. It is an extremely beautiful
shrub for the back of a mixed or shrub
border. Where there is enough room,
it makes an attractive specimen. Plant it
in full sun or partial shade in any
moderately fertile, well-drained soil.

◊ ◖ ☼ ◐ Z6–8 H8–6
↕↔ to 15ft (5m)

CREPIS AUREA

Perennial

A pretty late-flowering plant for the rock garden, with a low rosette of rounded, toothed, light green leaves. In late summer and early autumn it produces hairy, wiry stems bearing yellow-orange, dandelion-like flowerheads that are attractive to late-flying beneficial insects. It is easy to grow in full sun and in any well-drained soil. It has a long taproot that enables it to survive dry summers.

◊ ☼ Z5–7 H7–5
‡ to 12in (30cm) ↔ to 6in (15cm)

GLADIOLUS PAPILIO

Cormous perennial

This is an attractive species of gladiolus that will add valuable late color to a mixed or herbaceous border. It blooms in late summer and early autumn, producing spikes of funnel-shaped flowers. These are pale yellow to greenish or golden yellow, often with soft purple blotches at the throat and purple-tinged outsides. The leaves are sword-shaped. Plant corms in spring in full sun in light, moderately fertile, well-drained soil. Mulch for winter where marginally hardy.

◊ ☼ Z8–10 H12–6
‡ to 3ft (1m) ↔ to 6in (15cm)

GLEDITSIA TRIACANTHOS *'Sunburst'*

Deciduous tree

This golden-leaved honeylocust is a conical tree with an open tracery of spreading branches. The delicate, ferny leaves are golden yellow in spring, later turning green, then brilliant yellow in autumn. 'Sunburst' is less vigorous and thorny than the species and makes a beautiful specimen for smaller gardens, especially in urban situations, since it tolerates pollution. Plant it in full sun in any well-drained, fertile soil.

◊ ☼ Z3–7 H7–1
↕ to 40ft (12m) ↔ to 30ft (10m)

HAMAMELIS VIRGINIANA

Deciduous shrub

Common witch hazel is an upright shrub with oval green leaves that turn bright yellow in autumn. As they begin to fall, small clusters of spidery yellow flowers are produced. Plant it in full sun or partial shade in moderately fertile, moist but well-drained, neutral to acidic soil. It prefers a site with some shelter from strong wind. Grow it as a specimen, at the back of a shrub border, or in a woodland garden.

◊ ◑ ☼ ◐ Z3–8 H8–1
↕↔ to 12ft (4m)

HELICHRYSUM SPLENDIDUM

Evergreen shrub

This clump-forming shrub has white-woolly stems and masses of tiny, silver-gray leaves. The deep yellow flowerheads appear at the tips of upright stems from late summer to autumn. They can be cut and dried for winter arrangements. It is drought tolerant and excellent for a hot, sunny bank or a mixed or herbaceous border. Grow in full sun in very well-drained, poor to moderately fertile soil. Trim each year in spring to keep it compact. It may not survive a wet winter.

◊ ☼ Z9–11 H12–1
↨↔ to 4ft (1.2m)

KIRENGESHOMA PALMATA

Perennial

This is a clump-forming perennial with dark stems bearing deeply lobed, slightly hairy, pale green leaves. In late summer and early autumn it produces nodding, tubular, pale yellow flowers with a waxy texture. Plant it in a shady situation in moist, acidic soil enriched with leaf mold. It is an elegant plant for a shady border or woodland garden and looks especially beautiful at the sides of streams or ponds.

◐ ☼ Z5–8 H8–5
↕ to 4ft (1.2m) ↔ to 30in (75cm)

LIQUIDAMBAR STYRACIFLUA
'Golden Treasure'

Deciduous tree

A slow-growing tree, this variegated sweet gum is grown mainly for its foliage. The deeply lobed, maplelike leaves are margined with rich yellow; in late autumn, they take on dramatic tints as they turn red and purple with golden margins. It tolerates partial shade, but the best autumn color develops in full sun. Plant in neutral to acidic, moderately fertile soil that is moist but well drained.

◊ ◊ ☼ ☼ Z6–9 H9–6
‡ to 30ft (10m) ↔ to 20ft (6m)

MALUS × ZUMI
'Golden Hornet'

Deciduous tree

An attractive crabapple, 'Golden Hornet' is valued for its spherical, golden yellow fruits that appear in autumn and remain on the bare branches well into winter. In spring it bears masses of white flowers that open from pink buds. Plant it in full sun in fertile, moist but well-drained soil. It is best grown as a specimen tree, sited where its pretty fruit can be fully appreciated. The slightly smaller variety *calocarpa* has bright red fruits.

◊ ◊ ☼ Z5–8 H8–5
‡ to 30ft (10m) ↔ to 25ft (8m)

PHYGELIUS × RECTUS
'Moonraker'

Evergreen shrub

This is a long-flowering, small shrub with glossy, dark green leaves and long, upright spikes of hanging, creamy yellow flowers from midsummer to autumn. Plant in full sun in fertile, moist but well-drained soil. Deadhead regularly to prolong flowering. Excellent in a mixed or herbaceous border and also good against a wall or fence. Where marginally hardy, provide a loose, deep winter mulch; it usually grows back from the base in spring.

○ ◑ ☼ Z8–9 H9–8
‡ to 3ft (1m) ↔ to 4ft (1.2m)

SAMBUCUS RACEMOSA
'Plumosa Aurea'

Deciduous shrub

The deeply cut yellow leaves of this red-berried elder are flushed bronze when young. The creamy flowers are borne in clusters in spring and are followed by red fruits in summer. Plant this shrub in a lightly shaded site, because the foliage may scorch in strong sun. Grow in moderately fertile, moist but well-drained soil. For the best foliage effects, prune it hard in spring to within a few buds of the base, then fertilize and mulch it.

○ ◑ ☼ Z3–7 H7–1
‡ to 10ft (3m) ↔ to 10ft (3m)

SOLIDAGO
'Golden Wings'

Perennial

This tall, upright goldenrod has stems
with narrow green leaves that are
topped in late summer and early
autumn by large, spreading clusters
of tiny, golden yellow flowers. It is one
of the most vigorous forms of goldenrod and is good for the back of a large
border or a wild garden. It attracts late-
flying beneficial insects. Plant it in full
sun in poor to moderately fertile, very
well-drained soil. The flowers are good
for cutting.

◊ ☼ Z5–9 H9–5
‡ to 6ft (2m) ↔ to 3ft (1m)

SORBUS
'Joseph Rock'

Deciduous tree

Suitable for the smaller garden, 'Joseph
Rock' grows quickly once established,
forming a crown of upright branches.
The finely divided, bright green leaves
turn brilliant shades of orange, red,
and purple during autumn, when it also
bears crops of particularly attractive,
creamy yellow berries that age to
golden yellow. There are clusters of
white flowers in spring. Plant it in full
sun or partial shade in fertile, moist but
well-drained, organic soil.

◊ ◊ ☼ ☀ Z7–8 H8–7
‡ to 30ft (10m) ↔ to 22ft (7m)

STERNBERGIA LUTEA

Bulbous perennial

The autumn daffodil bears deep yellow,
goblet-shaped flowers in autumn. The
narrow, dark green leaves appear with,
or just after, the flowers. Plant bulbs in
late summer in a warm, sunny site in
gritty, moderately fertile, very well-
drained soil. It is a beautiful plant for a
rock garden, but it is also suitable for a
container or a trough filled with gritty
soil mix. If conditions are suitable it will
spread to form clumps; leave bulbs
undisturbed, and do not divide unless
overcrowding impairs flowering.

◊ ☼ Z7–9 H9–7
‡ to 6in (15cm) ↔ to 3in (8cm)

TRICYRTIS OHSUMIENSIS

Perennial

The toad lily is a clump-forming
perennial with arching, slightly hairy
stems and pale green leaves. In early
autumn it produces star-shaped,
primrose yellow flowers covered with
numerous tiny brown spots. Plant in a
sheltered position in deep or partial
shade and in moist, organic, well-
drained soil. It is excellent for a damp
woodland or a shady border.

◊ ◑ ☼ Z6–9 H9–6
‡ to 20in (50cm) ↔ to 9in (23cm)

ACER CAMPESTRE

Deciduous tree

The field maple is a very underused tree that is ideal for planting in medium-sized gardens. It has a rounded crown of lobed, dark green leaves that take on autumn tints of apricot yellow and, in colder autumns, shades of orange and red. It tolerates pollution, clay, and shallow, alkaline soils. It can also be included in mixed hedges and wildlife gardens. Plant it in full sun or partial shade in any fertile, moist but well-drained soil.

◊ ◑ ☼ ☀ Z5–8 H8–5
↕ to 25ft (8m) ↔ to 12ft (4m)

ACER PLATANOIDES
'Palmatifidum'

Deciduous tree

An attractive form of Norway maple, this tree has five-lobed leaves, with the lobes drawn out into fine points. In autumn the leaves turn brilliant shades of orange and red. The conspicuous clusters of small flowers emerge in spring before the leaves. It is a large tree and needs plenty of space. Plant it in larger gardens in an open situation in full sun or partial shade in any fertile, moist but well-drained soil.

◊ ◑ ☼ ☀ Z5–8 H8–5
↕ to 70ft (20m) ↔ to 30ft (10m)

CHRYSANTHEMUM
'Amber Enbee Wedding'

Perennial

From late summer to midautumn, this
upright chrysanthemum produces warm
golden-amber flowers with yellow-green
centers. It is excellent for late color in a
mixed or herbaceous border. Grow
in full sun in moist but well-drained,
neutral to slightly acidic soil that has
been enriched with well-rotted organic
matter. Support the stems with stakes to
prevent them from falling over in wind
and heavy rain.

◊ ◊ ☼ Z3–9 H9–1
‡ to 4ft (1.2m) ↔ to 30in (75cm)

COTINUS
'Flame'

Deciduous shrub

Primarily grown for its stunning autumn
color, this bushy shrub or small tree
has oval, light green leaves that turn a
brilliant orange-red. In hot summers its
sprays of tiny flowers hover like a smoky
haze above the foliage. Grow it in a
shrub border or as a specimen in sun
or light shade in moist but well-drained,
moderately fertile soil. Cut back hard in
spring for the best foliage effects, and
fertilize and mulch after pruning.

◊ ◊ ☼ ☼ Z5–8 H8–5
‡ to 20ft (6m) ↔ to 15ft (5m)

EUPHORBIA GRIFFITHII
'Fireglow'

Perennial

The upright stems of this spurge are red when young and clothed with dark green, red-veined leaves. In early summer it produces clusters of yellow flowerheads surrounded by orange-red bracts The leaves turn fiery orange and red in autumn. Plant in light shade in moist, organic soil. It is good for woodland gardens or large shady borders. It can become invasive, and the milky sap may cause an allergic skin reaction.

◑ ☼ Z4–9 H9–1
‡ to 30in (75cm) ↔ to 3ft (1m)

HAMAMELIS VERNALIS
'Sandra'

Deciduous shrub

This vernal witch hazel has purple young leaves that gradually turn green as spring progresses, then, in autumn, they assume glorious shades of orange and red. The spidery yellow or reddish yellow flowers appear on the bare shoots during late winter and early spring. Plant it in full sun or partial shade in neutral to acidic, moist but well-drained soil. Best in a site that is not exposed to strong winds.

◔ ◑ ☼ ☀ Z4–8 H8–1
‡↔ to 15ft (5m)

HIPPOPHAE RHAMNOIDES

Deciduous shrub

Sea buckthorn is a vigorous shrub with narrow, silvery gray-green leaves and spiny branches. Inconspicuous spring flowers are followed in autumn, on female plants, by clusters of shining orange fruit. Grow male and female plants together to ensure fruiting. Grow in a mixed border or as an intruder-proof hedge. Plant in full sun in moist but well-drained soil. It thrives by the sea and tolerates exposed sites. If it becomes too large, it can be pruned hard in late summer or when dormant.

◊ ◊ ☼ Z3–8 H8–1
‡↔ to 20ft (6m)

LEONOTIS LEONURUS

Deciduous shrub

This frost-tender shrub with upright stems and lance-shaped leaves produces tiers of soft orange-red to scarlet flowers from autumn into early winter. Plant in full sun in moderately fertile, well-drained soil. Where not hardy it needs greenhouse protection in winter, but, if container grown, it can be moved to a sunny patio for summer. Cut pot-grown plants back hard in early spring to stimulate new growth. Outdoors, it may lose its leaves in winter.

◊ ☼ Z10–11 H12–1
‡ to 6ft (2m) ↔ to 3ft (1m)

Malus tschonoskii

Deciduous tree

Prized for its autumn color, this vigorous tree has a flame-shaped crown of rounded, glossy green leaves. It flowers in spring, bearing pink-flushed white flowers followed by red-tinged, yellow-green fruit. In autumn, the leaves take on spectacular shades of orange, scarlet, and purple. Plant it in full sun in moderately fertile, moist but well-drained soil. It makes a beautiful specimen tree for small to medium-sized gardens.

○ ◊ ◊ ☼ ☼ Z5–8 H8–5
‡ to 40ft (12m) ↔ to 22ft (7m)

Physalis alkekengi

Perennial

The Chinese lantern is a vigorously spreading perennial with triangular to diamond-shaped green leaves on upright stems. The nodding, creamy white flowers appear in midsummer and are followed by orange-red, papery pods that enclose orange fruits. Plant it in full sun or partial shade in fertile, well-drained soil. It can be grown in a border (although it can be invasive) and cut for dried arrangements.

○ ☼ ☼ Z5–8 H8–5
‡ to 30in (75cm) ↔ to 36in (90cm)

STIPA ARUNDINACEA

Perennial

Pheasant's tail grass is an evergreen that forms a loose tussock of arching, rather leathery, dark green leaves. As the season progresses the leaves begin to exhibit orange streaks; by winter, the entire clump has turned russet-brown. In summer, arching spikes of purplish green flowers appear; they also turn golden orange as they mature. Plant in full sun or partial shade in moderately fertile, well-drained soil. Cut back dead foliage and flowerheads in spring.

○ ☼ ◑ Z8–10 H10–8
↕ to 5ft (1.5m) ↔ to 4ft (1.2m)

ZELKOVA SERRATA

Deciduous tree

The Japanese zelkova is an elegant, wide-spreading tree that makes a fine specimen for a large garden. At maturity, the gray bark peels to reveal paler orange bark beneath. The coarsely toothed, dark green leaves rustle in the breeze and have wonderful autumn color in shades of yellow, orange, and red. Plant it in full sun or partial shade in deep, fertile, moist but well-drained soil. Choose a site that will give some protection from wind when young.

○ ◐ ☼ ◑ Z5–9 H9–5
↕ to 100ft (30m) ↔ to 80ft (25m)

WINTER

THE DARK, COLD months of winter need not be without cheer. A number of plants do flower in winter, and while few have large and exuberant blooms, several are prized for their scent – the witch hazels (*Hamamelis*), wintersweet (*Chimonanthus*), and early honeysuckles among them. Mahonias produce large sprays of highly fragrant flowers in the chill of winter, and the sweetly scented pink-white flowers of *Viburnum farreri* often appear during warm spells.

Consider, too, the many broadleaf evergreens that bring living color to the winter garden, such as hollies, pieris, rhododendrons, euonymus, osmanthus, sarcococcas, cherry laurels, camellias, boxwoods, barberries, viburnums, and skimmias. Some, such as the heaths and heathers (*Erica* and *Calluna*), assume vivid shades of orange, gold, and red in winter, often prompted or enhanced by periods of winter cold.

BARK AND SEEDHEADS

It is now that the branch structure of deciduous trees can be appreciated and the color and texture of the bark enjoyed, so often overlooked when trees are in full leaf. The snakebark maples, such as *Acer grosseri* var. *hersii*, are striped green and white, and the peeling, papery bark of *Acer griseum* glows coppery red in low winter light. Young stems of dogwoods also look dramatic at this time: vibrant red in *Cornus sanguinea* 'Winter Beauty' and *C. alba* 'Sibirica', while those of *C. alba* 'Kesselringii' are purple.

The dried seedheads of many plants have their part to play, most notably the silvery heads of pampas grass and miscanthus. Allow them to remain after the autumn cleanup; they can look magical when dusted with snow. Any lingering seeds will be appreciated by the birds, which will also be lured into the garden by berries on pyracanthas and cotoneasters.

ABELIOPHYLLUM DISTICHUM

Deciduous shrub

The so-called white forsythia has spreading branches clothed with oval, dark green leaves in summer. In late winter and early spring it produces clusters of small white flowers on bare branches that are invaluable for bringing fragrance into the winter garden. Plant it in a mixed border or as a free-standing shrub. Grow it in full sun in fertile, well-drained soil.

◊ ☼ *f* Z5–9 H9–5
↔ to 5ft (1.5m)

BETULA PAPYRIFERA

Deciduous tree

The paper birch has striking white bark that peels off in large sheets to expose the new, pale orange-brown bark beneath. Yellow, hanging catkins appear in spring, and the oval, dark green leaves turn attractive shades of yellow and orange in autumn. Plant it as a specimen tree; the white bark is seen at its best against a warm red brick wall or a dark background of evergreens. Grow in full sun or light shade in moderately fertile, moist but well-drained soil.

◊ ◐ ☼ ☀ Z2–7 H7–1
↕ to 70ft (20m) ↔ to 30ft (10m)

GALANTHUS ELWESII

Bulbous perennial

This is bigger than the common snowdrop in all its parts. It bears large, honey-scented white flowers with green blotches in late winter. It is a robust plant with broad, slightly twisted, waxy, bluish green leaves. Plant bulbs in early autumn in partial shade in organic, moist but well-drained soil. It does particularly well on alkaline soil. Grow in a woodland garden, naturalized in grass, or at the front of a mixed or herbaceous border. Divide large clumps after flowering while still in leaf.

◊ ◐ ☼ *f* Z3–9 H9–1

‡ to 6in (15cm) ↔ to 3in (8cm)

GALANTHUS NIVALIS

Bulbous perennial

The common snowdrop is a small plant with narrow, waxy leaves and hanging, sweetly scented flowers in winter. Plant the bulbs in early autumn. It can be grown beneath trees or shrubs or naturalized in grass or in a rock garden. It grows best in partial shade in organic, moist but well-drained soil, including alkaline. In suitable conditions it will self-seed freely to form extensive colonies. Divide large clumps after flowering while still in leaf.

◊ ◐ ☼ *f* Z3–9 H9–1

‡ to 6in (15cm) ↔ to 3in (8cm)

HELLEBORUS NIGER

Perennial

The Christmas rose is a clump-forming perennial with thick, leathery, dark green leaves that remain green over winter. The large, saucer-shaped white flowers appear in early winter and remain until early spring; they have green centers and yellow stamens and turn pink as they age. Plant in heavy, neutral to alkaline soil in partial shade. It thrives in a woodland garden and can be appreciated fully in a container placed close to the house. Slugs and snails can be a problem.

◑ ☼ ☀ Z4–8 H8–1
‡ to 12in (30cm) ↔ to 18in (45cm)

LONICERA FRAGRANTISSIMA

Deciduous shrub

This honeysuckle is a bushy, spreading shrub. In late winter and early spring it produces clusters of fragrant, creamy white flowers on bare branches, followed by dull red berries. In mild winters the oval leaves may be held through winter. Plant it in full sun or partial shade in any well-drained soil. It is suitable for planting in a shrub border and can be grown as a screen or in a mixed hedge. It is also effective flanking a frequently used entrance to make the most of its winter scent.

◊ ☼ ☀ ƒ Z5–8 H8–5
‡ to 6ft (2m) ↔ to 10ft (3m)

NARCISSUS CANTABRICUS

Bulbous perennial

The white hoop-petticoat is one of the earliest-flowering narcissus. The blooms have a funnel-shaped white trumpet surrounded by smaller outer petals. The leaves are narrow, dark green, and almost cylindrical. It needs sharp drainage and dry conditions during its summer dormancy. Grow it in a raised bed or rock garden in very gritty soil, or in pots of one part grit to two parts soil-based potting mix, and keep it in a cold frame during the summer months.

◊ ☼ Z3–9 H9–1
‡ to 8in (20cm) ↔ to 2in (5cm)

RUBUS COCKBURNIANUS

Deciduous shrub

This is an outstanding ornamental bramble with prickly, deep purple stems that are covered with a striking, waxy white bloom. The dark green leaves are covered beneath with grayish white hairs. Plant it in full sun in well-drained, fertile soil. It can be grown in a wild garden or mixed border; the winter stems stand out best against a dark background. Cut canes to the ground each year in spring to promote plenty of new stems. Fertilize and mulch after pruning.

◊ ☼ Z5–9 H9–5
‡↔ to 8ft (2.5m)

SARCOCOCCA HOOKERIANA
'Purple Stem'

Evergreen shrub

The modest white flowers, tinted pink in this variety of Christmas box, emit a rich honey-like scent and are followed by blue-black fruit. The glossy, dark green leaves grow from purple shoots. It thrives in deep or partial shade in organic, moist but well-drained soil; it tolerates some sun in reliably moist soil. Excellent in a woodland garden or in a sheltered spot, where the fragrance intensifies in the still air.

○ ◊ ☼ ● ☀ *f* Z6–9 H9–6
‡ to 5ft (1.5m) ↔ to 6ft (2m)

SKIMMIA JAPONICA
'Wakehurst White'

Evergreen shrub

An attractive shrub with oval, glossy, dark green leaves. Clusters of small, fragrant white flowers open in spring. They are followed by spherical white fruit that persist into winter. Grow in a mixed border or woodland garden. Plant a male form nearby to ensure fruit, since male and female flowers are usually borne on separate plants. It prefers some shade but tolerates sun. Grow in moderately fertile, organic, moist but well-drained soil.

○ ◊ ☼ *f* Z7–9 H9–7
‡↔ to 20ft (6m)

VIBURNUM FARRERI

Deciduous shrub

This upright shrub has highly fragrant, white or pink-tinged flowers that appear on bare branches during mild spells in winter. The leaves emerge bronze-green, turn dark green as the season progresses, then take on shades of red-purple in autumn before they fall. Plant this viburnum in full sun or partial shade in fertile, moist but well-drained soil. Use it in a mixed or shrub border to disguise its deteriorating shape as it ages.

◊ ◊ ☼ ◑ ƒZ6–8 H8–6
‡ to 10ft (3m) ↔ to 8ft (2.5m)

VIBURNUM TINUS
'Eve Price'

Evergreen shrub

This is a justifiably popular shrub with large, oval, dark green leaves. It has dense clusters of pink buds (deep pink in 'Eve Price') that open in winter and early spring to white flowers. During summer it bears small, bluish black fruit. Plant in fertile, moist but well-drained soil in sun or light shade. Use it as a flowering hedge or screen, in a woodland garden, or in a mixed border. Trim hedges after flowering.

◊ ◊ ☼ ◑ Z8–10 H10–8
‡↔ to 10ft (3m)

CLEMATIS CIRRHOSA
'Freckles'

Climber

This interesting evergreen climber has
deeply divided leaves that turn bronze-
green during winter. In winter and early
spring it bears pale pink flowers that
are heavily spotted and streaked with
red within. They are followed by silky
seedheads. Grow in full sun – but with
the roots in shade – in organic, fertile,
moist but well-drained soil. It is ideal
for training over a pergola or wall or
through an old tree. Cut back after
flowering to keep it within bounds.

◌ ◑ ☼ ☀ Z7–9 H9–7
↕ to 10ft (3m)

CYCLAMEN COUM
Pewter Group

Perennial

This tuberous perennial has dark green
leaves with a pewter-silver sheen that
covers almost the entire surface. The
flowers appear from winter to early
spring; they range from pure white to
pink and carmine. Plant tubers 2in
(5cm) deep in sun or partial shade in
organic, rather gritty, moderately fertile,
well-drained soil with added leaf mold.
Excellent when grown beneath deciduous trees or shrubs.

◌ ☼ ☀ Z5–9 H9–5
↕ to 3in (8cm) ↔ to 4in (10cm)

DAPHNE MEZEREUM

Deciduous shrub

Mezereon is a compact, upright shrub
bearing masses of small, purplish pink,
fragrant flowers at the stem tips in late
winter and early spring before the
narrow bluish green leaves emerge.
They are followed by bright red, rather
fleshy, toxic fruits. Plant it in full sun
or partial shade in moderately fertile,
organic, neutral to alkaline soil.
It thrives in alkaline soil. Grow it in
a woodland garden, in a mixed or
shrub border, or on a sunny bank.

○ ☼ ☀ *f* Z5–8 H8–5
↕ to 4ft (1.2m) ↔ to 3ft (1m)

DAPHNE ODORA
'Aureomarginata'

Evergreen shrub

This is an extremely attractive, rounded
shrub with rather leathery, dark green
leaves set off by an irregular yellow
margin. In late winter and early spring
it produces small clusters of highly
fragrant white flowers that are deep
pinkish purple on the outside. Plant in
a site with shelter from wind. It grows
best in partial shade in neutral to
slightly alkaline soil that is moist but
well-drained and rich in organic matter.

○ ◑ ☀ *f* Z7–9 H9–7
↕↔ to 5ft (1.5m)

ERICA CARNEA
'Vivellii'

Evergreen shrub

An attractive heather with dark bronze-green leaves that become completely bronzed in winter. The spikes of deep purplish pink flowers age to magenta and appear abundantly from the middle of winter to midspring. Plant it in full sun or partial shade in peaty, well-drained soil. It will tolerate atmospheric pollution and alkaline soil. Cut back after flowering to keep it compact.

◊ ☼ ◐ Z5–7 H7–5
‡ to 6in (15cm) ↔ to 14in (35cm)

PRUNUS × SUBHIRTELLA
'Autumnalis Rosea'

Deciduous tree

This is a superb flowering cherry for the winter garden. Clusters of delicate, semidouble, blush pink flowers appear on a skeleton of bare, spreading branches during periods of mild weather from autumn and throughout winter until spring. The foliage is bronze-green when new in spring and turns yellow in autumn. Plant it as a specimen tree in full sun in fertile, moist but well-drained soil.

◊ ◊ ☼ Z6–8 H8–6
‡↔ to 25ft (8m)

RHODODENDRON
'Christmas Cheer'

Evergreen shrub

This is a compact rhododendron with
clusters of pink buds that open to pale
pink flowers. It flowers in mild weather
in winter and sometimes in early spring.
It is an old cultivar that was often pot-
grown and forced under cover for
flowers at Christmas, hence its name.
Plant it in organic, acidic, moist but
well-drained soil in a sheltered spot
in light shade. Mulch annually with
leaf mold or bark chips.

○ ◑ ☼ Z5–9 H9–5
↔ to 6ft (2m)

VIBURNUM × BODNANTENSE
'Dawn'

Deciduous shrub

This is one of the most reliable of all
winter-flowering shrubs. The fragrant,
deep pink flowers are produced on
bare branches during mild spells from
late autumn to early spring. The oval,
toothed leaves are bronze as they emerge
in spring, gradually turning to dark
green and finally red-bronze in autumn.
Plant in full sun or partial shade in
moderately fertile, moist but well-
drained soil. It is ideal as a specimen
or in a mixed border.

○ ◑ ☼ ◐ *f* Z7–8 H8–7
↕ to 10ft (3m) ↔ to 6ft (2m)

ACER GRISEUM

Deciduous tree

The paperbark maple is an elegant tree with a spreading crown of dark green leaves that turn to vivid shades of crimson, gold, and scarlet during autumn. When leafless, it reveals the beauty of its attractive bark – a rich mahogany red, peeling away on older trees to reveal the orange-red younger bark beneath. Plant it as a specimen tree or at the back of a mixed border in full sun or partial shade in fertile, moist but well-drained soil.

◊ ◊ ☼ ☼ Z4–8 H10–3
↕↔ to 30ft (10m)

ACER PENSYLVANICUM *'Erythrocladum'*

Deciduous tree

This snakebark maple is a beautiful tree with white-striped green bark that becomes a vivid salmon-pink in winter; the young shoots are an especially bright red-pink. It has three-lobed green leaves that turn to a warm shade of clear butter yellow in autumn. Plant it in full sun or dappled shade in fertile, moist but well-drained soil. It makes a wonderful specimen tree, and its beautiful bark is a highly distinctive winter feature.

◊ ◊ ☼ ☼ Z3–7 H7–1
↕ to 40ft (12m) ↔ to 30ft (10m)

ARBUTUS MENZIESII

Evergreen tree

The madroño is a broad, spreading tree with glossy, dark green, long-oval leaves. Its main attraction during the winter months is the bright reddish brown bark, which peels away to reveal the younger, smooth, olive green bark beneath. In early summer it bears upright clusters of waxy, creamy white flowers that are sometimes followed in autumn by orange-red fruit. Plant it in full sun or partial shade in a sheltered position with acidic, moist but well-drained soil.

◊ ◐ ☼ ☀ Z7–9 H9–7
‡↔ to 50ft (15m)

BERBERIS × OTTAWENSIS
'Superba'

Deciduous shrub

A large shrub with gracefully arching, spiny branches bearing red berries. The rounded leaves open purplish red and turn a brilliant crimson-red in autumn. In spring it bears clusters of pale yellow flowers. It is a tough shrub that can be planted in almost any well-drained soil and will grow happily in full sun or partial shade. Use it in a shrub or mixed border or as an intruder-proof hedge. Prune it hard to produce the best foliage coloration.

◊ ☼ ☀ Z5–9 H8–3
‡↔ to 8ft (2.5m)

BERGENIA
'Ballawley'

Perennial

This vigorous evergreen has large, leathery, dark green leaves flushed with red and bronze-purple in winter. In spring, upright stems bearing clusters of bright crimson flowers appear. Plant in a sheltered site in full sun or partial shade in organic, moist but well-drained soil. It is a superb groundcover plant for a woodland garden or for the front of a herbaceous border. Remove tattered leaves in spring. Divide clumps every 4–5 years to maintain vigor.

◊ ◐ ☼ ◑ Z3–8 H8–1
‡↔ to 24in (60cm)

BRASSICA OLERACEA
VAR. ACEPHALA

Biennial

The ornamental cabbages are grown for their attractive foliage in different combinations of green, red, pink, and white. Extremely striking as a bedding plant, they attain their deepest coloration during cold weather. Plant them in a sunny site, preferably in alkaline, fertile, well-drained soil, or in containers. Sow seed in spring, or buy young plants.

◊ ☼ Z13 H12–1
‡↔ to 18in (45cm)

CAMELLIA SASANQUA
'Crimson King'

Evergreen shrub

One of the earliest camellias to flower,
'Crimson King' has glossy, dark green
leaves and single, crimson-red flowers
from late autumn through winter; it is
often in bloom at Christmas. Grow in
a sheltered spot in dappled shade or
sun (but out of early morning sun)
in organic, acidic, moist but well-drained
soil. Where not hardy, grow under
cover in containers of acidic soil mix.

◊ ◗ ☼ ☀ Z7–8 H8–7
↕ to 20ft (6m) ↔ to 10ft (3m)

CORNUS ALBA
'Sibirica'

Deciduous shrub

This red-barked dogwood is an upright
shrub usually grown for its striking red
winter stems, but the dark green leaves
also turn bright red before falling in
autumn. Plant it in full sun in any
reasonably fertile soil. The new shoots
produce the brightest and longest-
lasting winter stem color, so cut all
stems back in early spring, just before
growth begins, to within two or three
buds from the ground. Fertilize and
mulch after pruning.

◊ ◗ ☼ Z2–8 H8–1
↕↔ to 10ft (3m)

CORNUS SANGUINEA
'Winter Beauty'

Deciduous shrub

The oval green leaves of this vigorous
shrub turn bright red in the autumn;
as they drop they reveal the vivid red
and orange winter shoots. Prune hard
in early spring to stimulate new growth,
which has the best color. Cut back to
within 2-3 buds from the base of the
plant, then fertilize and mulch. The
color develops best in full sun. This
dogwood thrives in any reasonably
fertile, well-drained soil.

◊ ☼ Z5–7 H7–5
‡ to 10ft (3m) ↔ to 8ft (2.5m)

COTONEASTER
CASHMIRIENSIS

Evergreen shrub

A low, mound-forming shrub with
glossy, dark green leaves. Pink buds
open in the summer to small white
flowers. They are followed by spherical,
deep red berries that persist into winter.
It is one of the smaller prostrate
cotoneasters and makes a compact
groundcover for a rock garden
or sunny bank. Plant it in full sun or
partial shade in any moderately fertile,
well-drained soil, including alkaline.
This plant is often sold as *C. cochleatus*.

◊ ☼ ☼ Z6–8 H8–6
‡ to 12in (30cm) ↔ to 6ft (2m)

COTONEASTER CONSPICUUS
'Decorus'

Evergreen shrub

This is an attractive, low-growing, spreading shrub with small, narrow, dark green leaves. The tiny white flowers appear in early summer and are followed by large quantities of conspicuous, spherical, bright red berries that last for most of the winter. Plant it in full sun or partial shade in moderately fertile, well-drained soil. It is ideal for planting on a dry, sunny bank, where it will provide color throughout winter.

◊ ☼ ◑ Z6–8 H8–6
↕ to 5ft (1.5m) ↔ to 8ft (2.5m)

COTONEASTER LACTEUS

Evergreen shrub

This is a substantial shrub with large, deeply veined, oval, dark green leaves with a yellowish white, woolly undersurface. The milky white flowers appear in large clusters in summer and are followed in autumn by large bunches of bright red berries that last well into winter. It makes a dense, ornamental hedge or can be grown in a mixed border. Trim lightly in late summer to keep in shape. Plant it in full sun or partial shade in any well-drained, moderately fertile soil.

◊ ☼ ◑ Z3–7 H7–1
↕↔ to 12ft (4m)

GAULTHERIA PROCUMBENS

Evergreen shrub

Wintergreen is a creeping shrub with underground stems and glossy, dark green leaves that smell strongly of wintergreen when crushed. The white or pink, urn-shaped flowers appear in summer and are followed in autumn by bright red, aromatic fruit. It prefers partial shade but will grow in full sun if provided with soil that is reliably moist. Grow in neutral to acidic, peaty soil. It is an excellent groundcover plant in damp woodland or shady borders.

◊ ☼ Z3–8 H8–1
↕ to 6in (15cm) ↔ to 3ft (1m)

HAMAMELIS × INTERMEDIA *'Diane'*

Deciduous shrub

This elegant shrub is grown for its clusters of fragrant flowers that appear on bare branches in late winter. They have threadlike, dark red petals. The rounded, bright green leaves turn red and yellow in autumn. Plant in full sun or partial shade in moderately fertile, neutral to acidic, moist but well-drained soils rich in organic matter. Grow in a shrub border or use as a specimen.

◊ ◊ ☼ ☼ *f* Z5–9 H9–5
↕↔ to 12ft (4m)

ILEX AQUIFOLIUM
'J.C. van Tol'

Evergreen tree

This is a form of English holly without any prickles. The leaves are dark green and very glossy and are carried on purple stems. It is a self-fertile female plant that produces its bright red berries through winter without the need for a male plant nearby. Plant it in full sun or partial shade in fertile, moist but well-drained soil. It grows happily in a woodland garden and can be used as a hedge or a specimen tree. Clip hedges in summer.

◊ ☼ ☀ Z7–9 H9–7
‡ to 20ft (6m) ↔ to 12ft (4m)

ILEX × MESERVEAE
'Blue Princess'

Evergreen shrub

An attractive hybrid holly with spiny, bluish green leaves and tiny white or pink flowers in late spring. It needs a male plant (such as 'Blue Prince') nearby to produce the glossy red fruit of autumn and winter. Grown in a woodland garden or use it to make an impenetrable hedge. Plant it in full sun or partial shade in fertile, organic, moist but well-drained soil. If grown as a hedge, it should be trimmed annually in summer.

◊ ◖ ☼ ☀ Z5–9 H9–5
‡↔ to 10ft (3m)

LEUCOTHOE
Scarletta

Evergreen shrub

This small to medium-sized, upright shrub has lance-shaped, rather leathery leaves. They are dark red-purple in spring, becoming dark green in summer before finally assuming red and bronze tints in winter. In spring it has clusters of tiny, narrowly pitcher-shaped white flowers. It should be grown in a shady position in acidic, organic, moist soil. It is ideal for a woodland garden or shady border.

◐ ☼ ☀ Z5–8 H8–5
‡ to 6ft (2m) ↔ to 10ft (3m)

PRUNUS SERRULA

Deciduous tree

This attractive flowering cherry is grown mainly for its tactile, rich coppery red bark, which is very shiny and particularly striking on a sunny winter's day. It has narrow, dark green leaves that turn yellow in autumn, and small, single, bowl-shaped white flowers in spring. It should be planted in full sun in moderately fertile, moist but well-drained soil. It looks particularly dramatic when grown as an avenue tree, but it also makes a handsome specimen in a smaller garden.

◐ ◐ ☼ Z6–8 H8–6
‡↔ to 30ft (10m)

SKIMMIA JAPONICA
'Rubella'

Evergreen shrub

This skimmia is a compact, dome-shaped shrub with red-edged, dark green leaves. It is a male plant that produces dense clusters of deep red buds from autumn to winter. In early spring the buds open to reveal small, fragrant white flowers. It is a good pollinator for female skimmias. Grow it in partial to deep shade in moderately fertile, moist but well-drained soil. Plant in a shrub border or woodland garden; it is also good in containers.

◊ ◊ ☼ ☀ ƒ Z7–9 H9–7
‡↔ to 20ft (6m)

SKIMMIA JAPONICA
'Nymans'

Evergreen shrub

This low-spreading shrub with dark green leaves is a female form noted for its large, red winter fruits that are borne very freely if the plant is grown with a male plant nearby. They form from the dense clusters of white spring flowers. Grow it in partial to deep shade in moderately fertile, moist but well-drained soil. Plant in a shrub border or wood-land garden. Like most skimmias, it is good in coastal and urban gardens and tolerates most soils.

◊ ◊ ☼ ☀ Z7–9 H9–7
‡ to 3ft (1m) ↔ to 6ft (2m)

BERGENIA CORDIFOLIA
'Purpurea'

Perennial

During late winter this evergreen produces dark, thick stems of deep magenta-purple flowers. It has substantial, leathery, midgreen leaves that turn reddish purple during winter. Plant it in full sun or partial shade in organic, moist but well-drained soil. It is suitable for the front of a herbaceous border or for a woodland garden. Remove tattered leaves in spring.

○ ◊ ☼ ☼ Z3–8 H8–1
‡↔ to 20in (50cm)

CORNUS ALBA
'Kesselringii'

Deciduous shrub

This striking shrub is especially valuable for its dramatic, purplish black winter stems. Bronzed leaves open in spring, turning green and then reddish purple in autumn. In spring it bears clusters of white flowers that are followed in autumn by white fruit. Cut back in early spring to within a few buds from the ground to stimulate the growth of new, more deeply colored shoots, then fertilize and mulch. Plant in sun in any well-drained, reasonably fertile soil.

○ ☼ Z2–8 H8–1
‡↔ to 10ft (3m)

CORYLUS MAXIMA
'Purpurea'

Deciduous shrub

This filbert forms a large, upright shrub
or small tree with dangling purple
catkins in winter. In spring the dark
purple leaves appear. In summer and
early autumn edible, purple-husked
nuts appear. It makes an attractive
specimen Grow in full sun for good
foliage color and abundant nuts.
It does best in fertile, well-drained soil,
and it grows well in alkaline soil.

○ ☼ Z4–9 H9–1
‡ to 20ft (6m) ↔ to 15ft (5m)

IRIS UNGUICULARIS

Perennial

A wonderful winter-flowering iris with
large, fragrant, pale lavender-purple or
deep violet-blue blooms marked by
a large patch of yellow on the lower
petals. It has upright stems and tough,
grasslike evergreen leaves. Grow it in a
rock garden or raised bed, on a terrace,
or at the foot of a warm, sunny wall.
Plant it in full sun in gritty, very well-
drained, neutral to alkaline soil.
Good for cutting.

○ ☼ *f* Z7–9 H9–7
‡ to 12in (30cm) ↔ indefinite

ACER GROSSERI
VAR. HERSII

Deciduous tree

This snakebark maple is an extremely attractive tree with upright, green-barked branches heavily marked with white striations, giving it the appearance of a snake's skin. The mid-green leaves are shallowly lobed and turn yellow and orange in autumn. Clusters of pale yellow flowers hang beneath the shoots in spring, followed by pink-brown autumn fruit. Plant it as a specimen in sun or partial shade in fertile, moist but well-drained soil.

◊ ◊ ☼ ☀ Z5–7 H7–5
‡↔ to 50ft (15m)

ACER PENSYLVANICUM

Deciduous tree

The moosewood maple looks equally attractive in winter and summer. In spring it produces long clusters of small, yellow-green flowers. The lobed, bright green leaves turn clear butter yellow in autumn, revealing the white-striped, jade green bark when they fall. Plant it in full sun or partial shade in moist but well-drained, fertile soil. Plant close to a walkway, where the bark can be appreciated during winter.

◊ ◊ ☼ ☀ Z3–7 H7–1
‡ to 40ft (12m) ↔ to 30ft (10m)

ARUM ITALICUM
'Marmoratum'

Perennial

The upright, dark green, arrow-shaped leaves, heavily mottled with paler green markings, last through winter. In early summer, greenish white hooded flowers appear, followed by spikes of bright orange-red berries. Grow in light shade or in sun with some shade from the hottest summer sun. Plant tubers in spring or autumn in organic, well-drained soil. It makes a good ground-cover beneath deciduous shrubs or in a woodland garden.

◊ ☼ Z6–9 H9–6
↕ to 10in (25cm) ↔ to 12in (30cm)

GARRYA ELLIPTICA

Evergreen shrub

The silk-tassel bush is a dense shrub with wavy-edged, leathery, grayish green leaves. Male and female flowers are borne on separate plants; the male plants are more attractive, with longer, dangling, gray-green catkins, measuring 8in (20cm) or more, that are borne in midwinter and early spring. Plant it in full sun or partial shade in fertile, well-drained soil. Excellent on a shady wall or shrub border and good as a specimen or as hedging in coastal gardens.

◊ ☼ ◐ Z8–10 H10–8
↕↔ to 12ft (4m)

HELLEBORUS VIRIDIS

Perennial

The green hellebore is a deciduous, clump-forming plant with very deeply divided, rather leathery, dark green leaves. In late winter and early spring it produces tall stems adorned with nodding, bright green flowers. It looks best when planted against a dark background and will grow in deep shade. Plant it in a woodland garden or a shrub border. It grows well in rather heavy, neutral or alkaline soil in dappled shade. It often self-seeds.

◊ ☼ ☀ Z6–8 H8–6
‡↔ to 12in (30cm)

RIBES LAURIFOLIUM

Evergreen shrub

This is a low-growing shrub with spreading branches bearing leathery, dark green leaves. In late winter and early spring it produces hanging clusters of greenish yellow flowers. Male and female flowers are borne on separate plants; if grown together, females produce black fruits. Plant it in a shrub border in sun or partial shade in moderately fertile, well-drained soil.

◊ ☼ ☀ Z7–9 H9–7
‡ to 3ft (1m) ↔ to 5ft (1.5m)

STACHYURUS PRAECOX

Deciduous shrub

The gracefully arching branches of
this spreading shrub produce hanging
chains of small, pale yellow flowers in
late winter and early spring. The similar
S. chinensis flowers about two weeks
later. Plant in full sun or partial shade
in fertile, organic, acidic, well-drained
soil, ideally against a wall or in a
woodland garden. When mature, cut
out the oldest shoots at the base after
flowering; this encourages the production of strong, new flowering stems.

○ ☼ ☀ Z7–9 H9–7
‡ to 12ft (4m) ↔ to 10ft (3m)

THUJA OCCIDENTALIS
'Hetz Midget'

Evergreen shrub

This dwarf conifer is a slow-growing
selection of the white cedar that forms
a dense, rounded mound of golden
green foliage that smells of apples
when crushed. It is ideal as a specimen
in a rock garden. Grow in full sun in
deep, moisture-retentive but well-
drained, fertile soil.

○ ◑ ☼ Z2–7 H7–1
‡↔ to 20in (50cm)

AZARA MICROPHYLLA

Evergreen tree

An upright, often shrubby small tree with oval, glossy, dark green leaves. In late winter and early spring it bears clusters of small, vanilla-scented yellow flowers. Plant it in full sun or partial shade in organic, well-drained, fertile soil. It can be grown in a shrub border but flowers best against a sheltered, sunny wall. When grown on a wall, train in the shoots when young to ensure good coverage. Prune back after flowering to within 2-4 buds of the woody framework of main stems.

○ ☼ ☀ *f* Z8–10 H10–8
‡ to 30ft (10m) ↔ to 12ft (4m)

CHIMONANTHUS PRAECOX *'Grandiflorus'*

Deciduous shrub

The wintersweet is an upright shrub with lance-shaped green leaves. It is especially valuable for the highly fragrant, nodding, deep yellow flowers that are stained red within. They appear on bare stems in winter and are excellent for cutting for winter posies. Plant it in full sun in fertile, well-drained soil in a sheltered place. Grow as a specimen or train it against a sunny wall. If wall-trained, shorten any outward-growing shoots after flowering.

○ ☼ *f* Z7–9 H9–7
‡ to 12ft (4m) ↔ to 10ft (3m)

CORNUS MAS

Deciduous shrub

The Cornelian cherry is a vigorous
shrub or small tree with spreading
branches and midgreen leaves that turn
red-purple in autumn. It is most
dramatic in the winter when it produces
an abundance of small yellow flowers
in clusters on bare branches. Bright red
fruit ripen in late summer. Grow as a
specimen or in a shrub border or
woodland garden. Plant in full sun or
partial shade in any moderately fertile,
well-drained soil.

◊ ☼ ☀ Z5–8 H8–5
↕↔ to 15ft (5m)

CORNUS STOLONIFERA
'Flaviramea'

Deciduous shrub

This vigorous dogwood forms a thicket
of bright yellow stems that create a
brilliant winter display. In summer,
small white flowers are followed by
white fruit in autumn, when the leaves
turn vivid orange and red before falling.
It looks beautiful at the side of ponds
or streams, especially if planted with
the red-stemmed *C. sanguinea*. Grow in
wet or moist soil in full sun. Cut back
to the base each year in early spring,
then fertilize and mulch it.

◊ ☼ Z2–8 H8–1
↕ to 6ft (2m) ↔ to 12ft (4m)

CORONILLA VALENTINA
SUBSP. GLAUCA

Evergreen shrub

A dense, bushy plant with divided, blue-green leaves. In late winter, early spring, and often again in late summer it produces clusters of bright yellow, pealike flowers. It is suitable in a shrub border or on a wall. Plant it in full sun in sandy, moderately fertile, well-drained soil. Where not hardy, grow in a container as a conservatory plant and move outdoors in summer

◊ ☼ Z8–9 H9–8
↔ to 32in (80cm)

HACQUETIA EPIPACTIS
Perennial

This is a low-growing, spreading perennial that produces tiny yellow flowers surrounded by a collar of bright emerald green, leaflike bracts in late winter and early spring. The brilliant green leaves develop fully only after flowering. It is suitable for planting in moist, shady situations, such as by pondsides or in a damp woodland garden. Plant it in organic, moist but well-drained, acidic or neutral soil. It is easily increased by dividing the clumps in spring.

◊ ◑ ☼ Z5–7 H7–5
↕ to 6in (15cm) ↔ to 12in (30cm)

HAMAMELIS
'Arnold Promise'

Deciduous shrub

This attractive winter-flowering shrub
produces a profusion of spidery,
bright yellow flowers on bare, upright
branches. It is excellent in a shrub
border or as a specimen. The vivid
green leaves turn red and gold in
autumn. Plant in full sun or partial
shade in fertile, neutral to acidic,
moist but well-drained soil.

◊ ◊ ☼ ☀ Z5–9 H9–5
↕↔ to 12ft (4m)

HAMAMELIS JAPONICA
'Sulphurea'

Deciduous shrub

This Japanese witch hazel is an upright,
branched shrub with rounded, glossy
green leaves that turn gold in autumn.
In midwinter the bare branches are
studded with small, sulfur yellow
flowers with very narrow petals. Plant it
in full sun or partial shade in fertile,
neutral to acidic, moist but well-drained
soil. Plant in groups in a woodland
garden or as a specimen.

◊ ◊ ☼ ☀ Z5–9 H9–5
↕↔ to 12ft (4m)

ILEX AQUIFOLIUM *'Bacciflava'*

Evergreen tree

'Bacciflava' is a female form of English holly with spiny, glossy, dark green leaves. If a male pollinator grows nearby, the tiny, insignificant flowers of spring and early summer give rise to yellow berries that last into winter. It forms an erect, pyramidal tree that is good as a specimen and is also suitable for hedging. Trim hedges in summer. Plant in full sun or partial shade in moist but well-drained, moderately fertile soil.

◊ ◊ ☼ ◑ Z7–9 H9–7
‡ to 70ft (20m) ↔ to 20ft (6m)

JASMINUM NUDIFLORUM

Deciduous shrub

The winter jasmine is one of the most beloved of winter-flowering shrubs. It has arching, scrambling, dark green stems and dark green leaves, each divided into three leaflets. It is very free-flowering, bearing bright yellow, six-petaled flowers from midwinter to early spring. It looks best when planted against a fence or trellis, but it needs tying in to a support. Plant in full sun or partial shade in fertile, well-drained soil. Trim after flowering to keep it dense, cutting back to strong buds.

◊ ☼ ◑ Z6–9 H9–6
‡↔ to 10ft (3m)

LUZULA SYLVATICA
'Aurea'

Perennial

This golden form of greater woodrush
is a clump-forming evergreen with
narrow, grasslike leaves. They are a
bright golden yellow in winter, fading
to yellow-green in summer. It is happy
in deep or partial shade in organic,
moist but well-drained, poor to moderately fertile soil. It tolerates dry soils.
Use as a groundcover or in a woodland
garden. It can be increased by division
in autumn and spring.

◊ ◊ ☼ ☼ Z5–9 H9–5
‡ to 32in (80cm) ↔ to 18in (45cm)

MAHONIA JAPONICA

Evergreen shrub

A beautiful winter-flowering shrub
with upright branches clothed in spiny,
divided, dark green leaves. It bears
drooping spikes of strongly fragrant,
lemon yellow flowers from late autumn
to early spring. These are followed by
an abundant crop of bluish black berries.
It provides a long season of interest in
a shrub border or woodland garden.
Plant it in a slightly shaded position
in organic, moist but well-drained soil.

◊ ◊ ☼ *f* Z7–8 H8–7
‡ to 6ft (2m) ↔ to 10ft (3m)

MAHONIA × MEDIA
'Charity'

Evergreen shrub

This is one of the most attractive forms of mahonia. It has large, dark green leaves divided into sharply toothed leaflets. Masses of sweetly scented, bright yellow flowers are borne in dense spikes from late autumn to early winter. Plant it in partial shade and moderately fertile, organic, moist but well-drained soil. It makes a dramatic specimen for planting in front of a wall or in a shrub border or woodland garden.

◊ ◊ ☼ *f* Z8–9 H9–8
‡ to 15ft (5m) ↔ to 12ft (4m)

NARCISSUS
'Rijnveld's Early Sensation'

Bulbous perennial

This golden yellow daffodil flowers in late winter, well before the other early flowering daffodils, such as 'February Gold'. It makes a valuable, long-flowering addition to the winter garden and should be planted in a bold group or naturalized in grass. Plant bulbs at three times their own depth in late summer. Grow in full sun in fertile, well-drained soil. Remove the flowers as they fade, or use them for cutting.

◊ ☼ Z3–9 H9–1
‡ to 14in (35cm)

PYRACANTHA
'Soleil d'Or'

Evergreen shrub

Firethorns have several seasons of
interest. This one has spiny red shoots
and glossy green leaves. In summer
it produces sprays of small white
flowers followed by yellow fruit that
last well into winter. Plant in full sun or
shade in fertile, well-drained soil. It can
be trained against a wall or fence or
grown as a free-standing shrub. It also
makes an excellent dense, impenetrable
hedge. Trim hedges in midspring
and summer.

○ ☼ ☀ Z7–9 H9–7
↕ to 10ft (3m) ↔ to 8ft (2.5m)

VIOLA × WITTROCKIANA
Universal Series

Perennial

Universal pansies are among the most
prolific of all winter-flowering plants,
flowering almost nonstop from early
winter to midspring if the weather
permits. The color range includes
yellow, blue, mauve, maroon, red, and
white, some with darker patches in the
center. Plant in sun in fertile, moist but
well-drained soil. Although perennial,
they are usually grown as annuals for
bedding. Use in borders, containers,
or hanging baskets.

○ ◐ ☼ Z4–8 H8–1
↕↔ to 8in (20cm)

CALLUNA VULGARIS
'Boskoop'

Evergreen shrub

This dense and compact heather bears spikes of lilac-pink flowers from midsummer to late autumn, then the foliage, which is golden throughout the summer, begins to assume vibrant orange-red winter tints that persist until the new growth emerges in spring. Grow in full sun in organic, well-drained, acidic soil. Cut plants back lightly in spring to keep them shapely. Excellent for a rock garden, it associates well with conifers and other heathers.

◊ ☀ Z5–7 H7–5
‡ to 12in (30cm) ↔ to 16in (40cm)

ILEX AQUIFOLIUM
'Amber'

Evergreen tree

This is one of the most attractive forms of the English holly, with virtually spine-free, glossy, bright green leaves. The tiny spring and early summer flowers give rise to profuse clusters of amber-yellow fruit. The tree is female and needs a male to be planted nearby to produce fruit. Plant it in full sun in well-drained, fertile soil. It can be grown as a hedge or as an attractive specimen tree. Trim in summer if grown as a hedge.

◊ ☀ Z7–9 H9–7
‡ to 20ft (6m) ↔ to 8ft (2.5m)

IRIS FOETIDISSIMA
Perennial

The stinking gladwyn is so called because the leaves smell unpleasant when crushed. It forms clumps of evergreen leaves and in early summer bears dull purple, yellow-tinged flowers. However, it really comes into its own when the seedpods ripen in autumn. They split to reveal glistening orange-red seeds that remain in place until winter. Grow in well-drained, moderately fertile, neutral to acidic soil. It is one of the toughest and most unique plants for dry shade.

◊ ☼ ☀ Z7–9 H9–7
‡ to 36in (90cm) ↔ indefinite

PYRACANTHA
'Orange Glow'

Evergreen shrub

This is a vigorous, upright shrub with spiny stems and glossy, dark green leaves. In late spring, clusters of small white flowers are followed by masses of orange berries that last until winter. Plant in full sun or shade in well-drained, moderately fertile soil. After flowering, shorten sideshoots back to two or three leaves to reveal the fruit. It can be trained against a wall and also makes an intruder-proof hedge. Trim hedges in spring and summer.

◊ ☼ ☀ Z7–9 H9–7
‡↔ to 10ft (3m)

ALL SEASONS

IT IS A GOOD IDEA to include a few reliable, undemanding plants that remain attractive in every season. They give the garden shape and structure and provide a backdrop for transient seasonal displays. Use them to liven up a border or to create focal points; shapely conifers, for example, can serve as "topiary" without the work. The cabbage palm (*Cordyline*) and New Zealand flax (*Phormium*) may appear as tender exotics but are tougher than they look. Their spiky shapes are portable in containers, and in borders they enhance a colorful display.

Climbers, like ivy (*Hedera*), can be used to disguise fences and sheds, to shield an unsightly compost pile by training it along a trellis, or as a groundcover. Evergreen groundcover plants play a valuable role in helping to suppress weeds: low-growing junipers, silvery artemisias, and heathers are all good choices; with minimal care, their foliage provides interest all year.

More visual punctuation may be obtained using grasses and bamboos, especially if you have plenty of space. Bamboos are normally grown as an elegant, rustling screen, but some, such as *Phyllostachys flexuosa*, grace the garden with the changing color of their stems.

A STRUCTURAL BACKBONE

Evergreen hedges and screens can surround the entire garden or divide it into sections. Boxwood (*Buxus*) and yew (*Taxus*) are traditional choices for clipped formal hedging and topiary, but hollies (*Ilex*) and firethorns (*Pyracantha*) form superb, impenetrable hedges and may also reward you with flowers and berries. Other conifers apart from yew can be used to create a tall screen, but choose with care; some can become a nuisance if they are allowed to grow too large, such as Leyland cypress, which can reach lofty heights in a surprisingly short time.

ARTEMISIA ARBORESCENS

Evergreen shrub

This small, aromatic, evergreen plant has very finely divided, silver-gray leaves that provide a foil for stronger flower colors in a sunny border or gravel garden. It also produces small yellow flowerheads in late summer and autumn. Plant it in a sunny site in moderately fertile, well-drained soil. It can become leggy and should be pruned hard in spring to keep it neat and compact. It dislikes excessive moisture in winters and benefits from a light, loose winter mulch.

◊ ☼ *f* Z5–8 H8–5
‡ to 3ft (1m) ↔ to 5ft (1.5m)

ARTEMISIA STELLERIANA
'Boughton Silver'

Perennial

This attractive evergreen forms a low, spreading clump of silver-gray leaves. It looks superb when planted against a background of darker foliage at the front of a border, or it can be used as path edging or in a gravel garden. The foliage looks better if the insignificant yellow flowers are removed well before they open in late summer. It prefers a position in full sun and well-drained, moderately fertile soil.

◊ ☼ Z3–7 H7–1
‡ to 6in (15cm) ↔ to 18in (45cm)

BALLOTA ACETABULOSA

Evergreen shrub

The upright, white-woolly stems of this compact woody plant are clothed with rounded, grayish green leaves. In summer it produces spires of small, purple-pink flowers. It grows well in hot, dry sites in full sun and poor, very well-drained soil. It may not survive cold, wet winters, but where it does, cut it back hard in the spring to keep it bushy. Grow it as a background for bright flower colors in a raised bed, gravel garden, or sunny border. *Ballota pseudodictamnus* is hardier.

◊ ☼ *f* Z8–9 H9–8
‡ to 24in (60cm) ↔ to 30in (75cm)

BETULA UTILIS
'Silver Shadow'

Deciduous tree

Birch trees are a year-round asset to a garden. They are valued for their graceful winter silhouette, attractive bark, yellow catkins in spring, and leaves that color yellow in the autumn. 'Silver Shadow' has silvery bark and makes a beautiful specimen tree, especially against a dark background of evergreen trees or shrubs. Plant it in sun or dappled shade in fertile, moist, well-drained soil.

◊ ◗ ☼ ☼ Z5–7 H7–5
‡ to 60ft (18m) ↔ to 30ft (10m)

CALLUNA VULGARIS
'Silver Queen'

Evergreen shrub

This is one of many heathers valued for year-round groundcover. It has silvery gray-green foliage and produces short spikes of pale mauve flowers in late summer and autumn. Plant in full sun in organic, well-drained, acidic soil, and cut the plants back in spring to keep them compact and bushy. Grow them together with other heathers and acid-soil-loving plants.

◊ ☼ Z5–7 H7–5
‡ to 16in (40cm) ↔ to 22in (55cm)

CONVOLVULUS CNEORUM

Evergreen shrub

This compact, bushy evergreen shrub has beautiful, silver-sheened leaves. It flowers from late spring to summer, producing delicate, funnel-shaped white flowers with yellow centers. Grow it in a warm, sunny, sheltered situation in poor, gritty, very well-drained soil. It is an excellent plant for a rock garden, container, raised bed, or sunny bank. Where not hardy, grow it in pots of gritty soil mix and move it into a cool greenhouse for the winter. Trim after flowering to keep it compact.

◊ ☼ Z8–10 H10–8
‡ to 24in (60cm) ↔ to 3ft (1m)

CORTADERIA SELLOANA
'Silver Comet'

Perennial grass

The arching clumps of tough, leathery evergreen leaves of pampas grass create an architectural presence throughout the year. The soft, silvery plumes arise in late summer and persist through winter. Grow it as a specimen in well-drained, fertile soil in full sun. Remove the old flowerheads and dead foliage before growth begins in spring; the leaves are sharp-edged, so wear tough gloves to protect your hands.

○ ☼ Z7–10 H10–7
↕ to 5ft (1.5m) ↔ to 3ft (1m)

EUONYMUS FORTUNEI
'Silver Queen'

Evergreen shrub

Valued for its year-round foliage, this compact shrub scrambles upward if given support. The oval, leathery leaves are pale yellow when young, later becoming green with an irregular white margin that flushes pink during cold weather. Excellent for brightening a dull corner, it is also very effective when grown against a wall. Plant it in full sun or light shade in any but waterlogged soil. Trim in midspring to keep it within bounds.

○ ◐ ☼ ◑ Z5–9 H9–5
↕ to 8ft (2.5m) ↔ to 5ft (1.5m)

HEBE PINGUIFOLIA
'Pagei'

Evergreen shrub

The purple stems of this tough hebe are clothed in silvery, blue-gray leaves that remain attractive throughout the year. It produces short spikes of small white flowers from late spring to summer. Plant it in full sun or partial shade in moderately fertile, moist, well-drained soil. Use it at the front of a mixed border, in a rock garden, or as a groundcover.

○ ◐ ☼ ☀ Z8–10 H10–8
↕ to 12in (30cm) ↔ to 36in (90cm)

SEDUM SPATHULIFOLIUM
'Cape Blanco'

Perennial

This evergreen stonecrop forms dense, low-growing mats of silvery-green foliage composed of rosettes of fleshy leaves covered in a waxy white bloom. The mats are spangled in summer with tiny, star-shaped yellow flowers. It is ideal for raised beds, troughs, and the tops of drystone walls. Grow it in gritty, poor to moderately fertile, very well-drained soil. The silvery foliage develops best in full sun, but the plant tolerates very light shade.

○ ☼ Z5–9 H9–5
↕ to 4in (10cm) ↔ to 24in (60cm)

SEMPERVIVUM ARACHNOIDEUM

Perennial

The cobweb hen and chickens is an evergreen mat-former with rosettes of fleshy, dark green, red-tipped leaves covered with a fine web of white hairs. In late summer it may produce sturdy stems with rose-red, star-shaped flowers at the tips. Each rosette dies after flowering, but younger rosettes readily fill the gap. Plant it in full sun in poor to moderately fertile, very well-drained soil. Grow it in a trough, pot, or rock garden or on a drystone wall.

◊ ☼ Z5–8 H8–5
↕ to 3in (8cm) ↔ to 12in (30cm)

STACHYS BYZANTINA

Evergreen perennial

Lambs' ears form an evergreen, soft-textured mat of bright, silvery white-woolly leaves. In summer it produces upright, hairy stems of pinkish purple flowers, but for the best foliage effect, remove these before the blooms open. It makes an excellent groundcover beside a path, at the front of a border, or in a gravel garden. It can become rather straggly, and old growth should be cut back in early spring. Grow it in a sunny situation in moderately fertile, well-drained soil.

◊ ☼ Z4–8 H8–1
↕ to 18in (45cm) ↔ to 24in (60cm)

AJUGA REPTANS
'Atropurpurea'

Perennial

This evergreen, mat-forming perennial is grown mostly for its glossy, bronze-purple leaves rather than the late spring spikes of blue flowers. The creeping stems root where they touch the soil, making this a superb groundcover that is relatively easy to control. Grow it in a partially shaded or sunny site in moist, moderately fertile soil. It is excellent in a woodland garden or shady border. 'Multicolor' has bronze-green and white leaves heavily suffused with purple.

◐ ☼ ☀ Z3–9 H9–1
↕ to 6in (15cm) ↔ to 3ft (1m)

CAREX COMANS
Bronze

Perennial

This attractive evergreen sedge forms a dense tussock of very narrow, almost hairlike, arching leaves in a warm, rich bronze-green. It will grow in sun or shade and in a wide range of soils but looks best when it is placed in a sunny position, where the color of its leaves will develop most fully. It produces rather inconspicuous brown flowers toward the end of the summer. Plant it beside a water garden or at the front of a herbaceous border.

◐ ☼ ☀ Z7–9 H9–7
↕ to 14in (35cm) ↔ to 30in (75cm)

CORDYLINE AUSTRALIS
Purpurea Group

Evergreen tree

The New Zealand cabbage palm is an
architectural specimen with narrow,
purplish green leaves. It develops a
trunk as it matures and may produce
creamy white summer flowers. It will
survive outdoors in mild climates.
Elsewhere, grow it in a container of
soil-based mix and move under cover
in winter. Outdoors, grow it in sun or
light shade in fertile, well-drained soil,
and protect it over winter during its
first few years.

○ ☼ ◑ Z10–15　H12–1
↕ to 10ft (3m) ↔ to 3ft (1m)

OPHIOPOGON PLANISCAPUS
'Nigrescens'

Perennial

The black lilyturf is a clump-forming,
grasslike perennial with dark purple,
almost black leaves. It looks superb
when planted as edging or in pale-
colored gravel. It is also suitable for
raised beds. In summer it produces
spikes of tiny, bell-shaped, purple-
flushed white flowers. Plant it in full
sun or partial shade in slightly acidic,
moist but well-drained soil.

○ ◐ ☼ ◑ Z6–10　H10–6
↕ to 8in (20cm) ↔ to 12in (30cm)

PHORMIUM TENAX
Purpureum Group

Perennial

New Zealand flax is an evergreen with large, leathery, sword-shaped leaves in a rich copper or deep purple-red hue. Tall, upright, architectural spikes of tubular, dark red flowers arise on plum-purple stems in summer. Grow it as a specimen plant or in a border in full sun and deep, fertile, moisture-retentive soil with shelter from wind. Where marginally hardy, provide a deep, dry mulch in winter. Phormiums do well in coastal gardens.

◐ ☼ Z9–10 H10–1
↕ to 8ft (2.5m) ↔ to 3ft (1m)

PITTOSPORUM TENUIFOLIUM
'Purpureum'

Evergreen shrub

The kohuhu is an evergreen shrub or small tree with black stems and wavy-edged, leathery purple leaves. In late spring it has tiny, scented, dark red, bell-shaped flowers. Plant it in full sun or partial shade in fertile, moist, well-drained soil. The leaf color is most intense in full sun. It is a superb hedge for coastal gardens, and the foliage is used in floral displays. Trim hedges in spring and early autumn.

◌ ◐ ☼ ƒZ9–10 H10–9
↕ to 30ft (10m) ↔ to 15ft (5m)

SALVIA OFFICINALIS
'Purpurascens'

Evergreen shrub

The purple sage forms a shrubby mound of aromatic, red-purple leaves and spikes of purple summer flowers that are very attractive to bees. It can be grown in an herb garden for culinary use, and it is also a useful foliage foil in a sunny border or gravel garden, where it associates well with silver-leaved plants. Grow it in full sun in moderately fertile, light, well-drained soil. Cut it back in spring and after flowering to keep it shapely.

◊ ☼ *f* Z5–8   H8–5
‡ to 32in (80cm) ↔ to 3ft (1m)

SEDUM SPATHULIFOLIUM
'Purpureum'

Evergreen perennial

This low-growing evergreen forms tight, dense mats of ground-covering foliage studded with starry yellow flowers in summer. The rosettes of fleshy, silvery gray leaves are flushed with purple and covered in a thick, waxy bloom. Grow it in a rock garden or trough, on top of a drystone wall, or in a raised bed. It grows best in full sun in gritty, very well-drained, poor to moderately fertile soil. It can easily be trimmed back occasionally to restrict its spread.

◊ ☼ Z5–9   H9–5
‡ to 4in (10cm) ↔ to 24in (60cm)

Festuca glauca
'Elijah Blue'

Perennial grass

This densely tufted evergreen grass forms a rounded clump of narrow, quite blue leaves with matching spikes of flowers in early summer. It makes a valuable color foil at the front of a border or in a gravel or rock garden. The best effects are achieved by planting it in groups of 3–5 plants. Grow it in full sun in poor to slightly fertile, well-drained, rather dry soil. Divide and replant it every 2–3 years in spring.

◊ ☼ Z4–8 H8–1
‡ to 12in (30cm) ↔ to 10in (25cm)

Juniperus squamata
'Blue Star'

Evergreen shrub

This low-growing conifer forms dense, compact mounds of sharply pointed, grayish blue leaves that retain their color throughout the year. The older stems have attractive reddish brown bark. It is ideal for growing as a ground-cover on a bank or in a gravel garden, and it combines well with other dwarf conifers and heathers. Plant it in full sun or very light shade in fertile, well-drained soil. It seldom needs pruning.

◊ ☼ ☀ Z5–8 H8–5
‡ to 16in (40cm) ↔ to 3ft (1m)

LEYMUS ARENARIUS

Perennial grass

This robust, tufted grass forms loose clumps of rather stiff, bright steel blue leaves adorned in summer by strong-stemmed heads of blue-gray flowers that age to buff. It spreads rapidly but can be confined in a container. It will develop the best color when grown in full sun in light, well-drained, slightly fertile soil, and it is ideal for creating foliage contrasts in a herbaceous or mixed border. Cut down the faded growth in spring, and trim back after flowering for improved foliage.

◊ ☼ Z4–9 H9–1
‡ to 5ft (1.5m) ↔ indefinite

RUTA GRAVEOLENS
'Jackman's Blue'

Evergreen shrub

This rounded shrub is grown for its deeply lobed, aromatic, blue-green leaves. In summer it produces small yellow flowers, but these should be removed before they bloom for the best foliage effect. It will grow well in a sunny position in moderately fertile, well-drained soil. It can also be grown in an herb garden or in a mixed or herbaceous border. Skin contact with the sap, especially in bright sunlight, can cause a severe reaction.

◊ ☼ ƒ Z5–9 H9–5
‡↔ to 24in (60cm)

ASPLENIUM SCOLOPENDRIUM

Perennial fern

The hart's tongue fern forms shuttlecock-like clumps of emerald green, lance-shaped fronds, which often have wavy margins. In summer, rust-colored spore cases are arranged herringbone-fashion on the undersides of the fronds. A beautiful fern for a shady wall, crevice, or border, it is also suitable for a woodland garden. Grow it in partial shade in a moist, preferably alkaline, well-drained soil. Divide large clumps in spring.

◊ ◊ ☼ Z6–8 H8–6
‡ to 30in (75cm) ↔ to 18in (45cm)

BLECHNUM PENNA-MARINA

Perennial fern

A tough but delicate-looking fern, this variety has long, slender fronds with many small, triangular, glossy, dark green leaflets. It spreads by means of underground stems and can form extensive colonies in ideal conditions. It forms a good year-round ground-cover in a woodland garden or a damp border, or site it in a shady spot by a wall. Grow it in partial shade in moist, fertile, slightly acidic soil.

◊ ☼ Z10–11 H12–10
‡ to 8in (20cm) ↔ indefinite

BUXUS SEMPERVIRENS

Evergreen shrub

Common boxwood is a slow-growing shrub with small, dark green leaves. It is widely grown as a hedge, planted in pots, or trimmed into balls, pyramids, or other topiary shapes. If left unpruned, it eventually forms a small, bushy tree. 'Suffruticosa' is best for dwarf hedges or for edging beds. Boxwood prefers partial shade but will tolerate full sun as long the soil does not dry out. Grow it in moist, well-drained soil; it thrives on alkaline soil or in pots of soil-based mix. Trim once a year in summer.

◊ ◊ ☼ ☀ Z6–8 H8–6
↕↔ to 15ft (5m)

CHUSQUEA CULEOU

Evergreen bamboo

This useful, slow-growing bamboo is less invasive than most and forms a fountain-shaped clump of cylindrical yellowish green stems; whiskery sheaves of narrow leaves arise at intervals on the stems. Plant it in sun or partial shade in moist but well-drained soil. Grow it in a sheltered site protected from wind, such as in a woodland garden or to disguise a fence. Old canes can be cut out and used for staking other plants.

◊ ◊ ☼ ☀ Z8–11 H12–8
↕ to 20ft (6m) ↔ to 8ft (2.5m)

EUCALYPTUS PAUCIFLORA *SUBSP.* NIPHOPHILA

Evergreen tree

The alpine snow gum is fast-growing once established and has attractive bark that peels to form a patchwork of green, gray, and cream. The leaves are blue-green and rounded in the juvenile form and lance-shaped when mature. Plant it in full sun in fertile, moist, well-drained soil. Grow it as a specimen tree or (in small gardens and borders) prune it hard every year in spring to produce a shrub with colorful young foliage. Fertilize and mulch after pruning.

◊ ◐ ☼ Z9–10 H10–9
‡↔ to 20ft (6m)

FARGESIA NITIDA

Evergreen bamboo

The fountain bamboo is slow-growing and produces erect, purplish green canes topped by narrow, lance-shaped, dark green leaves. It can be grown in a wild garden, but its spread may need to be restricted elsewhere. To achieve this, plant it in a large, bottomless container plunged up to its rim in the ground. Alternatively, chop back the rootstock using a sharpened spade every couple of years. Plant this bamboo in dappled shade in fertile, moist soil, and protect it from wind.

◐ ☼ Z7–10 H10–7
‡ to 15ft (5m) ↔ to 5ft (1.5m) or more

FATSIA JAPONICA

Evergreen shrub

A superb architectural shrub with huge, deeply lobed leaves and large heads of creamy white flowers in summer. Plant it in full sun or partial shade in fertile, moist but well-drained soil. It needs a sheltered position away from wind, which can damage the large leaves. It also benefits from a deep mulch to give some winter protection in its early years. Tolerant of pollution, it is suitable for urban gardens; it can be grown successfully by the coast, too.

◊ ◑ ☼ ☀ Z8–10 H10–8
↕↔ to 12ft (4m)

GRISELINIA LITTORALIS

Evergreen shrub

This vigorous shrub can become tree-like in mild areas, but it is more often grown as a hedge, valued for its rather leathery, glossy, emerald green leaves. Plant it in full sun in well-drained, fertile soil. Wind can damage it in exposed inland gardens, but it makes a good windbreak in mild coastal areas. Clip hedges in spring or, for a more informal effect, cut back with pruning shears.

◊ ☼ Z8–9 H9–8
↕ to 25ft (8m) ↔ to 15ft (5m)

HEBE CUPRESSOIDES
'Boughton Dome'

Evergreen shrub

A compact, dwarf hebe, this variety
forms a dense, rounded mound of
bright green leaves. Mature plants may
produce small spikes of white flowers.
It makes a neat specimen that needs
no pruning, or it can be grown in a
container, rock garden, or raised bed.
Plant it in full sun or partial shade in
poor to slightly fertile, moist, well-
drained, neutral to alkaline soil. It is
also tolerant of coastal conditions.

◊ ◊ ☼ ◑ Z8–9 H9–8
‡ to 12in (30cm) ↔ to 24in (60cm)

HEDERA HELIX
'Erecta'

Evergreen shrub

'Erecta' is an unusual nonclimbing form
of English ivy. It is shrublike, with
stiffly upright, spirelike stems clothed in
arrow-shaped, dark green leaves. It can
hold its own in a shrub border, and it
looks especially effective at the foot of
tree stumps or boulders. Plant it in
fertile, preferably alkaline, moist, well-
drained soil in sun or partial shade.
It usually needs very little pruning.

◊ ◊ ☼ ◑ Z5–11 H12–1
‡ to 3ft (1m) ↔ to 4ft (1.2m)

HEDERA HIBERNICA

Climber

Irish ivy is a vigorous, self-clinging, evergreen climber ideal for clothing unsightly walls, growing through large trees, or for using as a fast-growing groundcover. It has lobed, broadly oval, glossy dark green leaves with distinct, paler gray-green veins. Grow it in moist but well-drained, fertile, preferably alkaline soil in deep or partial shade. It needs no regular pruning but can be cut back hard at any time of year if it becomes necessary to restrict its spread.

◊ ◊ ☼ ☀ ◑ Z6–11 H12–1
‡ to 30ft (10m)

JUNIPERUS COMMUNIS '*Hibernica*'

Evergreen shrub

This juniper forms a narrow, tapering column of dense, prickly, bluish green foliage. It will grow happily in most well-drained soils, including alkaline ones. While some junipers tolerate some degree of shade, 'Hibernica' may become misshapen if not provided with position in full sun. It looks good in formal gardens, or plant it as a vertical accent in a large rock garden or a gravel garden. It does not need to be pruned.

◊ ☼ Z2–6 H6–1
‡ to 15ft (5m) ↔ to 12in (30cm)

JUNIPERUS PROCUMBENS

Evergreen shrub

The Bonin Island juniper is a creeping,
low-growing conifer that forms a
ground-hugging mound of yellowish
green, needlelike leaves. It makes a
superb groundcover for a bank or for
the edge of a gravel garden or patio.
It associates well with heathers and
more upright dwarf conifers and will
grow well in full sun or light shade
in any well-drained soil; it thrives
in sandy, alkaline, and dry soils.
It needs no pruning and should be
given space to spread.

◊ ☼ ☀ Z5–9 H9–5
‡ to 30in (75cm) ↔ to 6ft (2m)

LONICERA PILEATA

Evergreen shrub

The privet honeysuckle has glossy,
dark green, oval- to lance-shaped
leaves. In late spring it produces
clusters of creamy white, funnel-shaped
flowers that are followed by small,
translucent violet berries in summer.
Plant it in full sun or partial shade
in any well-drained soil. It makes a
good groundcover that requires little
attention and is suitable for coastal
gardens, since it tolerates salt spray.
In cold winters it may lose some
of its leaves.

◊ ☼ ☀ Z5–9 H9–5
‡ to 24in (60cm) ↔ to 8ft (2.5m)

PICEA MARIANA
'Nana'

Evergreen shrub

This is a slow-growing, dwarf form of
the black spruce that bears bluish gray
leaves. It forms a neat, rounded bush
suitable for growing in a gravel or rock
garden, on a patio, or with heathers.
Plant it in full sun in neutral to slightly
acidic, moderately fertile, well-drained
soil. It occasionally produces vigorous
upright shoots that mar the appearance
of the plant: cut them back to the base
as soon as they appear.

◊ ☼ Z3–6 H6–1
↕↔ to 20in (50cm)

PHYLLOSTACHYS FLEXUOSA

Evergreen bamboo

The zigzag bamboo forms clumps of
slender, arching canes that are bright
green when they emerge, later
becoming golden brown and finally
almost black as they mature. Grow in a
sheltered situation, such as a woodland
garden, and plant it in fertile, organic,
moist, well-drained soil in sun or
dappled shade. In milder areas clumps
will grow fast and require cutting back
with a sharp spade every 2-3 years.

◊ ◑ ☼ ◐ Z6–10 H10–6
↕ to 30ft (10m) ↔ indefinite

PINUS MUGO
'Mops'

Evergreen shrub

A diminutive selection of the Japanese dwarf mountain pine, 'Mops' forms a small, almost spherical shrub with upright branches covered in deep green, needlelike leaves. It produces tiny, oval, dark brown cones. Very slow growing, it is suitable for planting in a rock garden or with heathers and other dwarf conifers. Choose a site in full sun with well-drained soil. It requires very little or no pruning.

◊ ☼ Z3–7 H7–1
‡ to 3ft (1m) ↔ to 6ft (2m)

PITTOSPORUM TOBIRA

Evergreen shrub

The Japanese mock orange forms an upright shrub or small tree that bears leathery, shiny, dark green leaves. In late spring and early summer it produces clusters of scented, creamy white flowers. Where hardy, grow it in a sunny, sheltered site in fertile, moist, well-drained soil. In colder areas, grow it in a large container of soil-based mix, and move it to a cool conservatory or greenhouse over winter.

◊ ◊ ☼ *f* Z9–10 H10–9
‡ to 30ft (10m) ↔ to 10ft (3m)

POLYSTICHUM SETIFERUM
Divisilobum Group

Perennial fern

One of the most beautiful of all hardy ferns, this variety is a spreading evergreen with soft, feathery fronds divided into tiny pale green leaflets. It will flourish when planted in full or partial shade in fertile, moist but well-drained soil. Grow it in a mixed border beneath shrubs, in a dark, shady corner, or in a woodland garden.

◊ ◐ ☼ ☀ Z6–9 H9–6
‡ to 24in (60cm) ↔ to 18in (45cm)

SASA VEITCHII

Evergreen bamboo

This spreading bamboo needs plenty of space. Its purple canes bear dark green leaves during summer, but later in the year the margins dry out so that they appear variegated. Grow it in fertile, moist, well-drained soil in partial to deep shade; it tolerates sun in reliably moist soil. It is suitable for a woodland garden; elsewhere, to restrict it, plant it in a large bottomless container plunged in the ground to the rim. Alternatively, chop back clumps with a sharp spade every couple of years.

◊ ◐ ☼ ☀ Z6–10 H10–6
‡ to 4ft (1.2m) ↔ indefinite

STIPA GIGANTEA

Perennial grass

Golden oats is a magnificent evergreen grass that forms dense clumps of very narrow, dark green leaves. In summer, tall, slender but strong stems appear bearing clouds of tiny, glistening, purple-green flowers that age to gleaming gold. They make an attractive feature in the garden over winter, so wait until early spring to cut them down, along with any dead leaves. Grow as a specimen or as a gauzy screen at the back of a border. Best in full sun in fertile, well-drained soil.

○ ☼ Z8–10 H10–8
‡ to 8ft (2.5m) ↔ to 4ft (1.2m)

TAXUS BACCATA

Evergreen tree

The English yew can make a fairly large specimen tree, but it is also one of the finest species for hedging and topiary. It forms a dense, dark green hedge and impenetrable barrier. Plant in full sun or partial shade in fertile, moist but well-drained soil. This yew grows well in alkaline soil. Trim hedges once a year in late summer; renovate overgrown or misshapen hedges by cutting back hard in late summer.

○ ◑ ☼ ◕ Z7–8 H8–7
‡ to 70ft (20m) ↔ to 30ft (10m)

THUJA ORIENTALIS
'Aurea Nana'

Evergreen shrub

This is a dwarf, globe-shaped conifer with upright sprays of yellowish green leaves that become bronzed in autumn and winter. It is ideal for a raised bed or rock garden, for planting with heathers, and for growing as part of a collection of dwarf conifers. Plant it in full sun in moderately fertile, moist but well-drained soil. It needs little or no pruning.

○ ◐ ☼ Z6–9 H9–6
↕↔ to 24in (60cm)

VINCA MINOR

Evergreen shrub

This scrambling plant has glossy, dark green leaves and violet-blue flowers from spring to autumn. A few flowers may appear in the colder months of the year. It makes an excellent groundcover, with spreading stems that root wherever they touch the ground – it is, however, fairly easy to control. It grows well in any moderately fertile, well-drained soil in partial shade, but it flowers most freely in sun. *V. major* is considerably larger and much more vigorous.

○ ☼ Z4–9 H9–1
↕ to 8in (20cm) ↔ indefinite

ABIES NORDMANNIANA
'Golden Spreader'

Evergreen shrub

The Nordmann fir forms a very large ornamental tree, but 'Golden Spreader' is a dwarf, slow-growing form with spreading branches. The leaves on the inner parts of the plant are green, but those on the tips are bright golden yellow, giving a very attractive two-tone effect. It is suitable for growing in a rock or gravel garden. Plant in full sun in fertile, moist but well-drained, neutral or acidic soil.

◊ ◊ ☼ Z4–6 H6–1
‡ to 3ft (1m) ↔ to 5ft (1.5m)

AUCUBA JAPONICA
'Gold Dust'

Evergreen shrub

The spotted laurel is a rounded shrub with glossy green leaves variably spotted and splashed with golden yellow. If grown with a male plant, this female selection bears bright red berries in autumn. Aucubas are happy in most soils and tolerant of pollution and salt spray. It prefers partial shade but will tolerate deep shade and grows in any soil, except waterlogged. It can be planted as a hedge, which should be cut back with pruners in spring.

◊ ◊ ☼ Z6–10 H10–6
‡↔ to 10ft (3m)

BUXUS SEMPERVIRENS
'Elegantissima'

Evergreen shrub

This variegated form of common boxwood makes a neat, dome-shaped bush
that can also be used for hedging and
topiary. It grows best in dappled shade
but will also tolerate full sun. Grow it
in any well-drained, fertile soil, or as
trimmed specimens in pots of soil-based
mix. Trim hedges in summer. If older
bushes become ungainly, they can be
rejuvenated by hard pruning in spring,
followed by an application of general-
purpose fertilizer.

◊ ☼ Z6–8 H8–6
‡↔ to 5ft (1.5m)

CALLUNA VULGARIS
'Gold Haze'

Evergreen shrub

There are several forms of Scots heather
with golden yellow foliage. 'Gold Haze'
retains its brilliant color all year and in
summer produces long spikes of pure
white flowers. 'Ruth Sparkes' is more
compact, with double white flowers.
The golden leaves of 'Spitfire' turn red
during winter. All three are useful
groundcovers. Plant in full sun in
acidic, moist but well-drained, fertile
soil. Cut back in spring to keep
compact and bushy.

◊ ◐ ☼ Z5–7 H7–5
‡ to 18in (45cm) ↔ to 24in (60cm)

CAREX OSHIMENSIS
'Evergold'

Perennial

This sedge forms tussocks of narrow, arching, dark green leaves marked with a central stripe of rich golden yellow. In mid- to late spring it also produces spikes of dark brown flowers. Plant it in full sun or partial shade in fertile, moist but well-drained soil, although it tolerates dry conditions. It looks very good in containers, near water, and toward the front of a mixed or herbaceous border.

○ ◐ ☼ ☀ Z6–9 H9–6
‡ to 12in (30cm) ↔ to 14in (35cm)

CHAMAECYPARIS OBTUSA
'Crippsii'

Evergreen tree

A slow-growing form of the Hinoki cypress, this lovely specimen tree forms a broad column. The rich golden yellow color of its leaves is most strongly emphasized if it is planted against a background of darker foliage. Plant it in full sun in fertile, moist but well-drained, neutral or slightly acidic soil. It will also grow on alkaline soil. Pruning is rarely necessary.

○ ◐ ☼ Z4–8 H8–1
‡ to 50ft (15m) ↔ to 25ft (8m)

CHAMAECYPARIS PISIFERA '*Sungold*'

Evergreen tree

A form of Sawara cypress, this irregularly conical conifer has tiers of slightly drooping, threadlike, golden yellow shoots. There are several other cultivars with golden yellow foliage, but they tend to be scorched by cold winds and strong sun. Plant 'Sungold' in fertile, moist but well-drained, neutral to slightly acidic soil. A pretty specimen tree, it looks its best when planted against a dark background of evergreens.

◊ ◊ ☼ ☀ Z4–8 H8–1
‡ to 40ft (12m) ↔ to 15ft (5m)

CHOISYA TERNATA *Sundance*

Evergreen shrub

With its bright yellow leaves sharply divided into three leaflets, Sundance is one of the most dramatic evergreen shrubs for a mixed or shrub border. The color is more vibrant if it is planted in full sun, because the leaves are yellowish green in shade. Plant in well-drained, fertile soil, and provide shelter from wind.

◊ ☼ Z8–10 H10–8
‡↔ to 8ft (2.5m)

CORDYLINE AUSTRALIS
'Torbay Dazzler'

Evergreen tree

A decorative form of New Zealand cabbage palm, 'Torbay Dazzler' develops a slender trunk that bears a large cluster of creamy white variegated, sword-shaped leaves. In summer it may produce creamy white flowers. Plant it in fertile, well-drained soil in full sun or partial shade. Provide a loose, dry winter mulch in its early years. Where not hardy it can be grown as a container plant and overwintered in a frost-free conservatory or greenhouse.

◊ ☼ ☀ Z10–11 H12–1
‡ to 10ft (3m) ↔ to 3ft (1m)

CRYPTOMERIA JAPONICA
'Sekkan-sugi'

Evergreen shrub

This is a slow-growing type of Japanese cedar with creamy yellow foliage that turns almost white in winter. It is best planted in partial shade, because the pale foliage is easily scorched in strong sun. Plant it in fertile, moist but well-drained soil. It is best planted as a specimen tree. Unusual for a conifer, if it is cut back hard it will sprout again, so it can be safely pruned (within reason) if it outgrows its allotted space.

◊ ◊ ☀ Z6–9 H9–6
‡ to 25ft (8m) ↔ to 15ft (5m)

CUPRESSUS MACROCARPA
'Goldcrest'

Evergreen tree

'Goldcrest' is a striking conifer that forms
a narrow, column-shaped tree with
bright golden yellow leaves. Suitable for
a coastal garden, plant it in full sun in
any well-drained soil. It benefits from
shelter from wind. It makes an attractive
hedge that needs only gentle trimming
in late summer – take care not to cut
back into old wood.

◊ ☼ Z7–10 H10–7
↕ to 15ft (5m) ↔ to 8ft (2.5m)

ELAEAGNUS PUNGENS
'Maculata'

Evergreen shrub

This vigorous shrub has dark green,
glossy, leathery leaves with a bold,
central yellow blotch. In autumn it bears
clusters of small white, fragrant flowers.
Remove any shoots that revert to plain
green as soon as they appear and, in
spring, trim any stray stems that spoil
the shape of the plant. Suitable for
hedging, it is also tolerant of coastal
conditions. If grown as a hedge, trim it
in summer. Plant it in full sun or partial
shade in fairly fertile, well-drained soil.

◊ ☼ ◐ Z7–9 H9–7
↕ to 12ft (4m) ↔ to 15ft (5m)

ERICA CARNEA
'Foxhollow'

Evergreen shrub

Some heaths have especially attractive foliage, such as 'Foxhollow', which is yellow-green and has bronze-tipped young shoots. In cold winters its leaves are infused with shades of pinkish orange and red. In late winter and early spring it bears purple-pink flowers. Plant in full sun in moist but well-drained, fertile, acidic soil. It will also tolerate slightly alkaline soil. A lovely groundcover, give it a light clipping after flowering to keep it neat.

◊ ◑ ☼ Z5–7 H7–5
↕ to 6in (15cm) ↔ to 16in (40cm)

EUONYMUS FORTUNEI
'Emerald 'n' Gold'

Evergreen shrub

This robust and easily grown, dense shrub has glossy green leaves with bright yellow margins; during the cold winter months they take on pinkish tints. It grows in any soil, except waterlogged, and while it will tolerate shade, the leaf color is richer and stronger in full sun. A superb groundcover, it can also be grown in containers or as a low hedge, needing only a light trim in summer to keep it in shape.

◊ ◑ ☼ Z5–9 H9–5
↕ to 24in (60cm) ↔ to 36in (90cm)

HEBE OCHRACEA
'James Stirling'

Evergreen shrub

The tiny, scalelike leaves of the
whipcord hebe give it the appearance
of a dwarf conifer. The rich ochre-yellow
leaves look particularly attractive in
winter. In late spring and early summer
it bears clusters of small white flowers.
Plant it in a raised bed or on a rock
garden in full sun or partial shade in
moderately fertile, moist but well-
drained soil. It is a tough shrub that
is ideally suited to the conditions of
a coastal garden.

◊ ◊ ☼ ☀ Z8–10 H10–8
‡ to 18in (45cm) ↔ to 24in (60cm)

HEDERA COLCHICA
'Sulphur Heart'

Climber

This Persian ivy is a vigorous, self-
clinging climber with large, glossy,
evergreen leaves that are marked with
a central blotch of soft sulfur yellow.
It provides an excellent, fast-growing
cover for a shady wall and can also be
used as a groundcover. Grow in full sun
or partial shade in fertile, moist but well-
drained, preferably alkaline soil. It will
develop the most intense leaf color in
a sunny position. Cut back at any time
of year if necessary.

◊ ◊ ☼ ☀ Z5–10 H10–5
‡ to 15ft (5m)

HEDERA HELIX
'Buttercup'

Climber

An extremely attractive form of English ivy, this self-clinging evergreen climber has large, lobed, bright butter yellow leaves. In almost full sun the leaves really color up, while in shade they are a pale green. This makes for some interesting color effects, since the leaves overlap each other. Grow in fertile, moist but well-drained, preferably alkaline soil. An excellent wall plant, trim it back at any time of year if it exceeds its allotted space.

◊ ◊ ☼ ☼ Z5–10 H10–5
↕ to 6ft (2m)

ILEX AQUIFOLIUM
'Golden Milkboy'

Evergreen tree

A dense, upright tree, this striking holly makes a fine specimen or hedge. Its spiny, dark green leaves have irregular, golden yellow markings in the center. 'Golden Milkboy' is a male plant and does not produce berries, but it makes a good pollinator for female hollies. Plant in full sun or partial shade in fertile, moist but well-drained soil. For best leaf color, plant in full sun. Trim hedges in summer.

◊ ◊ ☼ ☼ Z7–9 H9–7
↕ to 20ft (6m) ↔ to 12ft (4m)

OSMANTHUS HETEROPHYLLUS
'Aureomarginatus'

Evergreen shrub

This rounded, slow-growing shrub has
pretty, glossy, hollylike leaves with
irregular dark green centers and bright
golden yellow margins. In late summer
and autumn it produces clusters of
small but very fragrant white flowers.
A welcome addition to the shrub border,
it makes a very good evergreen hedge.
Grow in full sun in fertile, well-drained
soil with some shelter from wind.
Trim hedges lightly in summer.

◊ ☼ *f* Z7–9 H9–7
‡↔ to 15ft (5m)

PHORMIUM TENAX
'Yellow Wave'

Perennial

The arching, sword-shaped leaves of this
large, clump-forming evergreen make a
bold focal point. They are a vibrant
yellow-green with a broad, central green
stripe. In summer, tall spikes of red-
purple flowers may appear. Plant in
full sun in moist but well-drained,
fertile soil. Where marginally hardy,
protect the crown by tucking in a thick
layer of dry mulch among the leaves.
Use as a specimen plant or in a mixed
border. Suitable for coastal gardens.

◊ ◑ ☼ Z9–10 H10–9
‡ to 10ft (3m) ↔ to 6ft (2m)

PINUS SYLVESTRIS
'Gold Coin'

Evergreen shrub

A diminutive, slow-growing version of the Scots pine, this dwarf conifer has greenish yellow, needlelike leaves that turn an intense shade of golden yellow in winter. A small rounded shrub, it is a good choice for a garden where space is limited; it is also ideally suited to a rock or gravel garden. Plant it in full sun in any moderately fertile, well-drained soil. It needs no pruning.

◊ ☼ Z3–7 H7–1
‡↔ to 6ft (2m)

PITTOSPORUM TENUIFOLIUM
'Abbotsbury Gold'

Evergreen shrub

This kohuhu is valued for its green-margined golden leaves. A bushy shrub or small tree, it is suitable for smaller gardens. It can be used for hedging, especially in coastal gardens, needing a trim once only in spring to keep it in shape. Grow in fertile, moist but well-drained soil. Provide shelter from wind.

◊ ◊ ☼ ☀ Z9–10 H10–9
‡ to 10ft (3m) ↔ to 5ft (1.5m)

PITTOSPORUM TENUIFOLIUM
'Irene Patterson'

Evergreen shrub

The emergent spring foliage of this
attractive shrub is cream, gradually
becoming marbled with dark green.
Slow-growing and mound-forming,
it makes an attractive specimen, but
it is also suitable as a hedging plant,
especially in wild and coastal gardens.
Trim to shape in spring. Plant in moist
but well-drained, fertile soil in full sun
or partial shade. Protect from wind,
and mulch young plants over winter.

◊ ◑ ☼ ☀ Z9–10 H10–9
‡ to 4ft (1.2m) ↔ to 24in (60cm)

THUJA PLICATA
'Stoneham Gold'

Evergreen shrub

This dwarf form of the Western red
cedar makes a small, cone-shaped bush.
The irregularly arranged sprays of
foliage are coppery bronze, becoming
golden yellow and then green as it
ages. It is slow-growing and makes a
good plant for a rock garden. Plant in
moist but well-drained, fertile soil in full
sun. It needs to be protected from wind
to avoid foliage scorch, especially in
its early years.

◊ ◑ ☼ Z6–8 H8–6
‡↔ to 6ft (2m)

INDEX

M

ACKNOWLEDGMENTS

Picture research: Samantha Nunn
Picture library: Richard Dabb, Lucy
Claxton, Charlotte Oster
Index: Michèle Clarke

The publisher would like to thank the
following for their kind permission to
reproduce their photographs:
(key: t=top, b=bottom)

17: Andrew Butler (b), Photos
Horticultural (t); 27: Harry Smith
Collection (t); 28: Garden Matters (t); 29:
Garden Matters (b), James Young (t); 30:
Andrew Lawson (t); 32: Juliette Wade (t);
33: John Glover (b), Harry Smith
Collection (t); 34: Juliette Wade (b); 38:
Garden Matters (t); 42: A-Z Botanical
Collection/Adrian Thomas (t), A-Z
Botanical Collection/Andrew Ackerley (b);
43: Garden Matters (b); 45: GPL/Sunniva
Harte (t); 51: Clive Nichols (b); 52: Photos
Horticultural (t); 58: GPL/Brian Carter (b);
65: RHS Garden Wisley (t); 77: Martin
Page (b); 78: James Young (b); 79: Photos
Horticultural (b); 81: GPL/Christopher
Fairweather (t); 91: Garden Matters (t);
106: GPL/Jacqui Hurst (b); 107: Martin
Page (b), Harry Smith Collection (t); 109:
James Young (t); 110:Garden Matters (t);
112: Roger Smith/DK (t); 117: Garden
Matters (t); 118: A-Z Botanical Collection
(b); 120: Photos Horticultural (t); 121:
Photos Horticultural (b, t); 122: John
Fielding (t); 123: Eric Crichton Photos (b);
124: A-Z Botanical Collection/Adrian
Thomas (b); 125: Andrew Lawson (b); 127:
Photos Horticultural (b); 130: GPL/Jacqui
Hurst (b); 132: James Young (b); 135:
Juliette Wade (b); 136: Martin Page (b);
137: A-Z Botanical Collection/Nina

McKenna (b); 141: Andrew Butler (t); 143:
A-Z Botanical Collection/Jack Coulthard
(t); 144: Roger Smith/DK (t); 149: Harry Smith
Collection (b); 160: John Fielding (b); 162:
Harry Smith Collection (t); 166: Andrew
Butler (t); 168: Juliette Wade (b); 173: C.
Andrew Henley (t); 174: Martin Page (b);
176: Roger Smith/DK (b); 185: Christine M.
Douglas (t); 188: Photos Horticultural (b);
192: Martin Page (t); 194: Photos
Horticultural (t), Roger Smith/DK (b); 196:
Roger Smith/DK (t); 198: Roger Smith/DK
(t); 200: Harry Smith Collection (t); 201:
Beth Chatto (t), Photos Horticultural (t);
202: GPL/Juliet Greene (t); 204: Eric
Crichton Photos (t); 205: GPL/Howard
Rice (t); 214: James Young (b); 217: Martin
Page (b); 220: James Young (b, t); 223:
Roger Smith/DK (t); 228: Garden Matters
(t); 229: Photos Horticultural (t); 232:
Photos Horticultural (b); 233: Harry Smith
Collection (b); 235: Photos Horticultural
(b); 239: GPL/Kim Blaxland (b); 240:
GPL/John Glover (t), Harry Smith Collection
(b), Harry Smith Collection (t); 253:
Michael Booher (b); 258: GPL/Linda
Burgess (b); 266: John Glover (t); 267:
Harry Smith Collection (b); 269: C. Andrew
Henley (b); 274: Harry Smith Collection
(t); 275: Roger Smith/DK (b); 278: A-Z
Botanical Collection/Derrick Ditchburn (t);
285: GPL/Jacqui Hurst (b); 286: Harry
Smith Collection (b); 300: Clive Nichols (b);
311: Christine M. Douglas (b), GPL/J. S
Sira (t); 313: Photos Horticultural (t); 315:
Clive Nichols (t); 317: Harry Smith
Collection (b); 331: GPL/Eric Crichton (t),
Harry Smith Collection (b); 337: C.
Andrew Henley (t), Photos Horticultural
(t); 338: Harry Smith Collection (b); 342:
Martin Page (b); 344: Harry Smith

Collection (b); 345: Photos Horticultural (b); 347: Photos Horticultural (b); 352: Photos Horticultural (b); 355: Photos Horticultural (b); 356: Photos Horticultural (b); 358: Eric Crichton Photos (b); 360: Clive Nichols (t); 361: Photos Horticultural (b); 362: Photos Horticultural (b); 363: Harry Smith Collection (t); 367: Harry Smith Collection (t); 368: Harry Smith Collection (t); 373: GPL/Howard Rice (b); 374: Juliette Wade (b); 379: Andrew Butler (t); 383: Photos Horticultural (b); 397: GPL/John Glover (t), GPL/Philippe Bonduel (b); 398: Harry Smith Collection (t);401: Clive Nichols/Jane Nichols (b); 406: Andrew Butler (b), Photos Horticultural (t); 408: Harry Smith Collection (t); 414: Clive Nichols (b); 422: Andrew Butler (b); 423: Juliette Wade (t); 424: Harry Smith Collection (t); 427: GPL/Ron Evans (t); 429: John Fielding (t); 430: Photos Horticultural (b); 431: Christine M. Douglas (t); 435: Andrew Lawson (b); 436: Clive Nichols (t); 437: Andrew Butler (t); 439: Andrew Lawson (t); 442: Andrew Butler (t); 445: Andrew Butler (t); 446: Roger Smith/DK (t); 458: Andrew Butler (t); 459: Beth Chatto (t), C. Andrew Henley (b); 462: Martin Page (b); 467: Photos Horticultural (t), Harry Smith Collection (b); 470: Andrew Butler (t); 472: Andrew Lawson; 478: GPL/Howard Rice (b); 480: GPL/Howard Rice (t); 482: Andrew Butler (t); 483: Clive Nichols (b), Photos Horticultural (t); 485: GPL/Neil Holmes (b); 486: Eric Crichton Photos (t); 487: Photos Horticultural (t); 489: Harry Smith Collection (b); 490: John Glover (b),

Photos Horticultural (t); 491: Andrew Lawson (t); 493: Photos Horticultural (b); 495: John Glover (b); 496: GPL/Howard Rice (t), Photos Horticultural (b); 499: Andrew Lawson (t); 502: Harry Smith Collection (t); 504: Roger Smith/DK (t); 506: John Glover (b); 509: Photos Horticultural (t); 512: Photos Horticultural (b); 513: Beth Chatto (b); 514: Martin Page (t); 518: Harry Smith Collection (b); 520: Roger Smith/DK (t); 521: Roger Smith/DK (t); 522: James Young (b); 523: Harry Smith Collection (t); 527: James Young (b); 531: James Young (t); 532: John Fielding (b); 536: GPL/J. S. Sira (b); 537: GPL/Jerry Pavia (t); 538: James Young (b); 539: Juliette Wade (b), GPL/Lamontagne (t); 540: John Glover (t); 542: James Young (t); 543: Photos Horticultural (b); 546: Andrew Butler (b); 547: Andrew Butler (t).

All other images © Dorling Kindersley.

For further information see:
www.dkimages.com

Dorling Kindersley would also like to thank the following for editorial assistance:
Zia Allaway, Chris Dyer, Lin Hawthorne, Letitia Luff, Robin Pridy; at the Royal Horticultural Society, Vincent Square: Barbara Haynes, Susanne Mitchell and Simon Maughan.

Visit the American Horticultural Society at **www.ahs.org**